THE *HIGH SCHOOL*

CHEMISTRY TUTOR®

SECOND EDITION

Staff of Research and Education Association
Dr. M. Fogiel, Chief Editor

Research and Education Association
61 Ethel Road West
Piscataway, New Jersey 08854

THE HIGH SCHOOL CHEMISTRY TUTOR®

REVISED PRINTING 1994

Printed in the United States of America

Library of Congress Card Catalog Number 85-63873

International Standard Book Number 0-87891-596-6

WHAT THIS BOOK IS FOR

For as long as chemistry has been taught in high schools, students have found this subject difficult to understand and learn. Despite the publication of hundreds of textbooks in this field, each one intended to provide an improvement over previous textbooks, students continue to remain perplexed, and the subject is often taken in class only to meet school/departmental requirements for a selected course of study.

In a study of the problem, REA found the following basic reasons underlying students' difficulties with chemistry taught in schools:

(a) No systematic rules of analysis have been developed which students may follow in a step-by-step manner to solve the usual problems encountered. This results from the fact that the numerous different conditions and principles which may be involved in a problem, lead to many possible different methods of solution. To prescribe a set of rules to be followed for each of the possible variations, would involve an enormous number of rules and steps to be searched through by students, and this task would perhaps be more burdensome than solving the problem directly with some accompanying trial and error to find the correct solution route.

(b) Textbooks currently available will usually explain a given principle in a few pages written by a professional who has an insight into the subject matter that is not shared by students. The explanations are often written in an abstract manner which leaves the students confused as to the application of the principle. The explanations given are not sufficiently detailed and extensive to make the student aware of the wide range of applications and different aspects of the principle being studied. The numerous possible variations of principles and their applications are usually not discussed, and it is left for the students to discover these for themselves while doing the exercises. Accordingly, the average student is expected to rediscover that which has been long known and practiced, but not published or explained extensively.

(c) The examples usually following the explanation of a topic are too few in number and too simple to enable the student to obtain a thorough grasp of the principles involved. The explanations do not provide sufficient basis to enable a student to solve problems that may be subsequently assigned for homework or given on examinations.

The examples are presented in abbreviated form which leaves out much material between steps, and requires that students derive the omitted material themselves. As a result, students find the examples difficult to understand--contrary to the purpose of the examples.

Examples are, furthermore, often worded in a confusing manner. They do not state the problem and then present the solution. Instead, they pass through a general discussion, never revealing what is to be solved for.

Examples, also, do not always include diagrams/graphs, wherever appropriate, and students do not obtain the training to draw diagrams or graphs to simplify and organize their thinking.

(d) Students can learn the subject only by doing the exercises themselves and reviewing them in class, to obtain experience in applying the principles with their different ramifications.

In doing the exercises by themselves, students find that they are required to devote considerably more time to chemistry than to other subjects of comparable credits, because they are uncertain with regard to the selection and application of the theorems and principles involved. It is also often necessary for students to discover those "tricks" not revealed in their texts (or review books), that make it possible to solve problems easily. Students must usually resort to methods of trial-and-error to discover these "tricks," and as a result they find that they may sometimes spend several hours in solving a single problem.

(e) When reviewing the exercises in classrooms, instructors usually request students to take turns in writing solutions on the board and explaining them to the class. Students often find it difficult to explain in a manner that holds the interest of the class, and enables the class to follow the material written on the board. The remaining students seated in the class are, furthermore, too occupied with copying the material from the board, to listen to the oral explanations and concentrate on the methods of solution.

This book is intended to aid students in chemistry in overcoming the difficulties described, by supplying detailed illustrations of the solution methods which are usually not apparent to students. The solution methods are illustrated by problems selected from those that are most often assigned for class work and given on examinations. The problems are arranged in order of complexity to enable students to learn and understand a particular topic by reviewing the problems in sequence. The problems are illustrated with detailed step-by-step explanations, to save the students the large amount of time that is often needed to fill in the gaps that are usually found between steps of illustrations in textbooks or review/outline books.

The staff of REA considers chemistry a subject that is best learned by allowing students to view the methods of analysis and solution techniques themselves. This approach to learning the subject matter is similar to that practiced in various scientific laboratories, particularly in the medical fields.

In using this book, students may review and study the illustrated problems at their own pace; they are not limited to the time allowed for explaining problems on the board in class.

When students want to look up a particular type of problem and solution, they can readily locate it in the book by referring to the index which has been extensively prepared. It is also possible to locate a particular type of problem by glancing at just the material within the boxed portions. To facilitate rapid scanning of the problems, each problem has a heavy border around it. Furthermore, each problem is identified with a number immediately above the problem at the right-hand margin.

To obtain maximum benefit from the book, students should familiarize themselves with the section, "How To Use This Book," located in the front pages.

To meet the objectives of this book, staff members of REA have selected problems usually encountered in assignments and examinations, and have solved each problem meticulously to illustrate the steps which are usually difficult for students to comprehend. Special gratitude is expressed to them for their efforts in this area, as well as to the numerous contributors who devoted brief periods of time to this work.

Gratitude is also expressed to the many persons involved in the difficult task of typing the manuscript with its endless changes, and to the REA art staff who prepared the numerous detailed illustrations together with the layout and physical features of the book.

The difficult task of coordinating the efforts of all persons was carried out by Carl Fuchs. His conscientious work deserves much appreciation. He also trained and supervised art and production personnel in the preparation of the book for printing.

Finally, special thanks are due to Helen Kaufmann for her unique talents in rendering those difficult border-line decisions and in making constructive suggestions related to the design and organization of the book.

Max Fogiel, PH. D.
Program Director

HOW TO USE THIS BOOK

This book can be an invaluable aid to students in algebra as a supplement to their textbooks. The book is subdivided into 29 chapters, each dealing with a separate topic. The subject matter is developed beginning with fundamental algebraic laws and operations and extending through systems of equations and applied problems.

TO LEARN AND UNDERSTAND A TOPIC THOROUGHLY

1. Refer to your class text and read there the section pertaining to the topic. You should become acquainted with the principles discussed there. These principles, however, may not be clear to you at that time.

2. Then locate the topic you are looking for by referring to the "Table of Contents" in front of this book.

3. Turn to the page where the topic begins and review the problems under each topic, in the order given. For each topic, the problems are arranged in order of complexity, from the simplest to the more difficult. Some problems may appear similar to others, but each problem has been selected to illustrate a different point or solution method.

To learn and understand a topic thoroughly and retain its contents, it will generally be necessary for students to review the problems several times. Repeated review is essential in order to gain experience in recognizing the principles that should be applied, and to select the best solution technique.

TO FIND A PARTICULAR PROBLEM

To locate one or more problems related to a particular subject matter, refer to the index. In using the index, be certain to note that the numbers given there refer to problem numbers, not to page numbers. This arrangement of the index is intended to facilitate finding a problem more rapidly, since two or more problems may appear on a page.

If a particular type of problem cannot be found readily, it is recommended that the student refer to the "Table of Contents" in the front pages, and then turn to the chapter which is applicable to the problem being sought. By scanning or glancing at the material that is boxed, it will generally be possible to find problems related to the one being sought, without consuming considerable time. After the problems have been located, the solutions can be reviewed and studied in detail. For this purpose of locating problems rapidly, students should acquaint themselves with the organization of the book as found in the "Table of Contents."

In preparing for an exam, locate the topics to be covered on the exam in the "Table of Contents," and then review the problems under those topics several times. This should equip the student with what might be needed for the exam.

CONTENTS

CHAPTER 1

UNITS OF MEASUREMENT

LENGTH

The Eiffel Tower is 984 feet high. Express this height in meters, in kilometers, in centimeters, and in millimeters.

<u>Solution</u>: A meter is equivalent to 39.370 inches. In this problem, the height of the tower in feet must be converted to inches and then the inches can be converted to meters. There are 12 inches in 1 foot. Therefore, feet can be converted to inches by using the factor 12 inches/1 foot.

$$984 \text{ feet} \times 12 \text{ inches/1 foot} = 118 \times 10^2 \text{ inches.}$$

Once the height is found in inches, this can be converted to meters by the factor 1 meter/39.370 inches.

$$11808 \text{ inches} \times 1 \text{ meter/39.370 inches} = 300 \text{ m.}$$

Therefore, the height in meters is 300 m.

There are 1,000 meters in one kilometer. Meters can be converted to kilometers by using the factor 1 km/1000 m.

$$300 \text{ m} \times 1 \text{ km/1000 m} = .300 \text{ km.}$$

As such, there are .300 kilometers in 300 m.

There are 100 centimeters in 1 meter, thus meters can be converted to centimeters by multiplying by the factor 100 cm/1 m.

$$300 \text{ m} \times 100 \text{ cm/1 m} = 300 \times 10^2 \text{ cm.}$$

There are 30,000 centimeters in 300 m.

There are 1,000 millimeters in 1 meter; therefore,

meters can be converted to millimeters by the factor 1000 mm./1 m.

$$300 \text{ m} \times 1,000 \text{ mm}/1 \text{ m} = 300 \times 10^3 \text{ mm}.$$

There are 300,000 millimeters in 300 meters.

● PROBLEM 1-2

The unaided eye can perceive objects which have a diameter of 0.1 mm. What is the diameter in inches?

Solution: From a standard table of conversion factors, one can find that 1 inch = 2.54 cm. Thus, cm can be converted to inches by multiplying by 1 inch/2.54 cm. Here, one is given the diameter in mm, which is .1 cm. Millimeters are converted to cm by multiplying the number of mm by .1 cm/1 mm. Solving for cm, you obtain:

$$0.1 \text{ mm} \times .1 \text{ cm}/1 \text{ mm} = .01 \text{ cm}.$$

Solving for inches:

$$.01 \text{ cm} \times \frac{1 \text{ inch}}{2.54 \text{ cm}} = 3.94 \times 10^{-3} \text{ inches}.$$

AREA

● PROBLEM 1-3

One cubic millimeter of oil is spread on the surface of water so that the oil film has an area of 1 square meter. What is the thickness of the oil film in angstrom units?

Solution: Since one is asked to give the final thickness of the film in angstroms, it is useful to convert the other dimensions given to angstroms first. $1\overset{o}{A} = 10^{-10}\text{m} = 10^{-7}$ mm. Therefore, 1 mm $= 1\overset{o}{A}/10^{-7} = 10^7\overset{o}{A}$.

Cubing both sides of this equation gives the number of cubic angstroms in 1 cubic millimeter.

$$(1 \text{ mm})^3 = (10^7\overset{o}{A})^3$$

$$1 \text{ mm}^3 = 10^{21}\overset{o}{A}^3 = \text{volume of oil}.$$

The final area of the film is given as 1 m². One

knows that $1 \text{ m} = 10^{10} \overset{\circ}{A}$; therefore, $1 \text{ m}^2 = (10^{10} \overset{\circ}{A})^2 = 10^{20} \overset{\circ}{A}^2$. The volume is equal to the area of the film multiplied by the thickness. Thus, one can find the thickness of the film by dividing the volume by the area.

$$\text{thickness} = \frac{10^{21} \overset{\circ}{A}^3}{10^{20} \overset{\circ}{A}^2} = 10 \; \overset{\circ}{A}.$$

● PROBLEM 1-4

How much area, in square meters, will one liter of paint cover if it is brushed out to a uniform thickness of 100 microns?

Solution: Because one is asked to give the final area in square meters, one should first convert the volume and thickness to meter units. One liter is equal to 1,000 cc. Since 1 m = 100 cm, one can convert centimeters to meter units by cubing both sides of the equality:

$$1\text{m}^3 = (100\text{cm})^3$$

$$1\text{m}^3 = 1.0 \times 10^6 \text{cc}$$

$$\frac{1\text{m}^3}{1.0 \times 10^6} = 1\text{cc}$$

$$10^{-6}\text{m}^3 = 1\text{cc}$$

Therefore, 1000 cc or 1 liter is equal to $10^{-6} \text{ m}^3 \times 1,000$ or 10^{-3} m^3. There are 10^6 microns in 1 m. Thus, 1 micron = 10^{-6} m and 100 microns = 10^{-4} m. The area of the film is equal to the volume divided by the thickness.

$$\text{Therefore, area} = \frac{10^{-3} \text{ m}^3}{10^{-4} \text{ m}} = 10 \text{ m}^2.$$

VOLUME

● PROBLEM 1-5

Determine the number of cubic centimeters in one cubic inch.

Solution: One meter equals 39.37 inches and, since there are 100 centimeters in 1 meter, there are 39.37 inches in 100 cm. Thus, 1 inch is equal to 100/39.37 cm.

$$1 \text{ inch} = \frac{100}{39.37} \text{ cm} = 2.54 \text{ cm}.$$

By cubing both sides of this equation, one can solve for the number of cubic centimeters in 1 cubic inch.

$$(1 \text{ inch})^3 = (2.54 \text{ cm})^3$$

$$1 \text{ inch}^3 = 16.4 \text{ cc}.$$

● **PROBLEM** 1-6

Calculate the number of liters in one cubic meter.

Solution: There are 1,000 milliliters (ml) or cubic centimeters (cc) in one liter. Thus, if one wishes to convert one cubic meter to liters, the cubic meter must be converted to cubic centimeters.

$$\begin{aligned} 1 \text{ meter} &= 100 \text{ centimeters} \\ (1 \text{ meter})^3 &= (100 \text{ centimeters})^3 \\ &= 1,000,000 \text{ centimeters}^3 \\ &= 1 \times 10^6 \text{ cubic centimeters} \end{aligned}$$

Cubic centimeters can be converted to liters by multiing the number of cubic centimeters by the factor 1 liter/1,000 cubic centimeters.

$$1 \times 10^6 \text{ cubic centimeters} \times 1 \text{ liter/1,000 cubic centimeters}$$

$$= 1,000 \text{ liters}.$$

There are 1,000 liters in one cubic meter.

● **PROBLEM** 1-7

What is the volume, in cubic centimeters, of a cube which is 150.0 mm along each edge?

Solution: There are 10 mm in 1 cm; therefore, millimeters can be converted to centimeters by multiplying the number of millimeters by 1 cm/10 mm.

length of edge in cm = 150 mm × 1 cm/10 mm = 15 cm.

The volume of a cube is equal to the length of the side cubed.

$$\text{volume} = (15 \text{ cm})^3 = 3375 \text{ cc}.$$

4

What volume (in cc) is occupied by a block of wood of dimensions 25.0 m × 10.0 cm × 300 mm. All edges are 90° to one another.

Solution: Since all of the edges are 90° to one another, one knows that the block is a rectangular solid. The volume of a rectangle is equal to the length times the width times the height. If one wishes to find the volume in cubic centimeters, the lengths of all of the sides must be first expressed in centimeters.

There are 100 cm in 1 m; thus, to convert meters to centimeters, the number of meters must be multiplied by 100 cm/1 m.

25.0 m × 100 cm/1 m = 2500 cm.

There are 10 mm in 1 cm; thus, to convert millimeters to centimeters, multiply the number of millimeters by 1 cm/10 mm.

300 mm × 1 cm/10 mm = 30 cm

Solving for the volume:

volume = 2500 cm × 10.0 cm × 30 cm = 7.50×10^5 cc.

A rectangular box is 5.00 in. wide, 8.00 in. long, and 6.0 in. deep. Calculate the volume in both cubic centimeters and in liters.

Solution: The volume of a solid is found by multiplying the height times the length times the width.

volume = (6.0 in) × (8.0 in) × (5.0 in) = 240 in^3.

From a standard conversion table, one finds that 1 inch = 2.54 cm. One finds the volume of cubic inches in cubic centimeters by cubing both sides of this equality.

1 inch = 2.54 cm

$(1 \text{ inch})^3 = (2.54 \text{cm})^3$

1 $inch^3$ = 16.4 cc.

Thus, one can convert the volume of the rectangle from cubic inches to cubic centimeters by multiplying the number of cubic inches by the conversion factor, 16.4 cc/1 $inch^3$.

volume of rectangle = 240 in^3 × 16.4 cc/1 in^3

= 3936 cc.

There are 1000 cc in 1 liter. Therefore, to convert from cubic centimeters to liters, multiply the number of cubic centimeters by 1 liter/1000 cc.

volume in liters = 3936 cc × 1 liter/1000 cc

= 3.936 liters.

MASS

● PROBLEM 1-10

A student made three successive weighings of an object as follows: 9.17 g, 9.15 g, and 9.20 g. What is the average weight of the object in milligrams?

Solution: The average of a set of weights is found by adding together all of the weights and then dividing by the number of weighings used.

$$\text{avg.} \atop \text{weight} = \frac{(9.17 \text{ g} + 9.15 \text{ g} + 9.20 \text{ g})}{3} = \frac{27.52 \text{ g}}{3} = 9.17 \text{ g.}$$

Now that the average weight in grams has been determined, convert it to milligrams using the conversion factor of 1,000 mg/g.

$$9.17 \text{ g} \times \frac{1000 \text{ mg}}{\text{g}} = 9170 \text{ mg.}$$

● PROBLEM 1-11

A silver dollar weighs about 0.943 ounces. Express this weight in grams, in kilograms, and in milligrams.

Solution: One ounce is equal to 28.35 g; thus, to convert from ounces to grams, one multiplies the number of ounces by the conversion factor, 28.35 g/1 ounce.

no. of grams = 0.943 ounces × 28.35 g/1 ounce

= 26.73 g.

There are 1,000 g in 1 kg; therefore, to convert from grams to kilograms, one multiplies the number of grams by 1 kg/1,000 g.

no. of kg = 26.73g × 1 kg/1000 g = .02673 kg.

There are 1,000 mg in one gram; thus, to convert from grams to milligrams, multiply the number of grams by the conversion factor, 1000 mg/1 g.

no. of mg = 26.73 g × 1000 mg/1 g = 26,730 mg.

● PROBLEM 1-12

It is estimated that 3×10^5 tons of sulfur dioxide, SO_2, enters the atmosphere daily owing to the burning of coal and petroleum products. Assuming an even distribution of the sulfur dioxide throughout the earth's atmosphere (which is not the case), calculate in parts per million by weight the concentration of SO_2 added daily to the atmosphere. The weight of the atmosphere is 4.5×10^{15} tons. (On the average, about 40 days are required for the removal of the SO_2 by rain).

Solution: Here, one is asked to find the number of tons of SO_2 per 10^6 tons, i.e. per million, of atmosphere. This is done by using the following ratio: Let x = no. of tons of SO_2 per 10^6 tons of atmosphere.

$$\frac{3.0 \times 10^5 \text{ tons } SO_2}{4.5 \times 10^{15} \text{ tons atm}} = \frac{x}{10^6 \text{ tons atm}}$$

$$x = \frac{3.0 \times 10^5 \text{ tons } SO_2 \times 10^6 \text{ tons atm}}{4.5 \times 10^{15} \text{ tons atm}}$$

$$x = 6.67 \times 10^{-5} \text{ tons } SO_2 \text{ or } 6.67 \times 10^{-5} \text{ ppm } SO_2.$$

DENSITY

● PROBLEM 1-13

The density of alcohol is 0.8 g/ml. What is the weight of 50 ml. of alcohol?

Solution: Density is defined as weight per unit volume.

$$\text{density} = \frac{\text{weight}}{\text{volume}} = \frac{g}{ml.}$$

7

Thus, one can solve for the weight of the alcohol by multiplying the density by the volume.

weight = density × volume

weight = 0.8 g/ml × 50 ml = 40 g.

● **PROBLEM** 1-14

Calculate the density of a block of wood which weighs 750 kg and has the dimensions 25 cm × 0.10 m × 50.0 m.

Solution: The density is a measure of weight per unit volume and is usually expressed in g/cc. Therefore, one must find the weight of this block in grams and the volume in cubic centimeters. The density is then found by dividing the weight by the volume.

1 kg = 1,000 g; therefore, 750 kg = 750 × 1,000 g

$= 7.5 \times 10^5$ g.   To find the volume in cubic centimeters, all of the dimensions must be converted to centimeters first.

1 m = 100 cm; thus, .10 m = 10 cm and

50.0 m = 5,000 cm.

Volume = 25 cm × 10 cm × 5,000 cm = 1.25×10^6 cc.

Solving for the density:

$$\text{density} = \frac{\text{weight}}{\text{volume}} = \frac{7.5 \times 10^5 \text{ g}}{1.25 \times 10^6} = .60 \text{ g/cc.}$$

● **PROBLEM** 1-15

The density of concentrated sulfuric acid is 1.85 g/ml. What volume of the acid would weigh 74.0 g?

Solution: Density is defined as weight per unit volume.

$$\text{density} = \frac{\text{weight}}{\text{volume}} = \frac{g}{ml}.$$

Therefore: $\text{volume} = \frac{\text{weight}}{\text{density}}$.

Solving for the volume:

$$\text{volume} = \frac{74.0 \text{ g}}{1.85 \text{ g/ml}} = 40.0 \text{ ml.}$$

One kilogram of metallic osmium, the "heaviest" substance known, occupies a volume of 44.5 cm³. Calculate the density of osmium in grams per cm³.

Solution: One is told that one kilogram of osmium occupies 44.5 cm³ and is then asked how many grams of osmium occupy one cm³. To find the density in grams per cm³, one kilogram must be first converted to grams after which this number of grams is divided by 44.5 cm³, the volume that they occupy. There are 1000 grams in one kilogram. As such, kilograms are converted to grams by multiplying the number of kilograms present by the factor 1,000 g/1 kg.

1 kg × 1,000/1 kg = 1,000 g.

Therefore, 1,000 g occupy 44.5 cm³. To find the number of grams present in 1 cm³, 1,000 g is divided by 44.5 cm³.

1000 g/44.5 cm³ = 22.5 g/cm³

The density of osmium is 22.5 g/cm³.

TEMPERATURE

Liquid helium boils at 4°K. What is the boiling temperature on the Fahrenheit scale?

Solution: The temperature in Kelvin is the temperature in degrees Centigrade added to 273. In this problem, the boiling point is given in °K. Hence, the temperature should be converted to °C and, then, to Fahrenheit using the relation

°F = 9/5 °C + 32

The boiling point of helium can be converted to °C by subtracting 273 from the boiling point in °K.

°C = °K - 273

°C = 4°K - 273 = - 269°C.

After the temperature is converted to the Centigrade scale, the temperature on the Fahrenheit scale can be determined.

9

$$°F = 9/5 \ °C + 32$$

$$°F = 9/5 \ (- \ 269°C) + 32 = - \ 452°F$$

The boiling point of helium on the Fahrenheit scale is 452°F.

● PROBLEM 1-18

The freezing point of silver is 960.8°C and the freezing point of gold is 1063.0°C. Convert these two readings to Kelvin (°K), Fahrenheit (°F), and Rankine (°R).

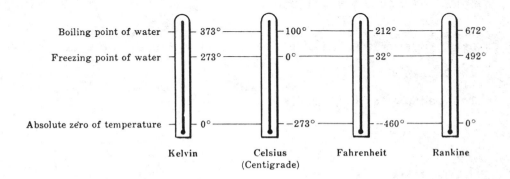

Solution: Kelvin: Temperatures measured in Celsius (°C) are converted to °K by adding 273.15 to the original measurement.

freezing point of silver = 960.8°C + 273.15 = 1234°K

freezing point of gold = 1063.0°C + 273.15 = 1336.2°K

Fahrenheit: °C are converted to °F by using the equation °F = 9/5 (°C) + 32.

freezing point of silver 9/5 (960.8°C) + 32 = 1761°F

freezing point of gold = 9/5 (1063.0°C) + 32 = 1945°F

Rankine: The Rankine scale is an absolute scale used by engineers. Its unit is the Fahrenheit degree. Absolute zero is equal to zero degrees Rankine. Convert °K to °R by using the equation

$$°R = 9/5 \ (°K)$$

freezing point of silver = 9/5 (1234°K) = 2221°R

freezing point of gold = 9/5 (1336.2°K) = 2405°R.

CHAPTER 2

GASES

PRESSURE

● PROBLEM 2-1

Given the setup in the figure, what would be the pressure of the gas (in atm) if P_{atm} is 745 Torr and P_{liq} is the equivalent of a mercury column 3.0 cm high?

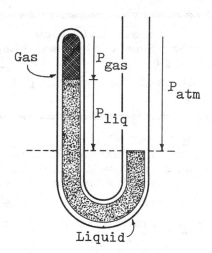

Gas

P_{gas}

P_{atm}

P_{liq}

Liquid

Solution: A manometer is used to measure the pressure of a trapped sample of gas. If the right hand tube is open to the atmosphere, the pressure which is exerted in the right-hand surface is atmospheric pressure, P_{atm}. If the liquid level is the same in both arms of the tube, the pressures must be equal; otherwise, there would be a flow of liquid from one arm to the other. At the level indicated by the dashed line in the figure, the pressure in the left arm is equal to the pressure of the trapped gas, P_{gas}, plus the pressure of the column of liquid above the dashed line, P_{liq}. One can write

$$P_{gas} = P_{atm} - P_{liq}$$

Here, one is given that P_{atm} is 745 Torr and that P_{liq} is equivalent to a mercury column 3.0 cm high. One wishes to find P_{gas} in atm, thus, one must convert 745 Torr to atm and find the P_{liq}. There are 760 Torr in 1 atm, which means

$$\text{no. of atm in } P_{atm} = \frac{745 \text{ Torr}}{760 \text{ Torr/1 atm}} = .98 \text{ atm}$$

One atmosphere pressure supports 76 cm of mercury, thus 3 cm of mercury supports 3/76 atm. Therefore, P_{liq} = 3 cm/76 cm/atm = .039 atm.

Solving for P_{gas}

$$P_{gas} = .980 \text{ atm} - .039 \text{ atm} = .941 \text{ atm}.$$

● **PROBLEM 2-2**

Consider the manometer, illustrated below, first constructed by Robert Boyle. When h = 40 mm, what is the pressure of the gas trapped in the volume, V_{gas}. The temperature is constant, and atmospheric pressure is P_{atm} = 1 atm.

Solution: We do not need to know any gas law to solve this problem. All we must realize is that the pressure exerted on the gas, P_{total}, is equal to the sum of the pressure exerted by the mercury, P_{Hg}, and the pressure exerted by the air, P_{atm}. Since 1 mm Hg = 1 torr and 1 atm = 760 torr,

P_{Hg} = 40 mm Hg = 40 torr and P_{atm} = 1 atm = 760 torr.

Then $P_{total} = P_{Hg} + P_{atm}$ = 40 torr + 760 torr = 800 torr.

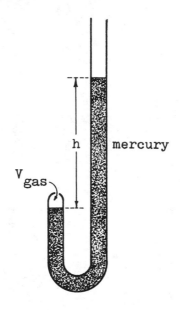

h mercury

V_{gas}

Consider gases confined by a liquid, as shown in the diagram below. Find an expression for the pressures P_1, P_2, and P_3 in terms of the density of the liquid, ρ (g/mℓ), the heights h_1 and h_3 (mm), and the barometric pressure P_{atm} (mm Hg).

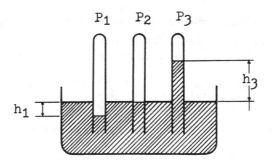

P_1 P_2 P_3

h_3

h_1

Solution: The device shown above is called a eudiometer. It is used to compare the pressures of several gases. The pressure of the confined gas is equal to the barometric pressure plus the pressure needed to depress the column of liquid (for P_1) <u>or</u> to the barometric pressure minus the pressure needed to support the column of liquid (for P_3). The pressure of the liquid column is given by

$$\begin{array}{l}\text{pressure} \\ \text{of liquid}\end{array} = \begin{array}{l}\text{height or depth of} \\ \text{column (mm)}\end{array} \times \rho \ (g/mℓ)(mℓ/cm^3) \ (cm/10mm)$$

Hence:

P_1 = barometric pressure + pressure needed to depress liquid

$$= P_{atm} + h_1 \times \rho \ (\ m\ell/cm^3) \ cm/10mm$$

$$= P_{atm} + 0.1 \ h_1 \ (g/cm^2) \ \rho$$

P_2 = barometric pressure + pressure needed to depress liquid (or - pressure needed to elevate liquid)

$$= P_{atm} + 0 \times \rho \times m\ell/cm^3 \times cm/10mm$$

$$= P_{atm}$$

P_3 = barometric pressure - pressure needed to elevate liquid

$$= P_{atm} - h_3 \times \rho \times m\ell/cm^3 \times cm/10mm$$

$$= P_{atm} - 0.1 \ h_3 \ (g/cm^2) \rho$$

● **PROBLEM 2-4**

(a) A diver descends to a depth of 15.0 m in pure water (density 1.00 g/cm^3). The barometric pressure is 1.02 standard atmospheres. What is the total pressure on the diver, expressed in atmospheres? (b) If, at the same barometric pressure, the water were the Dead Sea (1.20 g/cm^3), what would the total pressure be?

Solution: Pressure is defined as force per unit area. Atmospheric is measured by using a barometer (usually a mercury barometer; see figure). It is constructed by inverting a tube longer than 76 cm filled with mercury into a dish of mercury. The atmosphere will support only that height of mercury which exerts an equivalent pressure; any excess mercury will fall into the reservoir and leave a space with zero air pressure above it.

The pressure exerted on the diver from above is equal to the sum of the pressure exerted by the sea water and the pressure exerted by the atmosphere. One standard atmosphere equals the pressure exerted by exactly 76 cm (= exactly 760 mm) of mercury at 0°C

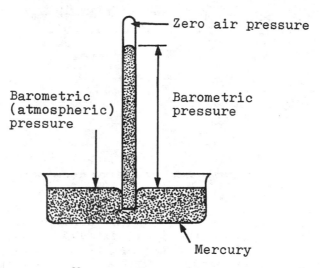

Zero air pressure

Barometric
(atmospheric)
pressure

Barometric
pressure

Mercury

Mercury Barometer

(density Hg = 13.5951 g/cm^3) and at standard gravity, 980.665 cm/s^2. Thus, 1 standard atm equals 13.5951 g/cm^3 × 76 cm (exactly) × 980.665 cm/s^2= 1.01325 × 10^6 dynes/cm^2 The pressure exerted by the water is found similarly: pressure of water = density × height × standard gravity

$$= 1.00 \text{ g/cm}^3 \times 1.5 \times 10^3 \text{ cm} \times 980.665 \text{ cm/s}^2$$

$$= 1.47 \times 10^6 \text{ dynes/cm}^2.$$

However, the problem states that atmospheric pressure is 1.02 standard atmospheres and, therefore, equals (1.02)(1.01325 × 10^6 dynes/cm^2) = 1.03 × 10^6 dynes/cm^2. To this atmospheric pressure, the pressure of the water is added to yield a total pressure of

$$(1.03 \times 10^6 \text{ dynes/cm}^2) + (1.47 \times 10^6 \text{ dynes/cm}^2)$$

$$= 2.50 \times 10^6 \text{ dynes/cm}^2.$$

This answer expressed in atmospheres gives

$$\frac{2.50 \times 10^6 \text{ dynes/cm}^2}{1.01 \times 10^6 \text{ dynes/cm}^2/\text{atm}} = 2.48 \text{ atm.}$$

(b) This part is very similar to part (a). The total pressure exerted is the pressure of the water plus the pressure of the atmosphere. The pressure of the atmosphere from part (a) is 1.03 × 10^6 dynes/cm^2. The pressure of the water must be calculated:

pressure of water = density × height × standard gravity

$$= 1.20 \text{ g/cm}^3 \times 1.5 \times 10^3 \text{ cm} \times 980.665 \text{ cm/s}^2$$

$$= 1.77 \times 10^6 \text{ dynes/cm}^2.$$

The total pressure is 1.77×10^6 dynes/cm^2 + 1.03 $\times 10^6$ dynes/cm^2 equals 2.80×10^6 dynes/cm^2.

This answer expressed in atmospheres is

$$\frac{2.80 \times 10^6 \text{ dynes/cm}^2}{1.01 \times 10^6 \text{ (dynes/cm}^2)/\text{atm}} = 2.77 \text{ atm.}$$

● **PROBLEM** 2-5

How many full strokes of a bicycle pump (chamber 4.0 cm diameter and 40.0 cm long) would you need to make in order to pump up an automobile tire from a gauge pressure of zero to 24 pounds per square inch(psi)(1.63 atm.)? Assume temperature stays constant at 25°C and atmospheric pressure is one atmosphere. Note, that gauge pressure measures only the excess over atmospheric pressure. A typical tire volume is about 25 liters.

Solution: One atmosphere equals 14.7 psi, therefore, the amount of pressure needed to fill the tire is 24 + 14.7 psi or 38.7 psi. Converting back to atm:

atm. contained in inflated tire = 38.7 psi × 1 atm/14.7 psi = 2.63 atm.

When the tire is deflated the pressure is 1 atm and the volume is 25 ℓ. Each atm of pressure occupies 25 ℓ. Therefore, the volume of the tire when inflated is 25ℓ × 2.63 atm.

Volume of inflated tire = 25ℓ × 2.63 = 65.75ℓ

Since there is 25ℓ present in the tire before inflation, the volume that the pump must contribute is 65.75 - 25ℓ or 40.75ℓ.

The volume of air forced into the tire at each stroke of the pump is equal to the volume of the pump.

Volume of pump = $\pi r^2 h = \pi \times (2cm)^2 \times 40$ cm = 503 cm^3/stroke

There are 1000 cm^3 in 1 liter, therefore 40750 cm^3 of air must be pumped into the tire. If 503 cm^3 is pumped in per stroke the number of strokes necessary to fill the tire is $\frac{40750 \text{ cm}^3}{503 \text{ cm}^3/\text{stroke}}$.

No. of strokes = $\frac{40750 \text{ cm}^3}{503 \text{ cm}^3/\text{stroke}}$ = 81 strokes.

BOYLE'S LAW, CHARLES' LAW, LAW OF GAY-LUSSAC

● **PROBLEM** 2-6

> 100 ml. of gas are enclosed in a cylinder under a pressure
> of 760 Torr. What would the volume of the same gas be at a
> pressure of 1520 Torr?

P = Pressure

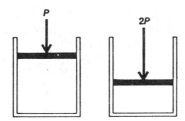

If the pressure on a gas is
doubled (at a constant temperature),
the volume is halved (Boyle's Law).

Solution: Since this problem deals with the pressure and
volume of a gas at a constant temperature, Boyle's law can
be used. Boyle's law states that the volume, V, of a given
mass of gas, at constant temperature, varies inversely with
the pressure, P. It can be stated as

$$V = k \times 1/P,$$

where k is a constant.

Hence, $k = PV$

For a particular system, at constant temperature, k
is constant. Therefore, if either the pressure or the
volume is changed, the other must adjust accordingly.

Here, P = 760 Torr   and   V = 100 ml   so

$k = 760 \times 100 = 76000$ Torr-ml.

If P is doubled to 1520 Torr, then

$k = 76000$ Torr-ml $= 1520$ Torr x V

$$V = \frac{76000 \text{ Torr-ml}}{1520 \text{ Torr}} = 50 \text{ ml}$$

Since k is a constant for a given system, another form of
Boyle's Law can be expressed as

$$P_1V_1 = P_2V_2$$

This says that the pressure of the original system times
the volume of the original system is equal to the new

pressure times the new volume. Here,

$$760 \text{ Torr} \times 100 \text{ ml} = 1520 \text{ Torr} \times V_2$$

$$50 \text{ ml} = V_2 .$$

What pressure is required to compress 5 liters of gas at 1 atm. pressure to 1 liter at a constant temperature?

Solution: In solving this problem, one uses Boyle's Law: The volume of a given mass of gas at constant temperature varies inversely with the pressure. This means that, for a given gas, the pressure and the volume are proportional; at a constant temperature, and their product equals a constant.

$$P \times V = K$$

where P is the pressure, V is the volume and K is a constant. From this one can propose the following equation

$$P_1V_1 = P_2V_2 ,$$

where P_1 is the original pressure, V_1 is the original volume, P_2 is the new pressure and V_2 is the new volume.

In this problem, one is asked to find the new pressure and is given the original pressure and volume and the new volume.

$$P_1V_1 = P_2V_2$$

$$1 \text{ atm} \times 5 \text{ liters} = P_2 \times 1 \text{ liter}$$

$$\frac{1 \text{ atm} \times 5 \text{ liters}}{1 \text{ liter}} = P_2$$

$$5 \text{ atm.} = P_2 .$$

P_1 = 1 atm.
V_1 = 5 liters
P_2 = ?

V_2 = 1 liter

A gaseous sample of neon, maintained at constant temperature, occupies 500 ml at 2.00 atm. Calculate the volume when the pressure is changed to each of the following: (a) 4.00 atm; (b) 760 torr; (c) 1.8×10^{-3} torr.

Solution: We need a relationship between volume and pressure. Such a relationship is provided by Boyle's

Law, which states that the product of pressure P and volume V of an ideal gas is a constant, k, or PV = k.

We must first determine k for the neon sample. We are given a value of P corresponding to a given value of V.

Therefore, $k = PV = 2.00$ atm $\times$ 500 ml = 2.00 atm $\times$ 0.500 ℓ = 1.00 ℓ-atm. Now that k is determined, we can obtain the value of V corresponding to the given values of P by using the formula $V = k/P$.

(a) $P = 4.00$ atm: $V = \dfrac{k}{P} = \dfrac{1.00 \ell\text{ -atm.}}{4.00\text{ atm}} = 0.25 \ell$

(b) $P = 760$ torr $= 760$ torr $\times \dfrac{1\text{ atm}}{760\text{ torr}} = 1$ atm :

$V = \dfrac{k}{P} = \dfrac{1.00 \ell\text{-atm.}}{1\text{ atm}} = 1.00 \ell$

(c) $P = 1.8 \times 10^{-3}$ torr $= 1.8 \times 10^{-3}$ torr $\times \dfrac{1\text{ atm}}{760\text{ torr}}$

$= 2.3 \times 10^{-6}$ atm:

$V = \dfrac{k}{P} = \dfrac{1.00 \ell\text{ -atm.}}{2.3 \times 10^{-6}\text{ atm}} = 4.35 \times 10^{5}\ \ell.$

● **PROBLEM** 2-9

A certain gas occupies a volume of 100 ml at a temperature of 20°C. What will its volume be at 10°C, if the pressure remains constant?

Solution: In a gaseous system, when the volume is changed by increasing the temperature, keeping the pressure constant, Charles' Law can be used to determine the new volume. Charles' Law states that, at a constant pressure, the volume of a given mass of gas is directly proportional to the absolute temperature. Charles Law may also be written

$$\frac{V_1}{T_1} = \frac{V_2}{T_2}$$

where V_1 is the volume at the original temperature T_1 and V_2 is the volume at the new temperature T_2.

To use Charles' Law, the temperature must be expressed on the absolute scale. The absolute temperature is calculated by adding 273 to the temperature in degrees Centigrade. In this problem, the centigrade temperatures are given and one must convert them to the absolute scale.

$T_1 = 20°C + 273 = 293°K$

$T_2 = 10°C + 273 = 283°K$

Using Charles' Law,

$V_1 = 100$ ml

$T_1 = 293°K$

$T_2 = 283°K$

$V_2 = ?$

$$\frac{V_1}{T_1} = \frac{V_2}{T_2} \qquad\qquad V_2 = \frac{V_1 T_2}{T_1}$$

$$V_2 = \frac{(100 \text{ ml})(283°K)}{293°K}$$

$V_2 = 96.6$ ml.

● **PROBLEM** 2-10

Assume that one cubic foot of air near a thermonuclear explosion is heated from 0°C to 546,000°C. To what volume does the air expand?

Solution: Charles' Law($V_1/T_1 = k$, where V_1 is the initial volume, T_1 the initial absolute temperature, and k is a constant)states that the volume is directly proportional to the temperature.

$$V \propto T$$

$\propto$ means 'is proportional to.'

The absolute temperature can be found by adding 273 to the temperature in °C.

$T_1 = 0 + 273 = 273$

$T_2 = 546,000 + 273 = 546,273$

Using the Charles' Law, one can set up the following ratio

$$\frac{V_1}{T_1} = \frac{V_2}{T_2} \, ,$$

where V_1 is the original volume, V_2 is the final volume, T_1 is the original temperature, and T_2 is the final temperature. Using this ratio, one can determine the final volume.

$$\frac{V_1}{T_1} = \frac{V_2}{T_2}$$

Substituting, one obtains

$$\frac{1 \ ft^3}{273} = \frac{V_2}{546,273}$$

$$V_2 = \frac{546,273}{273} \ (1 \ ft^3) = 2001 \ ft^3.$$

● **PROBLEM** 2-11

The volume of a sample of gaseous argon maintained at constant pressure was studied as a function of temperature and the following data was obtained:

Temperature, T (°K)	Volume, V (ℓ)
250	0.005
300	0.006
350	0.007

Calculate and confirm the Charles' Law constant for this system. Determine the temperature corresponding to a volume of 22.4 ℓ.

Solution: Charles' law states that the volume and absolute temperature of an ideal gas are directly proportional, i.e. $V = kT$, k is a constant. To determine the Charles' law constant k, we can use any one of the three sets of temperature-volume measurement. Choosing the first of these, we obtain

$$k = \frac{V}{T} = \frac{0.005 \ \ell}{250°K} = 2.00 \times 10^{-5} \ \ell{-}°K^{-1} \qquad \text{This value}$$

is confirmed by showing that the other two sets of data give the same value for k:

$$k = \frac{V}{T} = \frac{0.006 \ \ell}{300°K} = 2.00 \times 10^{-5} \ \ell{-}°K^{-1} \qquad \text{and}$$

$$k = \frac{V}{T} = \frac{0.007 \ \ell}{350°K} = 2.00 \times 10^{-5} \ \ell{-}°K^{-1}$$

To determine the temperature corresponding to

22.4 ℓ, we solve Charles' law for T, obtaining

$$T = \frac{V}{k} = \frac{22.4 \; \ell}{2.00 \times 10^{-5} \; \ell-°K^{-1}} = 1.12 \times 10^{6} \, °K$$

or about a million degrees Kelvin.

● **PROBLEM** 2-12

Consider the gas thermometer illustrated below. At 0°C, the volume of the gas is 1.25 liters. Assuming that the cross-sectional area of the graduated arm is 1 cm², what is the distance (in cm.) from the 0°C reading and a reading at 35°C?

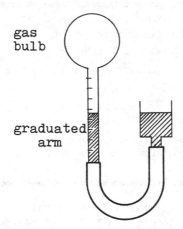

gas bulb

graduated arm

leveling bulb (adjust height until the liquid level in the leveling bulb is at the same height as the liquid level in the graduated arm)

Solution: Since volume, V, and absolute temperature, T, are the only two variables being considered, we can approach this problem by means of Charles' Law, V = kT, where k is the Charles' law constant, to be determined for our system.

We can determine k by using the initial values of 0°C (0°C = 273.15°K) and 1.25 liters (= 1250 ml = 1250 cm³). Then,

$$k = \frac{V}{T} = \frac{1250 \; cm^3}{273.15°K} = 4.576 \; cm^3-°K^{-1}$$

The volume at 35°C (308.15°K) can now be determined: V = kT = 4.576 cm³-°K⁻¹ × 308.15°K = 1410.1 cm³ = 1.410 ℓ. The difference between this volume and the initial volume is 1410.1 cm³ - 1250 cm³ = 160.1 cm³. This volume of liquid will be displaced in the graduated arm.

The difference in height of the liquid in the graduated arm, can now be calculated from the volume displaced and the cross-sectional area:

$$\text{height} = \frac{\text{volume}}{\text{area}} = \frac{160.1 \text{ cm}^3}{1 \text{ cm}^2} = 160.1 \text{ cm.}$$

The air in a tank has a pressure of 640 mm of Hg at 23°C. When placed in sunlight the temperature rose to 48°C. What was the pressure in the tank?

Solution: The law of Gay-Lussac deals with the relationship existing between pressure and the absolute temperature (°C + 273°), for a given mass of gas at constant volume. The relationship is expressed in the law of Gay-Lussac: volume constant, the pressure exerted by a given mass of gas varies directly with the absolute temperature. That is:

$$P \ \alpha \ T \text{ (volume and mass of gas constant).}$$

The variation that exists between pressure and temperature at different states can be expressed as

$$\frac{P_1}{T_1} = \frac{P_2}{T_2}$$

where P_1 = pressure of original state, T_1 = absolute temperature of original state, P_2 = pressure of final state, and T_2 = absolute temperature of final state.

Thus this problem is solved by substituting the given values into Gay-Lussac's Law.

P_1 = 640 mm Hg T_1 = 23°C + 273° = 296°K

P_2 = ? T_2 = 48°C + 273° = 321°K

Substituting and solving,

$$\frac{640 \text{ mm}}{296°K} = \frac{P_2}{321°K}$$

$$P_2 = 640 \text{ mm} \times \frac{321°K}{296°K}$$

$$= 694 \text{ mm of Hg.}$$

COMBINED GAS LAWS

Calculate the pressure required to compress 2 liters of a gas at 700 mm pressure and 20°C into a container of 0.1 liter capacity at a temperature of - 150°C.

Solution: One is dealing with changing volumes, pressures and temperatures of a gas. Therefore, this problem can be solved using the combined gas law. It states that as the pressure increases, the volume decreases and that as the temperature increases, the volume increases. These factors are related by the equation

$$\frac{P_1V_1}{T_1} = \frac{P_2V_2}{T_2}$$

where P_1, V_1 and T_1 are the initial pressure, volume and temperature and P_2, V_2, and T_2 are the final values.

For any problem dealing with gases, the first step always involves converting all of the temperatures to the degree Kelvin scale by the equation

$$°K = °C + 273$$

For this question

$$T_1 = 20°C = 20 + 273 = 293°K$$

$$T_2 = - 150°C = - 150 + 273 = 123°K.$$

This seems to indicate that the pressure would decrease. But one is also told that the volume decreases, which would have the effect of increasing the pressure. Therefore, one cannot predict the final change in volume.

For the sake of clarity, set up a table as given below.

P_1 = 700 mm	P_2 = ?
V_1 = 2 liters	V_2 = 0.1 liter
T_1 = 293°K	T_2 = 123°K

Since one is given 5 of the 6 values, it is possible to use the combined gas law equation to determine P_2

$$\frac{P_1V_1}{T_1} = \frac{P_2V_2}{T_2}$$

$$P_2 = \frac{T_2V_1P_1}{T_1V_2}$$

$$= \frac{123°K \ (2 \ liters) \ (700 \ mm)}{293°K \ (0.1 \ liter)}$$

$$= 5877 \ mm.$$

750 ml of gas at 300 torr pressure and 50°C is heated until the volume of gas is 2000 ml at a pressure of 700 torr. What is the final temperature of the gas?

<u>Solution</u>: Here, one is given a gaseous system involving pressure, volume and temperature, where two of the variables are changed in going from the original system to the final system. This indicates that the combined gas law should be used. It can be stated: For a given mass of gas, the volume is inversely proportional to the pressure and directly proportional to the absolute temperature. This gas law can also be stated

$$\frac{P_1V_1}{T_1} = \frac{P_2V_2}{T_2}$$

where P_1 is the original pressure, V_1 is the original volume, T_1 is the original absolute temperature, P_2 is the final pressure, V_2 is the final volume, and T_2 is the final absolute temperature.

In this problem, you are given the original pressure, volume and temperature and the final pressure and volume. You are asked to find the final temperature. The temperature in °C must be converted to the absolute scale before using the combined law. This can be done by adding 273 to the temperature in °C.

Converting the temperature:

$T_1 = 50 + 273 = 323°K$

Using the combined law:

$$\frac{P_1V_1}{T_1} = \frac{P_2V_2}{T_2}$$

$P_1 = 300 \ torr$	$P_2 = 700 \ torr$
$V_1 = 750 \ ml$	$V_2 = 2000 \ ml.$
$T_1 = 323°K$	$T_2 = ?$

$$\frac{(300 \ torr) \ (750 \ ml)}{323°K} = \frac{(700 \ torr) \ (2000 \ ml)}{T_2}$$

$$T_2 = \frac{(700 \ torr) \ (2000 \ ml) \ (323°K)}{(300 \ torr) \ (750 \ ml)}$$

25

$T_2 = 2010°K$

Convert T_2 to centigrade by subtracting 273 from it.

$2010 - 273 = 1737°C$.

500 liters of a gas at 27°C and 700 torr would occupy what volume at STP?

Solution: STP (Standard Temperature and Pressure) is defined as being 0°C and 760 torr, thus, in this problem, one is asked to find the new volume of a gas when the temperature and pressure are changed. One refers to the combined gas law in such a case. This law can be stated: For a given mass of gas, the volume is inversely proportional to the pressure and directly proportional to the absolute temperature. Stated algebraically

$$\frac{PV}{T} = K$$

where P is the pressure, V is the volume, T is the absolute temperature, and K is a constant. This means that if two of the variables are changed, the third changes so that the relation $PV/T = K$ remains true. This means that one can now state that

$$\frac{P_1V_1}{T_1} = \frac{P_2V_2}{T_2}$$

where P_1 is the original pressure, V_1 is the original volume, T_1 is the original temperature, P_2 is the new pressure, V_2 is the new volume, and T_2 is the new absolute temperature. In this problem, one is given the temperature on the Celsius scale. It must be converted to the absolute scale before using the combined gas law. This can be done by adding 273 to the temperature in °C.

$T_1 = 27 + 273 = 300°K$

$T_2 = 0 + 273 = 273°K$

One knows P_1, V_1, T_1, P_2, and T_2. One is asked to find V_2.

Using the Combined Gas Laws:

$$\frac{P_1V_1}{T_1} = \frac{P_2V_2}{T_2}$$

$P_1 = 700$ torr

$V_1 = 500$ liters

$$T_1 = 300°K$$

$$P_2 = 760 \text{ torr}$$

$$V_2 = ?$$

$$T_2 = 273°K$$

$$\frac{700 \text{ torr} \times 500 \text{ liters}}{300°K} = \frac{760 \text{ torr} \times V_2}{273°K}$$

$$V_2 = \frac{700 \text{ torr} \times 500 \text{ liters} \times 273°K}{760 \text{ torr} \times 300°K}$$

$$V_2 = 419 \text{ liters}.$$

● **PROBLEM** 2-17

A chemist has a certain amount of gas under a pressure of 33.3 atm; it occupies 30 ℓ at 273°C. For his research, however, the gas must be at standard conditions. Under standard conditions what will the volume of the gas be?

Solution: Standard conditions are defined to be 0°C and 1 atm. Hence, the gas is cooled and the pressure on it is decreased. The combined gas law relates pressure P, volume V and absolute temperature T.

$$k = \frac{PV}{T}$$

where k is a constant that is characteristic to the system. Hence,

$$\frac{P_I V_I}{T_I} = \frac{P_F V_F}{T_F}$$

where the subscript I indicates the initial values and the subscript F indicates the final states.

In this problem one is asked to solve for V_F. The temperatures in °C are converted to °K by adding 273.

$$T_I = 273°C + 273 = 546°K$$

$$T_F = \quad 0°C + 273 = 273°K$$

Solving for V_F:

$$\frac{(33.3 \text{ atm})(30 \text{ ℓ})}{(546°K)} = \frac{(1 \text{ atm})(V_F)}{(273°K)}$$

$$V_F = 499.5 \ \ell.$$

On a hot day, the pressure in an automobile tire increases. Assuming that the air in a tire at 59°F increases in pressure from 28.0 lbs/in^2 to 30.0 lbs/in$_i^2$, (a) what is the temperature of the air in the tire, assuming no change in volume? (b) What will the pressure be if the temperature rises to 106°F?

Solution: (a) Because pressure, volume, and temperature are involved, one thinks of the combined gas law. This law can be stated: For a given mass of gas, the volume is inversely proportional to the pressure and directly proportional to the absolute temperature. This law can be algebraically stated as:

$$\frac{PV}{T} = K,$$

where P is the pressure, V is the volume, T is the absolute temperature, and K is a constant. This means that if two of the parameters are changed, the third will adjust itself so that PV/T = K is still true. The following equation is thus true:

$$\frac{P_1 V_1}{T_1} = \frac{P_2 V_2}{T_2}$$

where P_1 is the original temperature, V_1 is the original volume, T_1 is the original absolute temperature, P_2 is the new pressure, V_2 is the new volume, and T_2 is the new absolute temperature. When $V_1 = V_2$, as in this problem, it follows from the formula that pressure is directly proportional to absolute temperature. In this case, the law can be written

$$\frac{P_1}{T_1} = \frac{P_2}{T_2}$$

In this problem, the temperature is given in °F, and must be converted to °K before it is used in the combined gas law. This is done by first converting it to °C and then adding 273.°F are converted to °C by use of the following equation:

$$°C = 5/9(°F - 32)$$

$$T_1 \text{ in } °C = 5/9 \ (59° - 32°) = 15°C$$

$$T_1 = 15 + 273 = 288°K.$$

One is given P_1, P_2, and T_1 and asked to find T_2.

$$\frac{P_1}{T_1} = \frac{P_2}{T_2}$$

P_1 = 28.0 lbs/in^2

T_1 = 288°K

P_2 = 30.0 lbs/in^2

T_2 = ?

$$\frac{28.0 \text{ lbs/in}^2}{288°K} = \frac{30.0 \text{ lbs/in}^2}{T_2}$$

$$T_2 = \frac{30.0 \text{ lbs/in}^2 \times 288°K}{28.0 \text{ lbs/in}^2} = 309°K.$$

The absolute temperature can now be converted to °F by first subtracting 273°, and then using the equation for conversion from °C to °F.

°F = 9/5 °C + 32

T_2 in °C = 309° - 273 = 36°C

T_2 in F = 9/5 (36°) + 32 = 97°F.

(b) One can again use the shortened form of the combined gas law, here:

$$\frac{P_1}{T_1} = \frac{P_2}{T_2}$$

Here, one is given T_1, T_2, and P_1 and asked to find P_2. The temperatures must be converted to the absolute scale before use. The same method as used in part (a) will be applied.

T_1 in °C = 5/9 (59 - 32) = 15°C

T_1 in °K = 15 + 273 = 288°K

T_2 in °C = 5/9 (106 - 32) = 41°C

T_2 = 41 + 273 = 314°K

The P_2 can now be found

$$\frac{P_1}{T_1} = \frac{P_2}{T_2}$$

P_1 = 28.0 lbs/in^2

T_1 = 288°K

P_2 = ?

T_2 = 314°K

$$\frac{28.0 \text{ lbs/in}^2}{288°K} = \frac{P_2}{314°K}$$

$$P_2 = \frac{314°K \times 28.0 \text{ lbs/in}^2}{288°K} = 30.5 \text{ lbs/in}^2.$$

AVOGADRO'S LAW-THE MOLE CONCEPT

● PROBLEM 2-19

How many moles are there in one atom?

Solution: A mole of atoms is defined as containing Avogadro's Number of atoms. Avogadro's number is 6.02×10^{23}. Therefore, the number of moles in one atom is equal to 1 atom divided by 6.02×10^{23} atoms/mole.

$$\text{No. of moles} = \frac{1 \text{ atom}}{6.02 \times 10^{23} \text{ atoms/mole}}$$

$$= 1.66 \times 10^{-24} \text{ moles}.$$

● PROBLEM 2-20

During the course of World War I, 1.1×10^8 kg of poison gas was fired on Allied soldiers by German troops. If the gas is assumed to be phosgene ($COCl_2$), how many molecules of gas does this correspond to?

Solution: To solve this problem we must convert mass to number of moles and then multiply by Avogadro's number to obtain the corresponding number of molecules.

The number of moles of gas is given by

$$\text{moles} = \frac{\text{mass (grams)}}{\text{molecular weight of } COCl_2 \text{ (g/mole)}}$$

The mass of gas is 1.1×10^8 kg = 1.1×10^8 kg $\times 10^3$ g/kg = 1.1×10^{11} g. The molecular weight of $COCl_2$ is obtained by adding the atomic weights (atm. wgt.) of its constituents. Thus,

$$\text{molecular weight } (COCl_2) = \text{atm wgt(C)} + \text{atm wgt(O)}$$
$$+ 2 \times \text{atm wgt(Cl)}$$

$$= 12.0 \text{ g/mole} + 16.0 \text{ g/mole}$$
$$+ 2 \times 35.5 \text{ g/mole}$$

$$= 99 \text{ g/mole}.$$

Hence, the number of moles of gas is

$$\text{moles} = \frac{\text{mass}}{\text{molecular weight}} = \frac{1.1 \times 10^{11} \text{ g}}{99 \text{ g/mole}}$$

$$\approx 1.1 \times 10^9 \text{ moles}.$$

Multiplying the number of moles by Avogadro's number, we obtain the number of molecules of gas:

number of molecules = moles × Avogadro's number

$$= 1.1 \times 10^9 \text{ moles} \times 6 \times 10^{23} \text{ molecules/mole}$$

$$= 6.6 \times 10^{32} \text{ molecules.}$$

● PROBLEM 2-21

An automobile travelling at 10 miles per hour produces 0.33 lb of CO gas per mile. How many moles of CO are produced per mile?

Solution: The number of moles of a substance is equal to the quotient of the mass (in grams) of that substance and its molecular weight (in g/mole), or

$$\text{moles} = \frac{\text{mass (g)}}{\text{molecular weight (g/mole)}}$$

The mass of CO is 0.33 lb = 0.33 lb × 454 g/lb = 150 g. The molecular weight of CO is the sum of the atomic weight of C and the atomic weight of O, or

molecular weight (CO) = atomic weight (C) + atomic weight (O)

$$= 12 \text{ g/mole} + 16 \text{ g/mole}$$

$$= 28 \text{ g/mole.}$$

Hence,

$$\text{moles} = \frac{\text{mass (g)}}{\text{molecular weight (g/mole)}} = \frac{150 \text{ g}}{28 \text{ g/mole}}$$

$$= 5.4 \text{ moles per mile.}$$

THE IDEAL GAS LAW

● PROBLEM 2-22

Three researchers studied 1 mole of an ideal gas at 273°K in order to determine the value of the gas constant, R. The first researcher found that at a pressure of 1 atm the gas occupies 22.4 ℓ. The second researcher found that the gas occupies 22.4 ℓ at a pressure of 760 torr. Finally, the third researcher reported the product of pressure and volume as 542 cal. What value for R did each researcher determine?

Solution: This problem is an application of the ideal gas equation, PV = n RT, where P = pressure, V = volume, n = number of moles, R = gas constant, and T = absolute temperature. Specifically, we are trying to determine R from the relation R = PV/nT. All three researchers worked with one mole of gas (n = 1) at T = 273°K. Their results are as follows:

First researcher: P = 1 atm, V = 22.4 ℓ.

$$R = \frac{PV}{nT} = \frac{1 \text{ atm} \times 22.4 \text{ } \ell}{1 \text{ mole} \times 273°K} = 0.0821 \frac{\ell\text{-atm}}{°K \text{ mole}}$$

Second researcher: P = 760 torr = 760 torr $\times \frac{1 \text{ atm}}{760 \text{ torr}}$ = 1 atm, V = 22.4 ℓ.

$$R = \frac{PV}{nT} = \frac{1 \text{ atm} \times 22.4 \text{ } \ell}{1 \text{ mole} \times 273°K} = 0.0821 \frac{\ell\text{-atm}}{°K \text{ mole}}$$

Third researcher: PV = 542 cal = nRT = 1 mole (R) (273°K)

$$R = \frac{PV}{nT} = \frac{542 \text{ cal}}{(1 \text{ mole}) (273°K)} = 1.99 \text{ cal/mole } °K.$$

● **PROBLEM** 2-23

How many moles of hydrogen gas are present in a 50 liter steel cylinder if the pressure is 10 atmospheres and the temperature is 27°C? R = .082 liter-atm/mole °K.

Solution: In this problem, one is asked to find the number of moles of hydrogen gas present where the volume, pressure and temperature are given. This would indicate that the Ideal Gas Law should be used because this law relates these quantities to each other. The Ideal Gas Law can be stated:

PV = nRT,

where P is the pressure, V is the volume, n is the number of moles, R is the gas constant (.082 liter-atm/mole °K), and T is the absolute temperature. Here, one is given the temperature in °C, which means it must be converted to the absolute scale. P, V, and R are also known. To convert a temperature in °C to the absolute scale, add 273 to the temperature in °C.

$$T = 27 + 273 = 300°K$$

Using the Ideal Gas Law:

$$PV = nRT \qquad \text{or} \qquad n = \frac{PV}{RT}$$

P = 10 atm

V = 50 liters

R = .082 liter-atm/mole °K

T = 300°K

n = number of moles of H_2 present

$$n = \frac{(10\ atm)(50\ liters)}{(.082\ liter\text{-}atm/mole\ °K)(300°K)}$$

= 20 moles.

● PROBLEM 2-24

The barometric pressure on the lunar surface is about 10^{-10} torr. At a temperature of 100°K, what volume of lunar atmosphere contains (a) 10^6 molecules of gas, and (b) 1 millimole of gas?

Solution: This problem is an application of the ideal gas equation, PV = nRT, where P = pressure, V = volume, n = number of moles, R = gas constant, and T = absolute temperature. Solving for V, V = nRT/P. In the first part of this problem, we use the definition

$n = \dfrac{\text{number of molecules}}{\text{Avogadro's number}} = \dfrac{N}{A}$. We must then substitute

into the formula V = nRT/P =(N/A)(RT/P)in order to obtain the volume corresponding to N molecules. In the second part of this problem we can use V = nRT/P directly, remembering that 1 millimole = 10^{-3} mole.

Hence, for the first part of the problem,

$$V = \frac{N}{A}\ \frac{RT}{P} = \frac{10^6\ \text{molecules}}{6.02 \times 10^{23}\ \text{molecules/mole}}$$

$$\times\ \frac{0.0821\ \ell\text{ -atm/°K - mole} \times 100°K}{1.316 \times 10^{-13}\ atm}$$

= 1.04×10^{-4} ℓ, where we have used P = 10^{-10} torr =

$$10^{-10} \text{ torr} \times \frac{1 \text{ atm}}{760 \text{ torr}} = 1.316 \times 10^{-13} \text{ atm}.$$

For the second part of the problem, $V = \frac{nRT}{P}$

$$= \frac{10^{-3} \text{ mole} \times .0821 \text{ } \ell - \text{atm}/^{\circ}\text{K} - \text{mole} \times 100^{\circ}\text{K}}{1.316 \times 10^{-13} \text{ atm}}$$

$$= 6.24 \times 10^{10} \text{ } \ell.$$

● **PROBLEM** 2-25

Describe the curve one would obtain by plotting pressure versus volume for an ideal gas in which the temperature and number of moles of gas are held constant.

Solution: This problem requires a plot of the ideal gas equation. This equation reads

$$PV = nRT,$$

where P = pressure of gas, V = volume of gas, n = number of moles of gas, R = gas constant, and T = absolute temperature of gas. Since R is a constant and n and T are held constant, the product nRT may be combined into a single constant, call it k. Then, PV = nRT = k, or

$$PV = k$$

which is the equation of a hyperbola. Plotting P on the abscissa axis and V on the ordinate axis, we obtain the following curve:

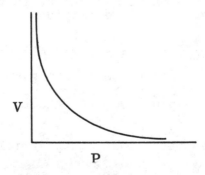

Note: Even if we did not know PV = k is the graph of a hyperbola, we could still obtain this graph. For example, if k is a constant, P and V must vary inversely with each other. In other words, if P is large, V must be small for k to remain constant. Likewise, if V is large, P must be small.

A sample of a gas exhibiting ideal behavior occupies a volume of 350 mℓ at 25.0°C and 600 torr. Determine its volume at 600°C and 25.0 torr.

Solution: We can solve this problem by determining the number of moles, n, of gas from the ideal gas equation, PV = nRT (where P = pressure, V = volume, n = number of moles, R = gas constant, and T = absolute temperature) by using the first set of conditions and then substituting this value of n along with P and T from the second set of conditions into the ideal gas equation and solving for V. However, we can save useless calculation by denoting the first and second sets of conditions by subscripts "1" and "2", respectively, to obtain

$$P_1V_1 = nRT_1, \quad \text{and} \quad P_2V_2 = nRT_2,$$

where n is the same in both cases. Dividing the second of these equations by the first we obtain

$$\frac{P_2V_2}{P_1V_1} = \frac{nRT_2}{nRT_1} \quad \text{or} \quad \frac{P_2V_2}{P_1V_1} = \frac{T_2}{T_1},$$

where we have cancelled n and R (both constant). Solving for V_2, we obtain

$$V_2 = \frac{P_1V_1}{P_2} \times \frac{T_2}{T_1}$$

$$= \frac{600 \text{ torr} \times 350 \text{ mℓ}}{25.0 \text{ torr}} \times \frac{873.15°K}{298.15°K}$$

$$= 24.6 \times 10^3 \text{ mℓ}$$

$$= 24.6 \text{ ℓ}.$$

A 3-liter bulb containing oxygen at 195 torr is connected to a 2-liter bulb containing nitrogen at 530 torr by means of a closed valve. The valve is opened and the two gases are allowed to equilibrate at constant temperature, T. Calculate the equilibrium pressure.

Solution: We will solve for the final or equilibrium pressure, P_f, by using the ideal gas law,

$$P_f = \frac{nRT}{V_f}$$

where n is the number of moles of O_2 $\left(n_{O_2}\right)$ plus the number of moles of N_2 $\left(n_{N_2}\right)$, that is, the total number of moles of gas, R is the gas constant, T the absolute temperature, and V_f the final volume (3 liters + 2 liters = 5 liters). We cannot solve this equation directly, since we do not know T.

The quantities n_{O_2} and n_{N_2} are calculated using the initial conditions and the ideal gas law,

$$n_a = \frac{P_a V_a}{RT}$$

where P_a is the original partial pressure of gas a and V_a is the volume initially occupied by gas a. Thus,

$$n_{O_2} = \frac{P_{O_2} V_{O_2}}{RT} = \frac{195 \text{ torr} \times 3 \text{ liters}}{RT} , \qquad \text{and}$$

$$n_{N_2} = \frac{P_{N_2} V_{N_2}}{RT} = \frac{530 \text{ torr} \times 2 \text{ liters}}{RT}$$

Multiplying both equations by RT and then adding,

$$n_{O_2} RT + n_{N_2} RT$$

$$= \left(\frac{195 \text{ torr} \times 3 \text{ liters}}{RT}\right) RT + \left(\frac{530 \text{ torr} \times 2 \text{ liters}}{RT}\right) RT$$

$$\left(n_{O_2} + n_{N_2}\right) RT = 195 \text{ torr} \times 3 \text{ liters} + 530 \text{ torr}$$
$$\times 2 \text{ liters}.$$

Dividing both sides by V_f, we obtain

$$\left(n_{O_2} + n_{N_2}\right) \frac{RT}{V_f} = \frac{195 \text{ torr} \times 3 \text{ liters} + 530 \text{ torr} \times 2 \text{ liters}}{V_f} .$$

But $n_{O_2} + n_{N_2} = n$, and $P_f = nRT/V_f$. Hence,

$$P_f = \frac{nRT}{V_f} = \left(n_{O_2} + n_{N_2}\right) \frac{RT}{V_f}$$

$$= \frac{195 \text{ torr} \times 3 \text{ liters} + 530 \text{ torr} \times 2 \text{ liters}}{V_f}$$

$$= \frac{195 \text{ torr} \times 3 \text{ liters} + 530 \text{ torr} \times 2 \text{ liters}}{5 \text{ liters}}$$

$$= 329 \text{ torr}.$$

A research worker isolated an unknown compound from one of his reaction products. This compound was a volatile liquid with a boiling point of 65°C. A .134 g sample of the liquid was vaporized and the gas was collected. The temperature of the collecting chamber was kept at 98°C in order that liquefaction would not occur. After all the sample was vaporized, the volume of the gas was measured as .0532 liters at 98°C and 737 mm. Calculate the molecular weight.

Solution: We are dealing with the variables m = mass, V = volume, P = pressure, and T = temperature. Whenever this occurs, it indicates that one should employ the ideal gas equation, PV = nRT, where n = moles and R = universal gas constant. An ideal gas is one in which the gas molecules take up no space and do not attract one another. Real gases do not completely meet these conditions, but at values in the neighborhood of standard conditions (0°C and 1 atm), the difference in the real and ideal values is small enough such that the ideal gas law is accurate enough to carry out the calculations.

One further bit of information is required. Since M.W. (Molecular Weight) does not appear anywhere in the equation, a relation must be found between M.W. and one of the 4 variables. The relation is n = moles = mass/M.W. Substituting this into the ideal gas equation we obtain

$$PV = \frac{m}{M.W.} \; RT$$

Solving for the molecular weight, we obtain:

$$MW = \frac{mRT}{PV}$$

m = mass of the sample = .134 g

R = gas constant = .082 liter - atm/mole - °K

T = 98°C = 273 + 98 = 371°K

V = 0.0532 ℓ

P = 737 mm. For the formula, P must be given in atmospheres. To do this, we multiply 737 mm by the conversion factor of $\frac{1 \text{ atm}}{760 \text{ mm}}$. Thus,

$$737 \text{ mm} = 737 \text{ mm} \cdot \frac{1 \text{ atm}}{760 \text{ mm}} = \frac{737}{760} \text{ atm.}$$

$$MW = \frac{(0.134)(0.082)(371)}{(737/760)(0.0532)} = 79.018 \text{ g/mole.}$$

Assuming ideal gas behavior, what is the molecular weight of a gas with a density of 2.50 g/liter at 98°C and .974 atm?

Solution: You must employ the ideal gas law to answer this question. This law, also called the equation of state for an ideal gas, relates pressure, volume, temperature, and moles to each other quantitatively. It states PV = nRT, where R is called the universal gas constant, P = pressure, V = volume, T = temperature in Kelvin, and n = number of moles. You can also write this equation as n/V = P/RT to determine moles per liter. By substituting,

$$\frac{.974 \text{ atm}}{(.0821 \text{ liter-atm/mole-°K})(371°K)} = .0320 \text{ moles/liter.}$$

Therefore, according to the above calculation, you know there are .0320 moles in one liter. However, the density is 2.50 g/liter. Hence, you can compare the two, and obtain the fact that .0320 moles weighs 2.50 g. From this, the molecule weight determination follows via a proportion. If 0.032 moles weighs 2.50 g, then 1 mole weighs x grams, which equals the molecular weight. In other words,

$\frac{.032}{2.50} = \frac{1}{x}$. Solving for x, we obtain x = 78.1 g.

● **PROBLEM** 2-30

A cylinder contains oxygen at a pressure of 10 atm and a temperature of 300°K. The volume of the cylinder is 10 liters. What is the mass of the oxygen?

Solution: In this problem, we are dealing with 4 variables ·· = mass, V = volume, P = pressure, and T = temperature. Three of them are given; we must calculate the fourth. These variables are governed by the ideal gas law.

An ideal gas is one in which the molecules have no attraction for one another and the molecules themselves occupy no space (a situation contrary to fact). Real gases do not completely satisfy either of these conditions, but under conditions close to STP (0°C and 1 atm), the real gases come very close to meeting these conditions. Therefore, the difference between the real and ideal values is small enough such that the ideal gas law equation can be used. It is:

PV = n RT

where n is the number of moles. Moles is defined as

grams/molecular weight. R is a gas constant equal to
.082 (liter)-(atm)/(°K)-(mole).

We are asked to find the mass of oxygen, yet there
is no value for mass in the ideal gas equation. Therefore, we must find an equation that involves mass and
moles. That equation is moles = grams/M.W. The molecular
weight of O_2 = 32 g/ mole. Therefore, substitute the
mole equation into the ideal gas equation

$$PV = nRT = \frac{M}{M.W.} RT$$

The only unknown value is mass and the solution is
arrived at by substituting in the appropriate values

$$(10 \text{ atm})(10 \text{ liter}) = \frac{m}{32} (.082)(300°K)$$

$$m = \frac{32 \times 10 \times 10}{.082 \times 300} = 130.08 \text{ grams.}$$

Metallic sodium violently liberates H_2 gas according to the
reaction

$$2Na(s) + 2H_2O(\ell) \rightarrow 2NaOH + H_2(g)$$

If you collect the gas at 25°C under 758 mm Hg of pressure, and it occupies 2.24 liters, (a) find the number of
moles of hydrogen produced, (b) find the number of moles
of water decomposed and (c) find the persent error in
(a) if the gaseous hydrogen had been collected dry,
assuming the vapor pressure of water is 23.8 mm at 25°C.
(R + .0821 ℓ-atm/mole K.)

Solution: (a) You want to determine the number of moles
of hydrogen gas liberated given its pressure, volume and
temperature. Therefore, you make use of the equation of state,
which indicates that PV = nRT, where P = pressure, V =
volume, R = universal gas constant, T = temperature in
Kelvin (Celsius plus 273°), and n = moles. Thus, to find
n, substitute into this equation and solve for n.

In 1 atm, there is 760 mm of pressure. You use
atmospheres as the units of pressure, since R is expressed
in atmospheres. Hence,

$$P = 758 \text{ mm} = \frac{758}{760} \text{ atms} = .997 \text{ atm.}$$

We are given R in the problem statement and that T = 298°K
and V = 2.24 ℓ. Substituting,

$$n = \frac{(.997)(2.24)}{(.0821)(298^\circ K)} = .0913 \text{ mole } H_2.$$

Now that you know how many moles of H_2 are liberated, you also know how much water decomposed via the stoichiometry of the reaction.

In (b), therefore, you make use of the equation

$$2Na(s) + 2H_2O(\ell) \rightarrow 2NaOH + H_2(g),$$

which tells you that for every mole of $H_2(g)$ produced you have 2 moles of H_2O decomposed. You calculated a release of .0913 moles of H_2. Therefore, $2 \times .0913 = .183$ mole of water must have decomposed. For (c) you must realize that if the hydrogen gas were wet (not dried), the pressure given is not the true pressure of the H_2. For in this pressure is included the vapor pressure of water. Thus, the actual pressure of H_2 is only $758 - 23.8 = 734.2$, where 23.8 was the given vapor pressure of water at 25°C. The % error is, then

$$\frac{23.8}{734.2} \times 100 = 3.24 \text{ \%.}$$

• PROBLEM 2-32

Compare the number of H_2 and N_2 molecules in two containers described as follows: (1) A 2-liter container of Hydrogen filled at 127°C and 5 atm. (2) A 5-liter container of nitrogen filled at 27°C and 3 atm.

Solution: Avogadro's Law states that equal numbers of molecules are contained in equal volumes of different gases if the pressure and temperature are the same. Therefore, if the conditions were the same, then there would be equal numbers of molecules of H_2 and N_2.

For reasons of clarity, it is useful to set up a table like that shown below.

gas	V	T	P
H_2	2 liters	400°K	5 atm
N_2	5 liters	300°K	3 atm

By using the general gas equation

$$PV = nRT$$

where n = number of moles, and R = 0.082 atm-liter/°K-mole, one can find the number of moles of H_2 and N_2.

Thus, for H_2

$$n = \frac{PV}{RT} = \frac{(5 \text{ atm})(2\ell)}{(0.082 \text{ atm-}\ell/\text{mole-}^\circ K)(400^\circ K)} = 0.305 \text{ moles}$$

for N_2

$$n = \frac{PV}{RT} = \frac{(3 \text{ atm})(5 \ell)}{(0.082 \text{ atm-}\ell/\text{mole-}^\circ K)(300^\circ K)} = 0.610 \text{ moles}.$$

There are twice as many moles of N_2 as there are of H_2. Since the number of molecules is directly proportional to the number of moles, then there are twice as many molecules of N_2 as molecules of H_2.

● **PROBLEM** 2-33

A 0.100 ℓ container maintained at constant temperature contains 5.0×10^{10} molecules of an ideal gas. How many molecules remain if the volume is changed to 0.005 ℓ? What volume is occupied by 10,000 molecules at the initial temperature and pressure?

Solution: Since only the volume changed and no molecules were added to or withdrawn from the system, the number of molecules at a volume of 0.005 ℓ is the same as that at a volume of 0.100 ℓ, or 5.0×10^{10} molecules.

In the second part of the problem we require a relationship between volume and number of molecules, taking into account the fact that the number of molecules can change. We will obtain such a relationship by modifying the ideal gas equation, $PV = nRT$, where P = pressure, V = volume, n = number of moles, R = gas constant, and T = absolute temperature. Since the number of moles is equal to the number of molecules, N, divided by Avogadro's number, A, or $n = N/A$, we can write the ideal gas equation as $PV = nRT = N/A \, RT$, or

$$PVA = NRT.$$

The initial and final pressure and temperature are the same. Also, A and R are constants. Denoting the initial volume and number of molecules by V_i and N_i, respectively, and the final volume and number of molecules by V_f and N_f, respectively, we obtain

$$PV_i A = N_i RT \quad \text{and} \quad PV_f A = N_f RT.$$

Dividing the second of these by the first we obtain

$$\frac{PV_f A}{PV_i A} = \frac{N_f RT}{N_i RT} \qquad \text{or} \qquad \frac{V_f}{V_i} = \frac{N_f}{N_i},$$

where we have cancelled all the constants. Solving for the

final volume we obtain

$$V_f = V_i \times \frac{N_f}{N_i} = 0.100 \; \ell \times \frac{10,000}{5 \times 10^{10}} = 2 \times 10^{-8} \; \ell.$$

● **PROBLEM** 2-34

At standard conditions, it is found that 28.0 g of carbon monoxide occupies 22.4 ℓ. What is the density of carbon monoxide at 20°C and 600 torr?

Solution: The density of carbon monoxide under STP or standard conditions (pressure = 1 atm or 760 torr and temperature = 0°C or 273.15°K) is ρ = mass/volume. 28 g of CO, carbon monoxide, represents one mole and a mole of any gas occupies 22.4 liters of volume under standard conditions. Thus, ρ = 28g/22.4 ℓ = 1.25 g/ℓ.

We can apply the equation $P/(\rho T)$ = constant, which holds for ideal gases of density ρ at pressure P and absolute temperature T. We will first determine the constant for our system and then use this value to calculate the density at 20°C = 293.15°K and 600 torr.

The value of the constant for our system is

$$\text{constant} = \frac{P}{\rho T} = \frac{760 \; \text{torr}}{1.25 \; \text{g/}\ell \times 273.15°K} = 2.225 \; \frac{\text{torr} - \ell}{\text{g} - °K}.$$

Hence, for our system, $\dfrac{P}{\rho T} = 2.225 \; \dfrac{\text{torr} - \ell}{\text{g} - °K}$ or

$\rho = \dfrac{P}{T} \times \dfrac{1}{2.225 \; \text{torr} - \ell/\text{g} - °K}$. At 20°C = 293.15°K and

600 torr, the density of CO is

$$\rho = \frac{P}{T} \times \frac{1}{2.225 \; \text{torr} - \ell/\text{g} - °K}$$

$$= \frac{600 \; \text{torr}}{293.15°K} \times \frac{1}{2.225 \; \text{torr} - \ell/\text{g} - °K} = .9198 \; \text{g/}\ell.$$

● **PROBLEM** 2-35

One gram of an unknown gaseous compound of boron (B, atomic weight = 10.8 g/mole) and hydrogen (H, atomic weight = 1.0 g/mole) occupies 0.820 liter at 1.00 atm at 276 K. What is the molecular formula of this compound?

Solution: The general formula for the compound is $B_a H_b$, where a and b are to be determined. To find these, we must first find the molecular weight of the compound by using the ideal gas law,

$$PV = nRT,$$

where P = pressure, V = volume, n = number of moles, R = gas constant, and T = absolute temperature. n equals the mass, m, divided by the molecular weight MW, $PV = nRT = \frac{m}{MW} RT$, or $MW = \frac{mRT}{PV}$.

$$MW = \frac{mRT}{PV} = \frac{1 \text{ g} \times 0.082 \text{ liter - atm/mole-}^{\circ}K \times 276^{\circ}K}{1.00 \text{ atm} \times 0.820 \text{ liter}}$$

$$= 27.6 \text{ g/mole.}$$

To find a and b, we use the relation $MW_{B_aH_b}$ = a × atomic weight of B plus b × atomic weight of H, or 27.6 g/mole = a × 10.8 g/mole + b × 1.0 g/mole.

By trial and error, we find that a = 2 and b = 6 (2 × 10.8 g/mole + 6 × 1.0 g/mole = 27.6 g/mole), so that the formula of our compound is B_2H_6 (diborane).

● PROBLEM 2-36

$KMnO_4$ is added to a 350 ml solution of an approximately 3% H_2O_2 solution. It is found that 3.94 cm^3 of O_2 gas is released. It is collected over H_2O at a pressure (barometric) of 0.941 atm and 28°C. Assuming that the pressure due to water vapor is 0.0373 atm, what is the actual concentration of the H_2O_2 solution?

Solution: The concentration of a solution is given in terms of molarity, i.e., moles/liter. This means that the number of moles of H_2O_2 must be determined, since you already know the volume.

To determine the number of moles of H_2O_2, you know that, when oxidized, 1 mole of H_2O_2 yields 1 mole of O_2. Thus, if you know the number of moles of O_2 produced, you also know the moles of H_2O_2 originally present. To find the number of moles of O_2, you must use the equation of state. This tells us PV = nRT, where P = pressure, V = volume, n = number of moles, R = universal gas constant, (.082057 1-atm mol^{-1} deg^{-1}), and T = temperature in degrees Kelvin (degree Celsius plus 273°). Hence,

$$n_{O_2} = \frac{PV}{RT}.$$

All the values needed to find n_{O_2} are known or can be calculated. The pressure of O_2 will not be .941 atm, since

43

this figure also includes vapor pressure from water. Therefore, the actual pressure of O_2 is .941 - .0373. That is, the difference between barometric and vapor pressure. Substituting, you obtain

$$n_{O_2} = \frac{(.941 - .0373)(3.94 \times 10^{-3})}{(.082)(301)} = 1.44 \times 10^{-4}$$

moles of O_2. This means there were originally 1.44×10^{-4} moles. Now, recalling the definition of molarity, which represents the concentration of a solution, you have

$$\frac{1.44 \times 10^{-4} \text{ moles}}{.350 \text{ liters}} = 4.12 \times 10^{-4} \text{ M}$$

which is the concentration of the H_2O_2 solution.

CHAPTER 3

GAS MIXTURES AND OTHER PHYSICAL PROPERTIES OF GASES

MOLE FRACTION

Calculate the mole fractions of ethyl alcohol, C_2H_5OH, and water in a solution made by dissolving 9.2 g of alcohol in 18 g of H_2O. M.W. of $H_2O = 18$, M.W. of $C_2H_5OH = 46$.

Solution: Mole fraction problems are similar to % composition problems. A mole fraction of a compound tells us what fraction of 1 mole of solution is due to that particular compound. Hence,

$$\text{mole fraction of solute} = \frac{\text{moles of solute}}{\text{moles of solute + moles of solvent}}$$

The solute is the substance being dissolved into or added to the solution. The solvent is the solution to which the solute is added.

The equation for finding mole fractions is:

$$\frac{\text{moles A}}{\text{moles A + moles B}} = \text{mole fraction A}$$

Moles are defined as grams/molecular weight (MW). Therefore, first find the number of moles of each compound present and then use the above equation.

$$\text{moles of } C_2H_5OH = \frac{9.2 \text{ g}}{46.0 \text{ g/mole}} = .2 \text{ mole}$$

$$\text{moles of } H_2O \quad = \frac{18 \text{ g}}{18 \text{ g/mole}} \quad = 1 \text{ mole}$$

$$\text{mole fraction of } C_2H_5OH = \frac{.2}{1 + .2} = .167$$

mole fraction of H_2O $= \dfrac{1}{1 + .2} = .833.$

Note, that the sum of the mole fractions is equal to 1.

● PROBLEM 3-2

Of the many compounds present in cigarette smoke, such as the carcinogen 3,4-benzo[a]pyrene, some of the more abundant are listed in the following table along with their mole fractions:

Component	Mole Fraction
H_2	0.016
O_2	0.12
CO	0.036
CO_2	0.079

What is the mass of carbon monoxide in a 35.0 ml puff of smoke at standard temperature and pressure (STP)?

Solution: Assuming ideal gas behavior, we will calculate the number of moles of ideal gas in a 35.0 ml volume. Using the mole fraction of CO in smoke, we will then obtain the number of moles of CO in a 35.0 ml volume and finally convert this to a mass.

The molar volume of an ideal gas is 22.4 liter/mole when STP conditions exist, i.e. when temp. = 0°C and pressure = 1 atm. Hence, the number of moles of ideal gas in a 35.0 ml volume is obtained by dividing this volume by the molar volume of gas, or 35.0 ml/22.4 liter/mole = 0.035 liter/22.4 liter/mole = 1.56×10^{-3} mole.

The mole fraction is defined by the equation

$$\text{mole fraction CO} = \frac{\text{moles CO}}{\text{total number of moles}}$$

solving for the number of moles of CO,

moles CO = mole fraction CO × total number of moles
$= 0.036 \times 1.56 \times 10^{-3}$ mole
$\equiv 5.6 \times 10^{-5}$ mole.

This is converted to a mass by multiplying by the molecular weight of CO (28 g/mole). Hence,

mass of CO = moles of CO × molecular weight of CO
$= 5.6 \times 10^{-5}$ mole × 28 g/mole
$= 1.6 \times 10^{-3}$ g.

It has been estimated that each square meter of the earth's surface supports 1×10^7 g of air above it. If air is 20% oxygen (O_2, molecular weight = 32 g/mole) by weight, approximately how many moles of O_2 are there above each square meter of the earth?

Solution: This problem is solved by first calculating what weight of oxygen is present in 1×10^7 g of air and then dividing by the molecular weight of oxygen to convert this mass to moles.

Using the definition of weight percent,

$$\text{weight \% of } O_2 = \frac{\text{weight of } O_2}{\text{total weight}} \times 100\%$$

$$20\% = \frac{\text{weight of } O_2}{1 \times 10^7 \text{ g}} \times 100\%$$

$$20 = \frac{\text{weight of } O_2}{1 \times 10^7 \text{ g}} \times 100$$

Solving for the weight of O_2,

$$\text{weight of } O_2 = \frac{20}{100} \times 1 \times 10^7 \text{ g} = 2 \times 10^6 \text{ g}.$$

The number of moles of O_2 is equal to the weight of O_2 divided by the molecular weight, or

$$\text{moles of } O_2 = \frac{\text{weight of } O_2}{\text{molecular weight}} = \frac{2 \times 10^6 \text{ g}}{32 \text{ g/mole}}$$

$$\cong 6 \times 10^4 \text{ moles}.$$

Therefore, each square meter of the earth's surface supports 6×10^4 moles of O_2.

DALTON'S LAW OF PARTIAL PRESSURES

A mixture of nitrogen and oxygen gas is collected by displacement of water at 30°C and 700 torr Hg pressure. If the partial pressure of nitrogen is 550 torr Hg, what is the partial pressure of oxygen? (Vapor pressure of H_2O at 30°C = 32 torr Hg.)

Solution: Here, one uses Dalton's Law of partial pressures. This law can be stated: Each of the gases in a gaseous mixture behaves independently of the other gases and exerts its own pressure; the total pressure of the mixture being the sum of the partial pressures exerted by each gas present. Stated algebraically

$$P_{total} = p_1 + p_2 + \ldots p_n$$

where P_{total} is the total pressure and p_1, p_2, ... p_n are the partial pressures of the gases present. In this problem, one is told that oxygen and nitrogen are collected over H_2O, which means that there will also be water vapor present in the gaseous mixture. In this case, the equation for the total pressure can be written

$$P_{total} = P_{O_2} + P_{N_2} + P_{H_2O}$$

One is given P_{total}, P_{N_2}, and P_{H_2O} and asked to find P_{O_2}. This can be done by using the law of partial pressures

$$P_{total} = P_{O_2} + P_{N_2} + P_{H_2O} \qquad P_{total} = 700 \text{ torr}$$

$$\qquad\qquad\qquad\qquad\qquad\qquad P_{O_2} = ?$$

$$700 \text{ torr} = P_{O_2} + 550 \text{ torr} + 32 \text{ torr} \qquad P_{N_2} = 550 \text{ torr}$$

$$P_{O_2} = (700 - 550 - 32) \text{torr} \qquad P_{H_2O} = 32 \text{ torr}$$

$$= 118 \text{ torr}$$

$$P_{O_2} = 118 \text{ torr.}$$

● **PROBLEM 3-5**

Methane is burnt in oxygen to produce carbon dioxide and water vapor according to the following reaction, $CH_{4 (g)} + 2O_{2 (g)} \rightarrow CO_{2 (g)} + 2H_2O_{(g)}$. The final pressure of the gaseous products was 6.25 torr. Calculate the partial pressure of the water vapor.

Solution: The partial pressure of each of the components in a mixture of gaseous substances will be equal to the product of the mole fraction of that component in the gas and the total pressure of the system. Given the total vapor pressure of the gases, one can calculate the mole fraction of the water vapor.

Let P_A = partial pressure of the water vapor, N_T = total number of moles of gases produced, N_A = number of moles of water vapor, and P_T = total pressure. This law can now be expressed in these terms:

$$P_A = \frac{N_A}{N_T} P_T \quad .$$ From the stoichiometry of the

equation, the total number of moles of products is 3.
Out of these 2 moles are water vapor. Thus, substituting,

$$P_A = 2/3 \ (6.25 \text{ torr}) = 4.16 \text{ torr of water vapor.}$$

A mixture of gaseous oxygen and nitrogen is stored at
atmospheric pressure in a 3.7 ℓ iron container maintained
at constant temperature. After all the oxygen has reacted with the iron walls of the container to form solid
iron oxide of negligible volume, the pressure is measured
at 450 torr. Determine the final volume of nitrogen and
the initial and final partial pressures of nitrogen and
oxygen.

Solution: The partial pressure of each component, which
is independent of any other component in a gaseous mixture
at a defined volume, is equal to the pressure each component would exert if it were the only gas in that volume.
The total pressure of a gaseous mixture is the sum of the
partial pressures of the components. These two definitions
are sufficient to solve this problem.

Once all the oxygen has reacted, no oxygen is present
in the gaseous phase, so that the final partial pressure
of oxygen is zero. By the second definition, final total
pressure = final partial pressure of N_2 + final partial
pressure of O_2

450 torr = final partial pressure of N_2 + 0 torr

or, final partial pressure of N_2 = 450 torr.

But since, after all the oxygen has reacted, only
nitrogen fills the entire volume, the final volume of
nitrogen is 3.7 ℓ. By the first definition, the initial
partial pressure of nitrogen is the same as the final
partial pressure of nitrogen, 450 torr. We now again
employ the second definition to determine the last remaining unknown quantity, the initial partial pressure
of oxygen. Proceeding, we obtain

initial total pressure = initial partial pressure of O_2
+ initial partial pressure of N_2

1 atm = initial partial pressure of O_2 + 450 torr

or, initial partial pressure of O_2 = 1 atm - 450 torr

$$= 760 \text{ torr} - 450 \text{ torr}$$

$$= 310 \text{ torr}.$$

Summarizing these results in tabular form we have:

	Initial	Final
partial pressure of O_2	310 torr	0 torr
partial pressure of N_2	450 torr	450 torr
total pressure	760 torr	450 torr

● **PROBLEM** 3-7

A cylinder contains 40 g He, 56 g N_2, and 40 g Ar. (a) What is the mole fraction of each gas in the mixture? (b) If the total pressure of the mixture is 10 atm, what is the partial pressure of He?

Solution: (a) The mole fraction of a component in a system is defined as the number of moles of that component divided by the sum of all the moles present in the system. Here, one must first calculate the number of moles present of each component, then the mole fractions can be found. The number of moles of each gas can be found by dividing the number of grams present of the gas by the molecular weight. (MW He = 4, MW N_2 = 28, MW Ar = 40.)

$$\text{no. of moles} = \frac{\text{no. of grams}}{\text{MW}}$$

$$\text{no. of moles of He} = \frac{40 \text{ g}}{4 \text{ g/mole}} = 10 \text{ moles}$$

$$\text{no. of moles of } N_2 = \frac{56 \text{ g}}{28 \text{ g/mole}} = 2 \text{ moles}$$

$$\text{no. of moles of Ar} = \frac{40 \text{ g}}{40 \text{ g/mole}} = 1 \text{ mole}$$

The total number of moles of gas in the system is the sum of the number of moles of the three gases. Thus, there are 13 moles of gas in the system. The mole fraction can now be found for each gas by dividing the number of moles of each gas by 13, the total number of moles

$$\text{mole fraction} = \frac{\text{no. of moles}}{\text{total no. of moles in system}}$$

$$\text{mole fraction of He} = \frac{10 \text{ moles}}{13 \text{ moles}} = .77$$

$$\text{mole fraction of } N_2 = \frac{2 \text{ moles}}{13 \text{ moles}} = .15$$

mole fraction of Ar = $\dfrac{1 \text{ mole}}{13 \text{ moles}}$ = .08

(b) In a system where various gases are present, the partial pressure of each gas is proportional to the mole fraction of the gas. The relationship between the partial pressure of a particular gas and the total pressure is

partial pressure = total pressure × mole fraction

In this problem, one is given the total pressure of the system and one has found the mole fraction of He. One can now find the partial pressure of He

partial pressure of He = 10 atm × .77 = 7.7 atm.

● PROBLEM 3-8

The composition of dry air by volume is 78.1% N_2, 20.9% O_2 and 1% other gases. Calculate the partial pressures, in atmospheres, in a tank of dry air compressed to 10.0 atmospheres.

Solution: A partial pressure is the individual pressure caused by one gas in a mixture of several gases. The total pressure, P_{total}, according to Dalton's Laws, is the sum of these individual partial pressure, p_1, p_2 and p_3. i.e. $P_{total} = p_1 + p_2 + p_3$.

The term dry air indicates that no water vapor is present.

The partial pressure is found by multiplying the percent of each gas in the volume by the total pressure.

partial pressure = proportion by volume × total pressure

P_{N_2} = .781 × 10 atm = 7.81 atm

P_{O_2} = .209 × 10 atm = 2.09 atm

$P_{other\ gases}$ = .010 × 10 atm = .1 atm.

The total pressure, as required, is 10 atm.

● PROBLEM 3-9

A sample of air held in a graduated cylinder over water has a volume of 88.3 ml at a temperature of 18.5°C and a pressure of 741 mm (see figure). What would the volume of the air be if it were dry and at the same temperature and pressure?

51

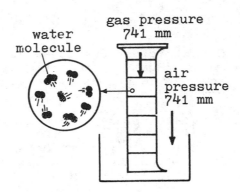

water molecule

gas pressure
741 mm

air pressure
741 mm

Solution: This problem is an application of Dalton's Law which states that the total pressure of a mixture, P_{total}, of gases is the sum of the individual partial pressures, P_1, P_2. Stated mathematically

$$P_{total} = P_1 + P_2 + P_3 \ldots$$

The mixture of gases in this problem is located in the cylinder and is made up of dry air and water vapor. At 18.5°C the vapor pressure of water is 16 mm. The pressures are related by the equation

$$P_{total} = P_{dry\ air} + P_{water\ vapor}$$

Using this equation, we can calculate $P_{dry\ air}$. Having

obtained this value, the problem becomes a direct pressure-volume relationship. As the volume increases, the pressure decreases and vice versa. These factors are related by the equation

$$P_1 V_1 = P_2 V_2$$

where P_1 and V_1 represent pressure and volume in the presence of water vapor, and P_2 and V_2 represent the same quantities for dry air. By Dalton's Law:

$$P_{dry\ air} = P_{total} - P_{water\ vapor}$$

$$= 741 - 16$$

$$= 725 \text{ mm when water vapor is present.}$$

If there is no water vapor present and the dry air were to exert the entire pressure of 741 mm then, we predict that the dry air volume will be smaller. Next substitute the values into the pressure-volume equation and solve for unknown volume V_2

$$V_2 = \frac{P_1 V_1}{P_2}$$

$$= \frac{725(88.3)}{741}$$

$$= 86.4 \text{ ml}$$

Therefore, as predicted the volume has decreased.

● PROBLEM 3-10

What would be the final partial pressure of oxygen in the following experiment? A collapsed polyethylene bag of 30 liters capacity is partially blown up by the addition of 10 liters of nitrogen gas measured at 0.965 atm and 298°K. Subsequently, enough oxygen is pumped into the bag so that, at 298°K and external pressure of 0.990 atm, the bag contains a full 30 liters. (assume ideal behavior.)

Solution: One should first find the number of moles of gas that fill a volume of 30 liters at .990 atm. One then solves for the number of moles of N_2 that was pumped in and the number of moles of O_2 that are needed to fill the bag. The partial pressures of these gases are equal to the mole fraction of the gas times the total pressure.

   To solve for the partial pressure of O_2 one should find:

   1) the total number of moles of gas that will fill 30 liters at .990 atm.

   2) the number of moles of N_2 present

   3) the partial pressure of N_2

   4) the partial pressure of O_2.

Solving:

   1) One uses the Ideal Gas Law to solve for the number of moles of gas needed to fill 30 liters at 298°K and .990 atm. The Ideal Gas Law can be stated as

$$PV = nRT \qquad \text{or} \qquad n = \frac{PV}{RT}$$

where n is the number of moles, P is the pressure, V is the volume, R is the gas constant (.082 liter-atm/mole-°K) and T is the absolute temperature. Solving for n in this system

P = .990 atm
V = 30 liters
R = .082 liter-atm/mole-°K
T = 298°K

$$n = \frac{.990 \text{ atm} \times 30 \text{ liters}}{.082 \text{ liter-atm/mole-}^\circ K \times 298^\circ K}$$

$$= 1.22 \text{ moles}$$

2) One also uses the Ideal Gas Law to find the number of moles of N_2 already present.

$$P = .965 \text{ atm}$$
$$V = 10 \text{ liters}$$
$$R = .082 \text{ liter-atm/mole-}^\circ K$$
$$T = 298^\circ K$$

$$n = \frac{.965 \text{ atm} \times 10 \text{ liters}}{.082 \text{ liter-atm/mole-}^\circ K \times 298^\circ K}$$

$$n = 0.395 \text{ moles.}$$

3) The partial pressure is related to the total pressure by the following

$$P_x = P_o X$$

where P_x is the partial pressure, P_o is the total original pressure and X is the mole fraction of the gas. The mole fraction is defined as the number of moles of the gas present divided by the total number of moles in the system. Solving for the partial pressure of N_2, P_{N_2},

$$P_N + P_o X \qquad\qquad P_{N_2} = ?$$

$$P_o = .990 \text{ atm}$$

$$X = .395/1.22$$

$$P_{N_2} = .990 \text{ atm} \times \frac{.395}{1.22}$$

$$P_{N_2} = .321 \text{ atm.}$$

4) The total pressure of the system is equal to the sum of the partial pressures. Thus, .990 atm is the sum of P_{N_2} and P_{O_2}. One has already found P_{N_2}, therefore, one can now solve for P_{O_2}

$$P_{O_2} = P_{total} - P_{N_2} \qquad\qquad P_{total} = .990 \text{ atm}$$

$$P_{N_2} = .321 \text{ atm}$$

$$P_{O_2} = .990 \text{ atm} - .321 \text{ atm}$$

$$P_{O_2} = .669 \text{ atm.}$$

200 mℓ of oxygen is collected over water at 25°C and 750 torr. If the oxygen thus obtained is dried at a constant temperature of 25°C and 750 torr, what volume will it occupy? What volume will be occupied by the water vapor removed from the oxygen if it is maintained at 25°C and 750 torr? (The equilibrium vapor pressure of water at 25°C is 28.3 torr.)

Solution: This problem will be approached by determining the partial pressures of oxygen and of water vapor in the initial mixture and then using these partial pressures to determine the separate volumes of each component.

The partial pressures exerted by the oxygen and the water vapor must add up to the total pressure. Since the partial pressure of water vapor is equal to its equilibrium vapor pressure, we can determine the partial pressure of oxygen:

total pressure = partial pressure of O_2 + partial pressure of water

750 torr = partial pressure of O_2 + 28.3 torr

or, partial pressure of O_2 = 750 torr - 28.3 torr
= 721.7 torr.

By definition, this partial pressure is the pressure the oxygen would exert if it filled the entire 200 mℓ volume. We must determine the volume this amount of oxygen would fill at 750 torr. To do this we use the relationship $P_1 V_1 = P_2 V_2$, which is valid for constant temperature and constant number of moles of gas. Let $P_1 = 721.7$ torr, $V_1 = 200$ mℓ, and $P_2 = 750$ torr. Then,

$$V_2 = \frac{P_1}{P_2} \times V_1 = \frac{721.7 \text{ torr}}{750 \text{ torr}} \times 200 \text{ mℓ} = 192.45 \text{ mℓ}.$$

Hence, the dried oxygen would occupy a volume of 192.45 mℓ.

We follow a similar procedure in calculating the volume that the water vapor would occupy at 750 torr. The vapor pressure of water, 28.3 torr, is the pressure the water vapor would exert if it filled the entire 200 mℓ volume. Again, applying the relationship $P_1 V_1 = P_2 V_2$, remembering that the only reason we can do so is that we have constant temperature and constant number of moles of gas, we can calculate the volume that the water vapor occupies under a pressure of 750 torr. Let $P_1 = 28.3$ torr, $V_1 = 200$ mℓ, and $P_2 = 750$ torr. Then the volume at 750 torr is

$$V_2 = \frac{P_1}{P_2} \times V_1 = \frac{28.3 \text{ torr}}{750 \text{ torr}} \times 200 \text{ mℓ} = 7.55 \text{ mℓ}.$$

As a check, we ascertain that the individual volumes at 750 torr add up to the total volume at 750 torr:

Volume of O_2 + volume of water = 192.45 ml + 7.55 ml

$$= 200 \text{ ml}.$$

• **PROBLEM** 3-12

Suppose 100 ml of oxygen were collected over water in the laboratory at a pressure of 700 torr and a temperature of 20°C. What would the volume of the dry oxygen gas be at STP?

Solution: STP means Standard Temperature and Pressure, which is 0°C and 760 torr. In this problem oxygen is gathered over water, therefore, Dalton's law of partial pressure (each of the gases in a gaseous mixture behaves independently of the other gases and exerts its own pressure, the total pressure of the mixture being the sum of the partial pressures exerted by each gas present; that is $P_{total} = p_1 + p_2 + p_3 \ldots p_n$) is used to calculate the original pressure of the oxygen. There is both water vapor and oxygen gas present.

After you obtain the original pressure of the oxygen, you can use the combined gas law to calculate the final volume of the oxygen. The combined gas law stated that for a given mass of gas, the volume is inversely proportional to the pressure and directly proportional to the absolute temperature. It can be written as follows:

$$\frac{P_1 V_1}{T_1} = \frac{P_2 V_2}{T_2}$$

where P_1 is the original pressure, V_1 is the original volume, T_1 is the original absolute temperature, P_2 is the final temperature, V_2 is the final volume, and T_2 is the final absolute temperature. You are given the temperature in °C, so it must be converted to the absolute temperature by adding 273.

(a) Finding the original pressure of oxygen. The partial pressure of water is 17.5 torr.

$$P_{total} = 700 \text{ torr} = P_{O_2} + P_{H_2O}$$

$$P_{O_2} = 700 - 17.5$$

$$= 682.5 \text{ torr}.$$

(b) Converting the temperature to the absolute scale.

$$T_1 = 20 + 273 = 293°K$$

$$T_2 = 0 + 273 = 273°K$$

(c) Using the combined law

$$\frac{P_1V_1}{T_1} = \frac{P_2V_2}{T_2}$$

$P_1 = 682.5$ torr $P_2 = 760$ torr

$V_1 = 100$ ml $V_2 = ?$

$T_1 = 293°K$ $T_2 = 273°K$

$$\frac{(682.5 \text{ torr})(100 \text{ ml})}{293°K} = \frac{(760 \text{ torr}) V_2}{273°K}.$$

$$V_2 = \frac{(682.5 \text{ torr})(100 \text{ ml})(273°K)}{(760 \text{ torr})(293°K)} = 83.7 \text{ ml.}$$

● PROBLEM 3-13

A sample of hydrogen is collected in a bottle over water. By carefully raising and lowering the bottle, the height of the water outside is adjusted so that it is just even with the water level inside (see figure). When a sample of gas was collected the initial conditions were: volume = 425 ml, pressure = 753 mm and the temperature of the water (and thus, the gas also) = 34°C. Calculate the volume of the hydrogen if it were dry and at a pressure of 760 mm and a temperature of 0°C (STP).

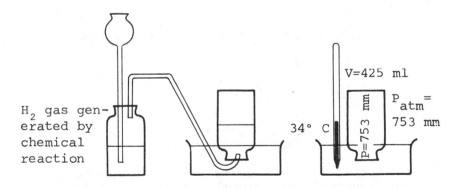

Solution: First, apply Dalton's Law and then make use of the Combined Gas Law to obtain the desired answer.

Dalton's Law states that the total pressure of a mixture of gases, P_{total}, is equal to the sum of the individual partial pressures, P_{H_2} and P_{H_2O}. In this example the individual gases are hydrogen and water vapor. Therefore, the total pressure is the sum of these two gases. At 35°C, the partial pressure of H_2O vapor is 40 mm,

$$P_{total} = P_{H_2} + P_{H_2O}$$

$$P_{H_2} = P_{total} - P_{H_2O}$$

$$= 753 - 40 = 713 \text{ mm}$$

This means that if no water vapor was present the H_2 gas would fill the container at 713 mm of pressure.

Since pressure is indirectly proportional to the volume of H_2 gas, the effect of changing the pressure of 713 mm to STP pressure (760 mm) is to decrease the volume.

In addition, however, the temperature of the H_2 gas is directly proportional to the volume of the gas, so that the effect of changing the temperature of (34°C + 273° =) 307°K to STP temperature (273°K) is also to decrease the volume of the gas. Therefore, we can predict that the net effect of changing the pressure and temperature of the gas to STP conditions is to decrease the volume.

Using the combined gas law equation to solve for the dry H_2 gas volume, V_2,

$$\frac{P_1 V_1}{T_1} = \frac{P_2 V_2}{T_2}$$

where $P_1 = 713$ mm $P_2 = 760$ mm

$V_1 = 425$ ml $V_2 = $ volume at STP

$T_1 = 307°K$ $T_2 = 273°K$

Thus, substituting,

$$V_2 = \frac{P_1 V_1 T_2}{P_2 T_1}$$

$$= \frac{(713 \text{ mm})(425 \text{ ml})(273°K)}{(760 \text{ mm})(307°K)} = 355 \text{ ml}.$$

We see that this answer is in total agreement with our prediction that the volume at STP, $V_2 = 355$ ml, is less than the volume at the initial conditions, $V_1 = 425$ ml.

CHAPTER 4

AVOGADRO'S HYPOTHESIS, CHEMICAL COMPOUNDS AND FORMULAS

● PROBLEM 4-1

How many mercury atoms would there be in a 100 g piece of swordfish said to contain 0.1 ppm (part per million by weight) of mercury?

Solution: One can find the number of atoms present by multiplying the number of moles of mercury by the number of atoms in 1 mole. The number of atoms in one mole is equal to Avogadro's Number or 6.02×10^{23} atoms/mole. To solve for the number of mercury atoms present find:

(1) the amount of mercury present

(2) the number of moles of mercury

(3) the number of atoms of mercury.

Solving:

(1) Because there is 0.1 ppm of mercury in the sword-fish, one multiplies 0.1×10^{-6} by the amount of fish present.

amount of mercury = $0.1 \times 10^{-6} \times 100$ g = 1.0×10^{-5} g.

(2) The number of moles is found by dividing the weight of the mercury present by the weight of one mole, the molecular weight (MW = 200.6)

no. of moles = $\dfrac{1.0 \times 10^{-5} \text{ g}}{200.6 \text{ g/mole}}$ = 4.99×10^{-8} moles.

(3) The number of atoms is found by multiplying the number of moles by the number of atoms in one mole, 6.02×10^{23} atoms.

no. of atoms = 4.99×10^{-8} moles $\times 6.02 \times 10^{23}$ atoms/mole

$$= 3.00 \times 10^{16} \text{ atoms.}$$

● **PROBLEM** 4-2

If the dot under a question mark has a mass of 1×10^{-6} g, and you assume it is carbon, how many atoms are required to make such a dot?

Solution: Two facts must be known to answer this question. You must determine the number of moles in the carbon dot. You must also remember the number of atoms in a mole of any substance, 6.02×10^{23} atoms/mole (Avogadro's number).

A mole is defined as the weight in grams of a substance divided by the atomic weight (or molecular weight).

The atomic weight of carbon is 12 g/mole. Therefore, in the dot you have

$\frac{1 \times 10^{-6} \text{ g}}{12 \text{ g/mole}}$ moles of carbon. Therefore, the number

of atoms in such a dot is the number of moles × Avogadro's number,

$$\left(\frac{1 \times 10^{-6} \text{ g}}{12 \text{ g/mole}} \right) 6.02 \times 10^{23} \text{ atoms/mole} = 5 \times 10^{16} \text{ atoms.}$$

● **PROBLEM** 4-3

What is the approximate number of molecules in a drop of water which weighs 0.09 g?

Solution: The number of molecules in a mole is defined to be 6.02×10^{23} molecules. Thus, to find the number of molecules in a drop of water, one must know the number of moles making up the drop. This is done by dividing the weight of the drop by the molecular weight of H_2O. (MW of H_2O = 18)

$$\text{number of moles} = \frac{0.09 \text{ g}}{18 \text{ g/mole}} = .005 \text{ moles.}$$

The number of molecules present is now found by multiplying the number of moles by Avogadro' number (6.02×10^{23}).

no. of molecules = .005 moles $\times 6.02 \times 10^{23}$ molecules/mole

$$= 3.01 \times 10^{21} \text{ molecules.}$$

60

What is the difference between the number of carbon atoms
in 1.00 g of C-12 isotope (atomic mass = 12.000 g/mole)
and 1.00 g of C-13 isotope (atomic mass = 13.003 g/mole)?

Solution: The difference in the number of carbon atoms
in each sample is equal to the difference in the number
of moles times Avogadro's number 6.02×10^{23}. Hence, we
must begin by calculating the number of moles of C-12
and of C-13 in 1.00 g samples of each.

The number of moles is equal to the mass divided
by the atomic weight. Therefore,

$$\text{moles C-12} = \frac{\text{mass C-12}}{\text{atomic mass C-12}} = \frac{1.00 \text{ g}}{12.000 \text{ g/mole}} = 0.083 \text{ mole}$$

$$\text{and moles C-13} = \frac{\text{mass C-13}}{\text{atomic mass C-13}}$$

$$= \frac{1.00 \text{ g}}{13.003 \text{ g/mole}} = 0.077 \text{ mole.}$$

The difference in the number of moles between the two
samples is (moles C-12) - (moles C-13) = 0.083 - 0.077 =
0.006 mole. Multiplying by Avogadro's number gives the
difference in the number of carbon atoms in the two samples:

$$\text{number of carbon atoms} = 0.006 \text{ mole} \times 6.02 \times 10^{23} \frac{\text{molecules}}{\text{mole}}$$

$$= 3.61 \times 10^{21} \text{ molecules.}$$

During a moon landing, one of the experiments performed
was the measurement of the intensity of solar wind. As
a collector, an aluminum strip of about 3000 cm^2 area
was used. It was found that in 100 min, a mass of 3.0×10^{-10} g of H atoms was collected (by the sticking of H
atoms to the strip). What was the intensity of the solar
wind (in numbers of atoms per cm^2 per second)?

Solution: The intensity of the solar wind is the number
of H atoms striking the unit area in unit time,

$$\text{intensity} = \frac{\text{number of atoms}}{\text{area} \times \text{time}} \quad .$$

We must determine the number of atoms. This is accomplished
by converting mass to moles and then multiplying by
Avogadro's number.

The number of moles is given by

$$\text{moles} = \frac{\text{mass of H atoms}}{\text{atomic weight of H}} = \frac{3.0 \times 10^{-10} \text{ g}}{1.0 \text{ g/mole}}$$

$$= 3.0 \times 10^{-10} \text{ mole.}$$

Since there are an Avogadro's number of atoms in one mole, the number of atoms in 3.0×10^{-10} mole is

$$\text{number of atoms} = \text{moles} \times \text{Avogadro's number}$$

$$= 3.0 \times 10^{-10} \text{ mole} \times 6 \times 10^{23} \text{atoms/mole}$$

$$= 18 \times 10^{13} \text{ atoms.}$$

The intensity of the solar wind is then

$$\text{intensity} = \frac{\text{number of atoms}}{\text{area} \times \text{time}} = \frac{18 \times 10^{13} \text{ atoms}}{3000 \text{ cm}^2 \times 100 \text{ min}}$$

$$= \frac{18 \times 10^{13} \text{ atoms}}{3000 \text{ cm}^2 \times 100 \text{ min} \times 60 \text{ sec/min}}$$

$$= 1 \times 10^7 \text{ atoms/cm}^2\text{-sec.}$$

● **PROBLEM** 4-6

The most abundant element in sea water is chlorine (Cl, atomic weight = 35.5 g/mole), which is present as chloride ion, Cl^-, in a concentration of 19 g Cl^- per 1 kg of sea water. If the volume of the earth's oceans is 1.4×10^{21} liters, how many moles of Cl^- are present in the oceans? Assume that the density of sea water is 1.0 g/cm^3.

Solution: The total number of moles of Cl^- is equal to the total mass of Cl^- divided by its atomic weight. Hence we must find the total mass of Cl^-. This will be done by determining the total mass of the oceans and using this value in conjunction with the concentration of Cl^- to find the total mass of Cl^-.

The volume of the oceans is 1.4×10^{21} liters = 1.4×10^{21} liters $\times 1000$ cm^3/liter = 1.4×10^{24} cm^3. Multiplying this volume by the density of sea water gives the total mass of the oceans, or 1.4×10^{24} cm^3 $\times 1.0$ g/cm^3 = 1.4×10^{24} g. Expressing this total mass as kilograms, we obtain

$$1.4 \times 10^{24} \text{ g} = 1.4 \times 10^{24} \text{ g} \times 10^{-3} \text{ kg/g} = 1.4 \times 10^{21} \text{ kg.}$$

For every kg of sea water, there are 19 g of Cl^-. Hence, for 1.4×10^{21} kg there are 1.4×10^{21} kg $\times$ 19 g Cl^-/kg of sea water = 2.7×10^{22} g Cl^-.

Therefore, the number of moles of Cl^- is

$$moles\ Cl^- = \frac{mass\ Cl^-}{atomic\ weight\ Cl^-}$$

$$= \frac{2.7 \times 10^{22}\ g}{35.5\ g/mole} = 7.6 \times 10^{20}\ moles.$$

A chemist wants to calculate Avogadro's number by the inspection of a solid cube of AgCl. The density of the cube is 5.56 g/cm^3. The spacing between the Ag^+ and Cl^- ions in the cube is 2.773×10^{-8} cm from their centers. From these data, perform this calculation.

Solution: To solve this problem, the following quantities must be determined: the volume of one mole of AgCl, cubic edge length of one mole, the number of ions on an edge, and the total number of ions. The total number of ions divided by 2 will yield Avogadro's number. From the atomic weights of Ag and Cl (107.868 amu and 35.453 amu) one mole of AgCl weighs 143.321 grams. Because density = mass/volume, the volume of one mole =

$$= \frac{143.321\ g/mole}{5.56\ g/cm^3} = 25.78\ cm^3/mole.$$

The volume of a cube = $(e)^3$, where "e" is the length of the cube edge. Therefore,

$$e = \sqrt[3]{25.78\ cm^3/moles} = 2.954\ cm/\sqrt[3]{mole}.$$

Because the spacing between ions is 2.77×10^{-8} cm, the number of ions along the edge is

$$\frac{2.954\ cm/\sqrt[3]{mole}}{2.773 \times 10^{-8}\ cm} = 1.065 \times 10^8\ ions/\sqrt[3]{mole}$$

The total number of ions in 1 mole of AgCl must be

$$(1.065 \times 10^8/\sqrt[3]{mole})^3 = 1.209 \times 10^{24}/mole.$$

This number is not Avogadro's number. Because you have two ions per formula unit, there is one Avogadro's number of Ag^+ and one Avogadro's number of Cl^-. It follows, therefore, that you must divide by two. As such,

$$\frac{1.209 \times 10^{24}/mole}{2} = 6.04 \times 10^{23}/mole = Avogadro's\ number.$$

ATOMIC AND MOLECULAR WEIGHTS

1.3625 g of an unknown metal X reacts with oxygen to form 1.4158 g of the oxide X_2O. What is the atomic mass of X?

Solution: This problem will be solved by calculating the mass and, from this, the number of moles of oxygen in the compound. The corresponding number of moles of metal is twice this amount. The molecular weight is the number of moles of metal divided by the weight of metal that was used.

The mass of oxygen in the compound is

mass O = mass oxide - mass X

= 1.4158 g - 1.3625 g = 0.0533 g.

The corresponding number of moles is

moles O = mass O ÷ atomic mass O

= 0.0533 g ÷ 15.9994 g/mole = 0.0033 mole.

Since, in the oxide, there are two moles of X per mole of O, the number of moles of X present is 2 × 0.0033 mole = 0.0066 mole X. Hence, 1.3625 g of X corresponds to 0.0066 mole X. The atomic mass of X is then:

$$\text{atomic mass X} = \frac{\text{mass X}}{\text{moles X}} = \frac{1.3625 \text{ g}}{0.0066 \text{ mole}} = 206.4394 \text{ g/mole}.$$

How many moles are present in 100 g quantities of each of the following? (a) $CaCO_3$, (b) H_2O, (c) HCl, (d) $Al_2(SO_4)_3$?

Solution: One can find the number of moles of a specific compound in a certain number of grams of that compound by dividing the number of grams present by the molecular weight. The molecular weight is defined as the weight of one mole or Avogadro's Number (6.02×10^{23}) of particles.

$$\text{number of moles} = \frac{\text{weight in grams of sample}}{\text{molecular weight}}$$

One calculates the molecular weight of a compound by adding together the molecular weights of the elements present. When calculating the molecular weight, one must take into account the number of atoms of each element in the compound. This is done by multiplying the molecular weight of the element by the number of atoms present of

the particular element. This method will be used in the
following examples. Once the molecular weight is determined, the number of moles present in 100 g of the compound
can be found by using the equation

$$\text{number of moles in 100 g} = \frac{100 \text{ g}}{\text{molecular weight}}$$

(a) $CaCO_3$

There is one atom of Ca present in $CaCO_3$. Thus, the
molecular weight of Ca, 40, is multiplied by one. There
is one atom of C. Thus the molecular weight, 12, of C
is multiplied by one. Because there are 3 atoms of O
present, the molecular weight of O, 16, is multiplied by 3.

1 atom of Ca	1×40	=	40
1 atom of C	1×12	=	12
3 atoms of O	3×16	=	48
molecular weight of $CaCO_3$		=	100

The number of moles of $CaCO_3$ in 100 g may now be found.

$$\text{number of moles in 100 g} = \frac{100 \text{ g}}{100 \text{ g/mole}} = 1 \text{ mole.}$$

(b) H_2O

(1) Calculation of molecular weight. The MW of H is
1 and the MW of O is 16.

2 atoms of H	2×1	=	2
1 atom of O	1×16	=	16
molecular weight of H_2O		=	18

(2) Calculation of number of moles in 100 g of H_2O.

$$\text{number of moles in 100 g} = \frac{100 \text{ g}}{18 \text{ g/mole}} = 5.55 \text{ moles.}$$

(c) HCl

MW of H = 1, MW of Cl = 35.5.

1 atom of H	1×1	=	1
1 atom of Cl	1×35.5	=	35.5
molecular weight of HCl		=	36.5

$$\text{number of moles of HCl in 100 g} = \frac{100 \text{ g}}{36.5 \text{ g/mole}} = 2.74 \text{ moles}$$

(d) $Al_2(SO_4)_3$

MW of Al = 27   MW of S = 32   MW of O = 16

2 atoms of Al	2×27	=	54
3 atoms of S	3×32	=	96
12 atoms of O	12×16	=	192
molecular weight of $Al_2(SO_4)_3$		=	342

number of moles of $Al_2(SO_4)_3$ in 100 g = $\dfrac{100 \text{ g}}{342 \text{ g/mole}}$

= .292 moles.

● **PROBLEM** 4-10

What is the molecular weight of a substance, each molecule of which contains 9 carbon atoms and 13 hydrogen atoms and 2.33×10^{-23} g of other components?

Solution: The molecular weight of a compound is the sum of the weights of the components of the compound. It is the weight of one mole of the substance, thus this compound weighs the sum of the weight of 9 moles of C, 13 moles H and $(6.02 \times 10^{23}) \times (2.33 \times 10^{-23}$ g). Because each molecule of the third substance weighs 2.33×10^{-23} g, one mole of it weighs $(6.02 \times 10^{23}) \times (2.33 \times 10^{-23}$ g). There are 6.02×10^{23} molecules of this other substance in one mole of the compound (Avogadro's number).

molecular weight = (9 × MW of C) + (13 × MW of H) +

$(2.33 \times 10^{-23}$g$)(6.02 \times 10^{23}$ /mole)

= (9 × 12.01 g/mole) + (13 × 1.00 g/mole)+

(14.03 g/mole)

= 108.09 g/mole + 13.0 g/mole +

14.03 g/mole

= 135.12 g/mole.

● **PROBLEM** 4-11

Determine the relative abundance of each isotope in naturally occurring gallium from the following data: At. wt. Ga = 69.72. Masses if isotopes ^{69}Ga = 68.926, ^{71}Ga = 70.925.

Solution: The relative abundance of the various isotopes of gallium can be found by using the following equation:

atomic weight of Ga = % of ^{69}Ga × at. wt. of ^{69}Ga +

% of ^{71}Ga × at wt. of ^{71}Ga

It is given that Ga consists only of the two isotopes ^{69}Ga and ^{71}Ga. Thus, if one lets x = fraction of ^{69}Ga, then 1 - x = fraction of ^{71}Ga. Using the above equation one can solve for x.

$69.72 = (x \times 68.926) + (1 - x) \times 70.925$

$69.72 = 68.926x + 70.925 - 70.925x$

$-1.205 = -1.999x$

$x = 1.2/2.0 = 0.60.$

This means that the ^{69}Ga makes up 60 % of Ga. ^{71}Ga makes up 1 - .60 or 40% of Ga.

● **PROBLEM** 4-12

One method for determining the molecular weight of large, biologically important molecules, is by measuring the density by standard procedures and determining the average volume occupied by a single molecule by X-ray crystallographic analysis. If a biochemist measures the density of a sample of deoxyribonucleic acid (DNA) as 1.1 g/cm^3 and X-ray analysis of the same sample estimates the volume of a single DNA molecule as 0.91×10^{-15} cm^3, what is the molecular weight of this type of DNA?

Solution: The number density (molecules/cm^3) is the reciprocal of the volume of a single molecule and is related to the density (g/cm^3) by the following formula:

$$\text{number density} = \frac{1}{\text{volume per molecule}}$$

$$= \frac{\text{density}}{\text{molecular weight}} \times \text{Avogadro's number}$$

The validity of this formula is readily seen by considering the dimensions of the quantities involved. Dividing the density (g/cm^3) by the molecular weight (g/mole) gives a quantity with units of

$$\frac{\text{g/cm}^3}{\text{g/mole}} = \text{mole/cm}^3 \text{ (molar density)}.$$

Multiplying this number by Avogadro's number (molecules/mole) gives a quantity with dimensions of

$$\frac{\text{mole}}{\text{cm}^3} \times \frac{\text{molecules}}{\text{mole}} = \text{molecules/cm}^3 \text{ (number density)}.$$

Solving for the molecular weight in the above expression we obtain

67

$$\text{molecular weight} = \text{density} \times \text{Avogadro's number} \times \text{volume}$$

$$\text{per molecule}$$

$$= 1.1 \text{ g/cm}^3 \times 6 \times 10^{23} \text{ molecules/mole} \times$$

$$\times \ 0.91 \times 10^{-15} \text{ cm}^3/\text{molecule}$$

$$= 6 \times 10^8 \text{ g/mole.}$$

● **PROBLEM** 4-13

When metal M is heated in halogen X_2, a compound MX_n is formed. In a given experiment, 1.00 g of titanium reacts with chlorine to give 3.22 g of compound. What is the corresponding value of n?

Solution: In the compound MX_n, there is one mole of M and n moles of X. In the compound here, one is given that 1.00 g of it is Ti (titanium) and that the compound weighs 3.22 g. This means that 3.22 g - 1.00 g or 2.22 g of the compound is Cl. To find the simplest formula for the compound, one must first determine the number of moles of each component present. This is done by dividing the weight present by the molecular weight

$$\text{no. of moles} = \frac{\text{no. of grams}}{\text{MW}}$$

For Ti: (MW = 47.9)

$$\text{no. of moles} = \frac{1.00 \text{ g}}{47.9 \text{ g/mole}} = 2.09 \times 10^{-2} \text{ moles.}$$

For Cl: (MW = 35.5)

$$\text{no. of moles} = \frac{2.22 \text{ g}}{35.5 \text{ g/mole}} = 6.25 \times 10^{-2} \text{ moles.}$$

Since the simplest formula for the compound is $TiCl_n$, n can be found using the following ratio.

$$\frac{1 \text{ Ti}}{n} = \frac{2.09 \times 10^{-2} \text{ moles Ti}}{6.25 \times 10^{-2} \text{ moles Cl}}$$

$$n = \frac{1 \text{ Ti} \times 6.25 \times 10^{-2} \text{ Cl}}{2.09 \times 10^{-2} \text{ Ti}} = 2.99 \text{ Cl}$$

The formula for the compound is therefore $TiCl_3$. 2.99 Cl is rounded off to the nearest whole number, 3.

If the density of ethylene is 1.25 g/liter at S.T.P. and the ratio of carbon to hydrogen atoms is 1 : 2, what is molecular weight and formula of ethylene?

Solution: This problem is solved once you know that at S.T.P. (Standard Temperature and Pressure, 0°C, and 1 atm) one mole of any gas occupies 22.4 liters. Assume that one mole of ethylene gas is present. Density = mass/volume. As such the mass of the gas = (1.25 g/ℓ)(22.4 ℓ) = 28.0 g. Therefore one mole of ethylene weighs 28 g.

From the ratio given in the question you know the molecular formula can be represented as $(CH_2)_x$. To obtain the actual molecular formula, look for a compound that has a molecular weight of 28 g yet maintains the carbon : hydrogen ratio of 1 : 2. By looking at the periodic table for atomic weights and through some arithmetic, you will find that the only formula that meets these requirements is $(CH_2)_2$ or C_2H_4. This formula can also be found by dividing the weight of 1 CH_2 into 28 g. This solves for x in the expression $(CH_2)_x$. MW of CH_2 = 14.

$$\text{no. of } CH_2 = \frac{28 \text{ g}}{14 \text{ g/}CH_2} = 2 \ CH_2 = C_2H_4.$$

Phosphorus (atomic weight = 30.97) combines with another element such that 1 g of phosphorus requires 0.7764 g of the other element. If the atomic ratio of phosphorus to the other element is 4 : 3, what is the atomic weight of the unknown element?

Solution: First determine how many moles of phosphorus reacted. From this, one can calculate the number of moles of the unknown element that reacted using the atomic ratio. This ratio represents the relative mole amounts. If the number of moles of the unknown element is determined, the atomic weigth can be calculated because the number of moles is equal to number of grams/atomic weight. (At. wt. of P = 30.97).

One can now determine the atomic weight of the unknown element. The number of moles of phosphorus that reacted

$$= \frac{1.0 \text{ g}}{30.97 \text{ g/mole}} = 0.03229 \text{ moles.}$$

Let x = the number of moles of the unknown element. The atomic ratio of phosphorus to the unknown element is 4 : 3. Thus,

$$\frac{4 \text{ atoms}}{3 \text{ atoms}} = \frac{.03229 \text{ moles}}{x} \quad . \quad \text{Solving,}$$

$$x = 0.02422 \text{ moles unknown element.}$$

Therefore, the atomic weight of the unknown element is equal to

$$\frac{0.7764 \text{ g}}{0.02422 \text{ moles}} = 32.06 \text{ g/mole.}$$

● **PROBLEM** 4-16

1.0g of scandium (Sc) combines with oxygen (O) to form 1.5338 g of oxide. Assuming the oxide contains two atoms of scandium for every three atoms of oxygen, calculate the atomic weight of Sc. Oxygen has an atomic weight of 15.9994 amu.

Solution: This problem can be solved once a proportion is set up.

The oxide weighs 1.5338 g and the Sc, 1.0 g. Therefore, the weight of the oxygen that reacted must be 1.5338 - 1 = .5338 g.

The problem stated that 3 oxygen atoms reacted for every 2 Sc atoms. Therefore, the total atomic weight of the oxygen in the compound is 3 × 15.9994.

Let y be the atomic weight of Sc, then 2y is the total weight involved in the formation of the oxide. Therefore, there is .5338 g of oxygen whose atoms (3 of them) have an atomic weight of 3 × 15.9994, reacting with 1 g of Sc whose atoms weigh 2y. This can be represented as

$$\frac{.5338 \text{ g}}{3(15.9994)} = \frac{1.00 \text{ g}}{2y}$$

Solving for y, results in 44.96, which is the atomic weight of scandium.

● **PROBLEM** 4-17

A given sample of pure compound contains 9.81 g of zinc, 1.8×10^{23} atoms of chromium and 0.60 mole of oxygen atoms. What is the simplest formula?

Solution: The simplest formula for this compound is found from the simplest ratio of moles Zn : moles Cr : moles O. One is given the number of moles of O but must find the number of moles of Zn and Cr. One is given that there is 9.81 g of Zn. One can find the number of moles by dividing

9.81 g by the MW of Zn. (MW of Zn = 65.4).

$$\text{no. of moles} = \frac{9.81 \text{ g}}{65.4 \text{ g/mole}} = 0.15 \text{ moles}$$

One is given that there are 1.8×10^{23} atoms of Cr present. The number of moles can be found by dividing the number of atoms by the number of atoms in one mole, 6.02×10^{23}.

$$\text{no. of moles} = \frac{1.8 \times 10^{23} \text{ atoms}}{6.02 \times 10^{23} \text{ atoms/mole}} = 0.30 \text{ moles}$$

The ratio of Zn : Cr : O is .15 : .30 : .60 or 1 : 2 : 4. The simplest formula is $ZnCr_2O_4$.

● **PROBLEM** 4-18

Two different compounds of elements A and B were found to have the following composition: first compound, 1.188 g of A combined with 0.711 g of B; second compound, 0.396 g of A combined with 0.474 g of B. (a) Show that these data are in accord with the law of multiple proportions. (b) If the formula for the first compound is AB_2, what is the formula for the second?

Solution: (a) The law of multiple proportions can be stated: When two elements combine to form more than one compound, the different weights of one that combine with a fixed weight of the other are in the ratio of small whole numbers. This means that if one solves for the expected amount of B that is used in forming the second compound from the ratio of A : B in experiment one, the experimental amount should be a multiple of the calculated value. This is seen more clearly after looking at the data.

In experiment 1, A combines with B in a ratio of 1.188 g A : 0.711 g B or 1 : .598. In experiment 2, A combined with B in a ratio of 0.396 A : 0.479 B or 1 : 1.20. The law of multiple proportions states that .598 should be a small multiple of 1.20. 1.20/.598 = 2, thus the law is supported.

(b) If the formula for the first compound is AB_2, one knows that the proportion of the number of moles of A to B is 1 : 2. Thus 1 unit volume of A weighs 1.188 g and 2 units of B weigh 0.711 g. Therefore, 1 unit of B weighs 0.711 g/2 = 0.356 g. Using this data, one solves for the number of units of A in the second compound by dividing the weight of A in compound 2 by 1.188 g.

$$\text{no. of units of A in compound 2} = \frac{.396 \text{ g}}{1.188 \text{ g/unit}} = .311 \text{ units}$$

no. of units of B in compound 2 = $\dfrac{.474 \text{ g}}{.356 \text{ g/unit}}$ = 1.331 units

The ratio of A to B in compound 2 can now be found. Let x = no. of B atoms

$$\frac{A}{B} = \frac{.311}{1.331} = \frac{1}{x}$$

$$x = \frac{1.331}{.331} = 4.0$$

Therefore, the second compound is AB_4. This result could also have been obtained by using the data from part (a). It was determined that twice as much B is present in the second compound. Thus, if the first compound is AB_2, then the second compound must be AB_4.

● **PROBLEM** 4-19

When 10.00 g of phosphorus was reacted with oxygen, it produced 17.77 g of a phosphorus oxide. This phosphorus oxide was found to have a molecular weight of approximately 220 in the vapor state. Determine its molecular formula.

Solution: The molecular formula of a substance indicates the relative number of atoms in a molecule of the substance. Therefore, to solve this problem, you must first calculate the ratios of the gram-atoms to each other, the empirical formula, and then extrapolate to the molecular formula via the molecular weight.

The number of gram-atoms of phosphorus (P) is

$$\frac{\text{wt. in grams of P}}{\text{atom weight}} = \frac{10}{30.97} = 0.323 \text{ gram-atoms P.}$$

For oxygen we have $\dfrac{7.77 \text{ g}}{16.00}$ = .484 gram - atoms.

The weight in grams of oxygen is 7.77 because the final product weighs 17.77 g and the phosphorus weighs 10.00 g. Since, the only other element is oxygen, its weight must be the difference.

The ratio of the gram-atoms of P and O is respectively 1 : 1.5 or 2 : 3. Therefore, the empirical formula of the oxide is P_2O_3.

To calculate the molecular formula, we must use the stated molecular weight of 220. We must look for a formula that totals to this molecular weight AND maintains the 2 : 3 ratio of P : O as expressed in the empirical formula. With some arithmetic, we find that the only formula that meets these two requirements is P_4O_6. 4 : 6 is the same as 2 : 3. The atomic weight of P and O is respectively 30.97 and 16. We have four P atoms for a total of 123.88 and we have 6 O atoms for a total of 96. Now add: 123.88 + 96 = 219.88, which is approximately 220.

Another method for determining the molecular formula is to divide the molecular weight of the molecule, 220, by the weight of 1 P_2O_3, 110.

$$\text{no. of } P_2O_3 = \frac{220 \text{ g}}{110 \text{ g/mole of } P_2O_3} = 2 \text{ moles of } P_2O_3.$$

The formula is, therefore 2 × P_2O_3 or P_4O_6.

A chemist reacts metal "B" with sulfur and obtains a compound of metal and sulfur. Assuming metal "B" weighed 2.435 g (MW = 121.75 amu), and the compound weighs 3.397 g, what is the simplest or empirical formula of the compound? The atomic weight of sulfur is 32.06 g/mole.

Solution: To calculate the simplest formula, one must know the mole ratio of the elements that reacted.

A mole is defined as the weight in grams of a substance divided by its atomic weight. The number of moles of "B"

$$= \frac{2.435 \text{ g}}{121.75 \text{ g/mole}} = .0200 \text{ moles of "B".}$$

The number of grams of sulfur that reacted must be 3.397 − 2.435 = .962 g.

The increase in weight can only be derived from the addition of sulfur.

The number of moles of sulfur is

$$\frac{0.962 \text{ g}}{32.06 \text{ g/mole}} = .0300 \text{ moles of sulfur.}$$

The ratio of "B" to sulfur moles is .0200 B/.0300 S = 2 : 3. Therefore, the simplest formula must be B_2S_3.

It has been determined experimentally that two elements, A and B react chemically to produce a compound or compounds. Experimental data obtained on combining proportions of the elements are:

	Grams of A	Grams of B	Grams of Compound
Experiment 1	6.08	4.00	10.08
Experiment 2	18.24	12.00	30.24
Experiment 3	3.04	2.00	5.04

(a) Which two laws of chemical change are illustrated by the above data? (b) If 80 g of element B combines with 355 g of a third element C, what weight of A will combine with 71 g of element C? (c) If element B is oxygen, what is the equivalent weight of element C?

Solution: (a) If one adds the weight of A to the weight of B and obtains the weight of the compound formed, the Law of Conservation of Mass is illustrated. This law states that there is no detectable gain or loss of mass in a chemical change. Using the data from the experiments described, you find the following:

For experiment 1   6.08 g A + 4.00 g B = 10.08 g of compound

6.08 + 4.00 = 10.08

For experiment 2   18.24 g A + 12.00 g B
$\qquad$ = 30.24 g of compound

18.24 + 12.00 = 30.24

For experiment 3   3.04 g A + 2.00 g B = 5.04 g compound

3.04 + 2.00 = 5.04

From these calculations one can see that the Law of Conservation of Mass is shown.

Another important law of chemistry is the Law of Definite Proportions. This law is stated: When elements combine to form a given compound, they do so in a fixed and invariable ratio by weight. One can check to see if this law is adhered to by calculating the ratio of the weight of A to the weight of B in the three experiments. If all of these ratios are equal, the Law of Definite Proportions is shown.

Experiment 1 $\dfrac{6.08 \text{ g A}}{4.00 \text{ g B}} = 1.5$

Experiment 2 $\dfrac{18.24 \text{ g A}}{12.00 \text{ g B}} = 1.5$

Experiment 3 $\dfrac{3.04 \text{ g A}}{2.00 \text{ g B}} = 1.5$

The Law of Definite Proportions is illustrated here.

(b) From the Law of Definite Proportions, one can

find the number of grams of B that will combine with 71 g of C. After this weight is found, one can find the number of grams of A that will react with 71 g of C by finding the amount of A that reacts with that amount of B. It is assumed that the amount of A that reacts with 71 g of C is equal to the amount of A that will react with the amount of B that reacts with 71 g of C. The amount of A that will react with this amount of B can be found by remembering, from the previous section of this problem, that A reacts with B in a ratio of 1.5.

(1) Finding the amount B that would react with 71 g of C.

One is told that 80 g of B reacts with 355 g of C. By the Law of Definite Proportions, a ratio can be set up to calculate the number of grams of B that will react with 71 g of C.

Let x = the number of grams of B that will react with 71 g of C.

$$\frac{80 \text{ g B}}{355 \text{ g C}} = \frac{x \text{ g B}}{71 \text{ g C}}$$

$$x = \frac{71 \times 80}{355} = 16.$$

16 grams of B will react with 71 g of C.

(2) It is assumed that the same amount of A that will react with 16 g of B will react with 71 g of C. Therefore, using the fact that the ratio of the amount of A that reacts to the amount of B is equal to 1.5 (this fact was obtained in part (1)), one can calculate the amount of A that will react with 71 g of C.

Let x = the number of grams of A that will react with 16 g of B.

$$\frac{x \text{ g A}}{16 \text{ g B}} = 1.5$$

$$x = 16 \times 1.5 = 24 \text{ g.}$$

24 g of A will react with 16 g of B or 71 g of C.

(c) In finding the equivalent weight of C when B is taken to be oxygen, the Law of Definite Proportions is used again. The equivalent weight of oxygen is 8. Knowing that 16 g of B react with 71 g of C, one can set up the following ratio

x = weight of C if the weight of B is taken to be 8.

$$\frac{71 \text{ g C}}{16 \text{ g B}} = \frac{x \text{ g C}}{8 \text{ g B}}$$

$$x = \frac{8 \times 71}{16} = 35.5 \text{ g.}$$

The equivalent weight of C when B is taken to be oxygen is 35.5 g.

EQUIVALENT WEIGHTS

● PROBLEM 4-22

If the atomic weight of oxygen was 50, what would its equivalent weight be?

<u>Solution</u>: The relationship of the atomic weight and the equivalent weight is

$$\frac{\text{Atomic weight}}{\text{Equivalent weight}} = \text{valence number}$$

The valence number is a measure of the number of atoms of hydrogen that will combine with one atom of the element. Two hydrogen atoms combine with one oxygen. The valence number of oxygen is therefore 2. One can now solve for the equivalent weight of oxygen when the atomic weight is taken as 50.

$$\frac{50}{\text{equivalent weight}} = 2$$

$$\text{equivalent weight} = \frac{50}{2} = 25.$$

● PROBLEM 4-23

A compound of vanadium and oxygen is analyzed and found to contain 56.0 % vanadium. What is the equivalent weight of vanadium in this compound?

<u>Solution</u>: To find the equivalent weight of vanadium one can use the Law of Definite Proportions. This law states that when elements combine to form a given compound, they do so in a fixed and invariable ratio by weight. This means that the ratio of the weight of vanadium to the weight of the oxygen that reacts is equal to the ratio of the equivalent weight of the vanadium to the equivalent weight of the oxygen.

$$\frac{\text{weight of V}}{\text{weight of O}} = \frac{\text{equivalent weight of V}}{\text{equivalent weight of O}}$$

Solving for the equivalent weight of vanadium in this compound, one assumes he has 100 g of the compound for calculations. Because 56 % of this compound is vanadium, it means that 56 g of it is vanadium. This indicates that (100 % – 56 %) = 44 % of the compound is oxygen and that in 100 g of the compound there are 44 g of oxygen.

Here one will assume that the equivalent weight of oxygen is its atomic number, 8. Solving for the equivalent weight of vanadium:

$$\frac{56 \text{ g}}{44 \text{ g}} = \frac{\text{equivalent weight of V}}{8}$$

$$\text{equivalent weight of V} = \frac{8 \times 56 \text{ g}}{44 \text{ g}} = 10.2$$

The equivalent weight of vanadium in this compound is 10.2.

It was found that a magnesium oxide contained .833 g of oxygen and 1.266 g of magnesium. Calculate the gram-equivalent weight of magnesium.

Solution: You begin this problem by establishing what is meant by the term gram-equivalent weight.

Gram-equivalent weight may be defined as the number of grams of an element that will involve a gain or loss of N electrons, i.e., the Avogadro's number (6.02×10^{23}) of electrons, when the element enters into chemical combination with another element. In this problem, you know that oxygen is present. Oxygen has an oxidation state of - 2. In a reaction, one mole of oxygen will gain two moles of electrons. The molecular weight of oxygen is 16 g/mole. Its equivalent weight becomes 16/2 = 8.00 g, since 2 moles of electrons will be gained and, by definition, equivalent weight is the amount of a substance that will gain or lose one mole of electrons.

The gram-equivalent weight of magnesium is that amount of the element that combines with 8.00 g of oxygen. You are told that 1.266 g Mg combines with .833 g O_2. If you let x = grams of Mg that will combine with 8.00 of oxygen, you can set up the following proportion:

$$\frac{1.266 \text{ g Mg}}{.833 \text{ g } O_2} = \frac{x \text{ g Mg}}{8.00 \text{ g } O_2}$$

Solving for x, you obtain x = 12.16 g of Mg, which is its gram-equivalent weight.

A chemist forms magnesium oxide by burning magnesium in oxygen. The oxide obtained weighed 1.2096 grams. It was formed from .7296 g of magnesium. Determine the mass equivalent of magnesium in this reaction.

<u>Solution</u>: An equivalent is defined as that mass of oxidizing or reducing agent that picks up or releases the Avogadro number of electrons in a particular reaction. One equivalent of any reducing agent reacts with one equivalent of any oxidizing agent. In this problem, the key is to determine the number of equivalents of oxygen involved. Once this is known, you also know the number of equivalents of magnesium.

Since the oxide weighed 1.2096 g and the magnesium weighed .7296 g, the mass of the combined oxygen must be 1.2096 - .7296 = .4800 g. Before the oxygen reacted, its oxidation state was zero. After the reaction, however, it was - 2. As such, each oxygen atom gained 2 electrons. Therefore, the Avogadro number of electrons will be taken up by one half of a mole of O atoms.

It follows, therefore, that there are 8.000 g per equivalent for oxygen, since 1 mole of oxygen atoms weighs 16 grams. It was found, however, that there were .4800 g of oxygen. As such

$$\frac{.4800 \text{ g}}{8.00 \text{ g/equiv}} = .0600 \text{ equiv of oxygen.}$$

This means that magnesium also has .06 equiv. 0.7296 g of Mg participated in the reaction. Therefore, the grams per equivalent of Mg =

$$\frac{.7296 \text{ g Mg}}{.060 \text{ equiv}} = 12.16 \text{ g/equiv.}$$

● **PROBLEM** 4-26

For the oxidation of VO by Fe_2O_3 to form V_2O_5 and FeO, what is the weight of one equivalent of VO and of Fe_2O_3?

<u>Solution</u>: The equation for this reaction is

$$2VO + 3Fe_2O_3 \rightarrow V_2O_5 + 6FeO$$

Here V is a reducing agent and Fe is an oxidizing agent. One equivalent of an oxidizing agent is defined as the mass of the substance that picks up the Avogadro number of electrons. One equivalent of a reducing agent is defined as that mass of the substance that releases the Avogadro number of electrons. The oxidation state of O is always - 2, thus the oxidation state of V in VO is + 2.

The oxidation state of V in V_2O_5 is + 5 because 5 O contribute (5 × - 2) or - 10, thus 2V must be + 10 and V is + 5. The half-reaction for V is

$$V^{+2} \rightarrow V^{+5} + 3e^-$$

This means that there are 3 equivalents per mole of

VO. One finds the weight of one equivalent by dividing the molecular weight by 3. (MW of VO = 66.94):

$$\text{weight of 1 equiv of V} = \frac{66.94 \text{ g/mole}}{3 \text{ equiv/mole}} = 22.31 \text{ g}$$

One uses a similar method for Fe. The oxidation state of O in Fe_2O_3 is (3 × - 2) or - 6, this means the 2Fe must be + 6 and Fe must be + 6/2 or + 3. The oxidation state of O in FeO is - 2, thus the oxidation state of Fe is + 2.

The half-reaction for the Fe is then

$$Fe^{+3} + 1e^- \rightarrow Fe^{+2}$$

In Fe_2O_3 there are 2 moles of Fe, therefore the half-reaction becomes

$$2Fe^{+3} + 2e^- \rightarrow 2Fe^{+2}$$

There are thus 2 equiv per mole of Fe_2O_3. The weight of one equivalent is equal to the weight of one mole Fe_2O_3 divided by 2. (MW of Fe_2O_3 = 159.70)

$$\text{wt of 1 equiv} = \frac{159.7 \text{ g/mole}}{2 \text{ equiv/mole}} = 79.85 \text{ g/equiv.}$$

● **PROBLEM** 4-27

In acting as a reducing agent a piece of metal M, weighing 16.00 g, gives up 2.25×10^{23} electrons. What is the weight of one equivalent of the metal?

Solution: One equivalent of a reducing agent is defined as that mass of the substance that releases the Avogadro number of electrons. Avogadro's number is 6.02×10^{23}, thus one can find the number of equivalents in 16.00 g of the metal by dividing 2.25×10^{23} by 6.02×10^{23}.

$$\text{no. of equiv} = \frac{2.25 \times 10^{23} \text{ electrons}}{6.02 \times 10^{23} \text{ electrons/equiv}} = .374 \text{ equiv.}$$

Thus, .374 equiv weigh 16.00 g, one can find the weight of one equivalent by dividing 16.0 g by 0.374 equiv.

$$\text{weight of 1 equiv} = \frac{16.0g}{0.374 \text{ equiv}} = 42.78 \text{ g/equiv.}$$

CHEMICAL COMPOSITION-WEIGHT AND VOLUME PERCENT

● **PROBLEM** 4-28

What is the simplest formula of a compound that is composed of 72.4 % iron and 27.6 % oxygen by weight?

Solution: For purposes of calculation, let us assume that there is 100 g of this compound present. This means that there are 72.4 g of Fe and 27.6 g O. The simplest formula for this compound is Fe_nO_m, where n is the number of moles of Fe present and m is the number of moles of O. One finds the number of moles by dividing the number of grams by the molecular weight.

$$\text{number of moles} = \frac{\text{number of grams}}{\text{MW}}$$

For Fe: n = number of moles present. MW = 55.8.

$$n = \frac{72.4 \text{ g}}{55.8 \text{ g/mole}} = 1.30 \text{ moles}$$

For O: m = number of moles present. MW = 16.0.

$$m = \frac{27.6 \text{ g}}{16.0 \text{ g/mole}} = 1.73 \text{ moles.}$$

One solves for the simplest formula by finding the ratio of Fe : O.

$$\frac{Fe}{O} = \frac{1.30}{1.73} = .75 = \frac{3}{4}$$

Therefore, n = 3 and m = 4.

The simplest formula is Fe_3O_4.

● **PROBLEM** 4-29

An unknown compound consists of 82.98 % potassium and 17.02 % oxygen. What is the empirical formula of the compound?

Solution: The empirical formula of any compound is the ratio of the atoms that make up the compound by weight. It is the simplest formula of a material that can be derived solely from its components. Therefore, we must determine the ratio of gram-atoms of potassium (K) to the number of gram-atoms of oxygen (O).

The number of gram-atoms of a substance equals the weight of the substance in grams divided by the weight per gram-atom of the substance. In other words,

$$\text{number of gram-atoms} = \frac{\text{weight in grams}}{\text{weight per gram-atom}}$$

In this problem, we are given the percentages of the elements that make up the compound. These percentages are, in reality, the weight in grams, since in the definition of weight, we imply percentage. The weight per gram atom is the atomic weight of the element which can be found in the periodic table of elements.

Therefore, the number of gram-atoms for potassium is

$$\frac{82.98 \text{ g} \quad \text{(wt of K)}}{39.10 \quad \text{(atomic weight)}} = 2.120 \text{ moles.}$$

For oxygen, the number of gram-atoms is

$$\frac{17.02 \text{ g} \quad \text{(wt of O)}}{16.00 \quad \text{(atomic wt)}} = 1.062 \text{ moles.}$$

Recall, the empirical formula is the ratio of the elements by weight. Consequently, the ratio of potassium to oxygen is 2 : 1, since the gram - atom ratios are respectively 2.120 : 1.062. Therefore, the empirical formula is K_2O.

● **PROBLEM** 4-30

A certain hydrate analyzes as follows: 29.7 % copper, 15.0 % sulfur, 2.8 % hydrogen, and 52.5 % oxygen. Determine the empirical formula of this hydrate from these percentages.

Solution: A hydrate is the chemical combination of water with another compound. For example, copper sulfate combines with water to form the hydrate of the composition $CuSO_4 \cdot 5H_2O$

$$CuSO_4 + 5H_2O \rightarrow CuSO_4 \cdot 5H_2O$$

One can find the empirical formula for a compound, when given the weight percents of the various elements making up the compound. This is done by finding the number of moles of each element in 100 g of the compound. The weight of each element is equal to the percent weight.

The number of moles is equal to the weight divided by the molecular weight of the element. In 100 g of this compound, there are 29.7 g Cu, 15.0 g S, 2.8 g H, and 52.5 g O. One can now determine the number of moles of each element present.

81

$$\text{number of moles} = \frac{\text{number of grams}}{\text{MW}}$$

MW of Cu = 63.5, MW of S = 32, MW of H = 1, MW of O = 16.

$$\text{number of moles of Cu} = \frac{29.7 \text{ g}}{63.5 \text{ g/mole}} = 0.47 \text{ moles}$$

$$\text{number of moles of S} = \frac{15.0 \text{ g}}{32.0 \text{ g/mole}} = 0.47 \text{ moles}$$

$$\text{number of moles of H} = \frac{2.8 \text{ g}}{1 \text{ g/mole}} = 2.8 \text{ moles}$$

$$\text{number of moles of O} = \frac{52.5 \text{ g}}{16 \text{ g/mole}} = 3.28 \text{ moles.}$$

To determine the empirical formula for this hydrate one must look at the ratio of Cu : S : H : O.

The ratio of the number of moles of these elements is

Cu : S : H : O

.47 : .47 : 2.8 : 3.28

To find the empirical formula, these numbers should be made into integers. This is done by making the lowest number equal to 1 and solving for the other three.

$$\frac{.47}{1} = \frac{.47}{x} \qquad x = \frac{.47}{.47} = 1$$

$$\frac{.47}{1} = \frac{2.8}{x} \qquad x = \frac{2.8}{.47} = 6$$

$$\frac{.47}{1} = \frac{3.28}{x} \qquad x = \frac{3.28}{.47} = 7$$

The ratio now becomes

Cu : S : H : O

1 : 1 : 6 : 7.

The empirical formula for the compound is $CuSH_6O_7$ or $CuSO_4 \cdot 3H_2O$.

● **PROBLEM** 4-31

A compound subjected to analysis was found to have the following composition by weight: 69.96 % carbon (atomic weight = 12.0 g/mole), 7.83 % hydrogen (atomic weight = 1.01 g/mole), and 22.21 % oxygen (atomic weight = 16.0 g/mole). If the molecular weight of this compound is 360 g/mole, what is its molecular formula?

<u>Solution</u>: Molecular formula may be defined as the formula stating the actual number of each type atom in a particular compound. Problems of this sort are solved by assuming a sample of some convenient mass and then calculating the number of moles of each atom in this sample. Once the number of moles has been calculated for each component, these numbers are divided by the greatest common factor in order to obtain the proportions in which the various components appear in the molecule (empirical formula). From this, we check to see if the elements, in those proportions, give the actual molecular weight. If they do, we have the actual molecular formula. If they do not, we multiply by a factor until their weights do give the molecular weight. There is no error in assuming a sample of definite mass, since the size of a sample of molecules does not affect the composition of the molecules.

Assume a sample weighing 100 g. Then the masses of C, H, and O in the sample are:

mass C = 69.96 % × 100 g = 69.96 g

mass $\widehat{H}$ = 7.83 % × 100 g = 7.83 g

mass O = 22.21 % × 100 g = 22.21 g

We convert the mass of each element to the corresponding number of moles by dividing by the atomic weight of that element. Thus, we obtain the following number of moles of each element:

moles C = 69.96 g/12.0 g/mole = 5.83 moles

moles H = 7.83 g/1.01 g/mole = 7.75 moles

moles O = 22.21 g/16.0 g/mole = 1.39 moles

The greatest common factor is 1.39 moles. Dividing the number of moles of each element by 1.39 moles, we obtain

$$\frac{\text{moles C}}{1.39 \text{ moles}} = \frac{5.83 \text{ moles}}{1.39 \text{ moles}} \cong 4.2$$

$$\frac{\text{moles H}}{1.39 \text{ moles}} = \frac{7.75 \text{ moles}}{1.39 \text{ moles}} \cong 5.6$$

$$\frac{\text{moles O}}{1.39 \text{ moles}} = \frac{1.39 \text{ moles}}{1.39 \text{ moles}} = 1.$$

Multiplying these numbers by 5 in order to get whole numbers we obtain:

Proportion of C atoms = 4.2 × 5 = 21

Proportion of H atoms = 5.6 × 5 = 28

Proportion of O atoms = $1 \times 5 = 5$.

Thus, the molecular formula of this compound is $C_{21}H_{28}O_5$. As a check, we determine the molecular weight of this compound to be

molecular weight = (21 x atomic weight of C)

$$+(28 \text{ x atomic weight of H})$$

$$+(5 \text{ x atomic weight of O})$$

$$=(21 \times 12.0 \text{ g/mole})+(28 \times 1.01 \text{ g/mole})$$

$$+(5 \times 16.0 \text{ g/mole})$$

$$\cong 360 \text{ g/mole},$$

which is the experimentally determined molecular weight.

● **PROBLEM 4-32**

The most common constituent of gasoline is iso-octane. It is a hydrocarbon, composed by weight of 84.12 % carbon, and 15.88 % hydrogen. Given that it contains 5.27×10^{21} molecules per gram, what is its molecular formula?

Solution: The molecular formula for iso-octane is C_nH_m, where n is the number of moles of C and m is the number of moles of H present in 1 mole of iso-octane. One can find n and m from the molecular weight of the compound. It is given that there are 5.27×10^{21} molecules/g present in one gram of the compound. One knows that there are 6.02×10^{23} molecules per mole. Thus,

$$MW = \frac{6.02 \times 10^{23} \text{ molecules/mole}}{5.27 \times 10^{21} \text{ molecules/g}} = 114.23 \text{ g/mole}$$

The C in this compound weighs 84.12 % of 114.23 g and the H weighs 15.88 % of 114.23 g.

weight of C = .8412 × 114.23 g/mole = 96.09 g/mole

weight of H = .1588 × 114.23 g/mole = 18.14 g/mole.

The number of moles of carbon present, n, is equal to 96.09 g divided by 12.01 g/mole, its atomic weight.

$$n = \frac{96.09 \text{ g}}{12.01 \text{ g/mole}} = 8.00 \text{ moles}$$

The percentage composition of each element present can now be calculated by considering what fraction by weight each element is of the total compound.

$$m = \frac{18.14 \text{ g}}{1 \text{ g/mole}} = 18.14 \text{ mole},$$

where 1 g/mole is the atomic weight of hydrogen.

The formula is C_8H_{18}, 18.14 is rounded off to the nearest whole number.

Calculate the percentage composition of aluminum sulfate, $Al_2(SO_4)_3$.

<u>Solution</u>: Because the formula of a compound is constant, the percentage composition of each element present can be calculated by using the parts by weight of each element in one molecular weight of the compound. The molecular weight of the compound can be calculated by adding together the weights of the various elements contained in the compound.

There are 2 atoms of aluminum present, and the molecular weight of aluminum is 27, so the contribution of the aluminum to the compound's total molecular weight is found by mulyipltying 27 by 2.

2 atoms of aluminum weigh 2 × 27 = 54

The weight contributions of the other elements present can be calculated in the same way.

The molecular weight of sulfur is 32, and there are 3 sulfur atoms present in the compound.

3 atoms of sulfur weigh 3 × 32 = 96

The molecular weight of oxygen is 16, and there are 12 oxygen atoms present in the compound.

12 atoms of oxygen weigh 12 × 16 = 192

The weights of the three elements contained in the compound are added together to find the total molecular weight of the compound.

2 atoms of aluminum	54
3 atoms of sulfur	96
12 atoms of oxygen	192
molecular weight of $Al_2(SO_4)_3$	342

The percentage composition of each element present can

now be calculated by considering what fraction by weight each element is of the total compound.

The weight of two atoms of aluminum is 54 so the fraction by weight of aluminum in the compound can be found by dividing 54 by 342, the molecular weight of the compound. The percentage is then found by multiplying this fraction by 100.

percentage composition of aluminum

$$= \frac{\text{weight of aluminum in compound}}{\text{molecular weight compound}} \times 100$$

percentage composition of aluminum $= \frac{54}{342} \times 100 = 15.8 \text{ \%}$.

The same method can be applied to the sulfur and oxygen.

percentage composition of sulfur $= \frac{96}{342} \times 100 = 28. 1\%$

percentage composition of oxygen $= \frac{192}{342} \times 100 = 56.1 \text{ \%}$

If the percent compositions of all the elements in a compound are added together they will equal 100.0.

percent composition of aluminum	15.8
percent composition of sulfur	28.1
percent composition of oxygen	56.1
	100.0

● **PROBLEM** 4-34

Two thirds of the atoms in a molecule of water (H_2O) are hydrogen. What percentage of the weight of a water molecule is the weight of the two hydrogen atoms? The atomic weight of hydrogen is 1.008 g/mole and of oxygen is 16.00 g/mole.

Solution: The most direct way to solve this composition problem is to consider the total weight of one molecule of water:

$$\text{mass}_{H_2O} = 2 \text{ mass}_H + \text{mass}_O$$

$$= 2(1.008 \text{ g/mole}) + 16.00 \text{ g/mole}$$

$$= 18.016 \text{ g/mole}.$$

The mass of two hydrogen atoms is $2 \times 1.008 =$

2.016 g/mole. Hence, the percentage mass of hydrogen in water is:

$$\% \text{ mass} = \frac{2 \text{ mass}_H}{\text{mass } H_2O} \times 100 \% = \frac{2.016 \text{ g/mole}}{18.016 \text{ g/mole}} \times 100 \%$$

$$= 11.19$$

● **PROBLEM** 4-35

Using the Periodic Table of Elements, find the following for sodium dihydrogen phosphate, NaH_2PO_4: (a) formula weight, (b) percent composition of oxygen, (c) weight in grams of 2.7 moles, and (d) percentage composition of oxygen in 2.7 moles.

Solution: This problem encompasses work in chemical stoichiometry. With this in mind, you proceed as follows:

(a) The formula weight = molecular weight, which is the sum of atomic masses of all the atoms in the substance. Na = 22.98, H = 1.008, O = 15.9999, and P = 30.97. Thus, formula weight = Na + 2H + P + 4O = 22.98 + 2(1.0080) + 30.97 + 4(15.9999) = 119.9.

(b) Percentage composition of oxygen is

$\dfrac{\text{total weight of oxygen in compound}}{\text{total weight of compound}}$

$$= \frac{4 \text{ oxygen atoms} \times 15.9994 \text{ mass/oxygen atom}}{119.9}$$

$$= .5334 \text{ g of oxygen or } 53.34 \% \text{ by weight in } NaH_2PO_4.$$

(c) Mole = $\dfrac{\text{mass of substance}}{\text{molecular weight}}$. You are given that there are 2.7 moles and you calculated the molecular weight. Thus, the weight in grams of 2.7 moles = (119.9 g/mole)(2.7 moles) = 324 g of NaH_2PO_4.

(d) Following a procedure similar to the one in part (b),

$\text{percent composition} = \dfrac{\text{no. of moles of O} \times \text{MW of O}}{\text{weight of comp/no. of moles}} \times 100$

$$= \frac{4 \text{ moles} \times 15.9 \text{ g/mole}}{324 \text{ g/2.7 moles}} \times 100$$

$$= 53.34 \%.$$

The percent composition of any element in any compound does not change when the amount of the compound present is changed.

What is the elemental percent composition (by weight) of a mixture that contains 20.0 g of $KAl(SO_4)_2$ and 60.0 g of K_2SO_4?

Solution: The elemental percent composition by weight is equal to the weight of the element present divided by the total weight of the mixture multiplied by 100.

$$\text{percent composition} = \frac{\text{wt of element}}{\text{total wt}} \times 100$$

The weight of the total mixture is equal to the sum of the weights of the $KAl(SO_4)_2$ and the K_2SO_4.

total weight = 20.0 g + 60.0 g = 80.0 g

The weights of the various elements present is found by dividing the molecular weight of the element multiplied by the number of atoms of that particular atom present in the molecule by the molecular weight of the compound, and then multiplying the quotient by the number of grams of the compound present.

Solving for the weights of the elements in $KAl(SO_4)_2$: MW = 258.12.

For K = MW = 39.1

$$\text{weight of K} = \frac{39.1 \text{ g/mole} \times 1}{258.12 \text{ g/mole}} \times 20.0 \text{ g} = 3.03 \text{ g.}$$

For Al: MW = 26.98

$$\text{weight of Al} = \frac{26.98 \text{ g/mole} \times 1}{258.12 \text{ g/mole}} \times 20.0 \text{ g} = 2.09 \text{ g.}$$

For S: MW = 32.06

$$\text{weight of S} = \frac{32.06 \text{ g/mole} \times 2 \text{ moles}}{258.12 \text{ g/mole}} \times 20.0 \text{ g} = 4.97 \text{ g.}$$

For O: MW = 16

$$\text{weight of O} = \frac{16 \text{ g/mole} \times 8 \text{ moles}}{258.12 \text{ g/mole}} \times 20.0 \text{ g} = 9.92 \text{ g.}$$

Solving for the weight of the elements in K_2SO_4: MW = 174.26

For K: MW = 39.1

$$\text{weight of K} = \frac{39.1 \text{ g/mole} \times 2 \text{ moles}}{174.26 \text{ g/mole}} \times 60.0 \text{ g} = 26.93 \text{ g}$$

For S; MW = 32.06

weight of S = $\frac{32.06 \text{ g/mole} \times 1 \text{ mole}}{174.26 \text{ g/mole}} \times 60.0 \text{ g} = 11.04 \text{ g}$

For O: MW = 16

weight of O = $\frac{16 \text{ g/mole} \times 4 \text{ moles}}{174.26 \text{ g/mole}} \times 60.0 \text{ g} = 22.04 \text{ g.}$

One can find the total weights of the various elements by taking the sum of their weights from the two compounds.

Total weight of K = 3.03 g + 26.93 g = 29.96 g

Total weight of Al = 2.09 g

Total weight of S = 4.97 g + 11.04 g = 16.01 g

Total weight of O = 9.92 g + 22.04 g = 31.96 g.

One can now determine the elemental percent composition of the mixture.

$$\% = \frac{\text{weight of element}}{\text{total weight of mixture}} \times 100$$

% of K = $\frac{29.96 \text{ g}}{80.0 \text{ g}} \times 100 = 37.45 \%$

% of Al = $\frac{2.09 \text{ g}}{80.0 \text{ g}} \times 100 = 2.61 \%$

% of S = $\frac{16.01 \text{ g}}{80.0 \text{ g}} \times 100 = 20.01 \%$

% of O = $\frac{31.96 \text{ g}}{80.0 \text{ g}} \times 100 = 39.95 \%.$

● **PROBLEM** 4-37

A 0.240 g sample of a compound of oxygen and element X was found by analysis to contain 0.096 g of X and 0.144 g of oxygen. (a) Calculate the percentage composition by weight. (b) Calculate from the above data, three possible atomic weights for X relative to oxygen (at. wt. = 16). (c) What additional information is needed to calculate the true atomic weight of X?

Solution: (a) The percent composition by weight of each element in the compound is found by dividing the weight of that element by the weight of the compound and then multiplying the quotient by 100. For O, therefore, you obtain the following percentage:

$\frac{.144 \text{ g}}{0.240 \text{ g}} \times 100 = 60 \% \text{ O}$

For X:

$$\frac{.096 \text{ g}}{0.240 \text{ g}} \times 100 = 40 \text{ \% X}$$

(b) If you assume that the compound is XO, you can solve for the molecular weight of X by using the following ratio. Let x = MW of X.

$$\frac{.144 \text{ g O}}{16.0 \text{ g/mole O}} = \frac{.096 \text{ g}}{X \text{ g/mole x}}$$

MW X = 10.7

If the compound is taken to be X_2O, there are twice as many X atoms present as O atoms. In solving for the molecular weight of X in this case, use the following ratio

$$\frac{.144 \text{ g}}{\text{weight of 1 mole of O}} = \frac{.096}{\text{weight of 2 moles of X}}$$

Let x = MW of X

$$\frac{.144 \text{ g}}{16.0} = \frac{.096 \text{ g}}{x}$$

$$x = \frac{16.0 \times .096 \text{ g}}{.144 \text{ g}}$$

$$x = 5.35.$$

Assume also that the formula for the compound might be XO_2. Then, the following ratio should be used: Let x = MW of X.

$$\frac{.144 \text{ g}}{\text{weight of 2 moles of O}} = \frac{.096}{\text{weight of 1 mole of X}}$$

$$\frac{.144 \text{ g}}{32.0} = \frac{.096 \text{ g}}{x}$$

$$x = \frac{.096 \text{ g} \times 32.0}{.144 \text{ g}} = 21.4.$$

(c) To solve for the true atomic weight of X, you must know the actual number of X atoms present per each O atom present.

● **PROBLEM** 4-38

A certain solution contains 5 % $FeSO_4$. How many pounds of Fe could be obtained from 1 ton of this solution?

Solution: If a solution contains 5 % $FeSO_4$, this means that 5 % of the total weight of the solution is $FeSO_4$.

In this problem, 5 % of a ton is FeSO₄. To determine the weight of Fe in this amount of FeSO₄, one must calculate the weight percent of Fe in FeSO₄. This is done by dividing the molecular weight of Fe by the molecular weight of FeSO₄ and multiplying the quotient by 100.

To solve this problem:

(1) Determine the percent weight of FeSO₄

(2) Determine the weight of 5 % of a ton

(3) Determine how much of this weight is Fe.

(1) The molecular weight of a compound is determined by adding together the weight contributed by the elements of which it is composed. MW of Fe = 55.8, MW of S = 32, MW of O = 16.

Thus, for FeSO₄,

1 atom of Fe	1 × 55.8	= 55.8
1 atom of S	1 × 32	= 32
4 atoms of O	4 × 16	= 64
molecular weight of FeSO₄		151.8

$$\text{percent weight of Fe in FeSO}_4 = \frac{\text{weight of Fe}}{\text{weight of FeSO}_4} \times 100$$

$$= \frac{55.8}{151.8} \times 100 = 37 \text{ %.}$$

37 % of FeSO₄ by weight is Fe.

(2) Determining 5 % of a ton. 1 ton = 2000 lbs.

5 % of a ton = .05 × 2000 lbs = 100 lbs.

Thus, 5 % of a ton is 100 lbs.

(3) Determining the weight of Fe in 100 lbs. 37 % of this is Fe.

weight of Fe = .37 × 100 lbs = 37 lbs.

● **PROBLEM** 4-39

The density of a 25.0 % sugar solution is 1.208 g/ml. What weight of sugar would be contained in 1.00 liter of this solution?

Solution: When a solution is said to be 25.0 % sugar, it means that 25.0 % of the weight of the solution is made up by the sugar. Thus one can determine the weight of the sugar in this solution by multiplying the total weight of the solution by .25. Here one is not given the weight of the solution but the density and the volume. The density is the weight of 1 ml of the solution, thus the weight of 1.0 liter or 1000 ml is equal to the volume 1000 ml times the density (1.208 g/ml).

weight of solution = 1000 ml × 1.208 g/ml = 1208 g.

The weight of the sugar in the solution can now be found.

weight of sugar = .25 × weight of solution

= .25 × 1208 g = 302 g.

● PROBLEM 4-40

What is the weight of 1.0 liter of carbon monoxide (CO) at STP?

Solution: At STP (Standard Temperature and Pressure, 0°C and 760 torr), a mole of any gas has a volume of 22.4 liters. This means that the gram molecular weight of a gas is contained in 22.4 liters. In this problem, one is looking for the weight of 1 liter of CO. The molecular weight of CO is 28 g. Because there are 28 g of CO in 22.4 liters of gas, 28 g must be divided by 22.4 to find the weight of one liter.

$$\text{weight of one liter} = \frac{\text{gram molecular weight}}{22.4}$$

$$\text{weight of 1 liter of CO} = \frac{28 \text{ g}}{22.4} = 1.25 \text{ g.}$$

● PROBLEM 4-41

Mammalian hemoglobin contains about 0.33 % iron (Fe, atomic weight = 56 g/mole) by weight. If the molecular weight of hemoglobin is 68,000 g/mole, how many iron atoms are there in each molecule of hemoglobin?

Solution: To solve this problem, we consider a one mole sample of hemoglobin. This assumption introduces no error, since the size of the hemoglobin sample does not affect the number of Fe atoms per molecule of hemoglobin. We then calculate the mass of Fe atoms in one mole of

hemoglobin and divide by the atomic weight of Fe to
obtain the number of moles of Fe per mole of hemoglobin.

Since the molecular weight of hemoglobin is
68,000 g/mole, the weight of one mole of hemoglobin is

68,000 g/mole × 1 mole = 68,000 g.

The weight of Fe in one mole of hemoglobin is then

weight Fe = % Fe by weight × weight of 1 mole of
$$\hspace{6cm} \text{hemoglobin}$$

$$= 0.33 \ \% \times 68,000 \ g = 224.4 \ g.$$

The number of moles of Fe corresponding to this
weight is found by dividing this weight of Fe by the
atomic weight of Fe to obtain

$$\text{moles Fe} = \frac{\text{weight Fe}}{\text{atomic weight Fe}} = \frac{224.4 \ g}{56 \ g/mole} = 4 \ \text{moles.}$$

Hence, there are 4 moles of Fe per mole of
hemoglobin. To convert from number of moles to number
of atoms or molecules, we multiply by Avogadro's number:
hence, 4 moles of Fe correspond to 4 moles × 6 × 10^{23}
atoms/mole = 24 × 10^{23} atoms of Fe and 1 mole of hemoglobin
corresponds to 1 mole × 6 × 10^{23} molecules/mole = 6 ×
10^{23} molecules of hemoglobin. Thus, the ratio of number
of atoms of Fe to molecules of hemoglobin is

$$\frac{24 \times 10^{23} \text{ atoms of Fe}}{6 \times 10^{23} \text{ molecules of hemoglobin}} = 4 \ \text{atoms Fe/molecule hemoglobin}$$

There are 4 atoms of Fe in every molecule of
hemoglobin.

● **PROBLEM** 4-42

The average bromine content of sea water is 0.0064%.
(a) How much sea water, in cubic feet, would be required to
obtain one pound of bromine? (b) What volume of chlorine
gas, measured at STP would be required to liberate
the bromine from one ton of salt water? One cubic foot
of sea water weighs about 63 pounds (28.35 kg)

Solution: (a) The weight of bromine in one cubic foot of
sea water is found by multiplying 63 pounds (the weight
of 1 cu.ft. of sea water) by 0.000064. This is because
bromine composes 0.0064 % of the weight of sea water.

weight of Br per 1 cubic ft (liter) = .000064 x 63 lb
$$\hspace{5cm} \text{(1.01 kg/liter)}$$
$$\hspace{4cm} = 4.032 \times 10^{-3} \text{ lb}$$

$$(6.46 \times 10^{-5} \text{ kg})$$

One can find the number of cubic feet of sea water necessary to extract 1 lb of Br by dividing 1 lb by the number of pounds of Br in one cubic foot.

$$\text{no. of cubic ft} = \frac{1 \text{ lb}}{4.032 \times 10^{-3} \text{ lb/cubic ft}}$$

$$= 248.02 \text{ cubic feet } (7022.93 \text{ liters})$$

(b) Since chlorine is more active than bromine, the latter may be liberated from its salt by treatment with chlorine.

$$2Br^- + Cl_2 \rightarrow 2Cl^- + Br_2$$

One mole of Cl_2 will liberate 2 moles of Br^-. Therefore, to find the volume of Cl_2 gas necessary to liberate the bromine in one ton of sea water, one must first calculate the amount of Br^- present in 1 ton of sea water. One is given that 1 cubic foot of sea water weighs 63 pounds. Thus the number of cubic feet of sea water in 1 ton can be found. (1 ton = 2000 lbs).

$$\text{no. of cubic feet} = \frac{2000 \text{ lbs}}{63 \text{ lbs/cubic feet}} = 31.75 \text{ cu.ft.}$$
$$(899 \text{ liters})$$

In the previous section one found that each cubic foot contains 4.032×10^{-3} lb of Br^-, thus one finds the amount of Br^- in 31.75 cu. ft. by multiplying the number of cubic feet by the weight of one cubic foot.

weight of Br^- in 1 ton sea water =

$$= 31.75 \text{ cu.ft.} \times 4.032 \times 10^{-3} \text{ lb/cu.ft.}$$

$$= .128 \text{ lb } (0.058 \text{ kg})$$

One finds the number of moles present by dividing .128 lb by the molecular weight in pounds. (MW of Br^- = 80 gr/mole.)

There are 454 g in 1 lb, therefore grams are converted to pounds by multiplying the number of grams by 1 lb/454 g.

$$\text{MW of } Br^- \text{ in lb} = 80 \text{ g/mole} \times \frac{1 \text{ lb}}{454 \text{ g}} = .1762 \text{ lb/mole}$$

One can now find the number of moles of Br^- present in one ton.

$$\text{no. of moles} = \frac{\text{weight of } Br^-}{\text{MW in lbs}}$$

$$\text{no. of moles} = \frac{.128 \text{ lbs}}{.1762 \text{ lbs/mole}} = .73 \text{ moles.}$$

From the equation one knows that ½ as many moles of Cl_2 are needed as Br^-. Therefore, the amount of Cl_2 used is equal to ½ of .73 moles or .365 moles. The volume of one mole of gas at STP (Standard Temperature and Pressure, 0°C and 1 atm) is defined to be 22.4 liters. Therefore, one can find the volume of Cl_2 gas required for the reaction by multiplying the number of moles of gas present by 22.4 liters.

volume of Cl_2 = .365 × 22.4 liters = 8.18 liters.

● **PROBLEM** 4-43

What mass of calcium (Ca, atomic mass = 40.08 g/mole) must be combined with 1.00 g of phosphorus (P, atomic mass = 30.97 g/mole) to form the compound Ca_3P_2?

Solution: From the formula of the compound we are trying to form, Ca_3P_2, we see that the ratio of moles of calcium to moles of phosphorus must be 3/2. By calculating the number of moles of P in 1.00 g, we can determine the required number of moles of Ca and then convert this to a mass.

The number of moles of P in 1.00 g is

$$\text{moles P} = \frac{\text{mass P}}{\text{atomic mass P}} = \frac{1.00 \text{ g}}{30.97 \text{ g/mole}} = 0.0322 \text{ mole.}$$

Then, using the ratio $\frac{\text{moles Ca}}{\text{moles P}} = \frac{3}{2}$ or moles Ca = $\frac{3}{2}$ moles P, the number of moles of Ca required to combine with 0.0322 mole P in a 3/2 ratio is

$$\text{moles Ca} = \frac{3}{2} \text{ moles P} = \frac{3}{2} \times 0.0332 \text{ mole} = 0.0483 \text{ mole.}$$

To convert this to a mass we multiply by the atomic mass, obtaining

mass Ca = moles Ca × atomic mass Ca

= 0.0483 mole × 40.08 g/mole = 1.94 g Ca.

● **PROBLEM** 4-44

Aluminum and oxygen react to form Al_2O_3. This oxide has a density = 3.97 g/ml and by chemical analysis is 47.1 weight-percent oxygen. The atomic mass of oxygen is 15.9999, what is the atomic mass of aluminum?

Solution: You can answer this question by setting up a proportion between the relative number of atoms in the oxide and the percentages by weight of the atoms in the compound. From Al_2O_3, you see there must be 2 atoms of Al for every 3 atoms of O. You are told that the atomic mass of oxygen is 15.9999. There exist only 2 elements in Al_2O_3. Thus, the weight-percent of the aluminum is 100 - 47.1 = 52.9. You have,

$$\frac{2 \text{ Al}}{3 \text{ O}} = \frac{\text{weight-percent Al}}{\text{weight-percent O}} = \frac{2 \text{ Al}}{3(15.9999)} = \frac{52.2}{47.1}$$

Solving for Al, which is the atomic mass, you obtain

$$Al = \frac{3}{2} (15.9999) \left(\frac{52.9}{47.1}\right) = 26.9 \text{ g/mole.}$$

● **PROBLEM** 4-45

On being heated in air a mixture of FeO and Fe_3O_4 picks up oxygen so as to be converted completely to Fe_2O_3. If the observed weight gain is 5.00 percent of the initial weight, what must have been the composition of the initial mixture?

Solution: One should first determine the weight percent increase when the mixture is 100 % FeO or 100 % Fe_3O_4. 5.0 % increase will be some mixture in between. 5 % will be equal to the sum of the products of the percent weight gained by each compound and the fractions of the mixture that each compound contributes.

The reaction of FeO and O to form Fe_2O_3 is

$$2FeO + \frac{1}{2} O_2 \rightarrow Fe_2O_3.$$

The percent weight increase for the reaction is found by dividing the weight of Fe_2O_3 by the weight of 2FeO. Weight of 2FeO is 144, weight of Fe_2O_3 is 160.

$$\frac{\text{weight of } Fe_2O_3}{\text{weight of 2FeO}} = \frac{160}{144} = 1.1111$$

The percent weight increase is equal to $(1.1111 - 1.0)$ X 100 = 11.11 %. This means that for each Fe_2O_3 formed by FeO there is an 11.11 % weight increase. One can solve for the weight increase for Fe_3O_4 by a similar method. The reaction is

$$2Fe_3O_4 + \frac{1}{2} O_2 \rightarrow 3Fe_2O_3$$

The weight of $2Fe_3O_4$ is 464, the weight of $3Fe_2O_3$ is 480.

$$\frac{\text{weight of } 3Fe_2O_3}{\text{weight of } 2Fe_3O_4} = \frac{480}{464} = 1.0345$$

percent weight increase $= (1.0345 - 1.0) \times 100 = 3.45$ %.

Thus when Fe_2O_3 is formed from Fe_3O_4 there is a 3.45 % weight increase. The final mixture must have a 5 % weight increase. Let x = fraction of mixture that is FeO.

Mixture weight gain = (fraction FeO) × (wt gain percent

for FeO) + (fraction Fe_3O_4) ×

(wt. gain percent for Fe_3O_4)

$5 = (x)(11.11) + (1 - x)(3.45)$

$5 = 11.11x + 3.45 - 3.45 x$

$1.55 = 7.66 x$

$\frac{1.55}{7.66} = x$

$.2024 = x$

$.7976 = 1 - x$

The initial mixture is, therefore 20.24 % FeO and 79.76 % Fe_3O_4.

● PROBLEM 4-46

Ethanol (C_2H_5OH, molecular weight = 46 g/mole) unlike most ingested substances, is absorbed directly by the stomach lining. If 44 g of pure ethanol (4 oz of whiskey or 5.5 oz of a martini) is consumed the resulting concentration of ethanol in the blood is 0.080 g ethanol/100 ml blood. What percent of the ingested ethanol is in the blood? Assume that the total blood volume of an adult is 7.0 liters.

Solution: We must first calculate the total mass of alcohol in the blood and then determine to what percent of the ingested mass of alcohol this corresponds.

The total mass of ethanol in the blood is equal to the product of the concentration of ethanol and the total blood volume or 0.080 g ethanol/100 ml blood × 7.0 liters blood = 0.080 g ethanol/100 ml blood × 7000 ml blood = 5.6 g ethanol. Note: 7 liters = 7000 ml since 1 ℓ = 1000 ml. This corresponds to

$\frac{5.6 \text{ g}}{44 \text{ g}} \times 100 \% = 13 \%$ of the ingested ethanol.

● PROBLEM 4-47

It is known that, when exposed to air, beryllium does not corrode but barium does. One explanation is that beryllium

97

(Be) forms a tightly protective oxide coat whereas barium (Ba) does not. The density of BeO = 3.01 g/cc and BaO = 5.72 g/cc, find what happens to the volume per atom when the metals become oxides. The density of Be = 1.86 g/cc and of Ba = 3.598 g/cc.

<u>Solution</u>: To solve this problem, first calculate the volume per atom of Be and Ba, and then compare it with the volume per atom of their oxides. From this comparison, expansion or shrinkage can be determined. The volume per atom of any element can be found by knowing the atomic weight, the number of atoms per mole and the density of the element.

Thus, there are Avogadro's number or 6.02×10^{23} atoms per mole. You are given the densities of the substances involved in this problem. Thus, by substitution you find volume of Be

$$= \frac{MW}{(6.02 \times 10^{23})(density)} = \frac{9.01 \text{ g/mole}}{6.02 \times 10^{23} \text{ a/mole} \times 1.86 \text{ g/cc}}$$

$$= 8.05 \times 10^{-24} \text{ cc/atom}$$

From similar computations, you find that

BeO = 1.38×10^{-23} cc/atom, Ba = 6.34×10^{-23} cc/atom, and BaO = 4.45×10^{-23}.

One can find the comparative size of BeO to Be by subtracting the volume per atom of Be from that of BeO. This difference is then divided by the volume of Be and multiplied by 100. This product gives the percentage increase in size of the initial and final atoms when Be is oxidized. A similar process is used for Ba.

For Be:

$$\frac{1.38 \times 10^{-23} \text{ cc} - 8.05 \times 10^{-24} \text{ cc}}{8.05 \times 10^{-24}} \times 100 = 71 \text{ \%}$$

For Ba:

$$\frac{4.45 \times 10^{-23} \text{ cc} - 6.34 \times 10^{-23}}{6.34 \times 10^{-23}} \times 100 = -30 \text{ \%}.$$

From a comparison of the atomic volumes of Be and BeO, you see that Be expands by 71 % when it forms the oxide. From a comparison of Ba and BaO, you see that Ba shrinks by 30 %, when it forms the oxide.

CHAPTER 5

STOICHIOMETRY/WEIGHT AND VOLUME CALCULATIONS

BALANCING EQUATIONS

● **PROBLEM** 5-1

Balance the equations: (a) $Ag_2O \rightarrow Ag + O_2$,
(b) $Zn + HCl \rightarrow ZnCl_2 + H_2$; (c) $NaOH + H_2SO_4 \rightarrow Na_2SO_4 + H_2O$.

Solution: When balancing chemical equations, one must make sure that there are the same number of atoms of each element on both the left and right side of the arrow. For example, $H_2 + O_2 \rightarrow H_2O$ is not a balanced equation because there are 2 O's on the left side and only one on the right. $2H_2 + O_2 \rightarrow 2H_2O$ is the balanced equation for water because there are the same number of H and O atoms on each side of the equation.

   (a) $Ag_2O \rightarrow Ag + O_2$ is not a balanced equation because there are 2 Ag on the left and only one on the right, and because there is only one O on the left and two O on the right. To balance this equation one must first multiply the left side by 2 to have 2 O's on each side.

$$2Ag_2O \rightarrow Ag + O_2$$

There are now 4 Ag on the left and only one on the right, thus the Ag, on the right must be multiplied by 4.

$$2Ag_2O \rightarrow 4Ag + O_2$$

The equation is now balanced.

   (b) $Zn + HCl \rightarrow ZnCl_2 + H_2$

In this equation, there are 2 H and 2 Cl on the right and only one of each on the left, therefore, the equation can be balanced by multiplying the HCl on the left by 2.

$$Zn + 2HCl \rightarrow ZnCl_2 + H_2$$

Because there are the same number of Zn, Cl, and H on both sides of the equation, it is balanced.

    (c) NaOH + H_2SO_4 → Na_2SO_4 + H_2O

Here, there are 1 Na, five O, 3 H and 1 S on the left and 2 Na, 1 S, five O, and 2 H on the right. To balance this equation, one can first adjust the Na by multiplying the NaOH by 2.

    $2NaOH + H_2SO_4$ → Na_2SO_4 + H_2O

There are now 2 Na, six O, 4 H, and 1 S on the left and 2 Na, five O, 2 H, and 1 S on the right. Because there are two more H and one more O on the left than on the right, you can balance this equation by multiplying the H_2O by 2.

    $2NaOH + H_2SO_4$ → Na_2SO_4 + $2H_2O$

The equation is now balanced.

● **PROBLEM** 5-2

Balance the following by filling in missing species and proper coefficient: (a) NaOH + _____ → $NaHSO_4$ + HOH, (b) PCl_3 + __HOH → _____ + 3HCl, (c) CH_4 + ____ → CCl_4 + 4HCl.

Solution: To balance chemical equations you must remember that ALL atoms (and charges) must be accounted for. The use of coefficients in front of compounds is a means to this end. Thus,

    (a) NaOH + _____ → $NaHSO_4$ + HOH

On the right side of the equation, you have 1 Na, 3 H's, 5 O's, and 1 S. This same number of elements must appear on the left side. However, on the left side, there exists only 1 Na, 1 O, and 1 H. You are missing 2 H's, 1 S, and 4 O's. The missing species is H_2SO_4, sulfuric acid. You could have anticipated this since a strong base (NaOH) reacting with a strong acid yields a salt ($NaHSO_4$) and water. The point is, however, that H_2SO_4 balances the equation by supplying all the missing atoms.

    (b) PCl_3 + 3HOH → _____ + 3HCl.

Here, the left side has 1 P, 3 Cl's, 6 H's, and 3 O's. The right has 3 H's and 3 Cl's. You are missing 1 P, 3 O's and 3 hydrogens. Therefore, $P(OH)_3$ is formed.

    (c) CH_4 + _____ → CCl_4 + 4HCl

Here, there are 1 C, 8 Cl's, and 4 H's on the right and 1 C and 4 H's on the left. The missing compound, therefore, contains 8 Cl's and thus it is 4 Cl_2. One knows that it is

4 Cl_2 rather than Cl_8 or $8Cl$ because elemental chlorine gas is a diatomic or 2 atom molecule.

CALCULATIONS USING CHEMICAL ARITHMETIC

● **PROBLEM** 5-3

Verify that the following data confirm the law of equivalent proportions: Nitrogen and oxygen react with hydrogen to form ammonia and water, respectively. 4.66 g of nitrogen is required for every gram of hydrogen in ammonia, and 8 g of oxygen for every gram of hydrogen in water. Nitrogen plus oxygen yields NO. Here, 14 g of nitrogen is required for every 16 g of oxygen.

<u>Solution</u>: To verify, you must show that when two elements (nitrogen and oxygen) combine with a third element (hydrogen), they will do so in a simple multiple of the proportions in which they combine with each other. Thus, the nitrogen to oxygen ratio in NO must be a ratio of small integers with the nitrogen and oxygen ratio in H_3N (ammonia) and H_2O (water).

For ammonia and water, $\dfrac{N}{O} = \dfrac{4.66 \text{ g}}{8.00 \text{ g}} = .582$

For NO, $\dfrac{N}{O} = \dfrac{14 \text{ g}}{16 \text{ g}} = .875.$

If .582 and .875 are a ratio of small integers to each other, you verify the law of equivalent proportions. Therefore,

$$\frac{.582}{.875} = .665 \approx \frac{2}{3} ,$$

concluding that they are a ratio.

● **PROBLEM** 5-4

A metal has an atomic weight of 24. When it reacts with a non-metal of atomic weight 80, it does so in a ratio of 1 atom to 2 atoms, respectively. With this information, how many grams of non-metal will combine with 33.3 g of metal. If 1 g of metal is reacted with 5 g of non-metal, find the amount of product produced.

<u>Solution</u>: To answer this problem, write out the reaction between the metal and non-metal, so that the relative number of moles that react can be determined. You can calculate the number of grams of material that react or are produced. You are told that 1 atom of metal reacts with 2 atoms of non-metal. Let X = non-metal and M =

metal. The compound is MX_2. The reaction is $M \rightarrow 2X + MX_2$. Determine the number of moles that react. You have 33 g of M with an atomic weight of 24.

Therefore, the number of moles $= \dfrac{33 \text{ g}}{24 \text{ g/mole}} = 1.375$ moles.

The above reaction states that for every 1 mole of M, 2 moles of X must be present. This means, therefore, that $2 \times 1.375 = 2.75$ moles of X must be present. The non-metal has an atomic weight of 80. Thus, recalling the definition a mole, 2.75 mole $= \dfrac{\text{grams}}{80 \text{ g/mole}}$. Solving for grams of X, you obtain $2.75 (80) = 220$ grams.

Let us consider the reaction with 1 g of M with 5 g of X to produce an unknown amount of MX_2. The solution is similar to the other, except that here you consider the concept of a limiting reagent. The amount of MX_2 produced from a combination will depend on the substance that exists in the smallest quantity. Thus, to solve this problem you compute the number of moles of M and X present. The smaller number, (based on reaction equation) is the one you employ in calculating the number of moles of MX_2 that will be generated. You have, therefore,

$$M_{\text{moles}} = \frac{1}{24} = .04166 \text{ moles M}$$

$$X_{\text{moles}} = \frac{5}{80} = .0625 \text{ moles X.}$$

Using 0.0625 moles X, only .03125 moles of MX_2 will be produced, since the equation informs you that 1 mole of MX_2 is produced for every two moles of X. For M, it is a 1 : 1 ratio, so that .04166 moles of MX_2 would be generated. Therefore, X is the limiting reagent. The atomic weight of MX_2 is 184. Thus, the amount produced is

184 g/mole (.03125 moles) = 5.75 g.

WEIGHT-WEIGHT PROBLEMS

• PROBLEM 5-5

Upon the addition of heat to an unknown amount of $KClO_3$, .96 g of oxygen was liberated. How much $KClO_3$ was present?

Solution: The key to answering this question is to write a balanced equation that illustrates this chemical reaction. From this, you can employ the mole concept to determine the weights of the substances involved.

Given that oxygen is liberated and that oxygen gas

exists as O_2 and not O, you can write the balanced equation

$$2KClO_3 \rightarrow 2KCl + 3O_2.$$

All atoms are accounted for. The coefficients indicate the relative number of moles that react. For example, every two moles of $KClO_3$ yield 3 moles of oxygen. A mole is defined as weight in grams of a substance divided by its atomic or molecular weight. Therefore, you have

$$\frac{.96 \text{ g}}{32 \text{ g/mole}} = .030 \text{ moles of oxygen. To calculate the}$$

weight of $KClO_3$, you look at the balanced equation.

You find that the number of moles of $KClO_3$ is 2/3 the number of moles of oxygen. As such, the number of

moles of $KClO_3$ = .030 $\left(\dfrac{2 \text{ moles } KClO_3}{3 \text{ moles } O_2}\right)$ = .020 moles of

$KClO_3$. Recalling the definition of a mole, the number of grams of $KClO_3$ (MW of $KClO_3$ = 122.55) is

.020 × (122.55 g/mole) = 2.5 g.

● PROBLEM 5-6

Determine the weights of CO_2 and H_2O produced on burning 104 g. of C_2H_2. Molecular weights are CO_2 = 44 and H_2O = 18. The equation for the reaction is

$$2C_2H_2 + 5O_2 \rightarrow 4CO_2 + 2H_2O$$

Solution: Two methods can be used to solve this problem. One is called the mole method and the other the proportion method.

Mole method: According to the equation, 2 moles of C_2H_2 react with 5 moles of O_2 to produce 4 moles of CO_2 and 2 moles of H_2O. Thus, in this problem, the first thing one has to determine is how many moles of C_2H_2 are contained in 104 g.

The molecular weight of C_2H_2 is 26, by dividing the amount of C_2H_2 present by the molecular weight of the compound, the number of moles present is found.

$$\text{number of moles of } C_2H_2 = \frac{\text{number of grams of } C_2H_2}{\text{molecular weight of } C_2H_2}$$

$$\text{number of moles of } C_2H_2 \text{ present} = \frac{104 \text{ g}}{26 \text{ g/mole}} = 4 \text{ moles.}$$

In the equation 2 moles of C_2H_2 are burned to form 4 moles of CO_2 and 2 moles of H_2O. Here there are 4 moles of C_2H_2 present, which is twice the amount in the empirical equation. Therefore, twice as much CO_2 and H_2O will be formed. 8 moles of CO_2 and 4 moles of H_2O will be formed.

$$2 \times (2C_2H_2 + 5O_2 \rightarrow 4CO_2 + 2H_2O)$$

$$= 4C_2H_2 + 10O_2 \rightarrow 8CO_2 + 4H_2O$$

To find the weight of 8 moles of CO_2, the molecular weight of CO_2 is multiplied by 8.

weight of CO_2 = number of moles present × molecular weight of CO_2.

weight of CO_2 = 8 moles × 44 g/mole = 352 g.

The same procedure can be followed for H_2O.

weight of H_2O = number of moles present × molecular weight of H_2O

weight of H_2O = 4 moles × 18 g/mole = 72 g.

Proportion method:

An alternate method of solution to this problem is the proportion method in which molecular weights (multiplied by the proper coefficients) are placed below the formula in the equation and the amounts of substances (given and unknown) are placed above. Here one has for CO_2:

$$\begin{array}{cccc} 104 \text{ g} & & X & \\ 2\,C_2H_2 & + \quad 5O_2 & \rightarrow \quad 4\,CO_2 & + \, 2\,H_2O \\ 2\times26 \text{ g} & & 4\times44 \text{ g} & \end{array}$$

This becomes $\dfrac{104 \text{ g}}{52 \text{ g}} = \dfrac{X}{176 \text{ g}}$

Solving for X one has

$$X = \frac{(104 \text{ g})(176 \text{ g})}{(52 \text{ g})} = 352 \text{ gr } CO_2$$

A similar method can be applied to the H_2O

$$\begin{array}{cccc} 104 \text{ g} & & & X \\ 2\,C_2H_2 & + \, 5O_2 & \rightarrow \quad 4CO_2 & + \, 2\,H_2O \\ 2\times26 \text{ g} & & & 2\times18 \text{ g} \end{array}$$

$$\frac{104 \text{ g}}{52 \text{ g}} = \frac{X}{36 \text{ g}}$$

$$X = \frac{(104 \text{ g})(36 \text{ g})}{(52 \text{ g})} = 72 \text{ g } H_2O.$$

Silver bromide, AgBr, used in photography, may be prepared
from $AgNO_3$ and NaBr. Calculate the weight of each required
for producing 93.3 lb of AgBr. (1 lb = 454 g.)

<u>Solution</u>: The reaction for the production of AgBr is
written

$$AgNO_3 + NaBr \rightarrow AgBr + NaNO_3$$

This means that one mole of each $AgNO_3$ and NaBr are needed
to form one mole of AgBr. In this problem, to determine
the number of pounds of $AgNO_3$ and NaBr used to form 93.9 lbs
of AgBr, one must first determine the number of moles of
AgBr in 93.9 lbs. There will be one mole of each NaBr
and $AgNO_3$ for each mole of AgBr formed. Once the number of
required moles of NaBr and $AgNO_3$ are found, the weights of
these compounds can be determined by multiplying the number
of moles by the molecular weight. To solve this problem:

(1) solve for the number of moles of AgBr in 93.9 lbs

(2) determine the weights of NaBr and $AgNO_3$ used.

Solving:

(1) Molecular weights are given in grams, therefore
the grams should be converted to pounds for use in this
problem. MW of AgBr = 188 g/mole.

There are 454 grams in one pound, thus grams can be
converted to pounds by using the conversion factor
1 lb/454 grams.

MW of AgBr in lbs = 188 × 1 lb/454 g = .41 lbs.

The number of moles in 93.9 lbs can be found by
dividing the 93.9 lbs by the molecular weight in pounds.

$$\text{no. of moles of AgBr} = \frac{93.9 \text{ lbs}}{.41 \text{ lbs/mole}} = 229 \text{ moles}$$

Therefore, 229 moles of each NaBr and $AgNO_3$ are needed to
produce 93.9 lbs of AgBr.

(2) The weight of NaBr and $AgNO_3$ used is equal to the
number of moles times the molecular weight. In this problem,
one wishes to find the weight in pounds not grams, thus
the molecular weights must be converted to pounds before
the conversion factor 1 lb/454 g can be used. MW of NaBr =
103, MW of $AgNO_3$ = 170.

MW of NaBr in lbs = 103 g/mole × 1 lb/454 g = .23 lbs/mole

MW of $AgNO_3$ in lbs = 170 g/mole × 1 lb/454 g

= .37 lbs/mole.

Since it has already been calculated that 229 moles of each of these compounds are needed, one can calculate the weight needed of each by multiplying the number of moles by the molecular weight.

weight of NaBr = .23 lbs/mole × 229 moles = 52.7 lbs.

weight of $AgNO_3$ = .37 lbs/mole × 229 moles = 84.7 lbs.

● **PROBLEM** 5-8

Heating of $NaNO_3$ decomposed it to $NaNO_2$ and O_2. How much $NaNO_3$ would you have to decompose to produce 1.50 g of O_2?

Solution: The equation for this reaction is:

$$2NaNO_3 \rightarrow 2NaNO_2 + O_2$$

This means that for every mole of O_2 produced, 2 moles of $NaNO_3$ must be decomposed. One is given that 1.50 g of O_2 is formed, thus one should determine the number of moles. The number of moles of $NaNO_3$ needed will be twice this amount. One can solve for the weight by multiplying the number of moles by the molecular weight of the compound.

The number of moles of O_2 can be found by dividing 1.50 g by the molecular weight of O_2 (MW = 32.0).

no. of moles = $\dfrac{1.50 \text{ g}}{32.0 \text{ g/mole}}$ = 4.69 × 10^{-2} moles.

The number of moles of $NaNO_3$ needed can be found by multiplying the number of moles of O_2 by 2.

no. of moles = 2 × 4.69 × 10^{-2} moles = 9.38 × 10^{-2} moles.

One finds the weight of $NaNO_3$ needed by multiplying the number of moles by the molecular weight (MW = 85).

weight of $NaNO_3$ = 85 g/mole × 9.38 × 10^{-2} moles = 7.97 g.

● **PROBLEM** 5-9

Baking powder consists of a mixture of cream of tartar (potassium hydrogen tartrate, $KHC_4H_4O_6$, molecular weight = 188 g/mole) and baking soda (sodium bicarbonate, $NaHCO_3$, molecular weight = 84 g/mole). These two components react according to the equation

$$KHC_4H_4O_6 + NaHCO_3 \rightarrow KNaC_4H_4O_6 + H_2O + CO_2.$$

How much baking soda must be added to 8.0 g of cream of

tartar for both materials to react completely?

Solution: From the equation, we know that one mole of NaHCO$_3$ reacts with one mole of KHC$_4$H$_4$O$_6$. Hence, if we convert 8.0 g of KHC$_4$H$_4$O$_6$ to moles, we know how many moles of NaHCO$_3$ must be added. Finally, all we need to do is to convert moles of NaHCO$_3$ to grams of NaHCO$_3$.

In order to convert from grams to moles, we use the relationship moles = mass/molecular weight. The number of moles of KHC$_4$H$_4$O$_6$ in 8.0 g is

$$\text{moles} = \frac{\text{mass}}{\text{molecular weight}} = \frac{8.0 \text{ g}}{188 \text{ g/mole}} = 4.3 \times 10^{-2} \text{ mole.}$$

Hence, we must add 4.3×10^{-2} mole of NaHCO$_3$. Using the relationship mass = moles × molecular weight, we find that 4.3×10^{-2} mole of NaHCO$_3$ corresponds to

$$4.3 \times 10^{-2} \text{ moles} \times 84 \text{ g/mole} = 3.6 \text{ g.}$$

Hence, 3.6 g of baking soda must be added.

● PROBLEM 5-10

Some solid CaO in a test tube picks up water vapor from the surroundings to change completely to Ca(OH)$_2$(s). An observed total initial weight (CaO + test tube) of 10.860 g goes eventually to 11.149 g. What is the weight of the test tube?

Solution: The equation for the reaction is

$$CaO + H_2O \rightarrow Ca(OH)_2$$

This means that one mole of H$_2$O reacts with one mole of CaO. The difference in the weights of the test tubes is the weight of the H$_2$O that the CaO absorbed.

weight of H$_2$O = 11.149 - 10.860 = .289 g.

One should now solve for the number of moles of H$_2$O because the number of moles of water equals the number of moles of CaO present. From this one can find the weight of the CaO and the test tube. The number of moles equals the number of grams divided by the molecular weight (MW of H$_2$O = 18.0).

$$\text{number of moles of H}_2\text{O} = \frac{.289 \text{ g}}{18.0 \text{ g/mole}} = .0161 \text{ moles}$$

Therefore, .0161 moles of CaO were originally present in the test tube. One finds the number of grams by multiplying by the molecular weight of CaO (MW of CaO = 56.08).

number of grams of CaO = .0161 moles × 56.08 g/mole

$$= .900 \text{ g.}$$

The weight of the test tube is equal to .900 g subtracted from the original weight of the test tube and material.

weight of test tube = 10.860 - .900 = 9.960 g.

● PROBLEM 5-11

"Hard" water contains small amounts of the salts calcium bicarbonate ($Ca(HCO_3)_2$) and calcium sulfate ($CaSO_4$, molecular weight = 136 g/mole). These react with soap before it has a chance to lather, which is responsible for its cleansing ability. $Ca(HCO_3)_2$ is removed by boiling to form insoluble $CaCO_3$. $CaSO_4$ is removed by reaction with washing soda (Na_2CO_3, molecular weight = 106 g/mole) according to the following equation:

$$CaSO_4 + Na_2CO_3 \rightarrow CaCO_3 + Na_2SO_4.$$

If the rivers surrounding New York City have a $CaSO_4$ concentration of 1.8×10^{-3} g/liter, how much Na_2CO_3 is required to "soften" (remove $CaSO_4$) the water consumed by the city in one day (about 6.8×10^9 liters)?

Solution: We must determine the amount of $CaSO_4$ present in 6.8×10^9 liters and, from this, the amount of Na_2CO_3 required to remove it.

The number of moles per liter, or molarity, of $CaSO_4$ corresponding to 1.8×10^{-3} g/liter is obtained by dividing this concentration by the molecular weight of $CaSO_4$. Multiplying by 6.8×10^9 liters gives the number of moles of $CaSO_4$ that must be removed. Hence,

$$\text{moles } CaSO_4 = \frac{\text{concentration (g/liter)}}{\text{molecular weight of } CaSO_4} \times 6.8 \times 10^9 \text{ liters}$$

$$= \frac{1.8 \times 10^{-3} \text{ g/liter}}{136 \text{ g/mole}} \times 6.8 \times 10^9 \text{ liters}$$

$$= 9.0 \times 10^4 \text{ moles.}$$

From the equation for the reaction between $CaSO_4$ and Na_2CO_3, we see that one mole of $CaSO_4$ reacts with one mole of $NaCO_3$. Hence, 9.0×10^4 moles of $NaCO_3$ are required to remove all the $CaSO_4$. To convert this to mass, we multiply by the molecular weight of Na_2CO_3 and obtain

mass Na_2CO_3 = moles Na_2CO_3 × molecular weight Na_2CO_3

$$= 9.0 \times 10^4 \text{ moles} \times 106 \text{ g/mole}$$

$$= 9.5 \times 10^6 \text{ g} = 9.5 \times 10^6 \text{ g} \times 1 \text{ kg/1000 g}$$

$$= 9.5 \times 10^3 \text{ kg,}$$

which is about 10 tons.

● **PROBLEM** 5-12

How many pounds of air (which is 23.19% O_2 and 75.46% N_2 by weight) would be needed to burn a pound of gasoline by a reaction whereby C_8H_{18} reacts with O_2 to form CO_2 and H_2O?

Solution: The equation for the reaction is

$$C_8H_{18} + 12 \tfrac{1}{2} O_2 \rightarrow 8 CO_2 + 9 H_2O$$

From the equation, one knows that 12.5 moles of O_2 are needed to burn 1 mole of gasoline. To solve for the number of pounds of air necessary to burn 1 pound of gasoline:

(1) find the number of moles in 1 pound of C_8H_{18}

(2) determine the number of moles of O_2 needed

(3) solve for the number of moles of O_2 in 1 pound of the air

(4) calculate the number of pounds of air needed.

Solving:

(1) The molecular weight of C_8H_{18} is 114.23 g/mole. There are 453.50 g in 1 lb, thus one can convert from grams to pounds by multiplying the number of grams by 1 lb/453.50 g.

$$\text{MW of } C_8H_{18} \text{ in lbs} = 114.23 \text{ g/mole} \times \frac{1 \text{ lb}}{453.50 \text{ g}}$$

$$= 2.52 \times 10^{-1} \text{ lbs/mole.}$$

One can find the number of moles in 1 lb by dividing 1 lb by the molecular weight of C_8H_{18} in lbs.

$$\text{no. of moles} = \frac{1 \text{ lb}}{2.52 \times 10^{-1} \text{ lbs/mole}} = 3.97 \text{ moles}$$

(2) One needs 12.5 times as much O_2 as C_8H_{18}.

$$\text{no. of moles of } O_2 \text{ needed} = 12.5 \times \text{no. of moles } C_8H_{18}$$

$$= 12.5 \times 3.97 \text{ moles} = 49.63 \text{ moles}$$

(3) In 1 lb of the air, there is .2319 lb O_2 and .7546 lb N_2. Thus, to find the number of moles of O_2 in one pound of the air, one must divide .2319 lb by the molecular weight of O_2 in pounds (MW of O_2 = 32 g/mole).

$$\text{MW in lbs of } O_2 = 32 \text{ g/mole} \times \frac{1 \text{ lb}}{453.5 \text{ g}}$$

$$= 7.06 \times 10^{-2} \text{ lb/mole}$$

$$\text{no. of moles} = \frac{.2319 \text{ lb}}{7.06 \times 10^{-2} \text{ lb/mole}} = 3.29 \text{ moles.}$$

(4) There are 3.29 moles of O_2 in one lb and 49.63 moles of O_2 are needed to burn 1 lb of gas.

$$\text{no. of lbs of air needed} = \frac{49.63 \text{ moles}}{3.29 \text{ moles/lb}} = 15.10 \text{ lbs.}$$

● **PROBLEM** 5-13

A lunar module used Aerozine 50 as fuel and nitrogen tetroxide (N_2O_4, molecular weight = 92.0 g/mole) as oxidizer. Aerozine 50 consists of 50 % by weight of hydrazine (N_2H_4, molecular weight = 32.0 g/mole) and 50 % by weight of unsymmetrical dimethylhydrazine ($(CH_3)_2N_2H_2$, molecular weight = 60.0 g/mole). The chief exhaust product was water (H_2O, molecular weight = 18.0 g/mole). Two o. ne reactions that led to the formation of water are the following:

$$2N_2H_4 + N_2O_4 \rightarrow 3N_2 + 4H_2O$$

$$(CH_3)_2N_2H_2 + 2N_2O_4 \rightarrow 2CO_2 + 3N_2 + 4H_2O.$$

If we assume that these reactions were the only ones in which water was formed, how much water was produced by the ascent of the lunar module if 2200 kg of Aerozine 50 were consumed in the process?

Solution: Aerozine 50 consists of N_2H_4 and $(CH_3)_2N_2H_2$. From the first reaction, we see that 2 moles of H_2O are produced per mole of N_2H_4 consumed, and, from the second reaction, we see that 4 moles of H_2O are produced per mole of $(CH_3)_2N_2H_2$ consumed. Thus, if we determine the number of moles of N_2H_4 and the number of moles of $(CH_3)_2N_2H_4$ in 2200 kg of Aerozine 50, we can calculate the number of moles of water, and, from this, the mass of water produced, since moles = grams (mass)/molecular weight.

Since N_2H_4 and $(CH_3)_2N_2H_1$ each form 50% of Aerozine 50 by weight, the mass of each component in 2200 kg of Aerozine 50 is

$$\text{mass } N_2H_4 = 50 \text{ % } \times 2200 \text{ kg} = 1100 \text{ kg} = 1.1 \times 10^6 \text{ g.}$$

mass $(CH_3)_2N_2H_2 = 50\ \% \times 2200$ kg $= 1100$ kg $= 1.1 \times 10^6$ g.

(there are 1000g per kg.)

To convert mass to moles, we divide by the molecular weight. Hence, 2200 kg of Aerozine 50 contains

moles $N_2H_4 = 1.1 \times 10^6$ g/32.0 g/mole $= 3.4 \times 10^4$ moles N_2H_4

moles $(CH_3)_2N_2H_2 = 1.1 \times 10^6$ g/60.0 g/mole

$$= 1.8 \times 10^4 \text{ moles } (CH_3)_2N_2H_2.$$

3.4×10^4 moles of N_2H_4 produces $2 \times 3.4 \times 10^4 = 6.8 \times 10^4$ moles of H_2O and 1.8×10^4 moles of $(CH_3)_2N_2H_2$ produces $4 \times 1.8 \times 10^4 = 7.2 \times 10^4$ moles of H_2O.

The total number of moles of H_2O produced is $6.8 \times 10^4 + 7.2 \times 10^4 = 1.4 \times 10^5$ moles. To convert this to mass, we multiply by the molecular weight of water. Hence,

1.4×10^5 moles $\times$ 18.0 g/mole $= 2.5 \times 10^6$ g

$$= 2.5 \times 10^3 \text{ kg of water were produced.}$$

● **PROBLEM** 5-14

It has been found that the following sequence can be used to prepare sodium sulfate, Na_2SO_4:

$$S(s) + O_2(g) \rightarrow SO_2(g)$$

$$2SO_2(g) + O_2(g) \rightarrow 2SO_3(g)$$

$$SO_3(g) + H_2O(\ell) \rightarrow H_2SO_4(\ell)$$

$$2NaOH + H_2SO_4 \rightarrow Na_2SO_4 + 2H_2O$$

If you performed this sequence of reactions, how many moles of Na_2SO_4 could possibly be produced if you start with 1 mole of sulfur? How many moles are possible with 4.5 g of water?

Solution: If you had the general equation,

$$aA + bB \rightarrow cC + dD,$$

a moles of A react with b moles of B to produce c moles of C and d moles of D. Thus, if you want to know how many grams of D will be produced, and you know how much A you have, calculate the number of moles of A present. From this, you can determine how many moles of D can be generated, since you know that a moles of A will produce d moles of D. With this in mind, you can proceed to answer these questions.

From the first equation you see that if you start
with 1 mole of sulfur (S) 1 mole of SO_2 can be generated
(since all the coefficients are one, although 1 is not
written). Now that 1 mole of SO_2 is generated, you proceed
to the second equation. It states that for every 2 moles of
SO_2, 2 moles of SO_3 are generated. Thus, in keeping with
this relative ratio, 1 mole of SO_3 can be generated from
one mole of SO_2. In the third reaction you again have 1
mole of SO_3 yielding 1 mole of H_2SO_4. At this point, you
have 1 mole of H_2SO_4 (from 1 mole of starting sulfur). The
last equation shows 1 mole of H_2SO_4 producing 1 mole of
Na_2SO_4. Therefore, if you were to start with 1 mole of S,
you would obtain 1 mole of Na_2SO_4.

Now let us consider H_2O. Water does not enter the
sequence until the third equation. This means you start with

$$SO_3(g) + H_2O (\ell) \rightarrow H_2SO_4(\ell).$$

If you have 4.5 g of H_2O (MW = 18 g/m), you possess
4.5 g/18 g/mole = .25 moles H_2O. From the reaction, 1 mole
of H_2O yields 1 mole of H_2SO_4. Thus, .25 moles of H_2SO_4
are generated from .25 moles of water. You have the same
1 : 1 ratio.

The last equation is also a 1:1 ratio.
Therefore, if you start with 4.5 grams of H_2O, .25 moles
of Na_2SO_4 will be produced.

● **PROBLEM** 5-15

When 4.90 g of $KClO_3$ was heated, it showed a weight loss
of 0.384 g. Find the percent of the original $KClO_3$ that
had decomposed.

Solution: To solve this problem, you need to determine
how many moles of $KClO_3$ decomposed. Once this is determined
calculate the initial number of moles of $KClO_3$ and divide
to obtain a percentage. To do this, a balanced equation
that illustrates this reaction must be written. Such an
equation is

$$2KClO_3(s) \rightarrow 2KCL(s) + 3O_2(g)$$

The weight loss of .384 g must be the amount of O_2
liberated. The number of moles of O_2 is this weight divided
by its molecular weight, or

$$\frac{.384 \text{ g}}{32 \text{ g/mole}} = .0120 \text{ moles of } O_2.$$

Going back to the original equation, you find that the
number of moles of $KClO_3$ is 2/3 that of O_2. Therefore, the
number of moles of $KClO_3$ that reacted is

$$(.0120 \text{ mol of } O_2) \left(\frac{2 \text{ mol } KClO_3}{3 \text{ mol } O_2} \right) = .0080 \text{ moles of } KClO_3.$$

The number of moles of $KClO_3$ that you started with, however, is

$$\frac{4.90 \text{ g}}{122.6 \text{ g/mole}} = .0400 \text{ moles, where } 122.6 \text{ g/mole is}$$

the molecular weight of $KClO_3$. Therefore, the percentage decomposition is

$$\frac{.0080}{.0400} \times 100 = 20\%.$$

● **PROBLEM** 5-16

Clay contains 30 % Al_2O_3, 55 % SiO_2, and 15 % H_2O. What weight of limestone is required per ton of clay to carry out the following chemical change?

$6CaCO_3$ + Al_2O_3 + SiO_2 → $3CaO \cdot Al_2O_3$ + $3CaO \cdot SiO_2$ + $6CO_2$.
(limestone)

Solution: From the coefficients in the reaction equation, one sees that for every mole of Al_2O_3 and SiO_2 present, 6 moles of $CaCO_3$ (limestone) are required for the reaction to occur. As such, to determine how much limestone is necessary to react with 1 ton of clay, compute the number of moles of Al_2O_3 and SiO_2 present. From this figure, the number of moles of $CaCO_3$ can be found. Because a mole is defined as grams divided by molecular weight (MW) the weight (grams) can be found once the molecular weight is calculated.

It is given that 1 ton or 2000 lb of clay will be used. Because clay contains 30 % Al_2O_3 and 55 % SiO_2, .30 × 2000 = 600 lbs of Al_2O_3 and .55 × 2000 = 1100 lbs of SiO_2 are present in one ton of clay. To calculate the mole amounts, one must convert lbs to grams. This can be done by using the conversion factor 454 g/lb. Thus, 600 lbs × 454 g/lb = 2724×10^2 grams of Al_2O_3 and 1100 × 454 g/lb = 4994×10^2 grams of SiO_2.

The MW of Al_2O_3 = 102 grams/mole. The MW of SiO_2 = 60 grams/mole. Therefore,

$$\text{moles of } Al_2O_3 = \frac{2724 \times 10^2 \text{ g}}{102 \text{ g/mole}} = 2.67 \times 10^3 \text{ moles}$$

and moles of $SiO_2 = \dfrac{4994 \times 10^2 \text{ g}}{60 \text{ g/mole}} = 8.32 \times 10^3 \text{ moles}$

Notice, in one ton of clay, the mole amounts of SiO_2 and Al_2O_3 are not equal. The mole amount of limestone re-

113

quired will be six times the mole amount of Al_2O_3, 2.67×10^3, and not SiO_2. The reason stems from the fact that Al_2O_3 is the limiting reagent. The amount of any reagent required (or product produced) depends only on the limiting reagent. SiO_2, with a mole of 8.3×10^3, is in excess; the amount of limestone required will not depend on it.

Consequently, moles of limestone = 6(moles of Al_2O_3) = $6(2.67 \times 10^3) = 1.60 \times 10^4$ moles. The molecular weight of $CaCO_3$ (limestone) = 100 g/mole. Grams of $CaCO_3$ required per ton of clay = (moles of $CaCO_3$)(MW of $CaCO_3$)

$$= (1.60 \times 10^4)(100) = 1.60 \times 10^6.$$

● **PROBLEM** 5-17

A chemist has a mixture of $KClO_3$, $KHCO_3$, K_2CO_3, and KCl. She heats 1,000 g of this mixture and notices that the following gases evolve: 18 g of water (H_2O), 132 g of CO_2, and 40 g of O_2 according to the following reactions:

$$2KClO_3 \rightarrow 2KCl + 3O_2$$

$$2KHCO_3 \rightarrow K_2O + H_2O + 2CO_2$$

$$K_2CO_3 \rightarrow K_2O + CO_2$$

The KCl is inert under these conditions. Assuming complete decomposition, determine the composition of the original mixture.

Solution: The solution of this problem involves the use of the mole concept and the ability to employ it using chemical (balanced) equations. You need to determine the number of moles of the gases generated from the masses given and their molecular weights. A mole = mass in grams/molecular weight. Once this is known, you can calculate the number of moles of substances in the mixture that had to exist to produce the given quantities. You proceed as follows:

The only source of the 18 g of H_2O is from

$$2KHCO_3 \rightarrow K_2O + H_2O + 2CO_2.$$

The molecular weight of H_2O = 18. Thus, you have 18 g/18 g/mole = 1 mole of H_2O. But the equation states that for every mole of H_2O, you originally had 2 moles of $KHCO_3$. Therefore, the mixture must have **had 2 moles of** $KHCO_3$. The molecular weight of $KHCO_3$ is 100.1 g. Therefore, the weight in grams of it was 2(100.1) = 200.21 g.

The O_2 is generated from only the reaction

$$2KClO_3 \rightarrow 2KCl + 3O_2.$$

You have 40 g of O_2 evolved. Molecular weight of O_2 = 32

114

Thus you have 40/32 = 1.25 moles of O_2. According to the equation, for every 3 moles of O_2 produced, there existed 2 moles of $KClO_3$. Thus you have 2/3(1.25) or .833 moles of $KClO_3$. Molecular weight of $KClO_3$ = 122.6. Therefore, the number of grams = (122.6)(.833) = 102.1g.

The CO_2 gas has two sources:

$$2KHCO_3 \rightarrow K_2O + H_2O + 2CO_2 \quad \text{and} \quad K_2CO_3 \rightarrow K_2O + CO_2.$$

From the water evolved, you already know that you have 200.21 g of $KHCO_3$. Its molecular weight is 100.1g. Thus, the number of moles of it is, 200.2/100.1 = 2. From the equation, however, you see that for every 2 moles of $KHCO_3$, you obtain 2 moles of CO_2. Maintaining this one to one ratio, 2 moles of CO_2 must be generated. The molecular weight of CO_2 is 44. Thus, from $KHCO_3$, 2(44) = 88 g of CO_2 produced. The total number of grams CO_2 evolved was given as 132 g. This means, therefore, that the other source of CO_2, K_2CO_3, must give off 132 - 88 = 44 grams of CO_2. You have

$$K_2CO_3 \rightarrow K_2O + CO_2$$

This equation shows a 1 : 1 mole ratio between K_2CO_3 and CO_2. You have 44 grams of CO_2 released or 1 mole, since the molecular weight of CO_2 is 44. Therefore, you must have 1 mole of K_2CO_3 in the mixture. The molecular weight of K_2CO_3 is 138.21. Thus, the number of grams is (1)(138.21) for K_2CO_3 = 138.21 g.

In summary, you have 200.14 g of $KHCO_3$, 102.12 g of $KClO_3$ and 138.21 g of K_2CO_3. The total mass of these substances = 440.47 g. The original mixture was 1000 g. Thus,

1000 - 440.47 = 559.53 g is the mass of the inert KCl.

REACTIONS WITH LIMITING REAGENTS

● PROBLEM 5-18

Chromic oxide (Cr_2O_3) may be reduced with hydrogen according to the equation

$$Cr_2O_3 + 3H_2 \rightarrow 2Cr + 3H_2O$$

(a) What weight of hydrogen would be required to reduce 7.6 g of Cr_2O_3? (b) For each mole of metallic chromium prepared, how many moles of hydrogen will be required? (c) What weight of metallic chromium can be prepared from one ton of Cr_2O_3? 1 lb = 454 g.

Solution: (a) From the equation for the reaction, one knows that it takes three moles of H_2 to reduce one mole of Cr_2O_3. Thus, in solving this problem one should first determine the number of moles of Cr_2O_3 in 7.6 g, then using the ratio

$$\frac{3}{1} = \frac{\text{number of moles of } H_2}{\text{number of moles of } Cr_2O_3}$$

One can find the number of moles of H_2 necessary to reduce 7.6 g of Cr_2O_3. After finding the number of moles of H_2 needed, one can obtain the weight by multiplying the number of moles by the molecular weight of H_2.

(1) Solving for the number of moles of Cr_2O_3 in 7.6 g. This is done by dividing 7.6 g by the molecular weight of Cr_2O_3 (MW = 152).

$$\text{no. of moles} = \frac{7.6 \text{ g}}{152 \text{ g/mole}} = .05 \text{ moles}$$

(2) determining the number of moles of H_2 necessary. The ratio

$$\frac{3}{1} = \frac{\text{number of moles of } H_2}{\text{number of moles of } Cr_2O_3}$$

will be used. This ratio was made using the stoichiometric coefficients of the equation for the reaction

$$\frac{3}{1} = \frac{\text{number of moles of } H_2}{.05 \text{ moles}}$$

$$\text{no. of moles of H} = \frac{.05 \text{ moles} \times 3}{1} = .15 \text{ moles}$$

(3) solving for the weight of H_2. (MW = 2.) The weight of a compound is found by multiplying the number of moles present by the molecular weight.

$$\text{weight of } H_2 = .15 \text{ moles} \times 2 \text{ g/mole} = .30 \text{ g}.$$

(b) From the equation for the reaction, it is seen that 3 moles of H_2 are needed to form 2 moles of Cr. This means that for every mole of Cr formed 3/2 this amount of H_2 is needed. Thus, 1.5 mole of H_2 is necessary to form one mole of Cr.

(c) Using the equation for the reaction, one is told that for every mole of Cr_2O_3 reduced 2 moles of Cr are formed. Thus, one must determine the number of moles in 1 ton of Cr_2O_3; there will be twice as many moles of Cr formed. After one knows the number of moles of Cr formed, one can determine its weight by multiplying the number of moles by the molecular weight of Cr.

(1) Determining the number of moles of Cr_2O_3 in 1 ton of the compound (1 ton = 2000 lbs). The number of moles is found by dividing the weight of the Cr_2O_3 present by its molecular weight. Because the molecular weight is given in

grams per mole it must be converted to pounds per mole before using it to determine the number of moles present. There are 454 g in one pound, thus grams can be converted to pounds by multiplying the number of grams by the conversion factor 1 lb/454 g. (MW of Cr_2O_3 = 152.)

MW of Cr_2O_3 in lbs = 152 g/mole × 1 lb/454 g

$$= .33 \text{ lbs/mole.}$$

(2) determining the number of moles of Cr_2O_3 in 1 ton. The number of moles present can be found by dividing 1 ton (2000 lbs) by the molecular weight in pounds.

$$\text{number of moles} = \frac{2000 \text{ lbs}}{.33 \text{ lbs/mole}} = 6060 \text{ moles}$$

Thus, there are twice this many moles of Cr produced.

number of moles of Cr = 2 × 6060 moles = 12120 moles

(3) finding the weight of Cr formed. One knows that 12,120 moles of Cr are produced. To find the weight of this quantity, the number of moles is multiplied by the molecular weight. To find the weight in pounds, one must first convert the molecular weight from grams to pounds. This is done by multiplying the molecular weight by the conversion factor 1 lb/454 g. This is used because there are 454 g in 1 lb (MW of Cr = 52).

MW of Cr in pounds = 52 g/mole × 1 lb/454 g

$$= 0.11 \text{ lb/mole.}$$

The weight of the Cr formed is now found by multiplying this molecular weight by the number of moles present.

weight = 0.11 lb/mole × 12120 moles = 1333 lbs.

● PROBLEM 5-19

How many moles of Al_2O_3 can be formed when a mixture of 0.36 moles of aluminum and 0.36 moles of oxygen is ignited? Which substance and how much of it is in excess of that required?

$$4Al + 3O_2 \rightarrow 2Al_2O_3$$

Solution: In this reaction 4 moles of Al and 3 moles of O_2 form 2 moles of Al_2O_3. One is told that 0.36 moles of Al and of O_2 are available for the reaction. One can see from the equation that a greater number of moles of Al are needed for the reaction than O_2. Thus, one should assume that all 0.36 moles of Al will be used, but not all 0.36 moles of the O_2. Since 4 moles of Al are needed for every

3 moles of O_2, the following ratio holds:

$$\frac{4}{3} = \frac{\text{number of moles of Al}}{\text{number of moles of } O_2}$$

If 0.36 moles of Al are used, one can solve for the number of moles of O_2 that are needed to react with them.

$$\frac{4}{3} = \frac{0.36 \text{ moles}}{\text{number of moles of } O_2}$$

$$\text{number of moles of } O_2 = \frac{3 \times 0.36}{4} = 0.27 \text{ moles}$$

Since only 0.27 moles of O_2 are needed, and there are 0.36 moles present, there is an excess of 0.09 moles of O_2.

From the reaction, one knows that there are 2 moles of Al_2O_3 formed for every 4 moles of Al reacted. Therefore, a ratio can be set up to determine the number of moles of Al_2O_3 formed from 0.36 moles of Al.

$$\frac{4}{2} = \frac{\text{number of moles of Al}}{\text{number of moles of } Al_2O_3}$$

If 0.36 moles of Al are reacted, one can determine the number of moles of Al_2O_3 formed.

$$\frac{4}{2} = \frac{0.36 \text{ moles}}{\text{number of moles of } Al_2O_3}$$

$$\text{number of moles of } Al_2O_3 = \frac{0.36 \times 2}{4} = 0.18 \text{ moles}$$

Note: One does not determine the moles of Al_2O_3 from O_2, since the latter is in excess.

● **PROBLEM** 5-20

What is the maximum weight of SO_3 that could be made from 25.0 g of SO_2 and 6.00 g of O_2 by the following reaction?

$$2SO_2 + O_2 \rightarrow 2SO_3$$

<u>Solution:</u> From the reaction, one knows that for every 2 moles of SO_3 formed, 2 moles of SO_2 and 1 mole of O_2 must react. Thus, to find the amount of SO_3 that can be formed, one must first know the number of moles of SO_2 and O_2 present. The number of moles is found by dividing the number of grams present by the molecular weight.

$$\text{number of moles} = \frac{\text{number of grams}}{\text{MW}}$$

For O_2:   MW = 32

$$\text{no. of moles} = \frac{6.0 \text{ g}}{32.0 \text{ g/mole}} = 1.88 \times 10^{-1} \text{ moles}$$

For SO_2: MW = 64.

$$\text{no. of moles} = \frac{25.0 \text{ g}}{64.0 \text{ g/mole}} = 3.91 \times 10^{-1} \text{ moles.}$$

Because 2 moles of SO_2 are needed to react with 1 mole of O_2, 3.76×10^{-1} moles of SO_2 will react with 1.88×10^{-1} moles of O_2. This means that $3.91 \times 10^{-1} - 3.76 \times 10^{-1}$ moles or $.15 \times 10^{-1}$ moles of SO_2 will remain unreacted. In this case, O_2 is called the limiting reagent because it determines the number of moles of SO_3 formed. There will be twice as many moles of SO_3 formed as there are O_2 reacting.

$$\text{no. of moles of } SO_3 \text{ formed} = 2 \times 1.88 \times 10^{-1} \text{ moles}$$

$$= 3.76 \times 10^{-1} \text{ moles.}$$

The weight is found by multiplying the number of moles formed by the molecular weight (MW of SO_3 = 80).

$$\text{weight of } SO_3 = 3.76 \times 10^{-1} \text{ moles} \times 80 \text{ g/mole} = 30.1 \text{ g.}$$

● **PROBLEM** 5-21

A chemist reacts ferric sulfate with barium chloride and obtains barium sulfate and ferric chloride. He writes the following balanced equation to express this reaction:

$$Fe_2(SO_4)_3 + 3BaCl_2 \rightarrow 3BaSO_4\downarrow + 2FeCl_3$$

(A) How much $BaCl_2$ should be used to react with 10 grams of $Fe_2(SO_4)_3$? (B) How much $Fe_2(SO_4)_3$ will be necessary to produce 100 g of $BaSO_4$? (C) From a mixture of 50 g of $Fe_2(SO_4)_3$ and 100 g of $BaCl_2$, how much $FeCl_3$ can be produced?

Solution: To answer these questions, you must understand the mole concept, and how it is used to calculate the amount of material required in a chemical reaction.

A mole is defined as the number of grams of a substance divided by its molecular weight. In other words,

$$\text{a mole} = \frac{\text{amount in grams of substance}}{\text{molecular weight of substance}}$$

In the given equation:

$$Fe_2(SO_4)_3 + 3BaCl_2 \rightarrow 3BaSO_4\downarrow + 2FeCl_3,$$

the numbers before each compound are termed coefficients

(the coefficient of $Fe_2(SO_4)_3$ is one, and by convention is not written). The equation is balanced. This means that all of the elements are equal in number on both sides of the equation. For example, we have a total of 12 oxygen atoms on the left and 12 on the right. Before doing any problem involving a chemical equation, we must always balance it.

All the atoms must be accounted for. The coefficients serve this purpose. After balancing, they also tell you the relative mole amounts that will react. In other words, in this reaction 1 mole of $Fe_2(SO_4)_3$ reacts with 3 moles of $BaCl_2$. For the reaction to occur, we must have a mole ratio of 1 : 3 between $Fe_2(SO_4)_3$ and $BaCl_2$. If such a condition exists, then the equation tells us that 3 moles of $BaSO_4$ will be produced per mole of $Fe_2(SO_4)_3$. In addition, 2 moles of $FeCl_3$ will also be produced. Therefore, the coefficients tell the relative number of moles of each substance that must be either present or produced.

With this information, we can now answer the questions.

(A) We have 10 grams of $Fe_2(SO_4)_3$ and want the number of grams of $BaCl_2$ that are required to **react** with it. The molecular weight of $Fe_2(SO_4)_3$ is 399.88 g/mole. This number is obtained by adding up all the atomic weights of the individual atoms in the formula. Recalling the definition of a mole, we have 10/399.88 moles of $Fe_2(SO_4)_3$.

The equation tells us that 3 moles of $BaCl_2$ react with one mole of $Fe_2(SO_4)_3$. Therefore, we must have 3 times the number of moles of $Fe_2(SO_4)_3$ or

$$3 \times \frac{10}{399.88} = \frac{30}{399.88} \cdot$$ The number of moles of $BaCl_2$

required is, therefore, $\frac{30}{399.88}$. The molecular weight of $BaCl_2$ is 208.24 g/mole. Recall, mole = number of grams/molecular weight. The number of grams of $BaCl_2$ required is, therefore,

$$\frac{30}{399.88} \text{ moles} \times 208.24 \text{ g/mole} = 15.62 \text{ grams}$$

(B) We want to produce 100 grams of $BaSO_4$. The molecular weight of $BaSO_4$ is 233.40 g/mole. Therefore, we want to produce 100/233.40 moles of $BaSO_4$. How much $Fe_2(SO_4)_3$ should be used? Again, we must go back to the equation and look at the coefficients to determine the mole requirements. We see that 3 moles of $BaSO_4$ are produced for every mole of $Fe_2(SO_4)_3$. Therefore, the required number of moles of $Fe_2(SO_4)_3$ is 1/3 the number of moles of $BaSO_4$ or

$$\frac{1}{3} \times \frac{100}{233.40} = \frac{100}{700.20} \cdot$$ The molecular weight of

$Fe_2(SO_4)_3$ is 399.88 g/mole. Consequently, the number of grams required of $Fe_2(SO_4)_3$ is

$$\frac{100}{700.20} \text{ mole} \times 399.88 \text{ g/mole} = 57.11 \text{ grams}$$

(C) In this question, we are working with a mixture of two substances to produce a third. The first thing is to compute the moles:

$$\text{Moles Fe}_2(\text{SO}_4)_3 = \frac{50.00 \text{ g}}{399.88 \text{ g/mole}} = .125 \text{ moles}$$

$$\text{Moles BaCl}_2 = \frac{100 \text{ g}}{208.24 \text{ g/mole}} = .48 \text{ moles}$$

Because we are dealing with two substances to yield one, we must also consider their mole ratios as well as with the product $FeCl_3$. The equation calls for three moles of $BaCl_2$ to react with one mole of $Fe_2(SO_4)_3$. We have .125 moles of $Fe_2(SO_4)_3$. 3 times this amount is .375 moles. However, you have .48 moles of $BaCl_2$. This means, therefore, that we have .48 - .375 or .105 moles of $BaCl_2$ that will not react. In other words, $BaCl_2$ is in excess. We always take the limiting reagent, which is $Fe_2(SO_4)_3$. The amount of $FeCl_3$ present will reflect the number of moles of $Fe_2(SO_4)_3$, and not $BaCl_2$.

Because 2 moles of $FeCl_3$ will be produced for every mole of $Fe_2(SO_4)_3$, .125 × 2 = .25 moles of $FeCl_3$ will be produced. The molecular weight of $FeCl_3$ is 162.20. Therefore, the maximum weight of $FeCl_3$ produced is .25(162.20) = 40.56 grams.

● PROBLEM 5-22

Through several successive reactions, a chemist uses carbon, CaO, HCl and H_2O to produce $C_6H_4Cl_2$. Assuming an efficiency of 65 %, how much $C_6H_4Cl_2$ can be produced from 500 grams of carbon? Assume that 1/3 of the carbon is lost as 3 moles CO.

Solution: In solving this problem, you must account for all carbon atoms and employ the mole concept. You need not be concerned with the actual sequence of reactions nor the roles of CaO and H_2O.

Dichlorobenzene, $C_6H_4Cl_2$, consists of 6 carbon atoms.

You can determine that there were originally 9 moles of carbon present since 3 moles of CO are produced and the carbon present in the CO represents 1/3 of the original amount of carbon present.

A mole is defined as weight in grams/molecular weight. The molecular weight of carbon is 12. You started with 500 grams. Therefore, the number of moles of carbon is 500/12. It is stated above, however, that for every 9 moles of C, 1 mole of $C_6H_4Cl_2$ was produced. Therefore, the number of moles of $C_6H_4Cl_2$ is 1/9 of the moles of carbon that you started with. Namely, the number of moles of $C_6H_4Cl_2$ is $1/9 \times 500/12$. The problem calls for an efficiency of 65 %. Therefore, we must multiply this number of moles by

$$\frac{65}{100} \quad \text{or,} \quad \frac{1}{9} \times \frac{500}{12} \times \frac{65}{100} \, .$$

The molecular weight of $C_6H_4Cl_2$ is 147. Recalling the definition of a mole, the weight of $C_6H_4Cl_2$ produced is

$$147 \times \frac{1}{9} \times \frac{500}{12} \times \frac{65}{100} = 442 \quad \text{grams.}$$

VOLUME-VOLUME PROBLEMS

● PROBLEM 5-23

Calculate the volume of O_2 necessary to burn 50 liters of CO completely. The balanced reaction is:

$$2CO + O_2 \rightarrow 2CO_2$$

Also, calculate the volume of CO_2 formed.

Solution: This is a volume-volume problem and the technique shown applies only to gases. It is assumed that all the gases must be at the same temperature and pressure. No molecular weights or molecular volumes are needed. One solves this problem by setting up a ratio between the actual volumes present and the mole volumes of the reacting compounds as shown in the equation below.

$$\frac{\text{volume CO present}}{\text{mole volume CO}} = \frac{\text{volume } O_2 \text{ needed}}{\text{mole volume } O_2}$$

The mole ratio for this reaction is 2 : 1, therefore, the mole volume ratio is 2 : 1. Substitute, to obtain

$$\frac{50 \text{ liters}}{2 \text{ liters}} = \frac{\text{volume } O_2}{1 \text{ liter}}$$

volume O_2 = 25 liters.

To find the volume of CO_2 produced, set up a similar proportion between CO and CO_2 or O_2 and CO_2. The mole ratio for CO and CO_2 is 1 : 1 and for O_2 and CO_2 is 1 : 2. Therefore use the equation

$$\frac{\text{volume reactant}}{\text{mole volume reactant}} = \frac{\text{volume } CO_2}{\text{mole volume } CO_2}$$

The values for CO as the reactant are:

$$\frac{50}{2} = \frac{\text{volume } CO_2}{2}$$

volume CO_2 = 50 liters.

The values of O_2 as the reactant are:

$$\frac{25}{1} = \frac{\text{volume } CO_2}{2}$$

volume CO_2 = 50 liters.

Calculate the volume of oxygen necessary to burn completely
100 cubic feet (1 cubic foot = 28.316 liters) of butane gas
according to the equation
$$2C_4H_{10} + 13O_2 \rightarrow 8CO_2 + 10H_2O$$

Solution: Since volumes are concerned, the procedure
for solving this problem is to set up a ratio between the
volumes present and the mole requirements. For this reaction, 2 moles of butane react with 13 moles of O_2.

When two gases are under the same temperature and
pressure conditions, a mole of either gas will occupy
the same volume. Therefore, since 13/2 times as many
moles of O_2 are required, the volume of O_2 must be 13/2
times that of methane.

Given the volume of methane is 1000 cu. ft., the
volume of $O_2 = \frac{13}{2}$ (1000) = 6500 cubic feet.$(1.84 \times 10^5$
liters)

WEIGHT-VOLUME PROBLEMS

Glucose-1-phosphate, essential to the metabolism of
carbohydrates in humans, has a molecular weight of
260 g/mole and a density of about 1.5 g/cm^3. What is
the volume occupied by one molecule of glucose-1-
phosphate?

Solution: In general, volume = mass/density. Hence, in
order to determine the volume, we must determine the mass
of one molecule of glucose-1-phosphate.

One mole of glucose-1-phosphate weighs 260 g
(this is the meaning of a molecular weight of 260 g/mole).
Since there is an Avogadro's number of molecules in a
mole (6.02×10^{23} molecules/mole), the mass of one

molecule of glucose-1-phosphate is given by

$$\text{mass} = \frac{\text{molecular weight}}{\text{Avogadro's number}} = \frac{260 \text{ g/mole}}{6 \times 10^{23} \text{ molecules/mole}}$$

$$= 4.3 \times 10^{-22} \text{ g/molecule.}$$

Hence, one molecule of glucose-1-phosphate weighs 4.3×10^{-22} g and has a volume of

$$\text{volume} = \frac{\text{mass}}{\text{density}} = \frac{4.3 \times 10^{-22} \text{ g}}{1.5 \text{ g/cm}^3} \cong 2.9 \times 10^{-22} \text{ cm}^3.$$

● **PROBLEM** 5-26

What is the weight of 1,000 cubic feet of air at STP?

Solution: To solve this problem, one must first recognize that air is a mixture of 80% N_2 and 20% O_2. One should also know that 22.4 cubic feet of any gas at STP weighs its ounce molecular weight. For example, in this problem,

    22.4 ft.^{3} of O_2 would weigh 32 oz.

    22.4 ft.^{3} of N_2 would weigh 28 oz.

Using this information, if one knows what 22.4 ft.^{3} of air weighs, then one can determine how much 1000 ft.^{3} of air weighs.

Since air is a mixture, one can find its ounce molecular weight by multiplying the per cent composition of each gas times each gas' ounce molecular weight and adding these two values:

  for N_2 : $(0.8)(\text{MW } N_2) = (0.8)(28 \text{ oz}) = 22.4 \text{ oz}$

  for O_2 : $(0.2)(\text{MW } O_2) = (0.2)(32 \text{ oz}) = 6.4 \text{ oz.}$

The ounce molecular weight for air is $22.4 + 6.4 = 28.8$ oz., and has a volume of 22.4 ft.^{3}

If 22.4 ft.^{3} of air has a weight of 28.8 oz then, the weight of 1000 ft.^{3} can be found through the following proportion:

$$\frac{22.4 \text{ ft.}^3}{28.8 \text{ oz.}} = \frac{1000 \text{ ft.}^3}{\text{unknown weight}}$$

Solving for the unknown weight of air

$$\text{weight of air} = \frac{(1000 \text{ ft.}^3)(28.8 \text{ oz.})}{(22.4 \text{ ft.}^3)} = 1.29 \times 10^3 \text{ oz.}$$

Chlorine may be prepared by the action of $KClO_3$ on HCl, and the reaction may be represented by the equation:

$$KClO_3 + 6HCl \rightarrow KCl + 3Cl_2 + 3H_2O$$

Calculate the weight of $KClO_3$ which would be required to produce 1.0 liter of Cl_2 gas at STP. R = .082 liter-atm/mole-°K.

Solution: From the equation one can see that 1 mole of $KClO_3$ reacts to form 3 moles of Cl_2. If one can find the number of moles of $KClO_3$, which will react to form 1 liter of Cl_2, then one can find its weight by multiplying the number of moles by the molecular weight of $KClO_3$. STP (Standard Temperature and Pressure) is defined as 0°C and 1 atm.

One can find the number of moles of Cl_2 in 1 liter by using the Ideal Gas Law

$$n = \frac{PV}{RT},$$

where P is the pressure, V is the volume, R is the gas constant (0.082 liter-atm/mole-°K), T is the absolute temperature and n is the number of moles. Here, T is given in °C; it can be converted to °K by adding 273 to it. You have, then,

$$T = 0 + 273 = 273°K.$$

One can now solve for the number of moles of Cl_2 produced.

$$n = \frac{PV}{RT}$$

P = 1 atm
V = 1 liter
R = 0.082 $\frac{\text{liter-atm}}{\text{mole-°K}}$
T = 273

$$n = \frac{1 \text{ atm} \times 1 \text{ liter}}{0.082 \frac{\text{liter-atm}}{\text{mole-°K}} \times 273°K} = .045 \text{ moles.}$$

From the equation for the reaction, the following ratio is determined.

$$\frac{3}{1} = \frac{\text{number of moles of } Cl_2}{\text{number of moles of } KClO_3}$$

One knows that 1 liter contains .045 moles Cl_2, and if you substitute this value into the above ratio, one can find the number of moles of $KClO_3$ reacted.

$$\frac{3}{1} = \frac{.045 \text{ moles}}{\text{number of moles of } KClO_3}$$

$$\text{number of moles of } KClO_3 = \frac{.045 \text{ moles} \times 1}{3} = .015 \text{ moles}$$

The weight of .015 moles of $KClO_3$ can be found by multiplying .015 moles by the molecular weight of $KClO_3$. (MW of $KClO_3$ = 122.5.)

What volume of hydrogen at STP is produced as sulfuric acid acts on 120 g. of metallic calcium. Equation for the reaction is

$$Ca + H_2SO_4 \rightarrow CaSO_4 + H_2$$

<u>Solution</u>: This problem may be solved by using either the mole method or the proportion method.

<u>Mole method</u>: In using the mole method, one looks at this equation and sees that for every mole of calcium acted on by H_2SO_4, one mole of hydrogen is produced.

This means that to find how much hyrdogen is produced, one must first find out how much calcium is present. There will be the same number of moles of hydrogen produced as there are calcium reacted. After one knows how many moles of hydrogen are produced, one can calculate the volume.

To calculate the number of moles of calcium present, one must divide the amount present by the molecular weight (molecular weight of Ca = 40).

$$\text{number of moles} = \frac{\text{number of grams present}}{\text{molecular weight}}$$

$$\text{number of moles of Ca} = \frac{120 \text{ g}}{40 \text{ g/mole}} = 3.00 \text{ moles}$$

Therefore, 3.00 moles of hydrogen gas are produced. At STP (Standard Temperature and Pressure), the volume of one mole of any gas occupies 22.4 liters. Thus, when 3 moles of gas are generated, as in this problem it occupies 3×22.4 liters = 67.2 liters.

<u>Proportion method</u>: In the proportion method, the molecular weights (multiplied by the proper coefficients) are placed below the formula in the equation and the amounts of substances (given and unknown) are placed above. In this case, because one is trying to find the volume of hydrogen and not its weight, the volume of one mole will be placed below the equation as shown.

120 g				X(Vol.)
Ca	+	H_2SO_4	$\rightarrow$ $CaSO_4$ +	H_2
40.0 g				22.4 liters

$$\frac{120 \text{ g}}{40.0 \text{ g}} = \frac{X}{22.4 \text{ liters}}$$

X = unknown volume of H_2 produced.

Solving for X:

$$X = \frac{(22.4 \text{ liters})(120 \text{ g})}{40.0 \text{ g}} = 67.2 \text{ liters.}$$

● PROBLEM 5-29

How many liters of phosphine (PH_3) gas at STP could be made from 30 g of calcium by use of the following sequence of reactions:

$$3Ca + 2P \rightarrow Ca_3P_2$$

$$Ca_3P_2 + 6HCl \rightarrow 2PH_3 + 3CaCl_2$$

(Molecular weights: Ca = 40, PH_3 = 34.)

Solution: From the stoichiometry of these two equations 3 moles of Ca will yield 2 moles of PH_3 gas. Thus, if one knows the number of moles of Ca, then one can determine the number of moles of PH_3 produced. The number of moles of Ca given is its weight divided by its molecular weight.

Therefore,

$$\text{number of moles Ca} = \frac{30 \text{ g Ca}}{40 \text{ g/mole}} = 0.75 \text{ moles}$$

From 0.75 moles of Ca, one produces 2/3 as much or 2/3(0.75) = 0.50 moles of PH_3 gas. At STP, one mole of any gas occupies 22.4 liters, hence, the total volume of PH_3 produced at STP

$$= (22.4 \text{ } \ell/\text{mole})(0.50 \text{ moles } PH_3) = 11.2 \text{ } \ell.$$

● PROBLEM 5-30

Nitroglycerin ($C_3H_5(NO_3)_3$) explodes according to the following reaction:

$$4C_3H_5(NO_3)_3(\ell) \rightarrow 12CO_2(g) + 6N_2(g) + O_2(g) + 10H_2O(g),$$

producing only gaseous products. What is the total volume of gaseous products produced at standard temperature and pressure (STP) when 454 g of nitroglycerin explodes? The molecular weight of nitroglycerin is 227 g/mole.

Solution: This problem is an application of the ideal gas equation, PV = nRT, where P = pressure, V = volume, n = number of moles, R = gas constant, and T = absolute temperature. Solving for V,

$$V = \frac{nRT}{P}$$

STP is, by definition, $0°C (= 273°K)$ and 1 atm pressure. Hence, $T = 273°K$ and $P = 1$ atm. Also, $R = 0.082$ liter-atm/mole-deg. We must find the number of moles, n, of gaseous products. The number of moles of nitroglycerin we started with is equal to its mass divided by the molecular weight, or 454 g/227 g/mole = 2 moles of nitroglycerin. Dividing the equation for the reaction of nitroglycerin by 2 (so that $4C_3H_5(NO_3)_3$ becomes $2C_3H_5(NO_3)_3$), we obtain:

$$2C_3H_5(NO_3)_3(l) \rightarrow 6CO_2(g) + 3N_2(g) + \tfrac{1}{2}O_2(g) + 5H_2O(g).$$

Thus, our 2 moles of nitroglycerin will produce a total of $6 + 3 + \tfrac{1}{2} + 5 = 14.5$ moles of gaseous products, so that n = 14.5 moles. Substituting the values of n, R, T, and P into the equation for V gives:

$$V = \frac{nRT}{P} = \frac{14.5 \text{ moles} \times 0.082 \text{ liter-atm/mole-deg} \times 273°K}{1 \text{ atm}}$$

$$= 325 \text{ liters.}$$

● PROBLEM 5-31

A chemist performs the following reaction:

$$2KClO_3(s) \rightarrow 2KCl(s) + 3O_2(g).$$

He collects the O_2 gas by water displacement at 20°C. He observes a pressure of 753 mm Hg. Assuming the pressure of water vapor is 17.5 mm Hg at 20°C and he started with 1.28 g of potassium chlorate ($KClO_3$), what volume of gas is produced? ($R = .0821$ l-atm/mole °K.)

Solution: You are asked to find the volume of gas produced and can do so using the equation of state, $PV = nRT$, where P = pressure, V = volume, n = number of moles, R = universal gas constant and T = temperature in Kelvin (Celsius plus 273°).

In the problem you are told the pressure at which the gas is collected, which must be modified due to the presence of water vapor and the temperature. If you knew n, you could substitute for the values in the equation of state and solve for V.

Your procedure will be to find the number of moles of gas produced. This can be determined from the reaction e-quation given and the use of stoichiometry. If you knew how many moles of $KClO_3$ you started with, you would know the number of moles of O_2 produced, since 3 moles of O_2 are generated for every 2 moles of $KClO_3$. You can deter-mine how many moles of $KClO_3$ you started with. You are told that the chemist has 1.28 g. Since the molecular weight of $KClO_3$ is 122.55 g, you have

$\frac{1.28}{122.55}$ = 1.045 × 10⁻² moles of $KClO_3$. Therefore,

from reaction there are $\frac{3}{2}$ (1.045 × 10⁻²) = 1.57 × 10⁻² moles of O_2 gas produced.

Now you go back to PV = nRT. Recall that the gas was collected by water displacement. Thus, it is saturated by water vapor. Hence, the pressure of O_2 is only 753 mm Hg - 17.5 mm Hg, or 735.5 mm where 17.5 mm Hg is the water vapor pressure. Since 1 atm = 760 mm,

$$(735.5 \text{ mm}) \left(\frac{1 \text{ atm}}{760 \text{ mm}} \right) = .968 \text{ atm.}$$

Now, substitute and solve for the volume V of O_2 produced. Rewriting and substituting,

$$V = \frac{nRT}{P} = \frac{(.0157)(.0821)(293^\circ K)}{.968} = .390 \text{ liters or 390 ml.}$$

CHAPTER 6

SOLIDS

PHASE DIAGRAMS

● PROBLEM 6-1

The diagram below is an example of a phase diagram for a pure substance. To what phases do the regions A, B, and C correspond?

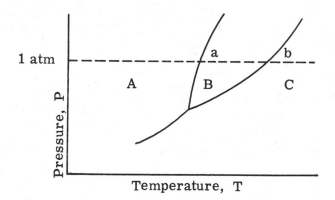

Solution: Following the 1 atm constant pressure line from left to right, we are proceeding from low values of the temperature to high values. Therefore, we will intersect the three regions in the order solid-liquid-vapor. The regions A, B, C hence correspond to the solid, liquid, and vapor phases, respectively. Point a denotes the normal freezing (melting) point of the substance and the point b denotes the normal boiling point.

Draw a labelled phase diagram for a substance Z which has the following properties; normal boiling point = 220°C, normal freezing point 80°C, and triple point 60°C and .20 atm. Predict the freezing and boiling, if the pressure were .80 atm?

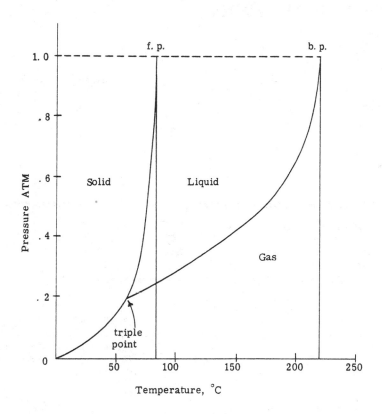

Temperature, °C

Solution: To draw this diagram you want to understand all the terms involved. The relation between solid, liquid, and gaseous states as a function of the given temperature and pressure can be summarized on a graph known as a phase diagram. From the given experimental observations, you can draw the diagram. The lines which separate the states in a diagram represent an equilibrium between the phases. The intersection of the three lines is called the triple point, where all three phases are in equilibrium with each other. By normal boiling and melting points you mean those readings taken at 1 atm. Thus, the phase diagram can be written as shown in the accompanying figure.

From the diagram you see that if the atm was .80, the b.p. and f.p. would drop, respectively, to 215°C and 85°C.

CHAPTER 7

PROPERTIES OF LIQUIDS

DENSITY

● **PROBLEM** 7-1

What volume of a block of wood (density = 0.80 g/cm³)
which weighs 1.0 kg, will be above the water surface
when the block is afloat? (Note: A floating object
displaces its own weight of water.)

Solution: Since a floating object displaces its own
weight in water, 1 kg of water is displaced by this
block of wood. One can find the volume of the block of
wood above the water by solving for the volume of the
block and subtracting the volume of 1 kg of water from
it. One uses the density to solve for the volume.

$$\text{density} = \frac{\text{weight}}{\text{volume}} = \frac{g}{cm^3}$$

Therefore:

$$\text{volume} = \frac{\text{weight}}{\text{density}}$$

Solving for the volume of the wood: 1 kg = 1000 g.

$$\text{volume} = \frac{1000 \text{ g}}{.80 \text{ g/cm}^3} = 1.25 \times 10^3 \text{ cm}^3$$

Solving for the volume of the water displaced:

By definition the density of water is 1.0 g/cm³.

$$\text{volume} = \frac{1000 \text{ g}}{1.0 \text{ g/cm}^3} = 1.00 \times 10^3 \text{ cm}^3$$

volume of wood above water = volume of wood - volume of
$$\text{water}$$

volume of wood above water = 1250 cm^3 - 1000 cm^3

$$= 250 \text{ cm}^3$$

● **PROBLEM** 7-2

A chemist dropped a 200 g object into a tank of water. It displaced 60 ml. of the water when it sunk to the bottom of the tank. In a similar experiment it displaced only 50 g of an oil into which it was dropped. Calculate the density of the object and the oil.

Solution: The density (ρ) of a substance is defined as its mass divided by its volume.

$$\rho = \frac{\text{mass}}{\text{volume}}$$

Thus, to solve for the densities of the object and the oil, one must first calculate their respective masses and volumes. The mass of the object is 200 g, but the volume is not given. An object dropped in any liquid displaces a volume of liquid equal to the volume of the object. The object displaces 60 ml of water; therefore, the volume of the object is 60 ml. Solving for the density of the object:

$$\rho = \frac{\text{mass}}{\text{volume}} = \frac{200 \text{ g}}{60 \text{ ml}} = 3.33 \text{ g/ml.}$$

One is given that the object displaces 50 g of the oil, and from the water experiment, it is known that the volume of the object is 60 ml. Since the object displaces the same volume of liquid as it occupies 60 ml of the oil weighs 50 g. Solving for the density of the oil:

$$\rho = \frac{\text{mass}}{\text{volume}} = \frac{50 \text{ g}}{60 \text{ ml}} = .833 \text{ g/ml.}$$

● **PROBLEM** 7-3

Assuming that the density of water is .9971 g/cm^3 at 25°C and that of ice at 0° is .917 g/cm^3, what percent of a water jug at 25°C should be left empty so that, if the water freezes, it will just fill the jug?

Solution: Density = $\frac{\text{mass}}{\text{volume}}$

When water freezes, the mass is constant, but its density decreases. This means, therefore, that an increase in volume occurs. To solve this problem you must determine the change in volume of water from 25° to 0°. Because you are given the densities of the substance at each temperature, you can say for 1 mole of H_2O (MW = 18)

$$\frac{mass}{volume} = \frac{18 \text{ g/mole}}{y} = \frac{0.997g}{cm^3} \text{ for water at 25°C and}$$

$$\frac{mass}{volume} = \frac{18 \text{ g/mole}}{x} = \frac{0.017g}{cm^3} \text{ for ice at 0°C.}$$

Rewriting, you have .997 y = 18 and .917 x = 18. Both expressions equal 18, which means .997 y = .917 x, or

$$\frac{x}{y} = \frac{.997}{.917} = 1.087.$$

This means, then, that at 0°C the volume is 1.087 times greater than the original at 25°C. If you let B equal the fraction of water to be put in the jug, then you can say 1.087 B = 1, or B = .920. In other words, only 92% of the jug should be filled at 25° to obtain a completely filled jug at 0°. This means that 8 % is empty space.

FREEZING POINT DEPRESSION AND BOILING POINT ELEVATION

● PROBLEM 7-4

The freezing point constant of toluene is 3.33°C per mole per 1000 g. Calculate the freezing point of a solution prepared by dissolving 0.4 mole of solute in 500 g of toluene. The freezing point of toluene is - 95.0°C.

Solution: The freezing point constant is defined as the number of degrees the freezing point will be lowered per 1000 g of solvent per mole of solute present. The freezing point depression is related to this constant by the following equation.

freezing pt depression = molality of solute × freezing pt constant

The molality is defined as the number of moles per 1000 g of solvent. Here, one is given that 0.4 moles of solute are added to 500 g of solvent, therefore there will be 0.8 moles in 1000 g.

$$\frac{0.4 \text{ moles}}{500 \text{ g}} = \frac{0.8 \text{ moles}}{1000 \text{ g}}$$

The molality of the solute is thus 0.8 m. One can

now find the freezing point depression. The freezing point constant for toluene is 3.33°.

freezing point depression = molality × 3.33°

$$= 0.8 × 3.33° = 2.66°$$

The freezing point of toluene is thus lowered by 2.66°.

freezing point of solution = (- 95°C) - 2.66° = - 97.66°C.

What is the freezing point of a solution of 92 g of alcohol (C_2H_5OH) and 500 g of H_2O?

Solution: The freezing point is dependent on the number of solute particles. One mole of a substance dissolved in 1000 g of water lowers the freezing point 1.86°. One uses the following equation to find the freezing point depression:

freezing pt. depression = molality of solute × 1.86°.

Now, one must find the molality of the alcohol. The molality is defined as the number of moles in 1000 g of H_2O. In this solution, there are 92 g of alcohol present. The number of moles is found by dividing 92 g by the molecular weight of the alcohol. MW of C_2H_5OH = 46.

$$\text{no. of moles} = \frac{92.0 \text{ g}}{46 \text{ g/mole}} = 2 \text{ moles}$$

There are 2 moles in 500 g of water.

In 1000 g of H_2O, there would be twice this amount or 4 moles. Therefore, the molality of the alcohol is 4 m.

One can now find the freezing point depression.

freezing pt. depression = molality × 1.86°

$$= 4 × 1.86° = 7.44°.$$

The freezing point of H_2O is 0°C.

freezing pt of solution = freezing pt of H_2O -
freezing pt of depression

$$= 0° - 7.44° = - 7.44°.$$

The molal freezing point constant for a certain liquid is 0.500°C. 26.4 g of a solute dissolved in 250 g of this liquid yields a solution which has a freezing point 0.125° below that of the pure liquid. Calculate the molecular weight of this solute.

Solution: A mole of a substance in 1000 g of H_2O gives a definite and known lowering of the freezing point. By determining the freezing point of a solution of known concentration, one can calculate the molecular weight of the dissolved substance. A general formula may be developed for this kind of calculation:

$$\text{molecular weight} = \frac{\text{grams solute}}{\text{kg of solvent}} \times \frac{K_f}{\Delta T_f}$$

where K_f is the freezing point constant and ΔT_f is change in the freezing point. Here, 26.4 g of a solute is dissolved in 250 g of liquid. One can find the number of grams of solute using the following ratio: (Note: there are 1000 g in 1 kg.) Let X = number of g of solute in 1000 g

$$\frac{26.4 \text{ g}}{250 \text{ g}} = \frac{X}{1000 \text{ g}}$$

$$X = \frac{1000 \text{ g} \times 26.4 \text{ g}}{250 \text{ g}} = 105.6 \text{ g}$$

One can now solve for the molecular weight.

$$\text{molecular weight} = \frac{105.6 \text{ g}}{1 \text{ kg}} \times \frac{0.500°C}{0.125°}$$

$$= 422.4 \text{ g}$$

A chemist wishes to determine the molecular weight and molecular formula of fructose (a sugar). He places .946 g of it in 150 g of H_2O (water) and finds that the freezing point of water is depressed to -0.0651°C. Determine the molecular weight and formula of fructose, assuming that the simplest formula of fructose is $(CH_2)O$.

Solution: To answer this question, you must know the

quantitative relationship for the depression of the
freezing point, ΔT_f. This relation can be expressed as

$\Delta T_f = k_f \times m$, where ΔT_f = the actual depression, k_f = molal
freezing point constant (-1.86 deg mol^{-1} for water) and m =
molality of the solution. Molality is defined as moles of
solute per 1 kg of solvent.

In this problem, water is the solvent and the
fructose compound is the solute. As such, you can express
the freezing point relationship as

$$\Delta T_f = k_f \times \frac{\frac{\text{grams solute}}{\text{molecular weight}}}{\text{grams solvent}} \times 1000, \qquad \text{where}$$

the numerator is the number of moles of solute. You possess
all of the unknowns, except the molecular weight, which can
be calculated. In other words, solve for the molecular weight
by substitution. Hence.

$$-0.0651°C = -1.86°C/\text{mole} \times \frac{\frac{.946 \text{ g}}{\text{mol. wt.}}}{150 \text{ g}} \times 1000 \text{ g/kg}$$

mol wt. = 180 g/mole.

To determine the molecular formula, you must figure
out what formula has a molecule weight of 180 g, and yet is
still a multiple of $(CH_2)O$.

Thus, one determines the weight of 1 $(CH_2)O$ and
divides this into 180 g. (MW of $(CH_2)O$ = 30.)

$$\text{no. of } (CH_2)O \text{ in fructose} = \frac{180 \text{ g}}{30 \text{ g}/(CH_2)O} = 6 \ (CH_2)O$$

Therefore, the formula for fructose is $6 \times (CH_2)O$
or $C_6H_{12}O_6$.

● **PROBLEM 7-8**

What is the approximate boiling point at standard pressure
of a solution prepared by dissolving 234 g of NaCl in
500 g of H_2O?

Solution: The boiling point of a solution is a colligative
property. This means that it depends on the ratio of number
of solute particles to number of solvent particles or
molality. Molality is defined as the number of moles of
solute divided by the number of kilograms of solvent.

When water is the solvent the boiling point constant,
K_b, is 0.52°. This means that when one mole of solute is in
1 kg of H_2O the boiling point of water is raised 0.52°.

boiling pt elevation = K_b × molality of solute

One can find the boiling point elevation once the molality of the NaCl is found. To determine the molality one must first determine the number of moles present. This is done by dividing the number of grams present by the molecular weight. (MW of NaCl = 58.5.)

$$\text{no. of moles} = \frac{234 \text{ g}}{58.5} = 4.0 \text{ moles}$$

There are 4.0 moles of NaCl in 500 g, or 0.5 kg, of H_2O. The molality can now be found.

$$\text{molality} = \frac{\text{moles of solute}}{\text{kg of solvent}}$$

$$\text{molality} = \frac{4.0 \text{ moles}}{0.5 \text{ kg}} = 8.0 \text{ m}$$

NaCl is an electrolyte which means that when it is placed in H_2O it dissociates into its ions.

$$NaCl \xrightleftharpoons{} Na^+ + Cl^-$$

This means that for every NaCl present, there are two ions formed. There are thus twice as many moles of particles as molecules of NaCl present. The effective molality is, therefore, twice the true molality.

effective molality = 2 × 8.0 m = 16.0 m

One can now solve for the boiling point elevation.

boiling point elevation = 0.52° × 16.0 m = 8.32°

The boiling point of the water is raised 8.32°. It was originally 100°C, therefore the new boiling point is 100°C + 8.32° = 108.32°C.

● **PROBLEM 7-9**

Give the approximate boiling points at sea level for the following: (a) 2 molal HBr; (b) Suspension of 100 g of powdered glass in one liter of water; (c) 1.2×10^{24} sucrose molecules/liter; (d) 0.5 molal $BaCl_2$.

Solution: The boiling point is a colligative property and, therefore, depends upon the number of particles present in 1 kg of solvent. The boiling point constant for water is 0.52°C. This means that for each mole of particles dissolved in 1 kg of H_2O the boiling point will be elevated by 0.52°C.

boiling pt. elevation = 0.52°C × molality of solute.

The molality is defined as the number of moles in one kg. of solvent.

(a) 2 molal HBr. HBr is a strong acid and will thus ionize completely when diluted with H_2O to form H^+ and Br^- ions.

$$HBr \rightleftarrows H^+ + Br^-$$

Therefore, 2 particles will be formed by each HBr that ionizes. The effective molality of the solution is then twice the molality of the HBr.

effective molality = 2 × 2 molal = 4 molal.

One can now find the boiling point elevation.

boiling pt. elevation = 0.52° × 4 molal = 2.1°

The normal boiling point of H_2O is 100°C the new boiling point is 100° + 2.1° or 102.1°C.

(b) Suspension of 100 g of powdered glass. These particles will not dissolve to their molecular components in H_2O, thus the boiling point of the water will not be changed.

(c) 1.2×10^{24} sucrose molecules/liter. One liter of H_2O weighs 1 kg, therefore, 1.2×10^{24} sucrose molecules are dissolved in 1 kg of H_2O. The number of moles present is equal to the number of molecules present divided by Avogadro's number, the number of particles in one mole.

$$\text{no. of moles} = \frac{1.2 \times 10^{24} \text{ molecules}}{6.02 \times 10^{23} \text{ molecules/mole}} = 2 \text{ moles}$$

Hence, there are 2 moles of sucrose in 1 kg of water, thus the solution is 2 molal. Sucrose does not ionize in water, therefore, the true molality is equal to the effective molality. Solving for the boiling point elevation:

boiling pt. elevation = 0.52° × 2 molal = 1.04°

The boiling point of this solution is 100° + 1.04° or 101.04°.

(d) 0.5 molal $BaCl_2$. $BaCl_2$ is a strong electrolyte and will completely ionize in H_2O.

$$BaCl_2 \rightleftarrows Ba^{++} + 2Cl^-$$

3 ions will be formed for each $BaCl_2$ present. The effective molality will therefore be 3 times the molality of unionized $BaCl_2$.

effective molality = 3 × 0.5 molal = 1.5 molal

One can now solve for the boiling point elevation.

boiling pt. elevation = 1.5 molal × 0.52° = 0.78°

   The boiling point of H_2O, 100°, will be raised 0.78°
to be 100.78°C.

● **PROBLEM** 7-10

The normal boiling point of benzene is 80.10°C. When 1 mole
of a solute is dissolved in 1000 g of benzene, the boiling
point of the resulting solution is 82.73°C. When 1.2 g of
elemental sulfur is dissolved in 50 g of benzene, the
boiling point of the solution is 80.36°C. What is the
molecular weight of sulfur?

Solution: In order to determine the molecular weight of
sulfur, we must determine how many moles of sulfur correspond to 1.2 g.

   When 1 mole of solute is added to 1000 g of benzene,
the normal boiling point is raised by 2.63°C, from 80.10°C
to 82.73°C. This corresponds to a concentration of 1 molal
(1 mole solute/1000 g solvent = 1 molal). The ratio of
sulfur to benzene in the sulfur-benzene solution is
1.2 g sulfur/50 g benzene = 0.024. Thus, adding 1.2 g of
sulfur to 50 g of benzene is equivalent to adding 24 g of
sulfur to 1000 g of benzene (because 24 g sulfur/1000 g
benzene is also 0.024).

   The observed boiling point elevation in the sulfur-
benzene solution is 0.26°C (from 80.10°C to 80.36°C).
This is the boiling point elevation one would obtain by
adding 24 g of sulfur to 1000 g of benzene. But this is
about one-tenth the rise one would obtain by adding 1 mole
of sulfur (the rise would then be 2.63°C), hence 24 g of
sulfur must correspond to about one-tenth of a mole.

   Thus, the apparent molecular weight of sulfur is

$$\frac{24 \text{ g}}{0.1 \text{ mole}} = 240 \text{ g/mole.}$$

RAOULT'S LAW AND VAPOR PRESSURE

● **PROBLEM** 7-11

You have two 1-liter containers connected to each other by
a valve which is closed. In one container, you have liquid
water in equilibrium with water vapor at 25°C. The other
container contains a vacuum. Suddenly, you open the valve.
Discuss the changes that take place, assuming temperature
is constant with regard to (a) the vapor pressure, (b) the
concentration of the water molecules in the vapor, (c) the

number of molecules in the vapor state.

Solution: The vapor pressure is the pressure exerted by
the gas molecules when they are in equilibrium with the
liquid. When the valve is opened some of the gas molecules
will move to the empty container. At this point the pressure will be less than the equilibrium pressure because the
concentration of the gas molecules will be lowered. Very
quickly, though, the equilibrium will be attained again by
the action of more liquid molecules vaporizing. Therefore,
the vapor pressure and the concentration of the gaseous
molecules of the system remains essentially unchanged.

Since the concentration of the gaseous molecules
remains unchanged when the volume of the system is doubled,
the number of molecules must also be doubled. This is true
because concentration is an expression of the number of
molecules per unit volume.

● **PROBLEM** 7-12

A chemist decides to find the vapor pressure of water by
the gas saturation method. 100 liters of N_2 gas is passed
through 65.44 g of water. After passage of the gas,
63.13 g remained. The temperature of the H_2O (water) is 25°C.
Find the vapor pressure of water at this temperature.

Solution: In the gas saturation method, a dry, unreactive gas
such as nitrogen or air is bubbled through a specific amount
of liquid maintained at constant temperature. After the gas
has been bubbled away, the loss in weight of the liquid is
determined. The weight loss is the number of grams of
liquid in the vapor state. There exists an equation that
relates the volume, pressure, weight loss, and molecular
weight of the liquid.

$P = \frac{g}{MV} RT$, where P = vapor pressure, g = grams of

vapor, M = molecular weight of liquid, R = universal gas
constant (.0821 $\frac{liter-atm}{mole\ °K}$, V = volume, and T = temperature
in Kelvin (Celsius plus 273°)

The pressure will be expressed in mm, so that you use
the conversion factor of $\frac{760\ mm}{atm}$. g = 65.44 − 63.13 = 2.31
grams or the weight of the liquid in the vapor state.

The molecular weight of water = 18.02 g/mole. Thus,

$$P = \frac{gRT}{MV} = \frac{(2.31\ grams)(.0821\ \frac{liter\ atm}{mole\ °K})(298°K)\ \frac{760\ mm}{1\ atm}}{(18.02\ g/mole)(200\ liters)}$$

= 23.8 mm = vapor pressure of H_2O.

When a swimmer leaves cold water on a warm, breezy day, he experiences a cooling effect. Why?

Solution: The equilibrium vapor pressure, is defined as the pressure exerted by the gas of that substance in equilibrium with the liquid state of the same substance. When the swimmer leaves the cold water, he is, coated with water. As the water evaporates a layer of gaseous water molecules form around the swimmer's body.

This vapor attains an equilibrium with the atmosphere which hinders further vaporization of the water. However, when the breeze comes, it blows away the vapor above the water, and thereby keeps the partial pressure of the vapor low above the skin. This, then, causes increased evaporation so that the partial pressure can be reestablished. This is true because the concentration and vapor pressure of the gaseous water molecules must be below a certain point for evaporation to occur. Once this pont has been reached no more liquid molecules of water can go into the gaseous state.

For the water to evaporate, it must go from a liquid to a gaseous phase, a process which requires heat. The water removes heat from the swimmer's body. Thus, the swimmer feels a cooling effect.

The vapor pressures of pure benzene and toluene at 60°C are 385 and 139 Torr, respectively. Calculate (a) the partial pressures of benzene and toluene, (b) the total vapor pressure of the solution, and (c) the mole fraction of toluene in the vapor above a solution with 0.60 mole fraction toluene.

Solution: The vapor pressure of benzene over solutions of benzene and toluene is directly proportional to the mole fraction of benzene in the solution. The vapor pressure of pure benzene is the proportionality constant. This is analogous to the vapor pressure of toluene. This is known as Raoult's law. It may be written as

$$P_1 = X_1 \ P_1^\circ$$

$$P_2 = X_2 \ P_2^\circ$$

where 1 and 2 refer to components 1 and 2, P_1 and P_2 represent the partial vapor pressure above the solution, P_1° and P_2°

are the vapor pressures of pure components, and X_1 and X_2 are their mole fractions. Solutions are called ideal if they obey Raoult's law.

The mole fraction of a component in the vapor is equal to its pressure fraction in the vapor. The total vapor pressure is the sum of the vapor's component partial pressures.

To solve this problem one must

1) calculate the partial pressures of benzene and toluene using Raoult's law

2) find the total vapor pressure of the solution by adding the partial pressures

3) find the mole fraction of toluene in the vapor.

One knows the mole fraction of toluene in the solution is 0.60 and, thus, one also knows the mole fraction of benzene is (1-0.60) or 0.40. Using Raoult's law:

$$P^\circ_{benzene} = 385 \text{ Torr} \qquad P^\circ_{Toluene} = 139$$

a) $P_{benzene} = (0.40)(385 \text{ Torr}) = 154.0 \text{ Torr}$

$P_{toluene} = (0.60)(139 \text{ Torr}) = 83.4 \text{ Torr}$

b) $P_{total} = 154.0 + 83.4 = 237.4 \text{ Torr}$

c) The mole fraction of toluene in the vapor =

$$X_{toluene, \, vap} = \frac{P_{toluene}}{P_{toluene} + P_{benzene}} = \frac{83.4}{237.4} = 0.351.$$

● **PROBLEM 7-15**

At 90°C, benzene has a vapor pressure of 1022 Torr, and toluene has a vapor pressure of 406 Torr. From this information, calculate the composition of the benzene-toluene solution that will boil at 1 atm pressure and 90°C, assuming that the solution is ideal.

Solution: A solution boils when the sum of the partial pressures of the components becomes equal to the applied pressure (i.e. total pressure). To solve this problem, one must realize that the applied pressure is atmospheric pressure, 760 Torr.

One can determine the partial pressure of benzene (P°_a) and of toluene (P°_b) by using Raoult's law. Raoult's law states that the partial pressure p of a gas is equal to its vapor pressure p° times its mole fraction X in the solution.

$$p = p^\circ X$$

Dalton's law of partial pressure states that the sum of the partial pressures of a system is equal to the toal pressure of the system. For this particular benzene-toluene solution to boil the total pressure of the system must equal atmospheric pressure 760 Torr. If one lets the mole fraction of benzene equal X_a, then the mole fraction toluene is equal to $1 - X_a$. One determines the partial pressures by substituting into Raoult's law

$$P_a = P_a^\circ (X_a)$$

$$P_b = P_b^\circ (1-X_a).$$

Then, substituting into Dalton's law:

$$760 \text{ Torr} = P_a + P_b$$

$$760 \text{ Torr} = 1022 \, X_a + 406 \, (1-X_a)$$

$$= 1022 \, X_a + 406 - 406 \, X_a$$
$$X_a = 0.574$$

The mole fraction of benzene in the liquid is 0.574 and the mole fraction of toluene is $(1-0.574)=0.426$.

● **PROBLEM** 7-16

A chemist dissolves 300 g of urea in 1000 g of water. Urea is NH_2CONH_2. Assuming the solution obeys Raoult's law, determine the following: a) The vapor pressure of the solvent at 0° and 100°C and b) The boiling and freezing point of the solution. The vapor pressure of pure water is 4.6 mm and 760 mm at 0°C and 100°C, respectively and the $K_f = 1.86$ C /mole and $K_b = .52$ C /mole .

Solution: To solve (a), you must employ Raoult's law, which states $P_{H_2O} = P^\circ_{H_2O} X_{H_2O}$, where P_{H_2O} = the partial pressure of water (the solvent), $P^\circ_{H_2O}$ = the vapor pressure of water when pure, and X_{H_2O} is the mole fraction of H_2O in the solution. The mole fraction is equal to $\dfrac{N_{H_2O}}{N_{solute} + N_{H_2O}}$, where N_{H_2O} = moles of H_2O, and N_{solute} = moles of solute. You are told the $P^\circ_{H_2O}$ for H_2O at the temperatures in question. Thus, to find the vapor pressures of the solution, you must calculate X_{H_2O} and substitute into Raoult's law

To calculate the concentration of urea, remember moles = $\dfrac{grams}{molecular\ weight}$. Since you have 300 grams of urea and the molecular weight of urea ia 60.06 g, you have $\dfrac{300}{60.06}$ or

4.995 moles of urea. Similarly, for water (MW=18), you have $\frac{1000 \text{ g}}{18 \text{ g/mole}}$ = 55.55 moles of water. Thus, the mole fraction of water = $\frac{55.55}{4.995 + 55.55}$ = .917. Therefore, at 0°,

$\left(P_{H_2O} = P^{\circ}_{H_2O} X_{H_2O} = (4.6 \text{ mm})(.917) = 4.2 \text{ mm} \right)$ at 760°,

$\left(P_{H_2O} = P^{\circ}_{H_2O} X_{H_2O} = (760)(.917) = 697 \text{ mm.} \right)$ To solve (b), you use the equations $\Delta T_f = K_f m$, where ΔT_f = freezing point depression, K_f = molal freezing pt. depression constant, and m = molality and $\Delta T_b = K_b m$, where ΔT_b = boiling point elevation, K_b = molal boiling point depression constant. If you find ΔT_f, you can calculate the freezing point, since the normal freezing point is decreased by this amount to give you the new freezing point. Boiling point works in the same way, except that you add to the normal boiling point. To calculate ΔT_f and ΔT_b, you must know molality. Molality = moles solvent per 1 kilogram solvent. You have 4.995 moles of urea and

1000 g of water or solvent, so that $\frac{4.995 \text{ mole}}{1 \text{ kg}} \approx$ 5 molal solution,

Thus, ΔT_f = (1.86)(5) = 9.3°C and ΔT_b = (.52)(5) = 2.6°C. Therefore, the freezing point is now 0.0°C - 9.3°C = -9.3°C and the boiling point is = 100°C + 2.6°C = 102.6°C.

● **PROBLEM** 7-17

The vapor pressure of benzene at 75°C is 640 torr. A solution of 3.68 g of a solute in 53.0 g benzene has a vapor pressure of 615 torr. Calculate the molecular weight of the solute. (MW of benzene = 78.0.)

Solution: At constant temperature, the lowering of the vapor pressure by a non-volatile solute is proportional to the concentration of the solute in the solution.

Hence, $P^0 - P = P^0 X_2$,

where P^0 is the original pressure, P is the final pressure and X_2 is the mole fraction of the solute. Here, one solves for the mole fraction of the solute, and from that, one can determine the molecular weight.

$$P^0 - P = P^0 X_2$$

X_2 = mole fraction

P^0 = 640 torr

P = 615 torr

$$640 \text{ torr} - 615 \text{ torr} = (640 \text{ torr}) \cdot X_2$$
$$25 \text{ torr} = (640 \text{ torr}) \cdot X_2$$
$$\frac{25 \text{ torr}}{640 \text{ torr}} = X_2$$

$$\text{mole fraction} = .039$$

Mole fraction is defined as the number of moles of each component divided by the sum of the number of moles in the solution.

mole fraction of solute =

$$= \frac{\text{no. of moles of solute}}{\text{no. of moles of solute} + \text{no. of moles of benzene}}$$

To find the number of moles of solute, one must first know the number of moles of benzene present. This is found by dividing the number of grams of benzene by the molecular weight of benzene. (MW = 78.)

$$\text{no. of moles of benzene} = \frac{\text{no. of grams}}{\text{MW}}$$

$$\text{no. of moles} = \frac{53.0 \text{ g}}{78.0 \text{ g/mole}} = .679 \text{ moles}$$

One can now solve for the number of moles of solute. Let X = moles of solute

$$\frac{\text{mole fraction}}{\text{of solute}} = \frac{\text{moles solute}}{\text{moles benzene} + \text{moles solute}}$$

$$.039 = \frac{X}{.679 + X}$$

$$.039 (.679 + X) = X$$

$$.265 + .039X = X$$

$$.265 = .961 \, X$$

$$.275 = X$$

Thus there are .275 moles of solute present. One is told that there are 3.68 g of this solute, therefore, there are .275 moles in 3.68 g. The molecular weight is found by dividing 3.68 g by 0.275 moles.

$$\text{molecular weight} = \frac{3.68 \text{ g}}{0.275 \text{ mole}} = 133.8 \text{ g/mole}.$$

OSMOTIC PRESSURE

● **PROBLEM** 7-18

A sugar solution was prepared by dissolving 9.0 g of sugar in 500 g of water. At 27°C, the osmotic pressure was measured as 2.46 atm. Determine the molecular weight of the sugar.

Solution: The molecular weight of the sugar is found by determining the concentration, C, of sugar from the equation for osmotic pressure,

$$\pi = CRT,$$

where π is the osmotic pressure, R = universal gas constant = 0.08206 liter-atm/mole- °K, and T is the absolute temperature.

The osmotic pressure is measured as π = 2.46 atm and the absolute temperature is T = 27°C + 273 = 300°K, hence

$$\pi = CRT,$$

2.46 atm = C × 0.08206 liter-atm/mole- °K × 300°K,

or $C = \dfrac{2.46 \text{ atm}}{0.08206 \text{ liter-atm/mole} - °K \times 300°K}$

= 0.10 mole/liter.

If we assume that the volume occupied by the sugar molecules in so small a concentration can be neglected, then in 1 liter of solution there is approximately 1 liter of water, or 1000 g of water, and

C = 0.10 mole/1000 g.

Therefore, there is 0.10 mole of sugar dissolved in 1000 g of water.

9.0 g of sugar dissolved in 500 g of water is equivalent to 18.0 g of sugar dissolved in 1000 g of water (9.0 g/500 g = 18.0 g/1000 g). But since C = 0.10 mole/1000 g, the 18.0 g of sugar must correspond to 0.10 mole of sugar. Therefore, the molecular weight of the sugar is

18 g/0.1 mole = 180 g/mole.

● **PROBLEM** 7-19

A chemist dissolves 10 g of an unknown protein in a liter of water at 25°C. The osmotic pressure is found to be 9.25 mmHg. What is the protein's molecular weight. Based upon the number of moles in 10 g of protein, what would the freezing point depression and boiling point elevation be? Assume R =

Universal Gas Constant = .0821 liter-atm/mole°K, k_f = 1.86°C/m, and k_b = .52°C/m.

Solution: The osmotic pressure (π) can be related to the molar concentration (C), Universal Gas Constant (R) and teperature (T) in degrees Kelvin of a solution via the formula π = CRT. After solving for C one can determine the molecular weight of the protein. Recall, C = moles/liter = N/V where N = moles and V = volume in liters. Hence, π = N/V RT. But N = moles = No. of grams/molecular wt = g/M.W. Rewriting,

$$\pi = \left(\frac{\frac{g}{M.W.}}{V}\right) RT \quad or \quad M.W. = \frac{gRT}{\pi V} .$$

Substituting for the known values,

$$M.W. = \frac{(10\ g)(.0821)(298°K)}{9.25\ mmHg\ (1)} \times \frac{760\ mm}{atm} = 20,100\ \frac{g}{mole} .$$

Note, you assumed a volume of 1 liter and multiplied by the conversion factor 760 mm/atm, since R is in atm. and π in mmHg. Now that you know that the molecular weight is 20,100, the number of moles in the 10 g of protein is 10/20,100 = 4.98×10^{-4} moles. To find the freezing point depression, ΔT_f, and boiling point elevation, ΔT_b, you must find the molality since $\Delta T_b = k_b m$ and $\Delta T_f = k_f m$, where k_f = molal freezing point depression constant k_b = molal boiling point elevation constant and m = molality. Molality = moles of solute per 1 kg solvent. Thus molality = .000498 mole/1 kg since in 1 liter of water you have 1000 ml which weighs 1 kg. Therefore,

$$\Delta T_f = (1.86°C)(.000498) = 9.3 \times 10^{-4}\ °C \qquad and$$

$$\Delta T_b = .52°C(.000498) = 2.59 \times 10^{-4}\ °C.$$

CHAPTER 8

SOLUTION CHEMISTRY

DENSITY AND FORMALITY

What are the mole fractions of solute and solvent in a solution prepared by dissolving 98 g H_2SO_4 (M.W. 98) in 162 g H_2O (M.W. 18)?

Solution: The mole fraction of solute is defined as the moles of solute divided by the sum of the number of moles of the solute and the number of moles of the solvent.

$$\text{Mole fraction of solute} = \frac{\text{moles of solute}}{\text{moles of solute+moles of solvent}}$$

The mole fraction of the solvent is defined similarly.

$$\text{Mole fraction of solvent} = \frac{\text{moles of solvent}}{\text{moles of solute+moles of solvent}}$$

Here, the solute is H_2SO_4 and the solvent is H_2O. One is given the amount of H_2SO_4 and H_2O in grams. Therefore, these quantities must be converted to moles. This can be done by dividing the number of grams available by the molecular weight.

$$\text{No. of moles} = \frac{\text{no. of grams}}{\text{MW}}$$

$$\text{No. of moles of } H_2SO_4 = \frac{98 \text{ g}}{98 \text{ g/mole}} = 1 \text{ mole}$$

149

No. of moles of $H_2O = \dfrac{162 \text{ g}}{18 \text{ g/mole}} = 9$ moles

Now that the number of moles of both solvent and solute are known, the mole fraction can be found.

Mole fraction of $H_2SO_4 = \dfrac{1 \text{ mole}}{1 \text{ mole} + 9 \text{ moles}} = 0.1$

Mole fraction of $H_2O = \dfrac{9 \text{ moles}}{1 \text{ mole} + 9 \text{ moles}} = 0.9$.

● **PROBLEM** 8-2

A wine has an acetic acid (CH_3COOH, 60 g/formula weight) content of 0.66% by weight. If the density of the wine is 1.11 g/ml, what is the formality of the acid?

Solution: This problem involves the correct interpretation of percent by weight. 0.66% by weight means 0.66×10^{-2} g acid per 100 g wine or 6.6×10^{-2} g acid per 1000 g wine. To convert 6.6×10^{-2} g acid to formula weight we divide by 60 g/formula weight and obtain 6.6×10^{-2} g/60 g/formula weight = 1.1×10^{-3} formula weight. To convert 1000 g wine to volume, we divide by the density of the wine and obtain 1000 g/1.11 g/ml = 900 ml = 0.90 liter. The formality is then

$$\text{formality} = \frac{\text{formula weights}}{\text{volume (liters)}} = \frac{1.10 \times 10^{-3} \text{ formula weight}}{0.90 \text{ liter}}$$

$$= 1.2 \times 10^{-3} \text{ formal} = 1.2 \times 10^{-3} \text{ F.}$$

MOLALITY

● **PROBLEM** 8-3

2.3 g of ethanol (C_2H_5OH, molecular weight = 46 g/mole) is added to 500 g of water. Determine the molality of the resulting solution.

Solution: This problem is a calculation of the molality of an aqueous solution. Molality is equal to the number of moles of solute per kilogram of solvent. In this case the solvent is water and the solute is ethanol.

Since 1 kg of water corresponds to twice the amount of water given in the problem it is desirable to calculate the amount of ethanol that would be added to 1 kg of water and still maintain the same concentration of 2.3 g ethanol per 500 g of water. For 2 × 500 g = 1000 g = 1 kg of water, we require 2 × 2.3 g = 4.6 g of ethanol.

We now know that our solution of 2.3 g ethanol in 500 g water corresponds to 4.6 g ethanol per 1 kg water, and all that remains to be done is to calculate the number of moles of ethanol in 4.6 g. We do this by dividing by the molecular weight to obtain 4.6 g/46 g/mole = 0.1 mole ethanol.

The concentration of the solution is then 0.1 mole ethanol/1 kg water = 0.1 molal.

● **PROBLEM 8-4**

Determine the mass of water to which 293 g of NaCl (formula weight = 58.5 g/mole) is added to obtain a 0.25 molal solution.

<u>Solution:</u>   To solve this problem we use the relationship

$$\text{molality} = \frac{\text{number of moles of solute}}{\text{kg of solvent}} \quad \text{or,}$$

$$\text{molality} = \frac{\text{moles of NaCl}}{\text{kg of water}} \quad .$$

The number of moles of NaCl in 293 g is determined by dividing 293 g by the formula weight of NaCl, or moles NaCl = mass NaCl/formula weight NaCl = 293 g/58.5 g/mole $\cong$ 5.0 moles NaCl. Then, solving for the kg of water,

$$\text{kg of water} = \frac{\text{moles of NaCl}}{\text{molality}} = \frac{5.0 \text{ moles NaCl}}{0.25 \text{ molal}} = 20 \text{ kg } H_2O.$$

MOLARITY

● **PROBLEM 8-5**

Calculate the molarity of a solution containing 10.0 grams of sulfuric acid in 500 ml of solution. (MW of H_2SO_4 = 98.1.)

<u>Solution:</u>   The molarity of a compound in a solution is defined as the number of moles of the compound in one liter of the solution. In this problem, one is told that there are 10.0 grams of H_2SO_4 present. One should first

calculate the number of moles that 10.0 g represents. This can be done by dividing 10.0 g by the molecular weight of H_2SO_4.

$$\text{number of moles} = \frac{\text{amount present in grams}}{\text{molecular weight}}$$

$$\text{number of moles of } H_2SO_4 = \frac{10.0 \text{ g}}{98.1 \text{ g/mole}} = 0.102 \text{ moles}$$

Since molarity is defined as the number of moles in one liter of solution, and since, one is told that there is 0.102 moles in 500 ml (½ of a liter), one should multiply the number of moles present by 2. This determines the number of moles in H_2SO_4 present in 1000 ml.

Number of moles in 1000 ml = 2 × 0.102 = 0.204.

Because molarity is defined as the number of moles in 1 liter, the molarity (M) here is 0.204 M.

Hydrogen peroxide solution for hair bleaching is usually prepared by mixing 5.0 g of hydrogen peroxide (H_2O_2, molecular weight = 34 g/mole) per 100 ml of solution. What is the molarity of this solution?

<u>Solution</u>:   Before employing the definition

$$\text{molarity} = \frac{\text{number of moles}}{\text{volume (liters)}}$$

we must convert 5.0 g of H_2O_2 to the corresponding number of moles. To do this, we use the formula

moles = mass/molecular weight.

Then,

$$\text{moles} = \frac{\text{mass}}{\text{molecular weight}}$$

$$= \frac{5.0 \text{ g}}{34 \text{ g/mole}} = 0.15 \text{ moles } H_2O_2$$

Converting 100 ml to liters, 100 ml = 100 ml × $\frac{1 \text{ liter}}{1000 \text{ ml}}$ = 0.10 liter. The molarity is then

$$\text{molarity} = \frac{\text{number of moles}}{\text{volume (liters)}} = \frac{0.15 \text{ moles}}{0.10 \text{ liters}}$$

$$= 1.5 \text{ moles/liter} = 1.5 \text{ molar} = 1.5 \text{ M}.$$

What mass of calcium bromide $CaBr_2$, is needed to prepare 150 ml of a 3.5 M solution? (M.W. of $CaBr_2$ = 200.618 g/mole)

Solution: M is the molarity of the solution and is defined as the number of moles of solute per liter. The solute is the substance being added to solution. A 1 M solution contains 1 mole of solute per liter (1000 ml) of solution.

We are asked to calculate the mass, however, no term for mass appears in the molarity equation. Therefore, a connection must be found between mass and another variable. The connection is the mole equation (moles = mass/M.W.). After substitution, the molarity equation reads

$$M = \frac{\frac{grams(mass)}{M.W.}}{liters}$$

grams = liters (M.W.)(M)

= .15ℓ (200.618 g/mole)(3.5 moles/ℓ)

= 105.32 g of $CaBr_2$.

A student has 50.00 mg crystal of $Ba(OH)_2 \cdot 8H_2O$ (M.W. = 315) and wants to make a solution of .12 M OH^-. How much water must the student add to obtain such a solution?

Solution: Molarity is defined as moles/liter. You are given the desired molarity, .12 M, and can calculate the number of moles of OH^- that would have to be present for this molarity. With these two known values, the volume (liters) can be obtained. You have 50 mg of $Ba(OH)_2 \cdot 8H_2O$ or (1 g/1000mg) 50 mg/315 g/mole = 1.59×10^{-4} moles of $Ba(OH)_2 \cdot 8H_2O$.

Now, $Ba(OH)_2 \cdot 8H_2O$ contains 2 moles of OH^-, which means that you have 3.18×10^{-4} moles of OH^- present in this crystal. Recalling, the stated definition of molarity, liters (volume) = moles/molarity. Therefore, the volume (liter) of water to be added =

$$= \frac{3.18 \times 10^{-4} \text{ moles}}{.120 \text{ moles/liter}} = 2.65 \times 10^{-3} \text{ liters}$$

or 2.65 ml total solution volume.

Determine the molarity of a 40.0% solution of HCl which has a density of 1.20 g/ml.

Solution: The molarity is defined as the number of moles of a compound present in 1 liter of solution. Here one is told that the density of this solution is 1.20 g/ml. This means that one ml of the solution weighs 1.20 g. The solution is 40.0% HCl, thus 40.0% of the 1.20 g is made up by HCl and 60% by H_2O. Here one finds the molarity of the HCl by: 1) determining the total weight of 1 liter of the solution, 2) calculating the weight of HCl present, and 3) finding the number of moles of HCl present in 1 liter (molarity).

Solving: 1) If 1 ml of this solution weight 1.20 g, 1000 ml (1 liter) is equal to 1000 × 1.20 g.

weight of solution = density × 1000 ml

$$= 1.20 \text{ g/ml} \times 1000 \text{ ml} = 1200 \text{ g}$$

2) 40.0% of this weight is taken up by HCl.

weight of HCl = weight of solution × .40

$$= 1200 \text{ g} \times .40 = 480 \text{ g}.$$

3) The molecular weight of HCl is 36.5 g/mole, thus the number of moles of HCl present in this 1 liter of solution is equal to the weight of the HCl present divided by its molecular weight.

no. of moles of HCl in 1 liter = $\dfrac{\text{weight of HCl}}{\text{MW}}$

$$= \frac{480 \text{ g}}{36.5 \text{ g/mole}} = 13.15 \text{ moles}$$

The solution is therefore 13.15 moles/liter in HCl or 13.15 M.

If 25 ml of .11 M sucrose is added to 10 ml of .52 M sucrose, what would be the resulting molarity?

Solution: In this problem one mixes two solutions of different concentrations and wishes to find the resulting molarity. The answer is obtained by first calculating the total number of moles present and then dividing this by the total volume.

Molarity is defined as moles ÷ volume. Therefore,

moles = Molarity × Volume

For the .11 M solution,

no. of moles = .11 moles/liter × .025 liter

$\qquad$ = .00275 moles

For the .52 M solution,

no. of moles = .52 moles/liter × .010 liter

$\qquad$ = .00520 moles

total no. of moles = .00275 + .00520 = .00795
total no. of liters = .025 + .010 = .035

Final Molarity = $\dfrac{.00795}{.035}$ = .23 M.

A chemist wants to dilute 50 ml of 3.50 M H_2SO_4 to 2.00 M H_2SO_4. To what volume must it be diluted?

Solution: Molarity is defined as the number of moles of solute per liter of solution. In other words,

$$\text{molarity} = \frac{\text{no. of moles of solute}}{\text{liters of solution}}.$$

In this problem you have a 50 ml solution of 3.50 M. In a liter there are 1000 ml. Thus, the number of liters in this solution is .05. Substituting, you have

$$3.50 \text{ M} = \frac{\text{no. of moles of } H_2SO_4}{.05 \text{ } \ell}$$

Solving for the number of moles, you obtain .175 moles of H_2SO_4.

When you dilute this mixture, you will still have .175 moles of the solute, H_2SO_4. You are only increasing the volume of the solvent, water. Therefore, in the diluted 2.0 M solution you wish to have

$$2.00 = \frac{.175}{\text{liters of solvent}}.$$

Solving for liters of solvent, you obtain .0875 liters or 87.5 ml. Thus, to dilute to a molarity of 2, the total volume must be 87.5 ml.

What is the mole fraction of H_2SO_4 in a 7.0 molar solution of H_2SO_4 which has a density of 1.39 g/ml?

Solution: The mole fraction of H_2SO_4 is equal to the number of moles of H_2SO_4 divided by the sum of the number of moles of H_2SO_4 and of H_2O.

$$\text{mole fraction of } H_2SO_4 = \frac{\text{moles of } H_2SO_4}{\text{moles of } H_2SO_4 + \text{moles of } H_2O}$$

Since the solution is 7.0 molar in H_2SO_4, you have 7 moles of H_2SO_4 per liter of solution. If one knows how much 7 moles of H_2SO_4 weighs, and how much one liter of the solution weighs, the weight of water can be determined by taking the difference between the quantities. The weight of one liter of the solution can be calculated by multiplying the density by the conversion factor 1000 ml/1 liter.

weight of 1 liter of the solution

$$= 1.39 \text{ g/ml} \times 1000 \text{ ml/liter} = 1390 \text{ g/}\ell.$$

weight of the water in a one liter solution

$$= \text{weight of the total solution}$$
$$- \text{ weight of 7 moles of } H_2SO_4$$

7 moles of H_2SO_4 weigh 7 times the molecular weight of H_2SO_4.

weight of 7 moles of H_2SO_4 = 7 × 98 g = 686 g.

Hence, weight of the water = 1390 g - 686 g = 704 g.

The number of moles of H_2O is found by dividing its weight by the molecular weight of H_2O.

$$\text{no. of moles of } H_2O = \frac{704 \text{ g}}{18 \text{ g/mol}} = 39 \text{ moles}$$

The number of moles of both components of the system is now known, therefore, the mole fraction of H_2SO_4 can be obtained.

$$\text{mole fraction } H_2SO_4 = \frac{\text{moles of } H_2SO_4}{\text{moles of } H_2SO_4 + \text{moles of } H_2O}$$

$$\text{mole fraction of } H_2SO_4 = \frac{7}{7 + 39} = 0.15.$$

You have 100-proof (50 percent alcohol by volume) bonded
Scotch whisky. Calculate its molarity, mole fraction,
and molality. If the temperature were to drop to - 10°C,
could you still drink the Scotch? Assume density =
.79 g/ml for ethyl alcohol (C_2H_5OH) and K_f = 1.86°C/m
for water.

Solution: To find molarity, mole fraction, and molality,
you need to know how many moles of alcohol are present in
the whiskey. You can obtain this from a calculation using
the density.

To find whether you can still drink the whisky at
- 10°C, requires you to know its freezing point, since
you cannot drink something if it is frozen. You can determine the freezing point of the Scotch by determining the
freezing point depression of the water containing the
alcohol. This is found from $\Delta T_f = K_f m$, where ΔT_f = the
depression, K_f = freezing point depression constant, and
m = molality.

You now proceed as follows:

You are told that 100 proof means 50 percent alcohol
by volume. This means that 1 liter of components possess
500 cm^3 of ethyl alcohol (a liter = 1000 cm^3). Density =
mass/volume. You know the density and volume, so that
mass of alcohol = density × volume = .79(500) = 395 g.

Molecular wt. of the alcohol = 46.07 g. Thus, you
have 395/46.07 = 8.57 moles of alcohol. Hence,

$$\text{molarity} = \frac{\text{moles of solute}}{\text{liters of solution}} = \frac{8.57}{1} = 8.57 \text{ M.}$$

$$\text{Molality} = \frac{\text{moles of solute}}{\text{kilograms of solvent}} \cdot$$

To find the number of grams of solvent, you need to use the
density again. In 1 liter of Scotch Whisky, you have 500 cm^3
of water. Density of water = 1 g/cm^3.

Thus, mass of water = 500 cm^3(1 g/cm^3) = 500 grams. Thus,

$$\text{Molality} = \frac{8.57}{\frac{500}{1000}} = 17.14 \text{ m}$$

You divided 500 by 1000 since molality is moles per
1000 g of solvent.

Mole fraction: (MW of H_2O = 18.) moles of H_2O = 500 g/18.0 g/mole.

Mole fraction of ethyl alcohol =

$$\frac{\text{moles ethyl alcohol}}{\text{moles ethyl alcohol + moles } H_2O} = \frac{8.57}{8.57 + \frac{500}{18}} = .2357.$$

Now, you answer whether the scotch can be consumed at - 10°C. You already calculated the molality. Thus, ΔT_f = k_f m = (1.86)(17.14) = 31.88°C. Thus, the freezing point of whisky is 0°C - 31.88°C = - 31.88°C. The temperature is only - 10°C, however. This means whisky is still a liquid and can be consumed.

NORMALITY

● **PROBLEM** 8-14

Calculate the normality of a solution containing 2.45 g of sulfuric acid in 2.00 liters of solution. (MW of H_2SO_4 = 98.1.)

<u>Solution</u>:   Normality is defined by the following equation.

$$\text{Normality} = \frac{\text{grams of solute}}{\text{equivalent weight} \times \text{liters of solution}}$$

In this problem, one is given the grams of solute (H_2SO_4) present and the number of liters of solution it is dissolved in. One equivalent of a substance is the weight in which the acid contains one gram atom of re-placeable hydrogen. This means that when the acid is dissolved in a solution, and it ionizes, that in one equivalent weight, one hydrogen atom is released. The equivalent weight for acids is defined as:

$$\text{equivalent weight} = \frac{MW}{\text{no. of replaceable H}}$$

When H_2SO_4 is dissolved in a solution, there are two replaceable H as shown in the following equation:

$$H_2SO_4 \overset{\leftarrow}{\rightarrow} 2H^+ + SO_4^=$$

This means that in calculating the equivalent weight for H_2SO_4 the molecular weight is divided by 2.

equivalent weight of H_2SO_4 = $\dfrac{98.1 \text{ g}}{2 \text{ equivalents}}$

$$= 49 \text{ g/equiv}$$

The normality can now be calculated.

Normality = $\dfrac{\text{grams of solute}}{\text{equiv. wt} \times \text{liters of soln}}$

Normality = $\dfrac{2.45 \text{ g}}{49 \text{ g/equiv} \times 2.0 \text{ liters}}$

$$= 0.025 \text{ equiv/liter.}$$

● **PROBLEM** 8-15

How many grams of sulfuric acid are contained in 3.00 liters of 0.500 N solution? (MW of H_2SO_4 = 98.1.)

Solution: The number of grams of sulfuric acid contained in this solution can be determined by using the definition of normality.

Normality = $\dfrac{\text{grams of solute}}{\text{equivalent weight} \times \text{liters of solution}}$

Here, one is given the normality (N) and the number of liters of solution. The equivalent weight for an acid is the molecular weight divided by the number of replaceable hydrogens,

equivalent weight = $\dfrac{\text{MW}}{\text{no. of replaceable H}}$

The number of replaceable hydrogens is determined by the number of hydrogens that will ionize when the acid is placed in solution. This number is 2 for H_2SO_4, as shown in the following equation:

$$H_2SO_4 \rightleftharpoons 2H^+ + SO_4^=$$

Once the number of replaceable hydrogen is known, the equivalent weight can be found.

equivalent weight = $\dfrac{\text{MW}}{\text{no. of replaceable H}}$

equivalent weight of H_2SO_4 = $\dfrac{98.1 \text{ g}}{2 \text{ equiv}}$ = 49 g/equiv.

At this point the number of grams of solute can be determined.

grams of solute = Normality × equiv weight × liters of
                                              solution

grams of H_2SO_4 = 0.500 equiv/ℓ × 49 g/equiv × 3.0 liter

                  = 73.5 g.

Calculate the normality of a solution 40 ml of which is
required to neutralize 0.56 g of KOH.

<u>Solution</u>:   KOH ionizes as shown in this equation.

$$KOH \overset{\leftarrow}{\rightarrow} K^+ + OH^-$$

    This means that for each KOH molecule ionized, one
OH^- ion is formed. Thus to neutralize the KOH one must
have 1 H^+ ion for each OH^- ion. Thus, one must first
determine the number of moles of KOH present in 0.56 g.
This is done by dividing 0.56 g by the molecular weight
of KOH (MW of KOH = 56)

number of moles of KOH = number of moles of OH^-

number of moles of KOH = $\dfrac{0.56 \text{ g}}{\text{MW}}$ = $\dfrac{0.56 \text{ g}}{56 \text{ g/mole}}$ = .01 mole

    Therefore, in the 40 ml of the solution there must
be .01 moles of H^+ ions. The normality of an acid is
defined as the number of equivalents of H^+ in 1 liter of
solution. An equivalent may be defined as the weight of
acid or base that produces 1 mole of H^+ or OH^- ions. In
this problem, equivalents = moles. There are 1000 ml in
1 liter, thus in 40 ml there are

40 ml × $\dfrac{1 \text{ liter}}{1000 \text{ ml}}$

number of liters = 40 ml × $\dfrac{1 \text{ liter}}{1000 \text{ ml}}$ = .04 liters.

    The normality can now be found.

normality = $\dfrac{\text{number of equivalents}}{\text{number of liters}}$

= $\dfrac{.01 \text{ equivalents}}{.04 \text{ liters}}$ = .25 N.

If 20 ml of 0.5 N salt solution is diluted to 1 liter, what is the new concentration?

Solution: When considering normality one must always keep in mind that it is a concentration defined as the number of equivalents per liter. Since the number of equivalents does not change during dilution, equivalents before dilution = equivalents after dilution, or in other words,

$$N_1 V_1 = N_2 V_2 \qquad 1 \text{ liter} = 1000 \text{ ml}$$

where N_1 is the normality of the initial solution, V_1 the initial volume, N_2 the final normality and V_2 is final volume.

Solving for the final normality:

$$(0.5)(0.020\ell) = N_2 (1\ell)$$

$$N_2 = \frac{(0.5)(0.020\ell)}{1 \ell}$$

$$= 0.01 \text{ N}$$

A sulfuric acid solution has a density of 1.8 g/ml and is 90% H_2SO_4 by weight. What weight of H_2SO_4 is present in 1000 ml of the solution? What is the molarity of the solution? the normality?

Solution: 1) Here one is asked to find the weight of H_2SO_4 in 1000 ml of the solution and told that the solution weighs 1.8 g/ml and that 90% of this weight is made up by H_2SO_4. The total weight of the solution is 1000 ml times the weight of one ml.

Hence, weight of solution = 1000 ml × 1.8 g/ml = 1800 g. H_2SO_4 makes up 90% of this weight.

weight of H_2SO_4 = .90 × weight of solution

$$= .90 \times 1800 \text{ g} = 1620 \text{ g}.$$

2) The molarity is defined as the number of moles in one liter of solution. One has already found that 1620 g of H_2SO_4 is present in 1 liter of the solution. Thus, to calculate molarity, one should determine the number of moles present in 1620 g. This is done by dividing 1620 g by the molecular weight of H_2SO_4. (MW

of $H_2SO_4 = 98.1$.)

$$\text{moles of } H_2SO_4 \text{ present} = \frac{1620 \text{ g}}{98.1 \text{ g/mole}} = 16.5 \text{ moles}$$

Since there is 1 liter of solution, the molarity of H_2SO_4 is 16.5 M.

3) The normality is defined as the number of moles of ionizable hydrogens per liter of solution. From the following equation one can see that there are 2 ionizable hydrogens for each molecule of H_2SO_4.

$$H_2SO_4 \rightleftharpoons 2H^+ + SO_4^=$$

Therefore if there are 16.5 moles of H_2SO_4 in one liter of the solution the normality is twice this amount.

normality of an acid = no. of ionizable H × molarity

$$= 2 \times 16.5 = 33.0 \text{ N.}$$

● **PROBLEM** 8-19

A solution is prepared by dissolving 464 g NaOH in water and then diluting to one liter. The density of the resulting solution is 1.37 g/ml. Express the concentration of NaOH as (a) percentage by weight, (b) molarity, (c) normality, (d) molality, (e) mole fraction.

Solution: (a) The percentage by weight of NaOH in this solution is found by dividing the weight of NaOH present, 464 g, by the weight of the solution and multiplying by 100. The weight of the solution is found by using the density of the solution. The density, 1.37 g/ml, tells the weight of 1 ml of solution, namely, 1.37 g. In one liter, there are 1000 ml, thus the weight of the solution is 1000 times the weight of one ml.

weight of 1 liter = 1000 ml × 1.37 g/ml = 1370 g.

The percentage by weight of the NaOH in the solution can now be found.

$$\text{percentage of NaOH} = \frac{\text{weight of NaOH}}{\text{weight of solution}} \times 100$$

$$= \frac{464 \text{ g}}{1370 \text{ g}} \times 100 = 33.9 \text{ \%.}$$

(b) The molarity is defined as the number of moles in one liter of solution. The molarity in this case can be found by determining the number of moles in 464 g of

162

NaOH, which is the amount of NaOH in one liter. The number of moles can be found by dividing 464 g by the molecular weight of NaOH. (MW of NaOH = 40.)

$$\text{no. of moles} = \frac{464 \text{ g}}{MW} = \frac{464 \text{ g}}{40 \text{ g/mole}} = 11.6 \text{ moles}.$$

The molarity of this solution is thus $11.6\,M$.

(c) The normality of a basic solution is the number of moles of ionizable OH^- ions in one liter of solution. There is one ionizable OH^- ion in each NaOH as shown by the equation:

$$NaOH \; \rightleftharpoons \; Na^+ + OH^-$$

Therefore, there are the same number of OH^- ions in the solution as NaOH molecules dissolved. Thus, the molarity equals the normality.

normality = molarity × 1 ionizable OH^-

normality = 11.6 N

(d) The molality is defined as the number of moles present in 1 kg of solvent. One has already found that the solution weighs 1370 g or 1.37 kg and that there are 11.6 moles of NaOH present. Therefore the molality can now be found.

$$\text{molality} = \frac{\text{no. of moles present}}{\text{no. of kg present}}$$

$$= \frac{11.6 \text{ moles}}{1.37 \text{ kg} = .339(1.370 \text{ kg})} = 12.8 \text{ m}$$

(e) The mole fraction is equal to the number of moles of each component divided by the total number of moles in the system. The components in this system are H_2O and NaOH. One already has found that there are 11.6 moles of NaOH present, but not the number of moles of H_2O. This can be found by determining the weight of the water and dividing it by its molecular weight. This solution weighs 1370 g, the NaOH weighs 464 g, thus the weight of the water is equal to the difference of these two figures,

weight of H_2O = weight of solution − weight of NaOH

= 1370 g − 464 g = 906 g.

One can now find the number of moles of H_2O present. (MW of H_2O = 18.)

$$\text{no. of moles} = \frac{906 \text{ g}}{18 \text{ g/mole}} = 50.3 \text{ moles}$$

The total number of moles in the system is the sum of the number of moles of H_2O and of the NaOH.

no. of moles in system = moles H_2O + moles NaOH

$$= 50.3 + 11.6 = 61.9 \text{ moles}$$

One can now find the mole fractions.

mole fraction = $\dfrac{\text{no. of moles of each component}}{\text{total no. of moles in system}}$

mole fraction of H_2O = $\dfrac{50.3}{61.9}$ = .81

mole fraction of NaOH = $\dfrac{11.6}{61.9}$ = .19.

NEUTRALIZATION

● **PROBLEM** 8-20

A mixture consisting only of KOH and $Ca(OH)_2$ is neutralized by acid. If it takes exactly 0.100 equivalents to neutralize 4.221 g of the mixture, what must have been its initial composition by weight?

Solution: One equivalent of an acid is the mass of acid required to furnish one mole of H_3O^+; one equivalent of a base is the mass of base required to furnish one mole of OH^- or to accept one mole of H_3O^+. Here one must find the mixture of KOH and $Ca(OH)_2$ that contains 0.100 equivalent of base. There is one equivalent for each OH^- in a molecule of base. Thus, there is 1 equivalent of base for each KOH. There are two for each $Ca(OH)_2$. Since one is given that there are 0.100 equivalent in 4.221 g of the mixture, one should solve for the equivalent per gram for KOH and $Ca(OH)_2$.

for KOH: MW = 56.1   equiv = 1

$\dfrac{\text{equiv}}{g} = \dfrac{1}{56.1} = 1.78 \times 10^{-2}$ equiv/g

For $Ca(OH)_2$ MW = 74.06   equiv = 2

$\dfrac{\text{equiv}}{g} = \dfrac{2}{74.06} = 2.70 \times 10^{-2}$ equiv/g.

There must be 0.100 equiv present. Let

x = number of grams of KOH

4.221 - x = number of grams of $Ca(OH)_2$

$$0.100 equiv. = \left(1.78 \times 10^{-2} \frac{equiv}{g}\right)(x) + \left(2.70 \times 10^{-2} \frac{equiv}{g}\right)x$$

$$(4.221 - x)$$

$$0.100 equiv. = 0.0178x \frac{equiv}{g} + .114\ equiv - .0270x \frac{equiv}{g}$$

$$0.100 equiv. = - .0092x \frac{equiv}{g} + .114\ equiv$$

$$-.014 equiv. = - .0092x \frac{equiv}{g}$$

$$\frac{- .014\ equiv}{- .0092\ equiv/g} = x$$

$$1.52\ g = x$$

$$2.701\ g = 4.221 - x$$

The original mixture contains 1.52 g KOH and 2.701 g $Ca(OH)_2$.

● **PROBLEM** 8-21

Calculate the volume of 0.3 N base necessary to neutralize 3 liters of 0.01 N nitric acid.

Solution: For neutralization to occur, there must be the same number of hydrogen ions as there are hydroxide ions. This is shown by the following equation

$$H^+ + OH^- \rightleftarrows H_2O$$

The H^+ ions come from the acid, the OH^- ions from the base. The number of H^+ and OH^- ions are equal to the number of equivalents.

Normality is defined as the number of equivalents of acid or base per liter of solution.

$$Normality = \frac{equivalents}{liter}$$

An equivalent is the number of grams of the acid or base multiplied by the number of replaceable hydrogens or hydroxides divided by the molecular weight of the acid or base.

$$\text{equivalent} = \frac{\text{grams of solute} \times \text{no. of replaceable H or OH}}{\text{MW of solute}}$$

The number of replaceable hydrogens or hydrodixes is defined as the number which ionize when the compound is placed in solution. For nitric acid, there is one replaceable hydrogen

$$HNO_3 \overset{\leftarrow}{\rightarrow} H^+ + NO_3^-$$

In brief, for neutralization there must be the same equivalent amount of base as there is acid. Because normality is defined as

$$\text{Normality} = \frac{\text{equivalents}}{\text{liters}}$$

equivalents are equal to the normality times the volume. Thus, the normality of the base times its volume equals the normality of the acid times its volume.

$$N_{base} \, V_{base} = N_{acid} \, V_{acid},$$

where N is the normality and V is the volume.

Here, $0.3 \text{ equiv/liter} \times V_{base} = 0.01 \text{ equiv/liter} \times 3 \text{ liters}$

$$V_{base} = \frac{0.01 \times 3 \text{ liters}}{0.3}$$

$$= 0.1 \text{ liter or } 100 \text{ M.}$$

● **PROBLEM** 8-22

What weight of $Ca(OH)_2$, calcium hydroxide is needed to neutralize 28.0 g of HCl. What weight of phosphoric acid would this weight of $Ca(OH)_2$ neutralize?

Solution: When we have neutralization problems, i.e., those where an acid reacts with a base, we must consider the meaning of equivalents. Equivalent weight may be defined as the molecular weight of a substance (grams/mole) divided by the number of protons (H^+) or hydroxyl (OH^-) ions available for reaction. In other words,

$$\text{Equivalent weight} = \frac{\text{molecular weight}}{\text{number of } H^+ \text{ or } OH^-}.$$

In a neutralization reaction, the number of equivalents of acid equals the number of equivalents of base.

The number of equivalents of acid and base are equal, thus, if we can calculate the number of equivalents of 1 reactant, we automatically know the number of equivalents present of the other reactant. To find this quantity use the equation

$$\text{no. of equivalents} = \frac{\text{grams}}{\text{grams/equivalent}}$$

The equivalent weight of HCl is

$$\frac{\text{M.W.}}{\text{no. of } H^+(OH^-)} = \frac{36.5}{1} = 36.5 \quad \text{and Ca(OH)}_2 \text{ is } \frac{74.1}{2} =$$

37 g/equiv.

$$\text{no. of equivalents HCl present} = \frac{28 \text{ g}}{36.5 \text{ g/equiv}} = .767$$

Therefore, there are also .767 equivalents of $Ca(OH)_2$. To find the grams of $Ca(OH)_2$ needed use

$$\text{no. of equiv} = \frac{\text{grams Ca(OH)}_2}{\text{grams/equiv}}$$

$$.767 = \frac{\text{grams}}{37}$$

grams $Ca(OH)_2$ = 28.4 need to neutralize 28 g of HCl.

The second half of the problem is answered in exactly the same way. We know then that there must also be .767 equiv of H_3PO_4 (phosphoric acid) present due to the fact .767 equiv of base $Ca(OH)_2$ is present. Recall, equivalents of an acid must equal the equivalents of a base for neutralization to occur. The M.W. of H_3PO_4 = 98.0 g, which yields a value of $\frac{98}{3}$ = 32.7 grams per equiv. Therefore,

$$\text{No. of equiv} = \frac{\text{grams } H_3PO_4}{\text{grams/equiv}}$$

$$.767 = \frac{\text{grams}}{32.7}$$

grams H_3PO_4 = 25.1 g needed to neutralize 28.4 g of $Ca(OH)_2$.

CHAPTER 9

EQUILIBRIUM

THE EQUILIBRIUM CONSTANT

Determine the equilibrium constant for the reaction
$H_2+I_2 \rightleftharpoons 2HI$ if the equilibrium concentrations are:
H_2, 0.9 moles/liter; I_2, 0.4 mole/liter; HI, 0.6 mole/liter.

Solution: The equilibrium constant (Keq) is defined as
the product of the concentrations of the products divided
by the product of the concentrations of the reactants.
These concentrations are brought to the power of the
stoichiometric coefficient of that component. For
example for the reaction $2A + B \rightleftharpoons 3C$ the equilibrium
constant can be expressed:

$$Keq = \frac{[C]^3}{[A]^2[B]}$$

where [] indicates concentration.

One can now express the equilibrium constant for the
reaction $H_2+I_2 \rightleftharpoons 2HI$ as

$$Keq = \frac{[HI]^2}{[H_2][I_2]}$$

One is given the concentrations of the components
for the system, thus one can solve for the equilibrium
constant.

$$Keq = \frac{[HI]^2}{[H_2][I_2]}$$

$[H_2]$ = 0.9 mole/liter

$[I_2]$ = 0.4 mole/liter

$[HI]$ = 0.6 mole/liter

168

$$Keq = \frac{[0.6 \text{ mole/liter}]^2}{[0.9 \text{ moles/liter}][0.4 \text{ moles/liter}]}$$

$$= \frac{0.36}{0.36} = 1.0$$

● **PROBLEM** 9-2

Given the reaction $A + B \rightleftarrows C + D$, find the equilibrium constant for this reaction if .7 moles of C are formed when 1 mole of A and 1 mole of B are initially present. For this same equilibrium, find the equilibrium composition when 1 mole each of A, B, C, and D are initially present.

Solution: In general, an equilibrium constant measures the ratio of the concentrations of products to reactants, each raised to the power of their respective coefficients in the chemical equation. Thus, for this reaction, the equilibrium constant, K, is equal to

$$\frac{[C][D]}{[A][B]} \quad .$$

You are asked to find K in the first part of this problem. Therefore, you must evaluate this expression. To do this, use stoichiometry. From the equation for the chemical reaction, you see that all the quantities are in equimolar amounts; 1:1:1:1 . It is given that .7 moles of C is produced. This means, therefore, that .7 mole of D must also be produced. If the equimolar quantities are to be maintained, then, .7 mole of each A and B must have been consumed. If you started 1with 1 mole of each, then .3 mole must be left. These mole amounts are the concentrations if you assume they are in a given amount of volume. Thus, substituting these values in

$$K = \frac{[C][D]}{[A][B]} \quad ,$$

you obtain

$$K = \frac{(.7)^2}{(.3)^2} = 5.44 \quad .$$

Therefore, you have calculated the equilibrium constant of this reaction to be 5.44.

The second part of this problem asks you to use this same equilibrium for a reaction that starts with 1 mole each of A, B, C, and D. To find its composition, determine the concentration of each species at equilibrium. This can be found from

$$K = \frac{[C][D]}{[A][B]} = 5.44 \quad .$$

To find the composition, assume X moles/liter (concentration) react. Thus, at equilibrium, both C and D have a final concentration of $1 + x$, since you started with 1 mole/liter and had x moles/liter of each produced. This means, therefore, that A's and B's initial concentration must be reduced by x moles/liter to $1 - x$. Substituting,

$$5.44 = \frac{(1+x)^2}{(1-x)^2} \quad .$$

Solving,

$$x = .40 \text{ moles/liter} \quad .$$

Thus, the concentration of both A and B = $1 - .4 = .6M$ and of both C and D = $1 + .4 = 1.4M$.

At a certain temperature, K_{eq} for the reaction $3C_2H_2 \underset{\leftarrow}{\rightarrow} C_6H_6$ is 4. If the equilibrium concentration of C_2H_2 is 0.5 mole/liter, what is the concentration of C_6H_6 ?

Solution: The equilibrium constant (Keq) for this reaction is stated:

$$K_{eq} = \frac{[C_6H_6]}{[C_2H_2]^3}$$

where [ ] indicate concentration. The $[C_2H_2]$ is brought to the third power because three moles of it react. Equilibrium is defined as the point where no more product is formed and no more reactant is dissipated; thus their concentrations remain constant. Here, one is given K_{eq} and $[C_2H_2]$ and asked to find $[C_6H_6]$. This can be done by substituting the given into the equation for the equilibrium constant.

$$K_{eq} = \frac{[C_6H_6]}{[C_2H_2]^3} \qquad \begin{array}{l} K_{eq} = 4 \\[4pt] [C_2H_2] = 0.5 \text{ moles/liter} \end{array}$$

$$4 = \frac{[C_6H_6]}{(0.5)^3}$$

$$[C_6H_6] = (0.5)^3 \times 4 = 0.5 \text{ moles/liter .}$$

The following reaction

$$2H_2S(g) \underset{\leftarrow}{\rightarrow} 2H_2(g) + S_2(g)$$

was allowed to proceed to equilibrium. The contents of the two-liter reaction vessel were then subjected to analysis and found to contain 1.0 mole H_2S, 0.20 mole H_2, and 0.80 mole S_2. What is the equilibrium constant K for this reaction?

Solution: This problem involves substitution into the equilibrium constant expression for this reaction,

$$K = \frac{[H_2]^2 [S_2]}{[H_2S]^2} \qquad .$$

The equilibrium concentration of the reactant and products are $[H_2S] = 1.0$ mole/2 liters $= 0.50$ M, $[H_2] = 0.20$ mole/2 liters $= 0.10$M, and $[S_2] = 0.80$ mole/2 liters $= 0.40$M, Hence, the value of the equilibrium constant is

$$K = \frac{[H_2]^2 [S_2]}{[H_2S]^2} = \frac{(0.10)^2(0.40)}{(0.50)^2} = 0.016$$

for this reaction.

EQUILIBRIUM CALCULATIONS

At 986°C, you have the following equilibrium:
$$CO_2(g) + H_2(g) \rightleftharpoons CO(g) + H_2O(g) .$$
Initially, 49.3 mole percent CO_2 is mixed with 50.7 mole per cent H_2 . At equilibrium, you find 21.4 mole percent CO_2 , 22.8 mole percent H_2 , and 27.9 mole percent of CO and H_2O . Find K. If you start with a mole percent ratio of 60:40, CO_2 to H_2 , find the equilibrium concentrations of both reactants and products.

Solution: An equilibrium constant K_{eq} measures the ratio of the concentrations of products to reactants, each raised to the power of their respective coefficients in the chemical equation. Thus, K_{eq} for this reaction =
$$\frac{[CO][H_2O]}{[CO_2][H_2]} .$$

If you assume each substance occupies the same volume in liters, the concentration can be expressed in moles because concentration = moles/liter , i.e., liters cancel out of the equilibrium constant expression. Thus, to find K , you need to find the number of moles of each of the products and reactants and then to substitute into the equilibrium expression. You are told the final product mole percents. The reactants, then, at equilibrium, have mole percents that equal their initial amounts minus the amount that decomposed to produce the products.

Thus, at equilibrium, $[CO_2]$ = 49.3 - 21.4 = 27.9, which was given. Similarily $[H_2]$ = 50.7 - 22.8 = 27.9, which was given. Thus, by substitution into

$$K = \frac{[CO][H_2O]}{[CO_2][H_2]} , \text{ you obtain } K = \frac{(.279)(.279)}{(.214)(.228)} = 1.60 ,$$

which is the equilibrium constant for this reaction.

The second part follows. You begin with a 60:40 ratio of $CO_2:H_2$, which means that initially you have .600 moles CO_2 and .400 moles H_2 . To find the equilibrium concentrations, let x = moles of CO formed. Thus, x = moles H_2O formed since coefficients tell us they are formed in equimolar amounts. The fact that moles of a product form, means that x moles of a reactant must have decomposed. Thus, at equilibrium, you have 0.600-x moles of CO_2 and 0.400-x moles of H_2 . Recalling,

$$K = \frac{[CO][H_2O]}{[CO_2][H_2]} \quad ,$$

you can now substitute these values to give $K = \frac{x^2}{(0.6-x)(0.4-x)}$.
From previous part, K = 1.60, therefore,

$$1.60 = \frac{x^2}{(0.6-x)(0.4-x)} \quad .$$

Solving, x = 0.267 . Thus, [CO] = [H_2O] = x = 0.267M, [CO_2] = 0.6-x = 0.333M and [H_2] = 0.4-x = 0.133M .

● **PROBLEM** 9-6

A chemist mixes nitric oxide and bromine to form nitrosyl bromide at 298° K, according to the equation $2NO_{(g)} + Br_{2(g)} \rightleftarrows$ $2NOBr_{(g)}$. Assuming K = 100, what is the quantity of nitrosyl bromide formed, if the reactants are at an initial pressure of 1 atm? R = 0.0821 liter-atm./mole° K .

<u>Solution</u>: You are given the equilibrium constant for this reaction and asked to calculate the quantity of nitrosyl bromide produced. The first step is to write out the equilibrium expression and equate it with the given value. For the general reaction,

$$xA + yB \rightarrow zC , \quad \text{K is defined} \quad \frac{[C]^2}{[B]^y[A]^x} \quad ,$$

where the brackets represent concentrations. For this reaction,

$$K = \frac{[NOBr]^2}{[NO]^2[Br_2]} = 100 \quad .$$

To find out how much NOBr is produced, you would have to know how many moles of NO and Br_2 were reacted. Once this is known, you can find the number of grams produced. You know that the equilibrium expression is based on concentration of reactants and products. Concentration is expressed in moles per liter. This means that if the volume of the NOBr and its concentration is known, you can find moles, since concentration X volume (liters) = moles. Let us represent the concentration as

$$\frac{N}{V} = \frac{moles}{Volume} \quad .$$

Thus, the equilibrium expression becomes

$$K = \frac{(N_{NOBr}/V)^2}{(N_{NO}/V)^2(N_{Br_2}/V)} \quad .$$

Let x = moles of NOBr formed. Then, x moles of NO and x/2 moles of Br_2 are consumed, since the coefficients of the reaction show a 2:2:1 ratio among NOBr:NO:Br_2. The equilibrium expression becomes

$$100 = \frac{N_{NOBr}^2 \, V}{N_{NO}^2 \, N_{Br_2}} = \frac{x^2 V}{(2-x)^2 (1-.5x)} \quad .$$

If x moles of NOBr form, and you started with 2 moles of NO, then, at equilibrium, you have left 2-x moles of NO . You started with only 1 mole of Br_2 and ½x moles of it form NOBr; thus you have 1-.5x moles left. Therefore, you need to determine only the volume to find the quantity NOBr formed. V can be found from the equation of state, PV = NRT , where P = pressure, V = volume, N = moles, R = universal gas constant, and T = temperature in kelvin (celsius plus 273°). You are told that the reactants are under a pressure of 1 atm. at 298° K . N = 3, since the coefficients inform you that a relative sum of 3 moles of reagents exist. You know R. Thus,

$$V = \frac{NRT}{P} = \frac{(3)(.0821)(298)}{1} = 73.4 \text{ liters } .$$

Now that V is known, the equilibrium expression becomes

$$\frac{x^2 (73.4)}{(2-x)^2 (1-0.5x)} = 100 \quad .$$

Solving for x, you obtain x = .923 moles = moles of NOBr formed. Molecular weight = 110. Grams produced = .923 × 110 = 101.53g.

● **PROBLEM** 9-7

> Two moles of gaseous NH_3 are introduced into a 1.0-liter vessel and allowed to undergo partial decomposition at high temperature according to the reaction
>
> $$2NH_3(g) \; \rightleftarrows \; N_2(g) + 3H_2(g) \; .$$
>
> At equilibrium, 1.0 mole of $NH_3(g)$ remains. What is the value of the equilibrium constant?

Solution: This problem involves substitution into the expression for the equilibrium constant for this reaction,

$$K = \frac{[N_2] \, [H_2]^3}{[NH_3]^2}$$

Since 1.0 mole of NH_3 remains, 2.0 - 1.0 = 1.0 mole of NH_3 was consumed. Also, since one mole of N_2 and three moles of H_2 are formed per 2 moles NH_3 consumed, at equilibrium, there are 3/2 moles of H_2 and 1/2 mole of N_2 . The equilibrium concentrations are therefore $[NH_3]$ = 1.0 mole/1.0 liter = 1.0m, $[N_2]$ = (1/2 mole)/(1.0 liter) = 0.5M, and $[H_2]$ = (3/2 moles)/(1.0 liter) = 1.5M.

Substituting these into the expression for K gives

$$K = \frac{[N_2][H_2]^3}{[NH_3]^2} = \frac{(0.5)(1.5)^3}{(1)^2}$$

$$= 1.6875 \quad .$$

For the reaction

$$CO_2(g) + H_2(g) \rightleftarrows CO(g) + H_2O(g),$$

the value of the equilibrium constant at $825°K$ is 0.137. If 5.0 moles of CO_2, 5.0 moles of H_2, 1.0 mole of CO, and 1.0 mole of H_2O are initially present, what is the composition of the equilibrium mixture?

Solution: This problem is an application of the expression for the equilibrium constant.

From the stoichiometry of the reaction, one mole of CO and one mole of H_2O are produced for one mole of CO_2 and one mole of H_2O that are reacted. Hence, if x moles of CO are produced at equilibrium, then x moles of H_2O are produced, x moles of CO_2 are consumed, and x moles of H_2 are consumed. Therefore, at equilibrium, there are $1+x$ moles of CO, $1+x$ moles of H_2O, $5-x$ moles of CO, and $5-x$ moles of H_2. If we let v denote the volume of the reaction vessel, the equilibrium concentrations are

$$[CO] = [H_2O] = (1+x)/v, \quad \text{and} \quad [CO_2] = [H_2] = (5-x)/v \ .$$

Substituting these values into the expression for the equilibrium constant gives

$$K = 0.137 = \frac{[CO][H_2O]}{[CO_2][H_2]} = \frac{[(1+x)/v][(1+x)/v]}{[(5-x)/v][(5-x)/v]} = \frac{(1+x)^2 v^2}{(5-x)^2 v^2} = \frac{1+2x+x^2}{25-10x+x^2} \ ,$$

or

$$0.137(25) - 0.137(10)x + 0.137x^2 = 1+2x+x^2$$

$$0.863x^2 + 3.370x - 2.425 = 0 \ .$$

Using the quadratic equation,

$$x = \frac{-3.370 \pm \sqrt{(3.370)^2 - 4(0.863)(-2.425)}}{2(0.863)}$$

or

$$x = 0.62 \ , \quad x = -4.52 \ .$$

The second of these is nonphysical and is therefore discarded.

The equilibrium concentrations are then

$$[CO] = 1+x = 1+0.62 = 1.62 \text{ moles}$$

$$[H_2O] = 1+x = 1+0.62 = 1.62 \text{ moles}$$

$$[CO_2] = 5-x = 5-0.62 = 4.38 \text{ moles}$$

$$[H_2] = 5-x = 5-0.62 = 4.38 \text{ moles.}$$

For the reaction

$$2HI(g) \rightleftarrows H_2(g) + I_2(g) \ ,$$

the value of the equilibrium constant at 700K is 0.0183. If 3.0 moles of HI are placed in a 5-liter vessel and allowed to decompose according to the above equation, what percentage of the original HI would remain undissociated at equilibrium?

Solution: This problem is an application of the equilibrium expression

$$K = \frac{[H_2] \ [I_2]}{[HI]^2} \ .$$

Since two moles of HI are involved in the production of one mole of H_2 and one mole of I_2 , if x moles of H_2 (and therefore x moles of I_2) are present at equilibrium, then 2x moles of HI have been consumed and 3-2x moles of HI remain. Therefore, at equilibrium, $[H_2] = [I_2] = $ x moles/ 5 liters and [HI] =

(3-2x) moles/5 liters.

Substituting these into the expression for K gives

$$K = 0.0183 = \frac{[H_2] \ [I_2]}{[HI]^2} = \frac{(x/5)(x/5)}{[(3-2x)/5]^2} = \frac{x^2}{(3-2x)^2} \times \frac{5^2}{5^2}$$

$$= \frac{x^2}{(3-2x)^2} = \frac{x^2}{9-12x + 4x^2} \ ,$$

or

$$9(0.0183) - 12(0.0183)x + 4(0.0183)x^2 = x^2$$

$$0.9268x^2 + 0.2196x - 0.1647 = 0 \ .$$

Using the quadratic formula,

$$x = \frac{-0.2196 \pm \sqrt{(0.2196)^2 - 4(0.9268)(-0.1647)}}{2(0.9268)}$$

or

x = -0.56, x = 0.32 .

Since negative moles are a nonphysical entity, the first answer is discarded and the second retained.

Thus, at equilibrium,

$$[H_2] = x = 0.32 \text{ mole}$$

$$[I_2] = x = 0.32 \text{ mole}$$

$$[HI] = 3-2x = 3-2(0.32) = 2.36 \text{ moles.}$$

Given the equilibria $H_2S + H_2O \rightleftarrows H_3O^+ + HS^-$ and $HS^- + H_2O \rightleftarrows H_3O^+ + S^{-2}$, find the final concentration of S^{-2}, if the final concentrations of H_3O^+ and H_2S are 0.3 M and 0.1 M, respectively.

$k_1 = 6.3 \times 10^{-8}$ for $H_2S + H_2O \rightleftarrows H_3O^+ + HS^-$ and

$k_2 = 1 \times 10^{-14}$ for $HS^- + H_2O \rightleftarrows H_3O^+ + S^{-2}$.

Solution: This problem can be solved by writing the equilibrium constant expressions for the equilibria. These expressions give the ratio of the concentrations of products to reactants, each raised to the power of its coefficient in the equilibrium equation.

Therefore, for $H_2S + H_2O \rightleftarrows H_3O^+ + HS^-$, we can write

$$k_1 = 6.3 \times 10^{-8} = \frac{[H_3O^+][HS^-]}{[H_2S]}$$

For $HS^- + H_2O \rightleftarrows H_3O^+ + S^{-2}$,

$$k_2 = 1 \times 10^{-14} = \frac{[H_3O^+][S^{-2}]}{[HS^-]}$$

Note: water concentration is not included in the equilibrium expression since its concentration is assumed to be constant.

One is not given any information concerning $[HS^-]$. $[HS^-]$ is common to both k_1 and k_2, so that if one solves one equation for $[HS^-]$ and substitutes it into the other equation, $[HS^-]$ is eliminated. Proceed as follows:

If one solves for $[HS^-]$ in k_1, one obtains

$$[HS^-] = \frac{k_1[H_2S]}{[H_3O^+]} = \frac{6.3 \times 10^{-8}\,[H_2S]}{[H_3O^+]}$$

Substituting this into k_2, one obtains

$$k_2 = 1 \times 10^{-14} = \frac{[H_3O^+][S^{-2}]}{[HS^-]} = \frac{[H_3O^+][S^{-2}]}{\dfrac{6.3 \times 10^{-8}[H_2S]}{[H_3O^+]}}$$

Rewriting in terms of $[S^{-2}]$,

$$[S^{-2}] = \frac{(1 \times 10^{-14})(6.3 \times 10^{-8})[H_2S]}{[H_3O^+]^2}$$

One is given that $[H_2S]$ and $[H_3O^+]$ equal 0.1 M and 0.3 M, respectively.

Therefore, one can substitute these values into this

equation to solve for $[S^{-2}]$.

$$[S^{-2}] = \frac{(1 \times 10^{-14})(6.3 \times 10^{-8})(0.1)}{(0.3)^2} = 7 \times 10^{-22} \text{ M.}$$

● **PROBLEM 9-11**

At $1000°K$, $K = 2.37 \times 10^{-3}$ for the reaction, $N_2(g) + 3H_2(g) \rightleftarrows 2NH_3(g)$. If you inject one mole of each N_2 and H_2 in a one-liter box at $1000°K$, what per cent of the H_2 will be converted to NH_3 at equilibrium?

Solution: To answer this question, determine the concentration of H_2 at equilibrium. Once this is known, subtract it from the initial concentration. The difference yields the amount that reacted to produce NH_3. By multiplying the quotient of the difference divided by the original amount of H_2 by 100, you obtain the per cent.

To find $[H_2]$ at equilibrium, employ the quilibrium constant expression. It states that K, the equilibrium constant, is equal to the concentration ratio of the products to reactants, each raised to the power of its coefficient in the chemical reaction. For this reaction, then,

$$K = 2.37 \times 10^{-3} = \frac{[NH_3]^2}{[H_2]^3[N_2]} \quad .$$

To find $[H_2]$, proceed as follows. Let x = amount of N_2 that dissociates. The initial concentrations of all species are 1M, since molarity = moles/liter, and 1 mole of each is placed in a one-liter box. If the N_2's initial concentration is one and x moles/liter dissociates, then, at equilibrium, there is $(1 - x)$ moles/liter left of N_2. In other words, at equilibrium, $[N_2] = 1 - x$. Now, from the chemical equation, it is seen that for every mole of N_2 that reacts, 3 moles of H_2 are necessary. Thus, when x moles/liter of N_2 dissociate, $3x$ moles/liter of H_2 are required. The initial concentration is 1, so that, at equilibrium

$$[H_2] = (1 - 3x) \text{ moles/liter.}$$

Notice, also, that for every mole/liter of nitrogen that dissociates, 2(mole/liter) of ammonia is obtained. Substituting these values into the equilibrium constant expression, one obtains

$$2.37 \times 10^{-3} = \frac{[NH_3]^2}{[N_2][H_2]^3} = \frac{(2x)^2}{(1-x)(1-3x)^3} \quad .$$

Solving for x, one obtains $x = .0217$ moles/liter of N_2 that dissociate. Thus, $[H_2] = 1 - 3x = .935$ moles/liter at equilibrium. The initial concentration was 1 mole/liter. The difference is the amount that dissociated, i.e., the H_2. The difference $= 1 - .935 = .065$. Thus, the percent that dissociated equals

$$\frac{.065M}{1M} \times 100 = 6.5\% \quad .$$

At 395 K, chlorine and carbon monoxide react to form phosgene, $COCl_2$, according to the equation

$$CO\ (g) + Cl_2\ (g) \rightleftarrows COCl_2\ (g).$$

The equilibrium partial pressures are p_{Cl_2} = 0.128 atm, p_{CO} = 0.116 atm, and p_{COCl_2} = 0.334 atm. Determine the equilibrium constant K_p for the dissociation of phosgene and the degree of dissociation at 395 K under a pressure of 1 atm.

Solution: After obtaining an expression for K_p for the dissociation of phosgene, the degree of dissociation under 1 atm of total pressure will be obtained by combining K_p with Dalton's law of partial pressures.

The dissociation of phosgene may be written as

$$COCl_2\ (g) \rightleftarrows CO\ (g) + Cl_2\ (g).$$

By definition, K_p is the product of the partial pressures of the products divided by the product of the partial pressure of the reactants. Hence,

$$K_p = \frac{p_{CO}\ p_{Cl_2}}{p_{COCl_2}} = \frac{(0.116\ atm)(0.128\ atm)}{(.334\ atm)}$$

$$= 0.0444\ atm.$$

K_p for the dissociation of phosgene is thus 0.0444 atm.

Let α denote the fraction of the original number of moles of phosgene that decomposed. Then, $1 - \alpha$ is the fraction of the original number of moles of phosgene remaining. From the stoichiometry of the dissociation reaction, one mole of CO and one mole of Cl_2 are formed for every mole of phosgene that decomposes. Thus, α moles of phosgene decomposes to α moles of CO and α moles of Cl_2.

From Dalton's law of partial pressures,

$$p_{COCl_2} = X_{COCl_2}\ p_T$$

$$p_{CO} = X_{CO}\ p_T \quad \text{and} \quad p_{Cl_2} = X_{Cl_2}\ p_T$$

where X_{COCl_2} is the mole fraction of phosgene, X_{CO} is the mole fraction of CO, X_{Cl_2} is the mole fraction of Cl_2, and p_T is the total pressure. Mole fraction may be defined as the number of moles of that particular substance divided by the total number of moles present. Since the total number of moles present after α moles of phosgene decomposes is

$(1 - \alpha)$ (from remaining phosgene)$+ \alpha$(from CO)$+ \alpha$(from Cl_2)

$$= 1 + \alpha$$

we have $\quad P_{COCl_2} = X_{COCl_2} \ P_T = \dfrac{1 - \alpha}{1 + \alpha} \ P_T$

$$P_{CO} = X_{CO} \ P_T = \dfrac{\alpha}{1 + \alpha} \ P_T$$

and $\quad P_{Cl_2} = X_{Cl_2} \ P_T = \dfrac{\alpha}{1 + \alpha} \ P_T.$

Substituting these into the expression for K_p, we obtain

$$K_p = \frac{P_{CO} \ P_{Cl_2}}{P_{COCl_2}} = \frac{\left[\dfrac{\alpha}{1 + \alpha} \ P_T\right]\left[\dfrac{\alpha}{1 + \alpha} \ P_T\right]}{\dfrac{1 - \alpha}{1 + \alpha} \ PT} = \frac{\alpha^2}{(1 + \alpha)(1 - \alpha)} \ P_T$$

$$= \frac{\alpha^2}{(1 - \alpha^2)} \ P_T \ ,$$

Now, the total pressure is $p_T = 1$ atm and K_p has been determined as $K_p = 0.0444$ atm. Hence,

$$K_p = \frac{\alpha^2}{1 - \alpha^2} \ P_T \ ,$$

$$0.0444 \ \text{atm} = \frac{\alpha^2}{1 - \alpha^2} \times 1 \ \text{atm},$$

$$0.0444 - 0.0444 \ \alpha^2 = \alpha^2 ,$$

or, $\quad \alpha = \left[\dfrac{0.0444}{1.0444}\right]^{\frac{1}{2}} = 0.206.$

The degree of dissociation of phosgene is equal to the fraction, α, of original moles that have dissociated. Hence, the degree of dissociation of phosgene at 395 K under a pressure of 1 atm is 0.206.

THE SHIFTING OF EQUILIBRIUM-LE CHATELIER'S PRINCIPLE

● **PROBLEM** 9-13

A solute of formula AB is slightly dissociated into A^+ and B^-. In this system, there is a dynamic equilibrium such that $A^+ + B^- \rightleftarrows AB$. Explain what happens if more acid is introduced into this system.

Solution: An acid is a species which, when added to a solvent (such as H_2O), dissociates into protons (H^+) and anions. In this particular case, the proton is represented as A^+. When more acid is added to this general solvent system, more A^+ is introduced. The increased concentration of A^+ places a stress on the equilibrium and the result is a shift in this equilibrium. According to Le Châtelier's principle, an equilibrium system will readjust to reduce a stress if one is applied. Thus, the equilibrium $A^+ + B^- \overset{\rightarrow}{\underset{\leftarrow}{}} AB$ will readjust to relieve the stress of the increased A^+ concentration. The stress is relieved by the reaction of A^+ with B^- to produce more AB. The concentration of B^- will decrease as compared to its concentration prior to the addition of the acid. Also, the concentration of the product AB will increase with the addition of the acid.

● PROBLEM 9-14

You are given a box in which $PCl_5(g)$, $PCl_3(g)$, and $Cl_2(g)$ are in equilibrium with each other at $546°K$. Assuming that the decomposition of PCl_5 to PCl_3 and Cl_2 is endothermic, what effect would there be on the concentration of PCl_5 in the box if each of the following changes were made? (a) Add Cl_2 to the box, (b) Reduce the volume of the box, and (c) Raise the temperature of the system.

Solution: You are told that the following equilibrium exists in the box $PCl_5 \overset{\rightarrow}{\underset{\leftarrow}{}} PCl_3 + Cl_2$ (all gases) and asked to see what happens to $[PCl_5]$ when certain changes are made. This necessitates the use of Le Chatelier's principle, which states that if a stress is applied to a system at equilibrium, then the system readjusts to reduce the stress. With this in mind, proceed as follows:

(a) Here, you are adding Cl_2 to the box. This results in a stress, since one of the components in the equilibrium has its concentration increased. According to Le Chatelier's principle, the system will act to relieve this increased concentration of Cl_2 - the stress. It can do so, if the Cl_2 combines with PCl_3 to produce more PCl_5. In this fashion, the stress is reduced, but the concentration of PCl_5 is increased.

(b) When the volume of the box is reduced, the concentration of the species is increased, i.e., the molecules are crowded closer together. Thus, a stress is applied. The stress can only be relieved (Le Chatelier's principle) if the molecules could be reduced in number. Notice, in our equilibrium expression you have 2 molecules, 1 each of PCl_3 and Cl_2, producing 1 molecule of PCl_5. In other words, the number of molecules is reduced if the equilibrium shifts to the left, so that more PCl_5 is pro-

180

duced. This is exactly what happens. As such, the $[PCl_5]$ increases.

(c) You are told that the decomposition of PCl_5 is endothermic (absorbing heat). In other words, if must absorb heat from the surroundings to proceed. If you increase the temperature, more heat is available, and the decomposition proceeds more readily, which means $[PCl_5]$ decreases. This fact can also be seen from the equilibrium constant of the reaction, K. This constant measures the ratio of products to reactants, each raised to the power of its coefficients in the chemical reaction. Now, when a reaction is endothermic, K is increased. For K to increase, the reactant's concentration must decrease. Again, therefore, you see that $[PCl_5]$ decreases.

● PROBLEM 9-15

At a certain temperature, an equilibrium mixture of
$$NO_2 + SO_2 \underset{\leftarrow}{\rightarrow} NO + SO_3$$
is analyzed and found to contain the following molar concentrations:

$[NO_2] = 0.100$, $[SO_2] = 0.300$, $[NO] = 2.00$, $[SO_3] = 0.600$.

If 0.500 moles of SO_2 are introduced at constant temperature, what will be the new concentrations of reactants and products when equilibrium is re-established?

Solution: Le Chatelier's principle states: If a stress is placed on a system in equilibrium, whereby the equilibrium is altered, that change will take place which tends to relieve or neutralize the effect of the added stress. Thus, in this reaction, if more SO_2 is added more NO and SO_3 will be formed. If stress is placed on the left side of the equation, the reaction will be forced to the right (and vice versa). One can determine the equilibrium constant (Keq) for this reaction by using the concentrations of the original mixture. The equilibrium constant is defined:

$$Keq = \frac{[NO][SO_3]}{[NO_2][SO_2]}$$

where [ ] indicate concentrations. Solving for Keq with

$[NO] = 2.00$ $[NO_2] = 0.100$
$[SO_3] = 0.600$ $[SO_2] = 0.300$,

one obtains
$$Keq = \frac{(2.00)(0.600)}{(0.100)(0.300)} = 40.0 .$$

One can solve for the new concentrations by using the Keq. From Le Chatelier's principle, one knows that when SO_2 is added to this mixture, the amounts of NO and SO_3 will increase. Let x = the number of moles by which NO and SO_3 will increase. For each mole of SO_3 and NO formed, one mole of SO_2 and one mole of NO_2 will react, thus the new concentrations of these components will be equal to the original concentrations less x moles. The new concentrations can be stated.

$$[NO] = 2.00 + x$$
$$[SO_3] = 0.600 + x$$
$$[NO_2] = 0.100 - x$$
$$[SO_2] = 0.300 + \text{the amount added} - x$$
$$= 0.300 + 0.500 - x = 0.800 - x \ .$$

Using the formula for the equilibrium constant, one can solve for x.

$$Keq = \frac{[NO][SO_3]}{[NO_2][SO_2]} = 40.0 \ .$$

Substituting,

$$40.0 = \frac{(2.00 + x)(0.600 + x)}{(0.100 - x)(0.800 - x)}$$

$$40.0 = \frac{1.20 + 2.6x + x^2}{.080 - 0.90x + x^2}$$

$$(0.80 - 0.90x + x^2)40 = 1.20 + 2.6x + x^2$$

$$3.20 - 36.0x + 40x^2 = 1.20 + 2.6x + x^2$$

$$2.0 - 38.6x + 38x^2 = 0 \ .$$

One can use the quadratic formula to solve for x.

$$ax^2 + bx + c = 0$$

$$x = \frac{-b \pm \sqrt{b^2 - 4ac}}{2a}$$

$$38x^2 - 38.6x + 2.0 = 0$$

$$x = \frac{38.6 \pm \sqrt{(38.6)^2 - 4 \times 2.0 \times 38}}{2 \times 38}$$

$$x = \frac{38.6 \pm 34.44}{76}$$

$$x = \frac{38.6 + 34.44}{76} = 0.96$$

or

$$x = \frac{38.6 - 34.44}{76} = 0.055$$

One cannot use x = 0.96 because $[NO_2]$ and $[SO_2]$ will be negative.

Concentrations cannot have negative values, which means x = .055. One can now find the new concentrations

$$[NO] = 2.00 + x = 2.055 \text{ moles}$$
$$[SO_3] = 0.600 + x = 0.65 \text{ moles}$$
$$[NO_2] = 0.100 - x = 0.045 \text{ moles}$$
$$[SO_2] = 0.800 - x = 0.745 \text{ moles}$$

CHAPTER 10

ACID-BASE EQUILIBRIA

ACIDS AND BASES

● PROBLEM 10-1

Can I^+ (the iodine cation) be called a Lewis base? Explain your answer.

Solution: A Lewis base may be defined as an electron pair donor. Writing out its electronic structure is the best way to answer this question, because it will show the existence of any available electron pairs.

The electronic structure of I^+ may be written as $[: \ddot{I} :]^+$. There are three available electron pairs. This might lead one to suspect that it is indeed a Lewis base. But note, I^+ does not have a complete octet of electrons, it does not obey the octet rule. According to this rule, atoms react to obtain an octet (8) of electrons. This confers stability.

Therefore, I^+ would certainly rather gain two more electrons than lose six. In reality, then, I^+ is an electron pair acceptor. Such substances are called Lewis acids.

● PROBLEM 10-2

Write the equations for the stepwise dissociation of pyrophosphoric acid, $H_4P_2O_7$. Identify all conjugate acid-base pairs.

Solution: Pyrophosphoric acid is an example of a polyprotic acid. Polyprotic acids furnish more than one proton per molecule. From its molecular formula, $H_4P_2O_7$, one can see there exist four hydrogen atoms. This might lead one to suspect that it is tetraprotic, i.e. having 4 protons that can be donated per molecule. This is in fact the case, which means there exist four dissociation reactions. In general, the equation for a dissociation reaction is,

$$HA + H_2O \rightarrow H_3O^+ + A^-.$$

Polyprotic acids follow this pattern. Thus, one can write the following equations for the step-wise dissociation of $H_4P_2O_7$.

(1) $H_4P_2O_7 + H_2O \rightarrow H_3O^+ + H_3P_2O_7^-$

(2) $H_3P_2O_7^- + H_2O \rightarrow H_3O^+ + H_2P_2O_7^{-2}$

(3) $H_2P_2O_7^{-2} + H_2O \rightarrow H_3O^+ + HP_2O_7^{-3}$

(4) $HP_2O_7^{-3} + H_2O \rightarrow H_3O^+ + P_2O_7^{-4}$

To identify all conjugate acid-base pairs, note the definition of the term. The base that results when an acid donates its proton is called the conjugate base. The acid that results when a base accepts a proton is called the conjugate acid. From these definitions, one sees that in all cases H_3O^+ is the conjugate acid of H_2O (the base in these reactions) and $H_3P_2O_7^-$, $H_2P_2O_7^{-2}$, $HP_2O_7^{-3}$ and $P_2O_7^{-4}$ are the conjugate bases of $H_4P_2O_7$, $H_3P_2O_7^-$, $H_2P_2O_7^{-2}$ and $HP_2O_7^{-3}$, respectively.

● **PROBLEM 10-3**

The dissociation sequence of the polyprotic acid H_3PO_4 shows three Bronsted-Lowry acids. Rank them in order of decreasing strengths.

<u>Solution</u>: Polyprotic acids are ones which furnish more than one proton per molecule. From its molecular formula, H_3PO_4, it is observed that there are 3 available hydrogen atoms available for release. In general, the equation for a dissociation reaction is

$$HA + H_2O \rightarrow H_3O^+ + A^-,$$

where HA is the acid and water is acting as a weak base. With this in mind, one can write the 3 dissociation reactions as

(1) $H_3PO_4 + H_2O \rightarrow H_3O^+ + H_2PO_4^-$

(2) $H_2PO_4^- + H_2O \rightarrow H_3O^+ + HPO_4^{-2}$

(3) $HPO_4^{-2} + H_2O \rightarrow H_3O^+ + PO_4^{-3}$

From this, one can see that the three acids are

H_3PO_4, $H_2PO_4^-$, and HPO_4^{-2}. The acids decrease in strength in the order of H_3PO_4, $H_2PO_4^-$, HPO_4^{-2}.

Ranking can be explained by noting that equivalent H-O bonds are being broken to give off H^+. The second and third protons that dissociate leave a progressively more negative ion. This means it is more difficult for the ion to dissociate in order to produce additional H^+ ions. This stems from the fact that the increased negativity results in increased attraction for the proton (H^+). In summary, as the negative charge of the acid increases, the weaker the acid becomes.

● **PROBLEM** 10-4

If you place $HClO_4$, HNO_3 or HCl in water, you find that they are strong acids. However, they show distinct differences in acidities when dissolved in acetic acid. Such an occurrence is referred to as the leveling effect of the solvent, water: a) Explain the basis for this leveling effect by comparing acid reactions in the water solvent system to the acetic acid solvent system. b) Discuss the leveling effect in terms of basicities instead of acidities.

Solution: (a) To explain the leveling effect, you must consider the relative acidic or basic properties of the species involved. In water, the general reaction for the acid is $HA + H_2O \rightleftharpoons H_3O^+ + A^-$. In acetic acid, however, the reaction is (assuming HA is a stronger acid than acetic acid (CH_3COOH), and the three acids given are) $HA + CH_3COOH \rightleftharpoons CH_3COOH_2^+ + A^-$. Let us consider the strengths of the acids in these two solvent systems. Water is less acidic, thus more basic and more strongly proton-attracting, than acetic acid. This means that when strong acids are dissolved the equilibrium will be shifted far to the right in water, but not as far in acetic acid. Thus, more products will be produced in the water solution than in the acetic acid. The acidities of the 3 given acids depend upon how much H^+ ion they produce. If the equilibrium is not shifted to the right, less H^+ ion is being produced. Thus, the acidicities of the three given acids will be less in acetic acid, since the equilibrium is shifted less to the right, and thus, not much H^+ ion is generated.

(b) The leveling effect can also be thought of in terms of basicity. For the two types of bases, you have $B + H_2O \rightleftharpoons BH^+ + OH^-$ in water and $B + CH_3COOH \rightleftharpoons BH^+ + CH_3COO^-$ in acetic acid. Now OH^- is a stronger base than CH_3COO^-, and, therefore, the equilibrium is further to the left in water than in acetic acid. Thus, when a base is added to water it will ionize less than in acetic acid.

THE AUTOIONIZATION OF WATER

A 0.10 M solution of HCl is prepared. What species of ions are present at equilibrium, and what will be their equilibrium concentrations?

<u>Solution</u>: Two processes are occurring simultaneously: the reaction of HCl with H_2O (dissociation of HCl) and the autoionization of H_2O.

HCl reacts with H_2O according to the equation

$$HCl + H_2O \rightleftarrows H_3O^+ + Cl^-.$$

For every mole of HCl that dissociates, one mole of Cl^- and one mole of H_3O^+ are produced. The initial concentration of HCl is 0.10 M. Thus, if we assume that HCl dissociates completely,

$$[H_3O^+] = 0.10 \text{ M} \quad \text{and} \quad [Cl^-] = 0.10 \text{ M}.$$

Water autoionizes according to the equation

$$H_2O + H_2O \rightleftarrows H_3O^+ + OH^-.$$

The water constant for this process is

$$K_w = 10^{-14} \text{ moles}^2/\text{liter}^2 = [H_3O^+][OH^-].$$

Hence, $[OH^-] = \dfrac{10^{-14} \text{ moles}^2/\text{liter}^2}{[H_3O^+]}$

Since $[H_3O^+]$ was determined to be 0.10 M = 10^{-1} M = 10^{-1} moles/liter,

$$[OH^-] = \frac{10^{-14} \text{ moles}^2/\text{liter}^2}{[H_3O^+]}$$

$$= \frac{10^{-14} \text{ moles}^2/\text{liter}^2}{10^{-1} \text{ moles/liter}} = 10^{-13} \text{ moles/liter} = 10^{-13} \text{ M}.$$

Hence, at equilibrium, H_3O^+, OH^-, and Cl^- are present in the concentrations

$$[H_3O^+] = 0.10 \text{ M}, \ [OH^-] = 10^{-13} \text{ M}, \ [Cl^-] = 0.10 \text{ M}.$$

A 0.10 M solution of NaOH is prepared. What species of ions are present at equlibrium, and what will be their equilibrium concentrations?

Solution: Two processes are occurring simultaneously, the dissociation of NaOH, and the autoionization of H_2O.

NaOH dissociates according to the equation

$$NaOH \; \overset{\rightarrow}{\leftarrow} \; Na^+ + OH^-.$$

For every mole of NaOH that dissociates, one mole of Na^+ and one mole of OH^- are produced. The initial concentration of NaOH is 0.10 M. Thus, if we assume that NaOH dissociates completely$[Na^+]$ = 0.10 M and $[OH^-]$ = 0.10 M.

Water autoionizes according to the equation

$$H_2O \; + H_2O \; \overset{\rightarrow}{\leftarrow} \; H_3O^+ + OH^-.$$

The water constant for this process is

$$K_w = 10^{-14} \text{ moles}^2/\text{liter}^2 = [H_3O^+][OH^-].$$

Hence, $[H_3O^+] = \dfrac{10^{-14} \text{ moles}^2/\text{liter}^2}{[OH^-]}$

Since $[OH^-]$ was determined to be 0.10 M = 10^{-1} M = 10^{-1} moles/liter, by substitution, we obtain

$$[H_3O^+] = \frac{10^{-14} \text{ moles}^2/\text{liter}^2}{[OH^-]} = \frac{10^{-14} \text{ moles}^2/\text{liter}^2}{10^{-1} \text{ moles/liter}}$$

$$= 10^{-13} \text{ moles/liter} = 10^{-13} \text{ M}.$$

Hence, at equilibrium, H_3O^+, OH^-, and Na^+ are present in the concentrations

$$[H_3O^+] = 10^{-13} \text{ M}, \; [OH^-] = 0.10 \text{ M}, \; [Na^+] = 0.10 \text{ M}.$$

AUTOPROTOLYSIS

Find the equation for the autoprotolysis of water. Indicate which species is the acid, the base, the conjugate acid, and the conjugate base.

Solution: One can begin by defining autoprotolysis. It may be defined as the donation of a proton from a molecule of one specie to another molecule of the same specie to produce positive and negative ions. Thus, for water, the equation is $H_2O + H_2O \rightarrow H_3O^+ + OH^-$. An acid is defined as a specie that donates protons. A base is a substance that accepts protons. From the equation, one sees that either water (H_2O) molecule can be the base or acid. A conjugate base is a specie obtained by abstracting a proton (H^+). If one abstracts a proton from water, one obtains OH^-. Thus, OH^- is the conjugate base. The conjugate acid is defined as the base plus a proton. It was stated that either H_2O molecule could be the base. If one adds a proton to one of them, one obtains H_3O^+. Thus, H_3O^+ is the conjugate acid.

● **PROBLEM** 10-8

Indicate the equilibrium equation and constant expression for the autoprotolysis of liquid ammonia. If $K_{NH_3} = 10^{-22}$, how many molecules of ammonia are ionized in 1 mole of ammonia? Assume a density of 0.771g/ml for ammonia.

Solution: Autoprotolysis is that phenomenon whereby an ammonia molecule can donate a proton to another NH_3 molecule to form positive and negative charged species. The equation of the autoprotolysis can be written $NH_3 + NH_3 \rightleftharpoons NH_4^+ + NH_2^-$ or

(i) $2NH_3 \rightleftharpoons NH_4^+ + NH_2^-$.

To find the constant expression, consider the equilibrium constant expression for the reaction:

$$K = \frac{[NH_4^+][NH_2^-]}{[NH_3]^2} \quad .$$

Note, though, that the concentration of NH_3 in pure ammonia is always constant. By analogy with the autoprotolysis of water (where the K_w expression is written $[OH^-][H_3O^+]$, - without $[H_2O]^2$ in the denominator), the constant expression for the autoprotolysis of NH_3 is

(ii) $K_{NH_3} = [NH_4^+][NH_2^-]$.

To find the number of molecules of ammonia ionized in 1 mole of ammonia, use the equation

$$K = \frac{[NH_4^+][NH_2^-]}{[NH_3]^2} \quad .$$

Let x be the number of moles of ammonia ionized. Then the NH_3 remaining nonionized is 1-x moles. Since each 2 ammonia molecules must ionize to produce one NH_4^+ and one NH_2^-, the number of NH_4^+ =

number of $NH_2^- = \frac{x}{2}$. Let V be the volume of one mole of ammonia. The concentration of NH_4^+ and NH_2^- can be rewritten as $\frac{x/2}{V}$, and the concentration of nonionized NH_3 is $\frac{1-x}{V}$. The equation for K can be rewritten as

(iii) $$K = \frac{(\frac{x/2}{V})(\frac{x/2}{V})}{(\frac{1-x}{V})^2} = \frac{x^2/4}{(1-x)^2} \cdot \frac{1/V^2}{1/V^2} = \frac{x^2}{4(1-x^2)} \quad .$$

x, the number of moles of ionized ammonia, can be calculated if K is known. To solve for K , consider a more general case of the equation

$$K = \frac{[NH_4^+][NH_2^-]}{[NH_3]^2} \quad .$$

The numerator $[NH_4^+][NH_2^-]$ is the constant expression for the auto-protolysis of NH_3 and must always equal K_{NH_3} . K_{NH_3} is given as 10^{-22} .

To find $[NH_3]^2$, use the fact that the density of ammonia is $0.771g/ml$. The mole weight of ammonia is $17.03g$. Thus, $0.771g$ is $\frac{0.771g}{17.03g/mole} = 0.0453$ moles of ammonia; and the density of ammonia is 0.0453 moles/ml. $= 45.3$ moles/liter. Thus, $[NH_3] = 45.3M$. Substitute these results in

$$K = \frac{[NH_4^+][NH_2^-]}{[NH_3]^2}$$

(iv) $$K = \frac{10^{-22}}{45.3^2} = 4.9 \times 10^{-26} \quad .$$

Substitute this value of K into (iii)

(v) $$4.9 \times 10^{-26} = \frac{x^2}{4(1-x^2)} \quad .$$

To simplify the problem, note that the dissociation of ammonia is very small and thus $x \ll 1$. Thus, approximate $1-x^2$ as 1. Then, (v) becomes

(vi) $$\frac{x^2}{4} = 4.9 \times 10^{-26} \quad .$$

Solve to obtain $x = 4.42 \times 10^{-13}$. This is the number of moles of NH_3 that ionized. To find the number of molecules, remember that 1 mole $= 6.02 \times 10^{23}$ molecules. Thus,

No. of molecules ionized $= (4.42 \times 10^{-13}$ moles$)(6.02 \times 10^{23}$ molecules/mole$)$
$= 2.66 \times 10^{11}$ molecules.

2.66×10^{11} molecules of ammonia are ionized.

pH

A) Determine the pH of a solution with a hydrogen ion concentration of 3.5×10^{-4}.

B) If a solution has a pH of 4.25, what is the hydrogen ion concentration?

Solution: To determine the acidity or basicity of an aqueous solution, the hydrogen ion concentration must be measured. The pH of a solution expresses this concentration. pH is defined as the negative logarithm of the hydrogen ion concentration. In other words, pH = (- log [H$^+$]), where the brackets around H$^+$ signify concentration. As such, to solve the problem, you must substitute into the equation. For part "A", you have
pH = -log [3.5×10^{-4}]
now -log [3.5×10^{-4}] = -log 3.5 - log 10^{-4}

$$= - .54 - (-4)$$

$$= - .54 + 4$$

$$= 3.46$$

It follows, then, that the pH = 3.46 for a hydrogen ion concentration of 3.5×10^{-4}. Part "B" is similar, but here you are given the pH and asked to find the ion concentration. Therefore, you have 4.25 = -log [H$^+$] or -4.25 = log [H$^+$]. Now. logarithm numbers give only positive mantissas. As such, -4.25 must be in the form of -5 + .75. If you take the antilogarithm of each, .75 is 5.6 and -5 is 10^{-5}, you obtain a hydrogen ion concentration of 5.6×10^{-5} mole/liter

Determine the pH of each of the following solutions: (a) 0.20 M HCl, (b) 0.10 M NaOH.

Solution: A pH scale has been devised to express the H$_3$O$^+$ concentration in solution. By definition,

$$pH = - \log [H_3O^+] \quad \text{or} \quad [H_3O^+] = 10^{-pH}$$

It has been shown that water dissociates to H$_3$O$^+$ and OH$^-$

ions to a small degree.

$$H_2O + H_2O \rightarrow H_3O^+ + OH^-.$$

The equilibrium constant is defined as K_w for this reaction and is expressed as $[H_3O^+][OH^-]$. The H_2O does not appear, since it is presumed to be a constant. From the dissociation equation, it can be seen that the concentration of H_3O^+ equals OH^-. By experimentation, K_w has been shown to equal 1.0×10^{-14}. This means that in water, therefore, H_3O^+ and OH^- each have a concentration of 1.0×10^{-7} M. With this information in mind, one can now solve the problem.

(a) The concentration of HCl is 0.20 M. Since HCl is a strong electrolyte, dissociation is complete. Therefore, the concentration of H_3O^+ is also 0.20 M = 2.0×10^{-1} M. By definition, then

$$pH = -\log (2.0 \times 10^{-1}) = 1 - 0.3 = 0.7.$$

(b) The $[OH^-]$ equals the concentration of NaOH, since it is also a strong electrolyte. One wants the pH, therefore, employ the expression for K_w.

$$[H_3O^+] = \frac{K_w}{[OH^-]} = \frac{1 \times 10^{-14}}{0.10} = 1.0 \times 10^{-13} \text{ M.}$$

Therefore, $pH = -\log (1.0 \times 10^{-13}) = 13.$

● **PROBLEM 10-11**

A certain solution has pH 3.89 at 0°C. Find pOH and $[OH^-]$.

Solution: pH is a measure of the $[H^+]$ and pOH is a measure of $[OH^-]$. Their product gives K_w, the ionization constant of water:

$$[H^+][OH^-] = K_w.$$

pH and pOH are related by the equation,

$$pOH + pH = pK_w.$$

At 0°C, $pK_w = 14.94$. Therefore:

$$pOH = pK_w - pH = 14.94 - 3.89 = 11.05.$$

To find $[OH^-]$ use the equation,

$$pOH = -\log [OH^-]$$

$11.05 = - \log [OH^-]$

$[OH^-] = 10^{-11.05} = 10^{-12+.95} = (10^{-12})(10^{.95})$.

Find the antilog of $10^{.95}$. It is 8.9 which gives

$[OH^-] = 8.9 \times 10^{-12}$.

Assuming complete ionization, calculate (a) the pH of
0.0001 N HCl, (b) the pOH of 0.0001 N KOH.

<u>Solution</u>: (a) pH is defined as the negative log of the
hydrogen ion concentration.

$pH = - \log [H^+]$

The normality of an acid is defined as the number of
equivalents of H^+ per liter of solution. The ionization of
HCl can be written

$$HCl \overset{\leftarrow}{\rightarrow} H^+ + Cl^-$$

This means that there is one H^+ for every HCl, and that
the concentration of H^+ equals the concentration of
completely ionized HCl.

$[H^+] = [HCl]$

We are told that $[HCl] = 0.0001$ N $= 1 \times 10^{-4}$ N. Therefore,
$[H^+] = 1 \times 10^{-4}$ N. We can now solve for pH. Note: In this
problem, normality = molarity (concentration), since equivalent weight=M.W.

$pH = - \log [H^+]$

$pH = - \log (1 \times 10^{-4}) = 4$.

The pH of this solution is 4.

(b) The pOH is defined as the negative log of the
OH^- ion concentration.

$pOH = - \log [OH^-]$.

The ionization of KOH can be stated

$$KOH \overset{\leftarrow}{\rightarrow} K^+ + OH^-$$

Therefore, one OH^- is formed for every KOH, and when KOH
is completely ionized, their concentrations are equal.

$[KOH] = [OH^-]$

We are told that [KOH] = 0.0001 N, thus [OH$^-$] = 0.0001 N (again, normality = molarity.)

Solving for pOH:

pOH = - log [OH$^-$]

= - log (0.0001) = - log (1 × 10^{-4}) = 4.

The pOH of this solution is 4.

● **PROBLEM** 10-13

What is the pH of a neutral solution at 50°C?
pK$_w$ = 13.26 at 50°C.

Solution: A neutral solution is defined as [H$^+$] = [OH$^-$]; an acid solution has [H$^+$] > [OH$^-$], and a basic solution has [H$^+$]< [OH$^-$]. For a solution at 25°, pK$_w$ = 14.

pK$_w$ indicates the amount of dissociation of water. To find the neutral pH, one lets pH = pOH = x. Since

pH + pOH = 2x = 14 = pK$_w$,

x = 7.

However, the solution in question is at 50°. At 50° pK$_w$ = 13.26. Therefore, to find the neutral pH,

pH + pOH = 2x = K$_w$ = 13.26

x = 6.63 = neutral pH.

● **PROBLEM** 10-14

Before the advent of pH meters, a urologist collected 1.3 liters of urine from a hospitalized patient over the course of a day. In order to calculate what the pH was a laboratory technician determined the number of equivalents of acid present in the sample. A given sample of urine contains 1.3 × 10^{-6} equivalents of dissociated acid. What is the pH of this sample?

Solution: To solve this problem, we have to note that 1 equivalent of H$^+$ is the same as 1 mole of H$^+$. We then determine [H$^+$] and from this the pH.

1.3 × 10^{-6} equivalent of H$^+$ is the same as 1.3 × 10^{-6} mole of H$^+$. The concentration of H$^+$ in the sample is then

193

$[H^+]$ = moles of H^+/volume

$= 1.3 \times 10^{-6}$ mole/1.3 liter $= 10^{-6}$ M.

The pH is defined as pH = $- \log [H^+]$, hence

pH = $- \log [H^+] = - \log (10^{-6}) = - (- 6) = 6$,

which is the pH of normal urine.

Both HCl and NaOH are strong electrolytes. What is the pH of the solution formed by adding 40 ml of 0.10 M NaOH to 10 ml of 0.45 M HCl?

Solution: We will solve this problem by considering the number of moles of H_3O^+ and of OH^- formed by the complete dissociation of HCl and NaOH, respectively.

If we assume that HCl and NaOH dissociate completely, then the concentration of H_3O^+ in the HCl solution is equal to the initial concentration of HCl, or $[H_3O^+]$ = 0.45 M, and the concentration of OH^- in the NaOH solution is equal to the initial concentration of NaOH, or $[OH^-]$ = 0.10 M. Since moles = concentration × volume, the number of moles of H_3O^+ in 10 ml of the acid solution is

moles $H_3O^+ = [H_3O^+] \times$ volume = 0.45 M × 10 ml

$= 0.45$ M × 0.01 liter

$= .0045$ mole $= 4.5 \times 10^{-3}$ mole.

Similarly, the number of moles of OH^- in 40 ml of the basic solution is

moles $OH^- = [OH^-] \times$ volume = 0.10 M × 40 ml

$= 0.10$ M × 0.04 liter

$= 0.004$ mole $= 4 \times 10^{-3}$ mole

H_3O^+ and OH^- neutralize each other according to the reaction

$$H_3O^+ + OH^- \rightarrow 2H_2O.$$

Ignoring the dissociation of water, we can assume that this reaction is complete. Hence, the 4×10^{-3} moles of OH^- will be neutralized by 4×10^{-3} moles of H_3O^+, leaving $4.5 \times 10^{-3} - 4.0 \times 10^{-3} = 0.5 \times 10^{-3} = 5 \times 10^{-4}$ mole of H_3O^+ remaining. Thus, when the two solutions are mixed, no OH^- remains and 5×10^{-4} mole of H_3O^+ remains. Since the final volume of the solution is 40 ml + 10 ml =

50 ml = 0.05 liter = 5×10^{-2} liter, the concentration of H_3O^+ is

$$[H_3O^+] = 5 \times 10^{-4} \text{ mole}/5 \times 10^{-2} \text{ liter} = 10^{-2} \text{ mole/liter}.$$

The pH is defined as pH = $- \log [H_3O^+]$, hence

$$pH = - \log [H_3O^+] = - \log (10^{-2}) = - (- 2) = 2.$$

THE IONIZATION CONSTANT

The ionization constant for acetic acid is 1.8×10^{-5}.

a) Calculate the concentration of H^+ ions in a 0.10 molar solution of acetic acid.
b) Calculate the concentration of H^+ ions in a 0.10 molar solution of acetic acid in which the concentration of acetate ions has been increased to 1.0 molar by addition of sodium acetate.

Solution: The ionization constant (Ka) is defined as the concentration of H^+ ions times the concentration of the conjugate base ions of a given acid divided by the concentration of unionized acid. For an acid, HA,

$$Ka = \frac{[H^+][A^-]}{[HA]} ,$$

where Ka is the ionization constant, $[H^+]$ is the concentration of H^+ ions, $[A^-]$ is the concentration of the conjugate base ions and $[HA]$ is the concentration of unionized acid. The Ka for acetic acid is stated as

$$Ka = \frac{[H^+][\text{acetate ion}]}{[\text{acetic acid}]} = 1.8 \times 10^{-5} .$$

The chemical formula for acetic acid is $HC_2H_3O_2$. When it is ionized, one H^+ is formed and one $C_2H_3O^-$ (acetate) is formed, thus the concentration of H^+ equals the concentration of $C_2H_3O^-$.

$$[H^+] = [C_2H_3O^-] .$$

The concentration of unionized acid is decreased when ionization occurs. The new concentration is equal to the concentration of H^+ subtracted from the concentration of unionized acid.

$$[HC_2H_3O] = 0.10 - [H^+] .$$

Since $[H^+]$ is small relative to 0.10, one may assume that $0.10 - [H^+]$ is approximately equal to 0.10.

$$0.10 - [H^+] \cong 0.10 .$$

Using this assumption, and the fact that $[H^+] = [C_2H_3O^-]$, Ka can be rewritten as

$$Ka = \frac{[H^+][H^+]}{0.10} = 1.8 \times 10^{-5} .$$

Solving for the concentration of H^+ :

$$[H^+]^2 = (1.0 \times 10^{-1})(1.8 \times 10^{-5}) = 1.8 \times 10^{-6}$$

$$[H^+] = \sqrt{1.8 \times 10^{-6}} = 1.3 \times 10^{-3} .$$

The concentration of H^+ is thus $1.3 \times 10^{-3} M$.

b)   When the acetate concentration is increased, the concentration of H^+ is lowered to maintain the same Ka . The Ka for acetic acid is stated as

$$Ka = \frac{[H^+][C_2H_3O^-]}{[HC_2H_3O]} = 1.8 \times 10^{-5}$$

As previously shown for acetic acid equilibria in a solution of 0.10 molar acid, the concentration of acid after ionization is

$$[HC_2H_3O] = 0.10 - [H^+] .$$

Because $[H^+]$ is very small compared to 0.10, $0.10 - [H^+] \cong 0.10$ and $[HC_2H_3O] = 0.10$.

In this problem, we are told that the concentration of acetate is held constant at 1.0 molar by addition of sodium acetate. Because one now knows the concentrations of the acetate and the acid, the concentration of H^+ can be found.

$$\frac{[H^+][C_2H_3O^-]}{[HC_2H_3O]} = 1.8 \times 10^{-5}$$

$$\frac{[H^+][1.0]}{[0.10]} = 1.8 \times 10^{-5}$$

$$[H^+] = 1.8 \times 10^{-6} .$$

● **PROBLEM** 10-17

Find the hydronium ion concentration of .1M HOAC (acetic acid) solution. Assume $k_a = 1.75 \times 10^{-5}$ for acetic acid.

Solution: You want to represent the equilibrium constant expression for the reaction, which necessitates a balanced equation. After writing the expression, you want to express the concentrations in terms of the same variables and solve for it. Begin by writing the balanced equation for the reaction of acetic acid in water. The acid will donate a proton (H^+) to the only available base, H_2O. Thus, $HOAC + H_2O \rightarrow H_3O^+ + OAC^-$. $[H_3O^+]$, the hydronium concentration, is the quantity you are looking for. The equilibrium constant expression measures the ratio of the concentrations of the products to the reactants, each raised to the power of their respective coefficients in the chemical equation. Thus, the constant, Ka, $= \frac{[OAC-][H_3O^+]}{[HOAC]}$. Note: H_2O is omitted, since it is considered a constant. Ka = 1.75 x 10^{-5}. Equating, $\frac{[OAC^-][H_3O^+]}{[HOAC]} = 1.75$ x 10^{-5}. Let x = concentration of H_3O^+. According to the reaction, $[H_3O^+]$ = $[OAC^-]$, thus, x = concentration of $[OAC^-]$, also. If the initial concentration of HOAC is .1 and X $\frac{moles}{liter}$ of $[H_3O^+]$ are formed, then you have $(.1-x)$ moles/liter of HOAC left. Substituting these variables into the equilibrium constant expression, you have

$$\frac{x^2}{.1-x} = 1.75 \times 10^{-5}.$$

Solving, $x = [H_3O^+] = 0.0013M$

● PROBLEM 10-18

The ionization constant for NH_4OH is 1.8×10^{-5}.

(a) Calculate the concentration of OH^- ions in a 1.0 molar solution of NH_4OH.

Solution: The ionization constant (K_b) is defined as the concentration of OH^- ions times the concentration of the conjugate acid ions of a given base divided by the concentration of unionized base. For a base, BA,

$$K_b = \frac{[B^-][A^+]}{[BA]},$$

where K_b is the ionization constant, $[B^-]$ is the concentration of ionized base ions, $[A^+]$ is the concentration of the conjugate acid, and $[BA]$ is the concentration of unionized base. The K_b for NH_4OH is stated as

$$K_b = \frac{[NH_4^+][OH^-]}{NH_4OH} = 1.8 \times 10^{-5}$$

When NH_4OH is ionized, one NH_4^+ ion is formed and one OH^- ion is formed,

$$NH_4OH \underset{\leftarrow}{\rightarrow} NH_4^+ + OH^-$$

Thus, the concentrations of each ion are equal.

$$[NH_4^+] = [OH^-]$$

The concentration of unionized base is decreased when ionization occurs. The new concentration is equal to the concentration of OH^- subtracted from the concentration of NH_4OH.

$$[NH_4OH] = 1.0 - [OH^-]$$

Since $[OH^-]$ is small relative to 1.0, one may assume that $1.0 - [OH^-]$ is approximately equal to 1.0

$$[NH_4OH] = 1.0 - [OH^-] \cong 1.0$$

Using this assumption, and the fact that $[OH^-] = [NH_4^+]$, K_b can be rewritten as

$$K_b = \frac{[OH^-][OH^-]}{1.0} = 1.8 \times 10^{-5}$$

Solving for $[OH^-]$:

$$\frac{[OH^-][OH^-]}{1.0} = 1.8 \times 10^{-5}$$

$$[OH^-]^2 = 1.8 \times 10^{-5}$$

$$[OH^-] = \sqrt{1.8 \times 10^{-5}} = 4.2 \times 10^{-3}$$

• **PROBLEM** 10-19

Find the degree of ionization of 0.05 M NH_3 in a solution of pH 11.0. $K_b = 1.76 \times 10^{-5}$.

Solution: The degree of ionization is the fraction of the total acid or base present (α) that ionizes. Namely,

$$\alpha = \frac{x}{c} ,$$

where x is the number of moles of acid or base that dissociate and c is the original number of moles present.

To solve this problem, let it first be stated that NH_3 is a base and that $[OH^-]$ can be calculated from the pH value.

The reaction equation is

$$NH_3 + H_2O \rightleftarrows NH_4^+ + OH^-.$$

After obtaining $[OH^-]$, $[NH_4^+]$ will be the only unknown in the equilibrium constant equation, which is

$$K_b = \frac{[NH_4^+][OH^-]}{[NH_3]} = 1.76 \times 10^{-5}.$$

To find $[OH^-]$, note that pOH $= - \log [OH^-]$ and that pH + pOH = 14. Substituting the given value of pH,

$$pOH = 14 - pH = 14 - 11 = 3.$$
Thus, $[OH^-] = - \log 3 = 1 \times 10^{-3}.$

Next, remember that for each x moles of NH_3 that dissociates, x moles of NH_4^+ will form. The problem becomes clearer if one observes what is happening from the table below.

$$NH_3 + H_2O \rightleftarrows NH_4^+ + OH^-$$

Before Reaction: 0.05   O   O   O

After Reaction: 0.05-x   x 1×10^{-3}

Upon substituting these values into the K_b equation, one obtains:

$$K_b = \frac{[NH_4^+][OH^-]}{[NH_3]} = 1.76 \times 10^{-5} = \frac{x (10^{-3})}{0.05 - x} .$$

Solving for $[NH_4^+]$,

$$x = [NH_4^+] = 8.65 \times 10^{-4}.$$

198

[NH_4^+] also represents the unknown value in the degree of ionization equation, since its concentration must be the amount of NH_3 that was ionized. Thus,

$$\alpha = \frac{8.65 \times 10^{-4}}{0.05} = 1.73 \times 10^{-2}.$$

● **PROBLEM 10-20**

Given K_i for acetic acid is 1.8×10^{-5}, calculate the percentage of ionization of 0.5 M acetic acid. The dissociation reaction is

$$HC_2H_3O_2 \; \rightleftharpoons \; H^+ + C_2H_3O_2^-.$$

Solution: K_i is the ionization constant and indicates to what degree acids and bases will dissociate in solution. Acetic acid is a weak acid because K_i is so small. The larger the value of K_i, the greater the % dissociation and the stronger the acid. A useful range of values for K_i is given below.

Strength	Range
Very strong	greater than 1×10^3
strong	1×10^3 to 1×10^{-2}
weak	1×10^{-2} to 1×10^{-7}
very weak	less than 1×10^{-7}

K_i is calculated from the ratio of products to reactants, each raised to the power of its coefficient in the reaction equation;

$$K_i = \frac{[products]^{\text{reaction moles (or coefficient)}}}{[reactants]^{\text{reaction moles (or coefficient)}}}$$

From the chemical reaction,

$$K_i = \frac{[H^+][C_2H_3O_2^-]}{[HC_2H_3O_2]} = 1.8 \times 10^{-5}$$

To solve this problem, one uses the following method. Before the reaction begins, no dissociation occurs, so that only acetic acid is present, and in its full concentration of 0.5 M. After dissociation occurs, b number of moles/liter has dissociated to the products in equal amounts. Or b moles/liter of each H^+ and $C_2H_3O_2^-$ are produced since the coefficients of the reaction indicate that they are formed in equimolar amounts. If b moles/liter dissociate, then there are 0.5 - b moles/liter of acetic acid left.

This can be summarized as follows:

Before: 0.5 moles.   0   0

After: 0.5 - b   b   b

This gives a K_i of,

$$K_i = \frac{[b][b]}{[0.5 - b]} = 1.8 \times 10^{-5}.$$

Since K_i is so small, very few moles of acetic acid dissociate, which causes b to be insignificantly small. Therefore, 0.5 - b is approximately equal to 0.5, giving

$$K_i = \frac{[b][b]}{[0.5]} = 1.8 \times 10^{-5}.$$

Solving for b, one obtains:

$$b^2 = 9.0 \times 10^{-6}$$

$$b = 3.0 \times 10^{-3} \text{ mole of acetic acid ionized.}$$

Using the following equation to find % ionization:

$$\% \text{ ionization} = \frac{\text{number of moles ionized}}{\text{original number of moles of acetic acid}} \times 100$$

$$= \frac{3.0 \times 10^{-3}}{0.5} \times 100 = 0.60 \%.$$

● **PROBLEM** 10-21

A solution of 10.0 g of HF in 500 g H_2O freezes at - 1.98°C. Calculate the degree of ionization of HF. (M.W. HF = 20.0   The Freezing point depression of H_2O is 1.86°.)

Solution: When an acid is dissolved in solution, it dissociates into ions. For example, when one mole of HF is dissolved in H_2O, one mole of H^+ and one mole of F^- are present after complete dissociation. The freezing point of a solution is dependent on the number of particles in the solution, which means that the freezing point of a solution will be lowered more by a compound which ionizes than by the same amount of a compound which does not ionize. The degree of ionization of a compound is a measure of what percent of the compound is ionized when it is placed in a particular solution.

200

In this problem, one is told that when 10 g of HF is added to 500 g of H_2O the original freezing point of the water ($0°$) is lowered to $- 1.98°C$. The freezing point depression is related to the concentration of particles in the solution by the statement

freezing point depression = molality × freezing point
constant

The freezing point constant of water is $1.86°$. This means that one mole of a substance (except those substances which ionize) dissolved in 1000 g of water lowers the freezing point $1.86°$. Since HF ionizes, we cannot use its molality in this equation. You can use the effective molality, which is the sum of the molalities of H^+, F^- and HF. The molality of H^+ and F^- will be equal to the degree of ionization of the HF. The concentrations of H^+ and F^- will be equal because, when HF ionizes, one H^+ and one F^- will be formed. This reaction is given by the equation

$$HF \xrightarrow{\leftarrow} H^+ + F^-$$

To solve for the degree of ionization of HF, one must: (a) find the molality of HF as if it were not ionized, (b) define a variable for the molalities of H^+ and F^-; here, x will be used, (c) find the molality of HF after ionization is taken into account, (d) find the effective molality of the species, (e) use the effective molality in the freezing point depression e-quation to solve for x, the molality of H^+ and F^-.

(a) The molality of HF before ionization.

The molality is defined as the number of moles of solute in 1000 g of solvent. The number of moles of HF can be found by dividing the number of grams present by the molecular weight.

$$\text{number of moles} = \frac{\text{number of grams}}{\text{molecular weight}}$$

$$\text{moles of HF} = \frac{10.0 \text{ g}}{20.0 \text{ g/mole}} = 0.5 \text{ moles}$$

The molality can now be found by dividing the number of moles of HF by the number of kg of water present.

$$\text{molality} = \frac{\text{no. of moles of HF}}{\text{no. of kg of } H_2O}$$

$$\text{molality} = \frac{0.5 \text{ moles}}{0.500 \text{ kg}} = 1.0 \text{ moles/kg}$$

(b) x = molality of H^+ = molality of F^-

(c) After ionization of x molal of H^+ and F^-, the molality of HF will be $1.0 - x$.

(e) The effective molality of the species will be equal to the sum of the molalities of all of the species present.

The effective molality = molality of H^+ + molality of F^- + molality of HF

effective molality = x + x + (1.0 - x) = 1.0 + x.

To solve for x, the concentration of H^+ and F^-, the effective molality of the species will be used in the freezing point depression equation.

freezing point depreesion = eff. molality × freezing pt constant

The freezing point depression in this case is 1.98° and the freezing point constant of water is 1.86°. Solving the equation

$$1.98° = (1.0 + x) \times 1.86°$$

$$1.0 + x = \frac{1.98°}{1.86°}$$

$$x = .06$$

The percent of ionization is the molality of H^+ and F^- divided by the molality of the unionized HF multiplied by 100.

$$\text{degree of ionization} = \frac{\text{molality of ion}}{\text{molality of unionized species}} \times 100$$

$$\text{degree of ionization} = \frac{0.06}{1.00} \times 100 = 6\%$$

Hence, the HF in this solution is 6 % ionized.

THE DISSOCIATION CONSTANT

● **PROBLEM** 10-22

If 1 mole of HCl and 1 mole of $NaC_2H_3O_2$ are mixed in enough water to make one liter of solution, what will be the concentrations of the species in the final equilibrium? $K_{diss} = 1.8 \times 10^{-5}$ for $NaC_2H_3O_2$.

Solution: To answer this question, you must consider what is happening at equilibrium. This necessitates defining $K_{dissociation}$, which is an equilibrium constant

HCl and $NaC_2H_3O_2$ are strong electrolytes, which

means that, in solution, they are completely dissociated. You have, therefore, H^+, Cl^-, Na^+, and $C_2H_3O_2^-$ ions present in the solution. The Na^+ and Cl^- do not associate, and need not be considered. Thus, you must only consider the formation of $HC_2H_3O_2$ from H^+ and $C_2H_3O_2^-$. The equation for this reaction can be written

$$H^+ + C_2H_3O_2^- \rightleftharpoons HC_2H_3O_2$$

This reaction can proceed in both directions, an equilibrium exists, as the double arrow indicates. The equilibrium constant (K_{eq}) for this reaction is equal to

$$\frac{[HC_2H_3O_2]}{[H^+][C_2H_3O_2^-]} .$$

$K_{dissociation}$ measures the equilibrium quantitatively. The dissociation reaction for $HC_2H_3O_2$ can be written

$$HC_2H_3O_2 \rightleftharpoons H^+ + C_2H_3O_2^- .$$

The dissociation constant,

$$K_{diss} = \frac{[H^+][C_2H_3O_2^-]}{[HC_2H_3O_2]} = 1.8 \times 10^{-5}.$$

By examination, you can see that K_{eq} for the association reaction is equal to $1/K_{diss}$. Thus,

$$K_{eq} = \frac{1}{K_{diss}} = \frac{1}{1.8 \times 10^{-5}} = \frac{[HC_2H_3O_2]}{[H^+][C_2H_3O_2^-]}$$

To rewrite into a more convenient form for solving, take the reciprocal of each side.

$$1.8 \times 10^{-5} = \frac{[H^+][C_2H_3O_2^-]}{[HC_2H_3O_2]}$$

The final concentrations of the species, the unknowns, will be those at the equilibrium. Let y be the concentration of $HC_2H_3O_2$ at equilibrium. The concentrations of both H^+ and $C_2H_3O_2^-$ can be represented by 1 - y. Initially, you started with 1 mole/liter of each, therefore, each y mole/liter that associates to form $HC_2H_3O_2$ must be subtracted from the initial concentration. You can now substitute these variables into the expression for K_{diss} to obtain

$$\frac{(1 - y)(1 - y)}{y} = 1.8 \times 10^{-5}$$

Solving for y, using the quadratic formula, you obtain y = .996. Therefore, the concentrations of the species are

$$[H^+] = 1 - y = .004 \text{ M}$$

$$[C_2H_3O_2^-] = .004 \text{ M}$$

$$[HC_2H_3O_2] = .996 \text{ M}.$$

● **PROBLEM** 10-23

Given a solution of 1.00M $HC_2H_3O_2$, what is the concentration of all solute species? What is the percentage of acid that dissociated? Assume $K_{diss} = 1.8 \times 10^{-5}$.

<u>Solution</u>: Determine the equilibrium equation, write an equilibriam constant expression, and substitute the concentrations of the species into the expression.

By definition, an acid is a substance which donates protons (H^+). Since water is the only other species in the solution, it must act as a base; it receives protons.

$$HC_2H_3O_2 + H_2O \rightleftarrows H_3O^+ + C_2H_3O_2^- .$$

There is a constant called $K_{dissociation}$, which measures the extent of the $HC_2H_3O_2$ donation of protons. For the general reaction,

$$HA + H_2O \rightarrow H_3O^+ + A^- , \quad K_{diss} = \frac{[A^-][H_3O^+]}{[HA]} .$$

For the reaction in this problem, you have

$$\frac{[C_2H_3O_2^-][H_3O^+]}{[HC_2H_3O_2]} = K_{diss} = 1.8 \times 10^{-5} .$$

You are asked to find these concentrations. Let x = the moles per liter of $HC_2H_3O_2$ that dissociated. From the chemical equation, you see that x must also be the concentration of H_3O^+ and $C_2H_3O_2^-$, since for each mole of $HC_2H_3O_2$ that dissociates, one mole of H_3O^+ and one mole of $C_2H_3O_2^-$ is produced. With this in mind, you can represent $[HC_2H_3O_2]$ as 1-x, since you started with 1M of $HC_2H_3O_2$ and x moles per liter dissociate. You have left 1-x moles per liter. Now substituting, you obtain

$$\frac{[H_3O^+][C_2H_3O_2^-]}{[HC_2H_3O_2]} = 1.8 \times 10^{-5} = \frac{x \cdot x}{1-x} .$$

Solving for x, you obtain $x = .0042$. Therefore, the concentrations of the species are

$$[HC_2H_3O_2] = 1 - .0042 = .9958M$$

$$[H_3O^+] = x = .0042M$$

$$[C_2H_3O_2^-] = x = .0042M$$

The percentage of acid that dissociated is, thus,

$$\frac{.0042}{1} \times 100 = .42\% .$$

Sulfuryl chloride decomposes according to the equation,

$$SO_2Cl_2(g) \rightleftharpoons SO_2(g) + Cl_2(g) .$$

Given that at $300°$ K and 1 atm pressure, the degree of dissociation is .121, find the equilibrium constant, K_p. What will be the degree of dissociation when pressure = 10 atm?

Solution: To find the equilibrium constant, K_p, one uses the expression for K_p. This is the product of the pressures of the products divided by pressure of the reactant. These pressures are brought to the powers of their coefficients. From this, employ Dalton's law concerning partial pressures to help solve for K_p.

At p = 10 atm, assume K_p is pressure-independent because of ideal gas behavior. This, then, allows the determination of the degree of dissociation from the K_p expression.

Thus, one commences by the definition of K_p.

$$K_p = \frac{P_{SO_2} \, P_{Cl_2}}{P_{SO_2Cl_2}}$$

To find K_p, evaluate these partial pressures. To do this, use Raoult's law, which states partial pressure of gas = mole fraction of gas in mixture times total pressure, i.e., $p = Xp_T$. The P_T is given as 1 atm. Thus, the key is to determine or represent the mole fraction X. Let "a" = the degree of dissociation of SO_2Cl_2. From the chemical equation, it is seen that SO_2 and Cl_2 are formed in equimolar amounts. Thus, at equilibrium there are "a" moles of both SO_2 and Cl_2. Starting with 1 mole of SO_2Cl_2 and "a" moles dissociated, then, at equilibrium, there remain 1 - a moles. In the mixture, therefore, total number of moles = (1-a) + a + a = (1+a). Thus, $P_{SO_2Cl_2} = X_{SO_2Cl_2} P_T = \left(\frac{1-a}{1+a}\right) P_T$,

$P_{SO_2} = P_{Cl_2} = \frac{a}{1+a} P_T$. Therefore,

$$K_p = \frac{P_{SO_2} \, P_{Cl_2}}{P_{SO_2} \, Cl_2} = \frac{\left(\frac{a}{1+a}\right) P_T \left(\frac{a}{1+a}\right) P_T}{\left(\frac{1-a}{1+a}\right) P_T}$$

This can be simplified to

$$K_p = \frac{a^2}{1-a^2} P_T .$$

Given the degree of dissociation, a, is equal to .121 and P_T = 1 atm; K_p therefore, equal

$$\frac{(.121)^2}{1-(.121)^2} (1) = 1.49 \times 10^{-2} .$$

At 10 atm, then,

$$K_p = \frac{a^2}{1-a^2} (10) = 1.49 \times 10^{-2} .$$

Solving for a, $a = .0386$.

THE HYDROLYSIS CONSTANT

● PROBLEM 10-25

If the hydrolysis constant of Al^{3+} is 1.4×10^{-5}, what is the concentration of H_3O^+ in 0.1 M $AlCl_3$?

Solution: Hydrolysis refers to the action of the salts of weak acids and bases with water to form acidic or basic solutions. Consequently, to answer this question, write out the reaction, which illustrates this hydrolysis, and write out an equilibrium constant expression. From this, the concentration of H_3O^+ can be defined. The net hydrolysis reaction is

$$AlCl_3 \rightarrow Al^{3+} + 3\ Cl^-$$

$$Al^{3+} + 2H_2O \rightleftarrows AlOH^{2+} + H_3O^+$$

$$K_{hyd} = 1.4 \times 10^{-5} = \frac{[H_3O^+][AlOH^{3+}]}{[Al^{2+}]} .$$

Water is excluded in this expression since it is considered as a constant. Let x = the moles/liter of $[H_3O^+]$. Since H_3O^+ and $AlOH^{2+}$ are formed in equal mole amounts, the concentration of $[AlOH^{2+}]$ can also be represented by x. If one starts with 0.1 M of Al^{3+}, and x moles/liter of it forms H_3O^+ (and $AlOH^{2+}$), one is left with 0.1 - x at equilibrium. Substituting these representations into the K_{hyd} expression,

$$\frac{x \cdot x}{0.1 - x} = 1.4 \times 10^{-5}.$$

If one solves for x, the answer is $x = 1.2 \times 10^{-3}$ M, which equals $[H_3O^+]$.

● PROBLEM 10-26

Calculate the hydrolysis constants of the ammonium and cyanide ions, assuming $K_w = 1 \times 10^{-14}$ and $K_a = 4.93 \times 10^{-10}$

for HCN and $K_b = 1.77 \times 10^{-5}$ for NH_3. For each, determine the percent hydrolysis in a .1M solution.

<u>Solution</u>: To find the hydrolysis constant, you must know what it defines. Hydrolysis is the process whereby an acid or base is regenerated from its salt by the action of water. The hydrolysis constant measures the extent of this process. Quantitatively, it is defined as being equal to $\dfrac{K_w}{K_a \text{ or } K_b}$, where K_w = the equilibrium constant for the autodissociation of water, K_a = dissociation of acid, and K_b = dissociation of base. You are given K_w, K_a, and K_b. Thus, the hydrolysis constants can be easily found by substitution. Let K_h = hydrolysis constant.

For cyanide ion: $K_h = \dfrac{K_w}{K_a} = \dfrac{1 \times 10^{-14}}{4.93 \times 10^{-10}} = 2.02 \times 10^{-5}$

For ammonium ion: $K_h = \dfrac{K_w}{K_b} = \dfrac{1 \times 10^{-14}}{1.77 \times 10^{-5}} = 5.64 \times 10^{-10}$

To find the percent hydrolysis in a .1M solution, write the hydrolysis reaction and express the hydrolysis constant just calculated in those terms. After this, represent the concentrations of the hydrolysis products in terms of variables and solve. For cyanide ion: The hydrolysis reaction is $CN^- + H_2O \rightleftarrows HCN + OH^-$. Therefore,

$K_h = \dfrac{[HCN][OH^-]}{[CN^-]}$. But you calculated that $K_h = 2.02 \times 10^{-5}$.

Equating, $2.02 \times 10^{-5} = \dfrac{[HCN][OH^-]}{[CN^-]}$. You start with a .1M solution of CN^-. Let x = [HCN] formed. Thus, x = [OH⁻] also, since they are formed in equimolar amounts. If x moles/liter of substance are formed from CN^-, then, at equilibrium you have .1-x moles/liter left. Substituting these values, $2.02 \times 10^{-5} = \dfrac{x \cdot x}{.1-x}$

Solving, $x = 1.4 \times 10^{-3}$M. The percent is just 100 times $\dfrac{x}{.10M}$ since the initial concentration is .10M, so that you have 1.4% hydrolysis in a .1M solution.

For ammonium ion: The hydrolysis reaction is $NH_4^+ + H_2O \rightleftarrows NH_3 + H_3O^+$. K_h for this reaction = $\dfrac{[NH_3][H_3O^+]}{[NH_4^+]}$ The calculated $K_h = 5.6 \times 10^{-10}$. Equating, $5.6 \times 10^{-10} = \dfrac{[NH_3][H_3O^+]}{[NH_4^+]}$.

From this point, you follow the same reasoning as was used with the cyanide.

Solving:

Let $x = [NH_3]$

$$5.6 \times 10^{-10} = \frac{(x)(x)}{(.1-x)}$$

$$x^2 = (5.6 \times 10^{-11}) - (5.6 \times 10^{-10})x$$

$$x^2 + (5.6 \times 10^{-10})x - 5.6 \times 10^{-11} = 0$$

Using the quadratic formula one can solve for x, where $ax^2 + bx + c = 0$

$$x = \frac{-b \pm \sqrt{b^2 - 4\,ac}}{2a}$$

$$x = \frac{-5.6 \times 10^{-10} \pm \sqrt{(5.6 \times 10^{-10})^2 - 4(1)(-5.6 \times 10^{-11})}}{2\,(1)}$$

$$x = \frac{-5.6 \times 10^{-10} \pm \sqrt{2.24 \times 10^{-10}}}{2}$$

$$x = \frac{-5.6 \times 10^{-10} \pm 1.50 \times 10^{-5}}{2}$$

$$x = \frac{-1.50 \times 10^{-5}}{2} \text{ or } x = \frac{1.50 \times 10^{-5}}{2}$$

x cannot be negative, because concentration cannot be negative. Thus, $x = 7.5 \times 10^{-6}$

Solving for the percent:

$$\frac{7.5 \times 10^{-6}}{.1} \times 100\% = 7.5\%$$

Thus, you find that the percent hydrolysis is $7.5 \times 10^{-3}\%$.

● PROBLEM 10-27

What is the pH of a 1.0 M solution of the strong electrolyte sodium acetate? The dissociation constant of acetic acid is $K_a = 1.8 \times 10^{-5}$ mole/liter.

Solution: The first step is the determination of the hydrolysis constant for sodium acetate. From this we obtain the concentration of hydroxyl contributed by the

hydrolysis of sodium acetate. The concentration of hydronium ion, and consequently the pH, is determined by using the water constant.

The dissociation of acetic acid (HAc) into hydronium

ions and acetate ions (Ac$^-$) may be represented by the equation

$$HAc + H_2O \; \overset{\rightarrow}{\leftarrow} \; H_3O^+ + Ac^-.$$

The dissociation constant for this reaction is

$$K_a = \frac{[H_3O^+][Ac^-]}{[HAc]}$$

This constant and the water constant, $K_w = [H_3O^+][OH^-]$ $= 10^{-14}$ mole^2/liter^2 will be used to determine the hydrolysis constant for acetate.

Hydrolysis of acetate proceeds according to the following equation:

$$Ac^- + H_2O \; \overset{\rightarrow}{\leftarrow} \; HAc + OH^-.$$

The hydrolysis constant is $K_h = [HAc][OH^-]/[Ac^-]$. This may be rewritten in terms of K_a and K_w as follows:

$$K_h = \frac{[HAc][OH^-]}{[Ac^-]} = \frac{[HAc][OH^-]}{[Ac^-]} \times \frac{[H_3O^+]}{[H_3O^+]}$$

$$= \frac{[HAc]}{[Ac^-][H_3O^+]} \times [H_3O^+][OH^-] = \frac{1}{K_a} \times K_w = \frac{K_w}{K_a} \, . \quad \text{Hence,}$$

$$K_h = \frac{[HAc][OH^-]}{[Ac^-]} = \frac{K_w}{K_a}$$

$$= \frac{10^{-14} \text{ mole}^2/\text{liter}^2}{1.8 \times 10^{-5} \text{ mole/liter}} = 5.6 \times 10^{-10} \text{ mole/liter.}$$

Let the equilibrium concentration of HAc formed by the hydrolysis of acetate be x. Since one mole of OH$^-$ is formed per mole of HAc formed, the equilibrium concentration of OH$^-$ is also x. Furthermore, if we assume that sodium acetate dissociates completely, then the initial concentration of Ac$^-$ is equal to the concentration of sodium acetate (1.0 M) and the equilibrium concentration of acetate is 1.0 - x. Note that we have neglected the contribution to [OH$^-$] from the hydrolysis of water.

Substituting these concentrations into the expression for K_h, we obtain

$$K_h = 5.6 \times 10^{-10} \text{ mole/liter} = \frac{[HAc][OH^-]}{[Ac^-]}$$

$$= \frac{x \cdot x}{1.0 - x} = \frac{x^2}{1.0 - x}$$

To avoid use of the quadratic formula, we will assume that x is much smaller than 1.0 so that $1.0 - x \cong 1.0$. (This assumption will be justified later on in the solution). Hence, we obtain

$$5.6 \times 10^{-10} \text{ mole/liter} = \frac{x^2}{1.0 - x} \cong \frac{x^2}{1.0}$$

or $x = (1.0 \times 5.6 \times 10^{-10})^{\frac{1}{2}} = 2.4 \times 10^{-5}$ mole/liter.

Since $[OH^-] = x$, $[OH^-] = 2.4 \times 10^{-5}$ mole/liter. Hence, x is much smaller than 1.0, justifying our earlier assumption.

We will find $[H_3O^+]$ by use of the water constant, $K_w = [H_3O^+][OH^-]$, or,

$$[H_3O^+] = \frac{K_w}{[OH^-]} = \frac{10^{-14} \text{ mole}^2/\text{liter}^2}{2.4 \times 10^{-5} \text{ mole/liter}}$$

$$= 4.2 \times 10^{-9} \text{ mole/liter}.$$

The pH is then

$$pH = - \log [H_3O^+] = - \log (4.2 \times 10^{-9})$$

$$= - (- 9.4) = 9.4.$$

NEUTRALIZATION

● **PROBLEM** 10-28

Assuming complete neutralization, calculate the number of milliliters of 0.025 M H_3PO_4 required to neutralize 25 ml of 0.030 M $Ca(OH)_2$.

Solution: This problem can be solved by two methods: mole method or equivalent method.

Mole Method

This method requires one to write out the balanced equation that illustrates the neutralization reaction. The balanced equation is $3Ca(OH)_2 + 2H_3PO_4 \rightarrow Ca_3(PO_4)_2 + 6H_2O$. From this equation, one can see that 2 moles of H_3PO_4 react for every 3 moles of $Ca(OH)_2$. This means that one must first calculate how many moles of $Ca(OH)_2$ are involved. The molarity of the $Ca(OH)_2$ is 0.030. (Molarity = no. of moles/liters.)

As given, the $Ca(OH)_2$ solution is 25 ml or 0.025 liters. Therefore, the number of moles of $Ca(OH)_2$ is

(0.030)(0.025) = 0.00075 moles. As the balanced equation indicates, the number of moles of H_3PO_4 is 2/3 the moles of $Ca(OH)_2$ or 2/3 (0.00075) = 0.00050 moles of H_3PO_4.

From the definition of molarity for H_3PO_4 one has

$$0.025 \text{ M} = \frac{0.00050 \text{ moles}}{\text{liters}} .$$

The molarity, 0.025, is given. Solving for liters, one obtains 0.020 liters or 20 ml. The key to solving this problem with the mole method, is to write a balanced equation, which will indicate the relative amounts of moles required for complete neutralization .

Equivalent Method

This method requires that one consider normality and the definition of an equivalent. An equivalent is defined as the molecular weight or mass of an acid or base that furnished one mole of protons (H^+) or hydroxyl (OH^-) ions. For example, the number of equivalents contained in a mole of H_2SO_4 is 98/2 or 49. Since each mole of H_2SO_4 produces two protons, divide the molecular weight by 2.

The number of equivalents of an acid must equal that of the base in a neutralization reaction. Normality is defined as equivalents of solute per liter. In this problem, it is given that there are 25 ml of 0.03 $Ca(OH)_2$.

To solve the problem, determine how many equivalents are present. The number of moles of $Ca(OH)_2$ is (0.025)(0.03) or 0.00075 from the definition of molarity. The molecular weight of $Ca(OH)_2$ is 74.08. Therefore, there are (0.00075)(74.08) or 0.06 grams of $Ca(OH)_2$.

The number of equivalents per gram is 74.08/2 since two OH^- can be produced. The number of equivalents is

$$\frac{(0.00075)(74.08) \text{g}}{\left(\frac{74.08}{2} \text{ g/equiv} \right)} = 0.0015 \text{ equiv of } Ca(OH)_2 .$$

This indicates that 0.0015 equivalents of H_3PO_4 are required. The molarity of H_3PO_4 is 0.025 M, which means its normality is 0.075 N, because there are 3 ionizable protons per mole. Recalling the definition of normality, there are

$$0.075 \text{ N} = 0.0015 \text{ equiv/liters}$$

The reason one knows that there is 0.0015 equiv in the H_3PO_4 present is because one knows that for the neutralization to occur the number of equivalents of acid must equal the number of equivalents of base. In this problem, one has already calculated that there are

0.0015 equiv of base present. Thus,

volume = 0.20 ℓ or 20 ml.

A 50 ml solution of sulfuric acid was found to contain
0.490 g of H_2SO_4. This solution was titrated against a
sodium hydroxide solution of unknown concentration.
12.5 ml of the acid solution was required to neutralize
20.0 ml of the base. What is the concentration of the
sodium hydroxide solution.

Solution: At the neutralization point, the number of
equivalents of acid in the 12.5 ml volume is equal to the
number of equivalents of base in the 20.0 ml volume. Since
the normality is defined as the number of equivalents per
liter of solution, the number of equivalents is equal to
the normality times the volume, at the neutralization
point we have

$$N_a V_a = N_b V_b$$

where N_a = normality of acid, V_a = volume of acid, N_b =
normality of base, V_b = volume of base.

The normality of the 50.0 ml (0.050 ℓ) sulfuric acid
solution is

$$N_a = \frac{\text{number of equivalents in } 0.050 \ \ell}{0.05 \ \ell}$$

$$= \frac{\text{mass of acid/gram equivalent weight}}{0.05 \ \ell}$$

The gram equivalent weight of sulfuric acid is
49.0 g/equivalent, because there are 2 equiv per molecule.
The MW of H_2SO_4 is 98 g/mole.

$$N_a = \frac{\text{mass of acid/gram equivalent weight}}{0.05 \ \ell}$$

$$= \frac{0.490 \ g/49.0 \ g/\text{equivalent}}{0.05 \ \ell} = 0.200 \ \text{equivalent}/\ell$$

$$= 0.200 \ N$$

The normality of the base is then found as follows:

$$N_a V_a = N_b V_b$$

$$N_b = \frac{N_a V_a}{V_b} = \frac{0.200 \ N \times 12.5 \ ml}{20.0 \ ml} = 0.125 \ N.$$

Therefore, the sodium hydroxide solution is 0.125 N, which because there is 1 ionizable OH^- in NaOH, is equal to 0.125 M.

● **PROBLEM** 10-30

A potato peeling solution was found to be 2.56 M in NaOH (formula weight = 40.0 g/mole) at the end of the day. To operate, the solution must be at least 10 % NaOH by weight (100 g NaOH per 1000 g of solution). What weight percent corresponds to 2.56 M? The density of a 2.56 M solution of NaOH is about 1.10 g/ml.

Solution: To solve this problem, the concentration 2.56 M must be converted to a weight-weight basis. 2.56 M = 2.56 moles NaOH/1 liter solution = 2.56 moles NaOH/1000 ml solution. To obtain the mass corresponding to 2.56 moles of NaOH, we multiply by the formula weight of NaOH, or, 2.56 moles × 40.0 g/moles = 102.4 g NaOH.

To obtain the mass of NaOH contained in 1000 ml of solution, we multiply by the density of the solution, 1000 ml × 1.10 g/ml = 1100 g. Hence,

$$2.56 \ M = \frac{2.56 \ moles \ NaOH}{1000 \ ml \ solution} = \frac{102.4 \ g \ NaOH}{1100 \ g \ solution} ;$$

$$\frac{102.4 \ g \ NaOH}{1100 \ g \ solution} \times 100 \ \% = 9.3 \ \% \ by \ weight.$$

Since this is less than 10 % by weight, the solution is no longer capable of peeling potatoes.

● **PROBLEM** 10-31

50 ml of rhubarb juice is titrated against 0.25 N NaOH. 20 ml of NaOH solution is required for neutralization. Assuming the acidity of the juice is due to oxalic acid $(H_2C_2O_4)$ determine (a) the weight of oxalic acid per liter of juice, (b) normality of the juice.

Solution: (a) For the neutralization to occur, there must be the same number of OH^- ions as there are H^+ ions present.

$$H^+ + OH^- \overset{\rightarrow}{\leftarrow} H_2O$$

The normality of a base is defined as the number of

equivalents of base in one liter of solution. An equivalent is the weight of an acid or base that produces one mole of H^+ or OH^- ions, respectively. When NaOH ionizes, there is 1 OH^- ion formed by each NaOH that ionizes.

$$NaOH \overset{\leftarrow}{\rightarrow} OH^- + Na^+$$

Therefore, in a 0.25 N NaOH solution there are 0.25 equivalents of OH^-, which, in this case is also the number of moles. 20 ml is 0.02 liters. The number of moles of NaOH present will equal the number of liters of solution times the molarity of the solution. As previously indicated, normality equals molarity. Thus,

no. of moles = no. of liters × normality

$$= 0.02 \text{ liters} \times \frac{.25 \text{ moles}}{\text{liter}} = 0.005 \text{ moles.}$$

Thus, there must be 0.005 moles of H^+ ions from the oxalic acid to neutralize the NaOH. When oxalic acid ionizes, there are 2 H^+ ions formed for each molecule ionized.

$$H_2C_2O_4 = 2H^+ + C_2O_4$$

Therefore, each mole of oxalic acid ionizes 2 moles of NaOH. Thus, for neutralization to occur, only one half as much oxalic acid is needed as NaOH. There are 0.005 moles of NaOH, present, therefore, 0.0025 moles of oxalic acid is needed to neutralize it. One now knows that there are 0.0025 moles of oxalic acid in the 50 ml of rhubarb juice. One can find the number of moles in 1 liter by multiplying 0.0025 moles/50 ml by the conversion factor 1000 ml/1 liter.

$$\text{no. of moles/liter of oxalic acid} = \frac{0.0025 \text{ moles}}{50 \text{ ml}} \times \frac{1000 \text{ ml}}{1 \text{ liter}}$$

$$= 0.05 \text{ moles/liter.}$$

Since there are 0.05 moles of $H_2C_2O_4$ in 1 liter of juice, one can find the weight of $H_2C_2O_4$ in this quantity of juice by multiplying 0.05 moles by the MW of $H_2C_2O_4$. (MW = 90).

weight of $H_2C_2O_4$ in 1 liter = 0.05 moles × 90 g/moles

$$= 4.5 \text{ g}$$

(b) For titrations, the following relation is found:

$$N_{acid} V_{acid} = N_{base} V_{base}$$

where N_{acid} is the normality of the acid, V_{acid} is the volume of the acid, N_{base} is the normality of the base, and V_{base} is the volume of the base.

Here, one is given N_{base}, V_{base}, and V_{acid}. One is asked to find N_{acid}.

$N_b = .25$ N

$V_b = 20$ ml

$N_a = ?$

$V_a = 50$ ml

$N_a V_a = N_b V_b$

$N_a \times 50$ ml $= .25$ N $\times 20$ ml

$N_a = \dfrac{0.25 \text{ N} \times 20 \text{ ml}}{50 \text{ ml}} = 0.10$ N.

CHAPTER 11

THERMODYNAMICS I

● PROBLEM 11-1

For the system described by the following diagram, is the forward reaction exothermic or endothermic?

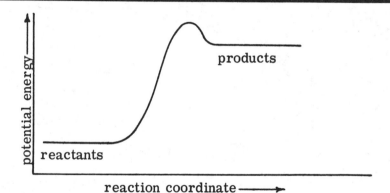

Solution: By observing the diagram, we see that the products are at a higher potential energy than the re-actants, thus energy must have been absorbed during the course of the reaction. The only mechanism by which this can occur is absorption of heat and subsequent conversion of heat into potential energy. Hence, the reaction absorbs heat and is therefore endothermic.

BOND ENERGIES

● PROBLEM 11-2

Given for hydrogen peroxide, H_2O_2:

$$HO - OH(g) \rightarrow 2OH(g) \qquad \Delta H^{\circ}_{diss} = 51 \text{ Kcal/mole}$$

From this value and the following data calculate:
(a) ΔH°_f of OH(g). (b) C-O bond energy; ΔH°_{diss} in

Solution: (a) ΔH^o_{diss} for this reaction is equal to the ΔH^o_f of the reactants subtracted from the ΔH^o_f of the products, where ΔH^o equals enthalpy or heat content.

$$\Delta H^o_{diss} = 2 \times \Delta H^o_f \text{ OH} - \Delta H^o_f \text{ HO-OH} = 51 \text{ Kcal/mole}$$

$$2 \times \Delta H^o_f \text{ OH} = 51 \text{ Kcal/mole} + \Delta H^o_f \text{ HO-OH}$$

$$\Delta H^o_f \text{ OH} = \frac{51 \text{ Kcal/mole} - 32.58 \text{ Kcal/mole}}{2}$$

$$\Delta H^o_f \text{ OH} = \frac{18.42 \text{ Kcal/mole}}{2} = 9.21 \text{ Kcal/mole.}$$

(b) CH_3OH dissociates by breaking the C-O bond:

$$CH_3OH(g) \rightarrow CH_3^+(g) + OH^-(g)$$

Therefore, the bond energy of the C-O bond equals ΔH^o_{diss}. ΔH^o_{diss} equals the sum of the ΔH's of the products minus the ΔH's of the reactants. Thus,

bond energy of C-O = ΔH^o_f of $CH_3^+(g)$ + ΔH^o_f of $OH^-(g)$ −

$$\Delta H^o_f \text{ of } CH_3OH(g).$$

bond energy of C-O = 34.0 Kcal/mole + 9.21 Kcal/mole

$$+ 47.96 \text{ Kcal/mole}$$

$$= 91.17 \text{ Kcal/mole.}$$

● **PROBLEM 11-3**

Using the following table of bond energies, calculate the energy change in the following:

(a) $2H_2(g) + O_2(g) \rightarrow 2H_2O(g)$
(b) $CH_4(g) + 2O_2(g) \rightarrow CO_2(g) + 2H_2O(g)$

(c) $CH_4(g) + Cl_2(g) \rightarrow CH_3Cl(g) + HCl(g)$

(d) $C_2H_6(g) + Cl_2(g) \rightarrow C_2H_5Cl(g) + HCl(g)$.

Bond Energies (in kcal per mole)

H–H	104	C–O	83
H–F	135	C=O	178
H–Cl	103	C–Cl	79
H–Br	88	C–F	105
H–I	71	Si–O	106
Li–H	58	Si–F	136
Cl–Cl	58	C–C	83
C–H	87	C=C	146
O–H	111	C≡C	199
O=O	118	N≡N	225
P–Cl	78		

Solution: When using the bond energies to calculate the net energy change in a reaction, the net energy change is equal to the total bond energy of the bonds formed subtracted from the bond energy of bonds broken. This method is illustrated in the following examples.

a) $2H_2(g) + O_2(g) \rightarrow 2H_2O(g)$

There are two H_2 bonds and 1 O_2 bond broken and 4 O-H bonds formed here.

$2H-H(g) + O = O(g) \rightarrow 2 H-O-H(g)$

net bond energy =(2 x bond energy of H-H)+(1 x bond energy of O=O)-(4 x bond energy of O-H)

The following bond energies can be found in the table.

Bond	Bond energy (Kcal/mole)
H — H	104
O = O	118
O — H	111

The net energy or heat evolved in the reaction can be found using these values.

net bond energy = $[(2\times104)+(1\times118)]-(4\times111)$

$$\Delta H = (208 + 118) - 444 = -118 \text{ Kcal.}$$

Thus when this reaction occurs 118 Kcal are released. The following examples will be solved in a similar manner.

b) $CH_4(g) + 2O_2 \rightarrow CO_2(g) + 2H_2O(g)$

This reaction can be rewritten

H
|
H — C — H (g) + 2 O=O (g) → O=C=O(g) + 2H-o-H(g)
|
H

This means that there are 4 C-H bonds and 2 O=O bonds broken and 2 O=C bonds and 4 O-H bonds formed.

net energy = [(4 × bond energy of C-H) + (2 × bond energy of O=O)] - [(2 × bond energy of C=O) + (4 × bond energy of O-H)]

The following bond energies are used.

Bond	Bond energy (Kcal/mole)
O — H	111
O = C	178
O = O	118
C — H	87

One can now determine the heat evolved in this reaction.

net energy = [(4 × 87) + (2 × 118)] - [(2 × 178) + 4 × 111]

ΔH = - 216 Kcal.

c) $CH_4(g) + Cl_2(g) \rightarrow CH_3Cl(g) + HCl(g)$

This equation can be rewritten

H_3C-H (g) + Cl-Cl (g) $\rightarrow$ H_3C-Cl (g) + H-Cl (g)

This means that there is 1 C-H and 1 Cl-Cl bond broken and 1 C-Cl and 1 H-Cl bond formed.

net energy = (1 × bond energy of C-H + 1 × bond energy of Cl-Cl) - (1 × bond energy of C-Cl + 1 × bond energy of H-Cl)

The following bond energies are used.

Bond	Bond energy (Kcal/mole)
C - H	87
Cl - Cl	58
C - Cl	79
H - Cl	103

The heat evolved can now be determined.

net energy = ΔH = [(1 × 87) + (1 × 58)] - [(1 × 79)+(1×103)]

= (87 + 58) - (79 + 103)

= - 37 Kcal.

d) $C_2H_6(g) + Cl_2(g) \rightarrow C_2H_5Cl(g) + HCl(g)$

This can be rewritten as

$$H_3C - \overset{\overset{\displaystyle H}{|}}{\underset{\underset{\displaystyle H}{|}}{C}} - H(g) + Cl-Cl \ (g) \ \rightarrow \ H_3C - \overset{\overset{\displaystyle H}{|}}{\underset{\underset{\displaystyle H}{|}}{C}} - Cl(g) + H-Cl \ (g)$$

Thus, there is 1 C-H and 1 Cl-Cl bond broken and 1 C-Cl and 1 H-Cl bond formed.

The net energy for the reaction can be determined by using the following values.

Bond	Bond energy (Kcal/mole)
C - H	87
Cl - Cl	58
C - Cl	79
H - Cl	103

The net energy can now be found.

net energy = ΔH = $[(1 \times 87) + (1 \times 58)] - [(1 \times 79) + (1 \times 103)]$

$$= (87 + 58) - (79 + 103)$$

$$= -37 \ Kcal.$$

HEAT CAPACITY

● **PROBLEM 11-4**

What is the heat capacity of uranium? Its atomic heat is 26 J/mole and its atomic weight is 238 g/mole.

Solution: The atomic heat of a solid element at room temperature is defined as the amount of heat required to raise the temperature of one mole of an element by one degree Celsius. The heat capacity, or specific heat, is the amount of heat required to raise the temperature of one gram of a substance by one degree Celsius. These two quantities can be related by the equation,

atomic heat = atomic weight × heat capacity.

Thus, to find the heat capacity of uranium, substitute the given values of atomic heat and weight.

heat capacity of uranium = 26 J/mole C°/238 g/mole

$$= 0.11 \ J/g°C.$$

Calculate the quantity of heat required to raise the
temperature of one gallon of water (3.78 liters) from
10° to 80°C.

Solution: The unit of heat is called the calorie. It is
defined as the quantity of heat necessary to raise the
temperature of one gram of water one degree centigrade.
In this problem, one is told that 3.78 liters of water are
heated from 10°C to 80°C. If one subtracts the final temperature from the original temperature, one can find the
number of degrees the temperature of the water is raised.

number of °C the temperature is raised =

final temperature - original temperature

no. of °C the temperature is raised = 80°C - 10°C = 70°C.

One must now determine the number of grams in
3.78 liters of water. Because 1 milliliter of water weighs
one gram, one must determine the number of milliliters in
3.78 liters of water. There are 1000 milliliters in
1 liter; therefore, liters can be converted to milliliters
by multiplying the number of liters present by the factor
1000 ml/1 liter.

3.78 liters × 1000 ml/1 liter = 3780 ml

Because number of ml = number of grams for water,
there are 3780 g of water present in 3.78 liters. One now
knows that 3780 g of water have been raised 70°C in temperature. Remembering the definition for calorie, one can

find the number of calories absorbed in this process by
multiplying the number of grams of water by the number of
degrees the temperature was raised by the factor
1 calorie/1g - 1°C, the specific heat of water.

number of calories absorbed = 3780 g × 70°C ×

1 calorie/1g - 1°C

= 265,000 calories

There are 1000 calories in 1 kilocalorie, so that
calories can be converted to kilocalories by multiplying
the number of calories by the factor 1 Kcal/1000 cal.

265,000 cal × 1 Kcal/1000 cal = 265 Kcal.

265 Kcal are absorbed in this process.

A piece of iron weighing 20.0 g at a temperature of 95.0°C
was placed in 100.0 g of water at 25.0°C. Assuming that no
heat is lost to the surroundings, what is the resulting
temperature of the iron and water? Specific heats: iron =
.108 cal/g-C°; water = 1.0 cal/g-C°.

<u>Solution</u>:   The heat lost by the iron must be equal to the
heat gained by the water. One solves for the heat lost by
the iron by multiplying the number of grams of Fe by the
number of degrees the temperature dropped by the specific
heat of iron. The specific heat of a substance is defined
as the amount of heat energy required to raise the temperature of 1 g of a substance by 1°C. The specific heat
for iron is .108 cal/g°C.Let t = the final temperature of
the system.

amount of heat lost by the iron = .108 cal/g-°C × 20.0 g

$$× (95.0°C - t)$$

The amount of heat gained by the water is the specific
heat of water multiplied by the weight of the water
multiplied by the rise in the temperature. The specific heat
of water is 1.0 cal/g-C°. Let t = final temperature of the
system.

amount of heat gained by water = 1.0 cal/g-°C × 100 g

$$× (t - 25°C)$$

Solving for t:

amount of heat lost by the iron = amount of heat gained by
the water. Therefore,

$$(.108 \text{ cal/g°C})(20.0 \text{ g})(95°C-t)=(1 \text{ cal/g°C})(100 \text{ g})(t-25°C)$$

$$205.2 \text{ cal} - (2.16 \text{ cal/°C})t = (100 \text{ cal/°C})t - 2500 \text{ cal}$$

$$2705.2 \text{ cal} = (102.16 \text{ cal/°C})t$$

$$\frac{2705.2 \text{ cal}}{102.16 \text{ cal/°C}} = t$$

$$26.48°C = t.$$

A container has the dimensions 2.5 m × 50 cm × 60 mm.
If it is filled with water at 32°F, how many kilocalories
will be necessary to heat the water to the boiling point?
(212°F)

Solution: A kilocalorie is defined as the amount of heat necessary to raise the temperature of 1 kg of water 1°C. Thus, to solve for the number of kilocalories necessary, one must first solve for the number of grams present and the number of °C that the temperature is raised. One cubic cm of water weighs 1 gram. Thus, if one solves for the volume in terms of cubic centimeters, the weight is then quickly determined. One can solve for the volume in cubic centimeters after converting the lengths of dimensions to centimeters. 1 m = 100 cm, therefore 2.5 m = 250 cm.

If 1 cm = 10 mm, then 60 mm = 6 cm.

Solving for the volume:

volume = 250 cm × 50 cm × 6 cm = 7.50×10^4 cc.

Therefore, the weight of the water is 7.5×10^4 g. 1 kg = 1000 g, thus 7.5×10^4 g = 75 kg.

To convert from °F to °C one uses the following formula:

°C = 5/9 (°F - 32)

Solving for °C when t = 32°F:

°C = 5/9 (32 - 32) = 0°C.

When t = 212°F.

°C = 5/9(212-32) = 5/9(180) = 100°C.

Therefore, the change in temperature is 100° - 0° or 100°C.

Solving for the number of kilocalories needed:

no. of Kcal = $\frac{1 \text{ Kcal}}{°C \text{ kg}}$ × 100°C × 75 kg = 7.5×10^3 Kcal.

ENTHALPY

● **PROBLEM** 11-8

Using the information in the following table, determine $\Delta H°$ for the reactions:
a) $3Fe_2O_3(s) + CO(g) \rightarrow 2Fe_3O_4(s) + CO_2(g)$
b) $Fe_3O_4(s) + CO(g) \rightarrow 3FeO(s) + CO_2(g)$
c) $FeO(s) + CO(g) \rightarrow Fe(s) + CO_2(g)$

Heats of Formation

Compound	$\Delta H°$ (Kcal/mole)
CO (g)	- 26.4

CO_2 (g)	- 94.1
Fe_2O_3 (s)	- 197
Fe_3O_4 (s)	- 267
FeO (s)	- 63.7

Solution: The energy change involved in the formation of one mole of a compound from its elements in their normal state is called the heat of formation. Thus, $\Delta H°$ for a reaction can be found by subtracting the sum of the $\Delta H°$'s for the reactants from the sum of the $\Delta H°$'s for the products.

$\Delta H°$ = $\Delta H°$ of the products - $\Delta H°$ of the reactants

a) 3 Fe_2O_3 (s) + CO(g) → 2 Fe_3O_4 (s) + CO_2 (g)

When more than one mole of a compound is either reacted or formed in a reaction, the $\Delta H°$ for that compound is multiplied by the number of moles present in solving for the $\Delta H°$ of the reaction.

For this reaction:

$\Delta H°$ = $(2 \times \Delta H°$ of $Fe_3O_4 + \Delta H°$ of $CO_2) - (3 \times \Delta H°$ of $Fe_2O_3 + \Delta H°$ of CO)

$\Delta H°$ = $[2 \times (-267) + (-94.1)] - [3 \times (-197) + -26.4)]$

= - 10.7 Kcal.

b) Fe_3O_4 (s) + CO(g) → 3FeO(s) + CO_2 (g)

$\Delta H°$ = $(3 \times \Delta H°$ of FeO+ $\Delta H°$ of CO_2) - ($\Delta H°$ of Fe_3O_4 + $\Delta H°$ of CO)

$\Delta H°$ = $(3 \times (- 63.7) + (- 94.1)) - ((- 267) + (- 26.4))$

= 8.2 Kcal.

c) FeO(s) + CO(g) → Fe(s) + CO_2 (g)

$\Delta H°$ = ($\Delta H°$ of Fe + $\Delta H°$ of CO_2) - ($\Delta H°$ of FeO + $\Delta H°$ of CO)

The $\Delta H°$ of any element is 0. Thus, the $\Delta H°$ of Fe is 0.

$\Delta H°$ = $(0 + (- 94.1)) - ((- 63.7) + (- 26.4))$

= - 4.0 Kcal.

● PROBLEM 11-9

Given the following reactions:	
S(s) + O_2(g) → SO_2 (g)	ΔH = - 71.0 Kcal
SO_2 (g) + ½O_2 (g) → SO_3 (g)	ΔH = - 23.5 Kcal
calculate ΔH for the reaction:	
S(s) + 1½O_2 (g) → SO_3 (g)	

Solution: The heat of a given chemical change is the same

whether the reaction proceeds in one or several steps;
in other words, the energy change is independent of the
path taken by the reaction. The heat for a given reaction
is the algebraic sum of the heats of any sequence of reactions which will yield the reaction in question. For this
problem, one can add the 2 reactions together to obtain
the third. The ΔH is found for the third reaction by adding
the ΔH's of the other two.

$$\begin{array}{r} \Delta H = -71.0 \text{ Kcal} \\ + \Delta H = -23.5 \text{ Kcal} \\ \hline -94.5 \text{ Kcal} \end{array}$$

$$\begin{array}{l} \quad S(s) + O_2(g) \rightarrow SO_2(g) \\ + \quad SO_2(g) + \frac{1}{2}O_2(g) \rightarrow SO_3(g) \\ \hline S(s) + O_2(g) + SO_2(g) + \frac{1}{2}O_2(g) \rightarrow SO_2(g) + SO_3(g) \end{array}$$

This equation can be simplified by subtracting $SO_2(g)$
from each side and adding O_2 and $\frac{1}{2}O_2$ together. You have,
therefore

$$S(s) + \left[O_2(g) + \frac{1}{2}O_2(g) \right] + SO_2(g) - SO_2(g) \rightarrow SO_3(g) + SO_2(g) - SO_2(g)$$

or $S(s) + 1\frac{1}{2}O_2(g) \rightarrow SO_3(g)$

The ΔH for this reaction is -94.5 Kcal, as shown
above.

● PROBLEM 11-10

You are given the following reactions at 25°C:
$2NaHCO_3(s) \rightarrow Na_2CO_3(s) + CO_2(g) + H_2O(\ell)$, $\Delta H =$
30.92 Kcal/mole. $\Delta H^\circ_{Na_2CO_3(s)} = -270.3$, $\Delta H^\circ_{CO_2(g)} =$
-94.0 and $\Delta H^\circ_{H_2O(\ell)} = -68.4$ Kcal/mole, what is the
standard enthalpy of formation for $NaHCO_3(s)$?

Solution: The ΔH° for a reaction is an indication of the
amount of heat released (or absorbed) when the reactants
are converted to products. In general, ΔH° for a reaction
will be the sum of the heats of formation of products
minus the sum of the heats of formation of reactants, each
of which is multiplied by its coefficient in the equation.
Because you are given this sum and the ΔH° (heats of
formation) of all products, the standard enthalpy of
formation of $NaHCO_3$ can be found. Proceed as follows:

$$\Delta H^\circ = \Delta H^\circ_{Na_2CO_3(s)} + \Delta H^\circ_{CO_2(g)} + \Delta H^\circ_{H_2O(\ell)} - 2\Delta H^\circ_{NaHCO_3(s)}$$

Substituting known values,

$$30.92 = (-270.3) + (-94.0) + (-44.8) - 2\Delta H^\circ_{NaHCO_3(s)} .$$

Solving for $\Delta H^{\circ}_{NaHCO_3(s)}$, you obtain

$$\Delta H^{\circ}_{NaHCO_3(s)} = (-270.3 - 94.0 - 44.8 - 30.9)/2$$

$$= -440.0/2 = -220.0 \text{ Kcal/mole,}$$

which is its standard enthalpy of formation.

● **PROBLEM** 11-11

Calculate the standard enthalpy change, ΔH°, for the combustion of ammonia, $NH_3(g)$, to give nitric oxide, $NO(g)$, and water $H_2O(\ell)$. The enthalpies of formation, ΔH°_f, are -68.32 Kcal/mole for $H_2O(\ell)$, -11.02 Kcal/mole for $NH_3(g)$, and 21.57 Kcal/mole for $NO(g)$.

Solution: The enthalpy change, ΔH, refers to the change in heat content between the products and the reactants of a chemical reaction. The symbol ΔH° is the enthalpy change for a reaction in which each reactant and product is in its standard state at a specified reference temperature (the common reference temperature is 25°C).

The standard enthalpy of formation, ΔH°_f, of a substance is defined as the change in enthalpy for the reaction in which one mole of the compound is formed from its elements at standard conditions.

For any chemical reaction, the change in enthalpy, ΔH, may be expressed as

$$\Delta H_{reaction} = \sum H_{products} - \sum H_{reactants}$$

(where the symbol $\sum H$ means the summation of the enthalpies of each substance).

To solve this problem, one must first write and balance the equation for the combustion of $NH_3(g)$:

$$4 \ NH_3(g) + 5O_2(g) \rightarrow 4NO(g) + 6 \ H_2O(\ell)$$

From the balanced equation, one knows that 4 moles of $NH_3(g)$ reacts with 5 moles of $O_2(g)$ to form 4 moles of $NO(g)$ and 6 moles of $H_2O(\ell)$. For the combustion of 4 moles of $NH_3(g)$:

$$4 \cdot \Delta H^{\circ}_{f, \ NH_3(g)} = 4 \left(-11.02 \ \frac{Kcal}{mole} \right) = -44.08 \text{ Kcal}$$

$$5 \cdot \Delta H^{\circ}_{f, \ O_2(g)} = 5 \ (0) = 0$$

$$4 \cdot \Delta H^{\circ}_{f, \ NO(g)} = 4 \left(21.57 \ \frac{Kcal}{mole} \right) = 86.28 \text{ Kcal}$$

$$6 \cdot \Delta H^{\circ}_{f, \ H_2O(\ell)} = 6 \left(-68.32 \ \frac{Kcal}{mole} \right) = -409.92 \text{ Kcal}$$

Note: The ΔH°_f of all elements is zero. As such $\Delta H^\circ_{f, O_2(g)} = 0$.

Thus,

$$\Delta H^\circ = \left[4 \cdot \Delta H^\circ_{f, NO(g)} + 6 \cdot \Delta H^\circ_{f, H_2O(\ell)} \right] - \left[4 \cdot \Delta H^\circ_{f, NH_3(g)} + 5 \cdot \Delta H^\circ_{f, O_2(g)} \right]$$

$$= [(86.28 \text{ Kcal}) + (-409.92 \text{Kcal})] - [(-44.08 \text{Kcal}) + 0]$$

$$= - 279.56 \text{ Kcal.}$$

However, since this result is the standard enthalpy change for the combustion of 4 moles of $NH_3(g)$, one must divide - 279.56 Kcal/mole by 4 to give the combustion of 1 mole of NH_3,

$$\Delta H^\circ = \frac{- 279.56 \text{ Kcal}}{4 \text{ moles}} = - 69.89 \text{ Kcal/mole.}$$

● **PROBLEM** 11-12

Using the data from the accompanying figure, calculate the heat of reaction for the following process at 25°C:

a) $CaCl_2(s) + Na_2CO_3(s) \rightarrow 2NaCl(s) + CaCO_3(s)$

b) $H_2SO_4(1) + 2NaCl(s) \rightarrow Na_2SO_4(s) + 2HCl(g)$

Standard Heats of Formation, ΔH°, in kcal/mole at 25°C.

Substance	ΔH°
$CaCl_2$ (s)	-190. 0
Na_2CO_3 (s)	-270. 3
NaCl (s)	- 98. 2
$CaCO_3$ (s)	-288. 4
H_2SO_4 (1)	-193. 9
HCl (g)	- 22. 1
Na_2SO_4 (s)	-330. 9

Solution: Calculate the amount of heat released (or absorbed) from the heats of formation. In general, ΔH for a reaction will be the sum of the heats of formation of products minus the heats of formation of reactants, each of which is multiplied by its coefficient in the equation. Once ΔH is determined, ΔE can be found from $E = \Delta H - (\Delta n)RT$, where Δn = change of moles, R = universal gas constant and T = temperature in Kelvin (Celsius plus 273°)

Proceed as follows:

(a) $CaCl_2(s) + Na_2CO_3(s) \rightarrow 2NaCl(s) + CaCO_3(s)$

Thus,

$$\Delta H = 2\Delta H°_{NaCl(s)} + \Delta H°_{CaCO_3(s)} - \Delta H°_{CaCl_2(s)} - \Delta H°_{Na_2CO_3(s)}$$

$$= 2(-98.2) + (-288.4) - (-190.0) - (270.3)$$

$$= -24.5 \text{ Kcal/mole.}$$

$\Delta E = \Delta H - \Delta nRT$. But, in this reaction, no gases appear. This means ΔnRT becomes zero. As such, $\Delta E = \Delta H = -24.5$ Kcal/mole.

(b) $H_2SO_4(1) + 2NaCl(s) \rightarrow Na_2SO_4(s) + 2HCl(g)$

$$\Delta H = \Delta H°_{Na_2SO_4(s)} + 2\Delta H°_{HCl(g)} - \Delta H°_{H_2SO_4(1)} - 2\Delta H°_{NaCl(s)}$$

$$= (-330.9) + 2(-22.1) - (-193.9) - 2(-98.2) = +15.2 \text{ kcal/mole.}$$

ΔE = heat of reaction = $\Delta H - (\Delta n)RT$.

A gas, HCl, is involved in this reaction. Δn = moles products - moles reactants = 2 - 0 = 2

T = 25 + 273 = 298°K; R is in terms of cal. and ΔH in terms of Kcal, so that you must use the conversion factor of 1Kcal/1000 cal.

Thus, $\Delta E = -15.2 - (2)(1.987)(298)(1/1000)$

$$= - 15.2 - 1.2$$

$$= - 16.4 \text{ Kcal/mole.}$$

● **PROBLEM 11-13**

Calculate the quantity of heat required to (a) convert a liter of H_2O at 30°C to a liter of water at 60°C, and (b) heat a 1 kg block of aluminum from 30° to 60°C. Assume the specific heat of water and aluminum is, respectively, 1 cal/g°C and .215 cal/g°C.

Solution: When heat is added to a mass of unspecified substance, the temperature will rise. The quantitative relationship between the quantity of heat, expressed in kilocalories, and the rise in temperature - provided there is no phase change - is:

quantity of heat = mass × specific heat × ΔT,

where ΔT is the change in temperature and the specific heat equals the amount of heat required to raise the temperature of 1 g of any substance by 1°C.

(a) To find the mass of H_2O, remember that density = mass/volume, and the density of H_2O is one. Thus, mass = (1 liter H_2O)(1000 ml/liter)(1.00 g H_2O)/ml. H_2O). Therefore,

$$\text{quantity of heat} = (\text{mass})(\text{specific heat})(\Delta T)$$

$$\text{mass} = (1 \text{ } \ell \text{ } H_2O)(1000 \text{ ml}/\ell)(1 \text{ g/ml})$$

$$= 1000 \text{ g}$$

$$\text{specific heat} = 1 \text{ cal/g}^\circ C$$

$$\Delta T = (60 - 30)^\circ C$$

$$= 30^\circ C$$

$$\text{quantity of heat} = (1000 \text{ g})(1 \text{ cal/g}^\circ C)(30^\circ C)$$

$$= 30,000 \text{ cal} = 30 \text{ Kcal}$$

(b) A similar calculation can be used to determine the amount necessary to raise the temperature of the aluminum from 30 to 60°C.

$$\text{mass} = (1 \text{ kg Al})(1000 \text{ g/kg}) = 1000 \text{ g}$$

$$\text{specific heat} = .215 \text{ cal/g}^\circ C$$

$$\Delta T = (60 - 30)^\circ C$$

$$= 30^\circ C$$

$$\text{quantity of heat} = (1000 \text{ g})(.215 \text{ cal/g}^\circ C)(30^\circ C)$$

$$= 6450 \text{ cal} = 6.45 \text{ Kcal}.$$

● **PROBLEM 11-14**

Calculate ΔH_r° for the combustion of methane, CH_4. The balanced reaction is

$$CH_4(g) \quad + \quad 2O_2(g) \rightarrow CO_2(g) \quad + \quad 2H_2O(\ell)$$
$$\Delta H_f^o \text{ in KCal/mole} = -17.89, \quad 0 \quad , \quad -94.05 \quad , \quad 2(-68.32)$$

Solution: ΔH_r^o is the Standard Enthalpy Change of Reaction. Standard conditions are defined as 25°C and 1 atm.

Enthalpy is the heat content of a system. If the overall change in enthalpy is negative, then heat is given off to the surroundings and the reaction is called exothermic. When the change is positive, heat is absorbed and the reaction is endothermic. Endothermic compounds are often unstable and can sometimes explode. An endothermic compound, however, is a more efficient fuel because, upon combustion, it yields more heat energy.

ΔH_r^o is calculated using the enthalpies of formation, ΔH_f^o. The sum of enthalpies of formation of products minus the sum of the enthalpies of formation of reactants, where each product and reactant is multiplied by its molar amount in the reaction as indicated by the coefficients, gives the value of ΔH_r^o. In other words,

$$\Delta H_r^o = \sum \Delta H_f^o \text{ products} - \sum \Delta H_f^o \text{ reactants}$$

ΔH_f^o for elements is always zero. In this reaction, therefore, ΔH_f^o for O_2 is zero.

$$\sum \Delta H_f^o \text{ products} = -94.05 - 136.64$$

$$\sum \Delta H_f^o \text{ reactants} = -17.89 \text{ Kcal/mole}$$

$$\Delta H_r^o = -94.05 - 136.64 - (-17.89)$$
$$= -212.8 \text{ Kcal/mole } CH_4 \text{ burned}$$

This reaction is exothermic, because the $\Delta H_r^o = $ a negative value.

● PROBLEM 11-15

The hydrogen-filled dirigible "Hindenberg" had a gas volume of 1.4×10^8 liters. Assuming that it was filled to a pressure of 1 atm at 0°C, how much energy was released when it burned to gaseous products at a reaction temperature of 25°C? The standard heat of formation of water vapor at 25°C is -57.8 Kcal/mole.

Solution: The solution to this problem involves calculation of the heat of reaction for the combustion of hydrogen and the number of moles of hydrogen in the dirigible.

The combustion reaction is written

$$H_2(g) + \tfrac{1}{2} O_2(g) \rightarrow H_2O(g).$$

The heat of reaction at 25°C (298°K) is written

ΔH^o_{298} = sum of heats of formation of products - sum of heats of formation of reactants

$$= \Delta H^o_{f, H_2O} - \left(\Delta H^o_{f, H_2} + \Delta H^o_{f, O_2} \right)$$

Since the heats of formation of O_2 and H_2 are zero by definition, $\Delta H^o_{f,O_2} = \Delta H^o_{f, H_2} = 0$ Kcal/mole, the heat of reaction is equal to the heat of formation of water vapor:

$$\Delta H^o_{298} = \Delta H^o_{f, H_2O} = -57.8 \text{ Kcal/mole.}$$

Since ΔH^o_{298} is negative, the reaction is exothermic and - 57.8 Kcal are released per mole of water produced. But since one mole of water is formed per mole of hydrogen burned, - 57.8 Kcal are released per mole of hydrogen burned.

To calculate the number of moles of hydrogen present in the dirigible, we make use of the fact that at 0°C and 1 atm pressure, one mole of gas occupies 22.4 ℓ (molar volume of gas). Then

$$\text{number of moles of } H_2 = \frac{\text{volume of dirigible}}{\text{molar volume of } H_2}$$

$$= \frac{1.4 \times 10^8 \text{ ℓ}}{22.4 \text{ ℓ/mole}} = \frac{1.4 \times 10^8}{22.4} \text{ moles}$$

The heat released is then the absolute value of the heat of reaction (per mole) multiplied by the number of moles of gas.

$$\text{heat released} = \left| \Delta H^o_{298} \right| \times \text{number of moles of } H_2$$

$$= 57.8 \text{ Kcal/mole} \times \frac{1.4 \times 10^8}{22.4} \text{ moles}$$

$$= 360 \times 10^6 \text{ Kcal.}$$

(We use the absolute value of ΔH^o_{298} because the word "released" already takes into account the fact that the reaction is exothermic and therefore the sign of ΔH^o_{298} is negative.) Note that we have assumed that all of the hydrogen is burned.

231

It is known that 1 ton of TNT can produce 4.6×10^9 J of energy. A chemist wanted to obtain this much energy from acetylene (C_2H_2) and oxygen (O_2). How much C_2H_2 and O_2 would be required? The $\Delta H° = -2510$ KJ for the reaction between C_2H_2 and O_2.

Solution: The equation for this reaction is

$2 C_2H_2 + 5O_2 \rightarrow 4CO_2 + 2H_2O$, $\Delta H° = -2510$ KJ. In a chemical reaction, energy is usually liberated or absorbed. The $\Delta H°$ enthalpy, expresses this energy liberation or absorption quantitatively. The negative sign denotes the release of energy.

Two moles of acetylene and 5 moles of oxygen react to form 2510 KJ or 2510×10^3 J of energy. Similarly, 2x moles of acetylene and 5x moles of oxygen produce 2.510×10^6 x J of energy. In this case, the energy released must equal 4.6×10^9 J. Therefore,
2.510×10^6 x $= 4.6 \times 10^9$, or x $= 1.83 \times 10^3$.

From the equation for the reaction one knows that 2 moles of C_2H_2 and 5 moles of O_2 react to produce 2510 KJ. The calculations already done show that to produce as much energy as 1 ton of TNT there must be $1.83 \times 10^3 \times 2$ moles of C_2H_2 and $1.83 \times 10^3 \times 5$ moles of O_2 to form 4.6×10^9 J. To solve for the amount of each needed, multiply the number of moles by the molecular weight of the substance. (MW of $C_2H_2 = 26$).

wt of $C_2H_2 = (1.83 \times 10^3 \times 2)$ moles $\times 26$ g/moles

$= 9.52 \times 10^4$ g $= 9.52 \times 10^4$ g $\times 1.10 \times 10^{-6}$ tons/g

$= .1044$ tons.

(MW of $O_2 = 32$)

wt of $O_2 = (1.83 \times 10^3 \times 5)$ moles $\times 32$ g/mole

$= 5.86 \times 10^4$ g $= 5.86 \times 10^4$ g $\times 1.10 \times 10^{-6}$ tons/g

$= 0.646$ tons.

ENTHALPY CALCULATIONS USING THE FIRST LAW OF THERMODYNAMICS

● **PROBLEM** 11-17

Calculate $\Delta E°$ and $\Delta H°$ for the following reactions at 25°C:
(a) $4NH_3(g) + 5O_2(g) \rightarrow 4NO(g) + 6H_2O(\ell)$

(b) $H_2S(g) + 1\frac{1}{2}O_2(g) \rightarrow SO_2(g) + H_2O(l)$
Use the following values for ΔH° of the compounds

Compound	H° (Kcal/mole)
$H_2O(l)$	- 68.3
$SO_2(g)$	- 71.0
$H_2S(g)$	- 5.3
$NO(g)$	21.6
$NH_3(g)$	- 11.0

Solution: ΔH° may be defined as the heat released or absorbed as a reaction proceeds. ΔH° for a particular reaction is found by subtracting the sum of the ΔH°'s of the compounds reacting from the sum of the ΔH°'s of the products being formed, i.e., ΔH° = (ΔH° of products) - (ΔH° of reactants).

(1) Determination of the ΔH°'s for the reactions:

(a) $4NH_3(g) + 5O_2(g) \rightarrow 4NO(g) + 6H_2O(l)$. When more than one mole of a compound is reacted or formed, the ΔH° of the compound is multiplied by the number of moles present.
$\Delta H^\circ = (4 \times \Delta H^\circ$ of NO + 6 $\times \Delta H^\circ$ of H_2O) - (4 $\times \Delta H^\circ$ of NH_3 +

$$5 \times \Delta H^\circ \text{ of } O_2)$$

The ΔH° of any element is always 0. Thus, the ΔH° of O_2 is zero. Substituting,

$\Delta H^\circ = [(4 \times 21.6) + 6 \times(- 68.3)] - [(4 \times (- 11.0)) + (5 \times 0)]$

= - 279.40 Kcal.

(b) $H_2S(g) + 1\frac{1}{2}O_2(g) \rightarrow SO_2(g) + H_2O(l)$

$\Delta H^\circ = (\Delta H^\circ$ of $SO_2 + \Delta H^\circ$ of H_2O) - (ΔH° of $H_2S + 1\frac{1}{2} \Delta H^\circ$ of O_2)

$\Delta H^\circ = [(- 71.0) + (- 68.3)] - [(- 5.3) + (1\frac{1}{2} \times 0)]$

= - 134.0 Kcal

(2) Determination of ΔE: ΔE° is the change in energy of a given reaction. It is defined as the difference of the ΔH°'s of the reaction and the pressure times the change in volume occurring during the reaction, i.e.,

$\Delta E^\circ = \Delta H^\circ - P\Delta V$,

where P is the pressure and ΔV is the change in volume. One is not given the values for pressure or volume here, thus one uses the Ideal Gas Law to substitute ΔnRT for $P\Delta V$ where Δn is the change in the number of moles present, R is the gas constant (1.99 cal/mole-$^\circ$K) and T is the absolute temperature. The Ideal Gas Law states that

$P\Delta V = \Delta nRT$

Here, one is told that the reactions both occur at 25°C. This temperature can be converted to the absolute scale by adding 273 to 25°C.

$$T = 25 + 273 = 298°K.$$

Δn is found by subtracting the number of moles of compounds reacting from the number of moles formed. Caution: Only moles of gases are taken into account. Δn = number of moles formed - number of moles reacted.

One can solve for $\Delta E°$ in these two reactions.

(a) $4NH_3(g) + 5O_2(g) \rightarrow 4NO(g) + 6H_2O (\ell)$

$\Delta H°$ for this reaction was found to be - 279.40 Kcal. $\Delta H°$ must be converted to calories when R is used. Kcal are converted to cal by multiplying the number of Kcal by 1000 cal/1 Kcal.

Δn = (4 moles NO) - (4 moles NH_3 + 5 moles O_2)

$\quad$ = (4) - (4 + 5) = - 5 mole

$\quad \Delta E° = \Delta H° - \Delta nRT$ $\qquad \qquad \Delta H° = - 279.40$ Kcal

$\qquad \qquad \qquad \qquad \qquad \qquad \qquad \Delta n = 5$ moles

$\qquad \qquad \qquad \qquad \qquad \qquad \qquad R = 1.99$ cal/mole-°K

$\qquad \qquad \qquad \qquad \qquad \qquad \qquad T = 298°K$

$\Delta E° = - 279.4$ Kcal $\times \left[\dfrac{1000\ cal}{1\ Kcal}\right] - (- 5$ mole

$\qquad \qquad \qquad \qquad \qquad \times 1.99$ cal/mole °K $\times 298°K)$

$\quad = - 279,400$ cal $+ 2965$ cal

$\quad = - 276,435$ cal $= - 276.4$ Kcal.

(b) $H_2S(g) + 1\frac{1}{2}O_2(g) \rightarrow SO_2(g) + H_2O(\ell)$

$\Delta H° = - 134.0$ Kcal

$\Delta H°$ should be expressed in calories

$\Delta H°$ in cal $= - 134.0$ Kcal $\times 1000$ cal/1 Kcal

$\qquad \qquad = - 134,000$ cal

Δn = (no. of moles of SO_2)- (no. of moles of H_2S + no. of moles of O_2)

Δn = (1 mole of SO_2) - (1 mole of H_2S + 1 ½ moles of O_2)

$\quad = (1) - (1 + 1\frac{1}{2}) = - 1.5$ moles

$R = 1.99$ cal/mole °K

$T = 298°K$

$\Delta E° = \Delta H° - \Delta nRT$

$$= -134,000 \text{ cal} - (-1.5 \text{ moles} \times 1.99 \text{ cal/mole}°K \times 298°K)$$

$$= -134,000 \text{ cal} + 890 \text{ cal}$$

$$= -133,110 \text{ cal} = -133.1 \text{ Kcal.}$$

● **PROBLEM 11-18**

The equation for the burning of naphthalene is
$C_{10}H_8(s) + 12O_2(g) \rightarrow 10CO_2 + 4H_2O$ (ℓ). For every mole of
$C_{10}H_8$ burned, - 1226.7 Kcal is evolved at 25° in a fixed-
volume combustion chamber. $\Delta H°$ for $H_2O(\ell)$ =
- 64.4 Kcal/mole and H_2O (g) = - 57.8 Kcal/mole. Calculate
(a) the heat of reaction at constant temperature and
(b) ΔH for the case where all of the H_2O is gaseous.

Solution: This problem deals with the heat evolved
when a compound is heated with oxygen to form carbon
dioxide and water (the heat of combustion). The heat of
reaction, or combustion in this case, ΔH, is given by
the formula $\Delta H = \Delta E + \Delta nRT$, where ΔE = amount of heat
released per mole, Δn = change in moles, R = universal
gas constant and T = temperature in Kelvin (Celsius plus
273°). Thus, to answer (a) substitute these values and
solve for ΔE. Δn is moles of gas produced - moles of gas
reacted, which is 10 moles- 12 moles= -2 moles based on
the coefficients in the equation. T = 25° + 273 = 298°K.
Use R in terms of kilocalories. As such

$$\Delta H = -1226.7 \text{ kcal} + (-2 \text{ moles})(1.987 \text{ cal/mole °K})$$
$$(298°K)(1 \text{ Kcal/1000 cal})$$

$$= -1226.7 - 1.2 = -1227.9 \text{ Kcal/mole.}$$

To find (b), note that the reaction is the same,
except that H_2O is gaseous not liquid. You have, therefore, $4H_2O(liq) \rightarrow 4H_2O(g)$. The ΔH, change in enthalpy,
for this conversion is $4\Delta H°(liq) -4H°\Delta(g)$ of H_2O =
$4(-57.8) - 4(-68.4) = 42.4$ Kcal/mole. It follows,then,
that the resulting

$$\Delta H = -1227.9 + 42.4 = -1185.5 \text{ Kcal/mole.}$$

● **PROBLEM 11-19**

A chemist expands an ideal gas against a constant external pressure of 700 mmHg, and finds its volume changes
from 50 to 150 liters. He finds that 1.55 Kcal of heat
have been absorbed in the process. Determine the internal
energy change that took place. 24.217 cal = 1 liter-atm.

Solution: The internal energy change of a system at
constant pressure is given by the formula $\Delta E = \Delta H - P\Delta V$,

where ΔE = change in internal energy, ΔH = enthalpy or heat absorbed or released, P = pressure and ΔV = change in volume.

In this problem, ΔV = 150 - 50 = 100 liters. The pressure, in atms, = (700 mm)(1 atm)/(760 mm) = .921 atm. To convert, liter-atm to kilocalories, multiply by 24.217 cal./liter-atm and then multiply by Kcal/1000 cal. Therefore,

$$\Delta E = 1.55 \text{ Kcal} - (.921 \text{ atm})(100 \text{ } \ell)(24.217 \text{ cal/liter-atm})$$
$$(\text{Kcal}/1000 \text{ cal})$$

$$= 1.55 - 2.23 = -.68 \text{ Kcal}.$$

HEATS OF FUSION AND VAPORIZATION

● PROBLEM 11-20

What weight of ice could be melted at 0°C by the heat liberated by condensing 100 g of steam at 100°C to liquid. Heat of vaporization = 540 cal/g, heat of fusion = 80 cal/g.

Solution: The quantity of heat necessary to convert 1 g of a liquid into a vapor is termed the heat of vaporization. For water, 540 calories are necessary to change liquid water at 100°C into vapor at 100°C. In this problem vapor is condensed, thus 540 cal of heat are evolved for each gram of liquid condensed.

no. of cal evolved in condensation = 540 cal/g × weight of vapor

Here 100 g of vapor is condensed. Thus,

no. of cal evolved = 540 cal/g × 100 g = 54000 cal

When ice melts, heat is absorbed. About 80 calories of heat are required to melt 1 g of ice, the heat of fusion. Here, 54000 cal are evolved in the condensation. Therefore, this is the amount of heat available to melt the ice. Because 80 cal are needed to melt 1 g of ice, one can find the number of grams of ice that can be melted by 54000 cal, by dividing 54000 cal by 80 cal/g.

no. of grams of ice melted = $\dfrac{54000 \text{ cal}}{80 \text{ cal/g}}$ = 675 g.

The following are physical properties of methyl alcohol, CH_3OH: freezing point - 98°C; boiling point 65°C; specific heat of liquid 0.570 cal/g - degree; heat of fusion 22.0 cal/g; and heat of vaporization 263 cal/g. Calculate the number of kilocalories required to convert one mole of methyl alcohol solid at - 98°C to vapor at 65°C.

Solution: There are three steps in this process: (1) melting the solid, (2) heating the liquid from - 98°C to 65°C, (3) vaporizing the liquid at 65°C.

Heat will be absorbed in each of these processes, thus one must calculate the heat absorbed in each process and then take the total.

(1) Heat absorbed in melting the solid.

To find the amount of heat absorbed when a compound is melted, one uses the heat of fusion. The heat of fusion for methyl alcohol is 22.0 cal/g. This means that for each gram of solid melted 22.0 cal of heat are absorbed. Here, one is melting one mole of CH_3OH. The molecular weight of CH_3OH is 32, thus one will calculate the heat absorbed when 32 g of CH_3OH is melted.

no. of cal absorbed = heat of fusion × no. of grams

no. of cal absorbed = 22.0 cal/g × 32 g = 704 cal.

(2) Heat absorbed in heating the liquid.

In determining the amount of heat absorbed in heating the liquid, one uses the specific heat of the liquid. For CH_3OH the specific heat is 0.570 cal/g-degree. This means that for each gram of CH_3OH raised 1 degree, 0.570 calories is absorbed. Here, the liquid is raised 65° - (- 98°) or 163°C. There are 32 g of CH_3OH heated.

no. of cal absorbed = no. of degrees × weight × specific heat

no. of cal absorbed = 163°× 32 g × 0.570 cal/g-°

= 2973 cal.

(3) Heat absorbed when the liquid is vaporized.

To calculate the amount of heat absorbed when the liquid is vaporized, one uses the heat of vaporization. The heat of vaporization for CH_3OH is 263 cal/g. This means that for each gram of CH_3OH vaporized, 263 calories are absorbed.

no. of cal absorbed = heat of vaporization × weight

no. of cal absorbed = 263 cal/g × 32 g = 8416 cal.

(4) To find the heat absorbed by the whole process,

the heat absorbed in these three steps must be added together.

total heat absorbed = heat absorbed in melting + heat
    absorbed in heating the liquid + heat absorbed in
    vaporization

total heat absorbed = 704 cal + 2973 cal + 8416 cal

                    = 12093 cal

Calories can be converted to kilocalories by multiplying the number of calories by 1 Kcal/1000 cal.

no. of Kcal = no. of cal × 1 Kcal/1000 cal

no. of Kcal = 12093 cal × 1 Kcal/1000 cal = 12.09 Kcal.

● **PROBLEM** 11-22

40 g of ice at 0°C is mixed with 100 g of water at 60°C. What is the final temperature after equilibrium has been established? Heat of fusion of H_2O = 80 cal/g, specific heat = 1 cal/g-°C.

Solution: In a determination of this kind, the heat lost by the water in cooling must be balanced by the heat gained by the ice in melting and in warming the resulting water (from the melted ice) to the final temperature. This means that the heat absorbed by the ice must equal the heat lost by the water at 60°C.

The heat absorbed by the ice is the combination of the heat absorbed by the ice in melting and the heat absorbed by the cold water to the new temperature. The heat absorbed when the ice melts can be calculated by taking into account the heat of fusion. The heat of fusion is defined as the number of calories absorbed when 1g of solid menlts. For water, 80 calories are absorbed for each gram of ice melted. Here 40 g of ice is melted. Therefore, the amount of heat absorbed by the ice is 40 times the heat of fusion.

40 g × 80 cal/g = 3200 cal.

As such, 3200 calories are absorbed when the ice melts. To find the amount of heat absorbed, when this water (from the melted ice) is heated to a new temperature, you must consider the specific heat of water. The specific heat is defined as the number of calories needed to raise 1 g of liquid 1 degree. The specific heat of water is 1, which means that for every gram of water raised 1 degree, 1 calorie is absorbed. In calculating the amount of heat absorbed by the water to the new temperature, let t = new temperature. To find the amount of heat absorbed, multiply the specific heat by 40 g, because 40 g of water is present, and by the new temperature, t, because the water will be raised t degrees from zero.

Amount of heat absorbed by liquid = 40 g × lcal/g-degree) ×t

= 40 t cal .

Therefore, 40 t calories will be absorbed by the melted ice. Thus, the amount of heat absorbed by the ice when it melts, and by the water when it is heated, is e-qual to the total amount of heat absorbed by the system.

Total amount of heat absorbed = 3200 cal + 40 t cal

= (3200 + 40 t) cal.

To find the amount of heat lost by the 100 g of water at 60°C, when it is cooled to a new temperature, t, the specific heat of water is also used. Here, it means that for every gram of water that is lowered one degree, 1 calorie of heat is released. Therefore, to find the amount of heat released by this water, the specific heat will be multiplied by 100 g, the amount of water present, and by 60-t°, which is the number of degrees that the tem-perature will drop.

(60-t)° × (1 cal/g-degree) × (100 g) = (6000 - 100t)cal.

To calculate t, one must set the amount of heat absorbed by the ice equal to the amount of heat lost by the water at 60°C.

amount of heat absorbed = amount of heat lost

amount of heat absorbed = (3200 + 40 t) cal

amount of heat lost = (6000 - 100 t) cal

(3200 + 40 t) cal = (6000 - 100 t) cal

140 t = 2800   t = 20°

Therefore, the final temperature is 20°C.

● **PROBLEM** 11-23

500 g of ice at 0°C is added to 500 g of water at 64°C. When the temperature of the mixture is 0°C, what weight of ice is still present? Heat of fusion of H_2O = 80cal/g.

Solution: The amount of heat used to melt the ice is equal to the amount of heat lost by the water. The amount of heat lost by the water is determined by using the specific heat of water. The specific heat of water is

1 cal/g-degree. This means that for each gram of water cooled 1 degree, 1 calorie of heat will be evolved. Here, 500 g of H_2O is lowered 64° - 0° or 64°. The heat evolved by the water can now be found.

$$\text{no. of calories evolved} = 1 \text{ cal/g-degree} \times 500 \text{ g} \times 64°$$

$$= 32000 \text{ cal.}$$

The heat of fusion is the quantity of heat necessary to liquefy 1 g of a solid substance at constant temperature at its melting point. Therefore, if the heat of fusion of water is 80 cal/g, then it takes 80 cal to melt one gram of ice. You found that 32000 calories are absorbed by the ice. The weight of ice melted by 32000 cal is found by dividing 32000 cal by 80 cal/g.

$$\text{no. of grams of ice} = \frac{32000 \text{ cal}}{80 \text{ cal/g}} = 400 \text{ g}$$

Thus 400 g of the ice is melted. Originally, there was 500 g of ice, therefore 100 g of ice is left.

● **PROBLEM** 11-24

Determine the heat needed to raise 60 g of Pb from 20°C to 360°C, given its specific heats are 0.0306 (solid) and 0.0375 (liquid). Its heat of fusion is 5.86 cal/g; its melting point is 327°C.

Solution: There are three heats involved in finding the amount of heat absorbed in raising the temperature of Pb from 20°C to 360°C. First, the amount of heat absorbed in raising the temperature of the solid from 20°C to 327°C (its melting point); then, the amount of heat absorbed in melting the compound; last, the amount of heat absorbed in raising the temperature of the liquid from 327°C to 360°C. The heat absorbed in these three processes are added together to find the amount of heat needed to bring Pb from 20°C to 360°C.

1) Raising the temperature of the solid from 20°C to 327°C.

The specific heat of solid Pb is used to calculate the amount of heat absorbed in this process. The specific heat is defined by the number of calories absorbed when one gram of mass is raised one degree. The specific heat of Pb as a solid is 0.0306. Here, 60 g of Pb is heated 307°C (327 - 20°C). Thus, the specific heat is multiplied by 60 and 307.

heat absorbed by solid = 60 × 307 × .0306 = 564 cal.

2) Heat needed to melt the solid.

To calculate the amount of heat needed to melt the solid, one needs to use the heat of fusion. The heat of fusion is the number of calories necessary to melt one gram of solid. The heat of fusion of Pb is 5.86 cal/g. There are 60 g of Pb, here. Thus, the heat of fusion must be multiplied by 60 g to find the amount of heat needed to melt the Pb.

heat needed to melt Pb = 60 g × 5.86 cal/g = 352 cal.

3) Heat absorbed in raising the temperature of the melted liquid from 327°C to 360°C.

Here the specific heat is used again, but because the Pb is now liquid, the specific heat for liquid Pb must be used. This is the amount of heat necessary to raise one gram of liquid one degree. 60 g Pb is heated 33°C (360°-327°); therefore, the specific heat must be multiplied by 60 and 33 to find the heat absorbed. The specific heat for liquid Pb is 0.0375.

heat absorbed by liquid Pb = 60 × 33 × 0.0375 = 74 cal.

The heat absorbed by the total process is the combination of the heats absorbed in these three processes.

Heat absorbed by solid	564 cal
Heat absorbed to melt solid	352 cal
Heat absorbed by liquid	74 cal
Total amount of heat needed	990 cal.

CHAPTER 12

THERMODYNAMICS II

ENTROPY

You are given the following absolute entropies, $S°$, for the reaction $CuO(s) + H_2(g) \rightarrow Cu(s) + H_2O(g)$ at 25°C:

$CuO(s)$	10.4 cal/mole
$H_2(g)$	31.2 cal/mole
$Cu(s)$	8.0 cal/g-atom
$H_2O(g)$	45.1 cal/mole

Is the ΔS favorable for this reaction, assuming standard conditions?

Solution: To find whether the reaction will proceed spontaneously, calculate the change in entropy, $\Delta S°$, for the reaction. When $\Delta S°$ is positive the reaction will proceed spontaneously. Remember, entropy is a measure of randomness and the natural order of the universe is for things to become more random, which necessitates a positive $S°$.

$$\Delta S° = S°_{products} - S°_{reactants}.$$

Thus for this reaction,

$$\Delta S° = S°_{Cu(s)} + S°_{H_2O(g)} - S°_{CuO(s)} - S°_{H_2(g)}$$

$$= 8 + 45.1 - 10.4 - 31.2 = + 11.5 \text{ cal/deg-mole.}$$

Since $\Delta S°$ is positive, the reaction will proceed spontaneously.

When mercury is vaporized at its boiling point at standard
pressure, the entropy change is 20.7 cal/mole-°K. Determine
the boiling point of Hg if the heat of vaporization is
65 cal/g.

Solution: When a process occurs at constant temperature,
the change in entropy, ΔS, is equal to the heat absorbed
divided by the absolute temperature at which the change
occurs, i.e.,

$$\Delta S = \frac{\Delta H}{T} \ ,$$

where ΔH is the heat of vaporization (in this case) and T
is the absolute temperature. T will be equal to the boiling
point of mercury in this problem.

Using this equation, one can solve for T after either
converting ΔH to cal/moles or converting ΔS to cal/g. Here,
one will convert ΔH from cal/g to cal/mole by multiplying
ΔH by the molecular weight of Hg. (MW of Hg = 200.6.)

ΔH in cal/moles = 65 cal/g × 200.6 g/mole

= 13039 cal/mole

One can now solve for T.

$$T = \frac{\Delta H}{\Delta S}$$ ΔH = 13039 cal/mole

ΔS = 20.7 cal/mole-°K

$$T = \frac{13039 \text{ cal/mole}}{20.7 \text{ cal/mole-°K}} = 630°K$$

T in °C = 630 - 273 = 357°C.

Calculate ΔS for the conversion of one mole of liquid water
to vapor at 100°C. Heat of vaporization = 540 cal/g.

Solution: When a process occurs at constant temperature,
the change in entropy (ΔS) is equal to the heat absorbed
divided by the absolute temperature at which the change
occurs.

$$\Delta S = \frac{\Delta H}{T}$$

In this problem, one is given ΔH and one can find T.

The absolute temperature is calculated by adding 273 to the temperature in °C.

$$T = 273 + 100 = 373°K$$

Because one mole of water is reacting here, and the heat of vaporization is given in cal/g, one must multiply the ΔH given by the molecular weight of water to find the ΔH in cal/mole.

The molecular weight of water is 18.

$$\Delta H = 540 \text{ cal/g} \times 18 \text{ g/mole} = 9720 \text{ cal/mole}$$

One can now calculate ΔS.

$$\Delta S = \frac{\Delta H}{T} \qquad\qquad \Delta H = 9720 \text{ cal/mole}$$
$$T = 373°K$$

$$\Delta S = \frac{9720 \text{ cal/mole}}{373°K} = 26.1 \text{ cal/mole-}°K$$

The change in entropy, when one mole of water is vaporized at 100°C, is 26.1 cal/mole-°K.

● **PROBLEM 12-4**

A chemist knows that the $\Delta H° = -485$ kJ for the reaction $2H_2(g) + O_2(g) \rightarrow 2H_2O(g)$ and that $\Delta H° = -537$ kJ for $H_2(g) + F_2(g) \rightarrow 2HF(g)$. With this information, he calculated the $\Delta H°$ for $2H_2O(g) + 2F_2(g) \rightarrow 4HF(g) + O_2(g)$ and predicted whether $\Delta S°$ was positive or negative. How?

Solution: Hess' Law states that the net heat change resulting from a particular chemical reaction is the same, independent of the steps involved in the transformation. Thus, $\Delta H°$ of the sum of two reactions equals the sum of the $\Delta H°$'s of each reaction. The chemist knows that

(i) $2H_2(g) + O_2(g) \rightarrow 2H_2O(g)$ $\qquad \Delta H° = -485$ kJ

(ii) $H_2(g) + F_2(g) \rightarrow 2HF(g)$ $\qquad \Delta H° = -537$ kJ

By doubling (ii) and adding to (i), the chemist obtains the desired equation

$$2H_2O \rightarrow 2H_2 + O_2 \quad \Delta H° = +485 \text{ kJ}$$

$$\underline{2(H_2 + F_2 \rightarrow 2HF)} \quad \Delta H° = -2(537)\text{kJ}$$

$$2H_2O + 2F_2 \rightarrow 4HF + O_2$$

The $\Delta H°$ for this reaction, according to Hess' Law, equals

$\Delta H^\circ {}_{(i)} + \Delta H^\circ {}_{(ii)} \times 2 = 485 + 2(-537) = -589$ kJ/moles.

Because the ΔH° for the overall reaction is negative, the reaction is spontaneous. The ΔS° is positive because as the reaction proceeds from reactants to products there is an increase in the number of moles present in the system. There are 4 moles of reactants and 5 moles of products.

FREE ENERGY

Hydrogen peroxide, H_2O_2, can be synthesized in two ways. The first method involves reduction of oxygen by hydrogen,

$$H_2(g) + O_2(g) \rightarrow H_2O_2(\ell).$$

The second method involves oxidation of water:

$$2H_2O(\ell) + O_2(g) \rightarrow 2H_2O_2(\ell).$$

Find the free energy of formation, ΔG°, for both processes and predict which process is more efficient for the commercial preparation of hydrogen peroxide.

Solution: The standard free energy change for a reaction is equal to the difference between the standard free energy of formation of the products and the standard free energy of formation of the reactants,

$$\Delta G^\circ = \Delta G^\circ_{products} - \Delta G^\circ_{reactants}.$$

The reaction with the more negative free energy change will be the more efficient, since it proceeds spontaneously as written. We will require the following standard free energies of formation:

$$\Delta G^\circ_{H_2O_2(\ell)} = -27.2 \text{ Kcal/mole}$$

$$\Delta G^\circ_{H_2O(\ell)} = -56.7 \text{ Kcal/mole}$$

$$\Delta G^\circ_{H_2(g)} = \Delta G^\circ_{O_2(g)} = 0 \text{ Kcal/mole}$$

For the first process
$$H_2(g) + O_2(g) \rightarrow H_2O_2(\ell),$$

the standard free energy change is

$$\Delta G^\circ = \Delta G^\circ_{products} - \Delta G^\circ_{reactants}$$

$$= \Delta G^\circ_{H_2O_2(\ell)} - \left[\Delta G^\circ_{H_2(g)} + \Delta G^\circ_{O_2(g)} \right]$$

$$= -27.2 \text{ Kcal/mole} - (0 \text{ Kcal/mole} + 0 \text{Kcal/mole})$$

$$= -27.2 \text{ Kcal/mole}$$

For the second process,

$$2H_2O\ (\ell) + O_2(g) \rightarrow 2H_2O_2(\ell),$$

the standard free energy change is

$$\Delta G^\circ = \Delta G^\circ_{products} - \Delta G^\circ_{reactants}$$

$$= 2\Delta G^\circ_{H_2O_2(\ell)} - \left[2\Delta G^\circ_{H_2O(\ell)} + \Delta G^\circ_{O_2(g)} \right]$$

$$= 2(-27.2 \text{ kcal/mole}) - (2 \times (-56.7)$$
$$\text{kcal/mole} + 0 \text{ kcal/mole})$$

$$= 59.0 \text{ Kcal/2 moles } H_2O_2 \text{ produced.}$$

$$= 29.5 \text{ Kcal/mole.}$$

Since the first process proceeds spontaneously as written (negative ΔG°) and the second process requires energy to proceed as written (positive ΔG°), the first method for preparing H_2O_2 is more efficient than the second.

● **PROBLEM** 12-6

For sublimation of iodine crystals,

$$I_2(s) \overset{\rightarrow}{\leftarrow} I_2(g),$$

at 25°C and atmospheric pressure, it is found that the change in enthalpy, $\Delta H = 9.41$ Kcal/mole and the change in entropy, $\Delta S = 20.6$ cal/deg-mole. At what temperature will solid iodine be in equilibrium with gaseous iodine?

Solution: Use the fact that the system is in a state of equilibrium. The change in Gibb's free energy is related to ΔH and ΔS by the equation

$$\Delta G = \Delta H - T\Delta S,$$

where T is the absolute temperature of the system. At

equilibrium, $\Delta G = 0$ and T is the equilibrium temperature, T_{equil}. Hence

$$\Delta G = \Delta H - T\Delta S,$$

$$0 = \Delta H - T_{equil} \Delta S,$$

or, $\quad T_{equil} = \dfrac{\Delta H}{\Delta S}$.

Therefore,

$$T_{equil} = \dfrac{\Delta H}{\Delta S} = \dfrac{9.41 \text{ Kcal/mole}}{20.6 \text{ cal/deg-mole}} = \dfrac{9410 \text{ cal/mole}}{20.6 \text{ cal/deg-mole}}$$

$$= 457 \text{ K},$$

or, $\quad T_{equil} = 457 - 273 = 184°C.$

EQUILIBRIUM CALCULATIONS

● **PROBLEM** 12-7

Calculate the equilibrium constant for the following re-action at 25°C or 298°K

$$C_{(graphite)} + 2H_2(g) \rightarrow CH_4(g)$$

$\Delta H°$ for this reaction is - 17,889 cal.

<u>Solution</u>: At equilibrium the equilibrium constant of any reaction is independent of the amount of pure solid (or liquid) phase.

To solve this problem (1) determine $\Delta S°$, the entropy change or randomness of the system. (2) Determine $\Delta G°$, the free energy or the energy available to do work, by using the formula: $\Delta G° = \Delta H° - T\Delta S°$, where $\Delta H°$ = the change in enthalpy or heat content, and T = absolute temperature (Celsius plus 273°). (3) Determine K_p, the equilibrium constant, by using $\Delta G° = - RT \ln K_p$.

The entropy change (from any entropy table) for this reaction is

$$\Delta S° \text{ of reaction} = \Delta S°_{products} - \Delta S°_{reactants}$$

$$= \Delta S°_{CH_4} - 2\Delta S°_{H_2} - \Delta S°_C$$

$$= 44.50 - 2(31.211) - 1.3609$$

247

$$= -19.28 \text{ cal/k}$$

$$\Delta G^\circ = \Delta H^\circ - T\Delta S^\circ$$

$$= -17,889 - (298)(-19.28)$$

$$= -12,143 \text{ cal.}$$

The equilibrium constant is thus

$$\Delta G^\circ = -RT \ln K_p = -(1.987 \text{ cal}^\circ K^{-1} \text{ mole}^{-1})(298^\circ K) \times$$
$$(2.303) \log K_p$$

$$-12,143 \text{ cal} = -1364 \log K_p$$

$$\log K_p = 8.90$$

$$K_p = 7.94 \times 10^8.$$

Given that k = 8.85 at 298°K and k = .0792 at 373°K, calculate the ΔH° for the reaction of the dimerization of NO_2 to N_2O_4. Namely, $2NO_2(g) \rightleftarrows N_2O_4(g)$.

Solution: ΔH° is the standard enthalpy change, a measure of the heat content of the system. It is quantitatively related to the equilibrium constants of a system at different temperations by the van't Hoff equation:

$$\log \frac{k_2}{k_1} = \frac{\Delta H^\circ}{19.15} \left(\frac{1}{T_1} - \frac{1}{T_2} \right) ,$$

where k_2 and k_1 are equilibrium constants, and T_1 and T_2 are temperatures in Kelvin. Given that $k_1 = 8.85$ at $T_1 = 298^\circ K$ and $k_2 = 0.0792$ at $373^\circ K$, one can find ΔH° by the substitution of these values in the equation. Thus,

$$\log \frac{.0792}{8.85} = \frac{\Delta H^\circ}{19.15} \left(\frac{1}{298} - \frac{1}{373} \right) .$$

Solving for ΔH°, one obtains

$$\Delta H^\circ = -58,200 \text{ J/mole} \quad \text{for the reaction.}$$

Calculate the enthalpy change, ΔH°, for the reaction

$$N_2(g) + O_2(g) = 2NO(g),$$

given the equilibrium constants 4.08×10^{-4} for a tem-

perature of 2000°K and 3.60 × 10⁻³ for a temperature of
2500°K.

Solution: The effect of temperature on chemical equilibrium is determined by $\Delta H°$ (enthalpy or heat content);
over moderate ranges in temperature, $\Delta H°$ is relatively
independent of temperature.

If, as in the case of this problem, $\Delta H°$ is independent of temperature then,

(1) $\Delta G° = - RT \ln k$,   where

$\Delta G°$ = standard free energy change,

R = gas constant,

T = absolute temperature

and k the equilibrium constant.

(2) $\Delta G° = \Delta H° - T\Delta S°$

(3) $\Delta H° - T\Delta S° = - RT \ln K$ or

$- \left[\dfrac{\Delta H° - T\Delta S°}{RT} \right] = \ln k$,   where $\Delta S°$ = the change in

entropy or randomness of system.

(4) $\dfrac{- \Delta H°}{RT} + \dfrac{\Delta S°}{R} = \ln k$

For two different temperatures, T_1 and T_2, equation
(4) becomes

$$\ln k_2 - \ln k_1 = \left[\dfrac{- \Delta H°}{RT_2} + \dfrac{\Delta S°}{R} \right] - \left[\dfrac{- \Delta H°}{RT_1} + \dfrac{\Delta S°}{R} \right]   \text{or}$$

$$\ln \dfrac{k_2}{k_1} = \dfrac{- \Delta H°}{RT_2} + \dfrac{\Delta H°}{RT_1}$$

$$\ln \dfrac{k_2}{k_1} = \dfrac{\Delta H° (T_2 - T_1)}{RT_2 \, T_1}   \text{or, finally,}$$

$$\log \dfrac{k_2}{k_1} = \dfrac{\Delta H° (T_2 - T_1)}{(2.303) \, R \, T_2 \, T_1}$$

Thus, $\log \dfrac{k_{2500°K}}{k_{2000°K}} = \log \dfrac{3.60 \times 10^{-3}}{4.08 \times 10^{-4}}$

$$= \dfrac{\Delta H° \, (2500 - 2000)°K}{(2.303)(1.987 \, cal°K^{-1} mole^{-1})(2500)°K \, (2000)°K}$$

$$\log 8.82 = .945 = \frac{H° \ (500°K)}{(2.303)(1.987)(5 \times 10^6) \, cal°K^{-1} \, mole^{-1} \, °K^2}$$

$$\frac{(0.945)(2.303)(1.987)(5 \times 10 \ )}{(500) \, mole \, cal^{-1}} = H°$$

$\Delta H° = 43,240 \ cal/mole.$

CHAPTER 13

ELECTROCHEMISTRY

REDOX REACTIONS

Balance the following reaction in basic aqueous solution:

$$SO_3^{2-} + CrO_4^{2-} \rightarrow SO_4^{2-} + Cr(OH)_3$$

<u>Solution</u>: Three rules can be used to balance oxidation-reduction reactions: (1) Balance charge by adding H^+ (in acid) or OH^- (in base). (2) Balance oxygen by adding water. (3) Balance atoms (of hydrogen) by adding hydrogen to the appropriate side. These 3 rules will balance the redox equation. You proceed as follows:

Reduction: $CrO_4^{2-} \rightarrow Cr(OH)_3$.

Add $2OH^-$, to the right side so that charge is balanced. You obtain

$$CrO_4^{2-} \rightarrow Cr(OH)_3 + 2OH^-.$$

Balance oxygens by adding one water molecule to left side. Thus,

$$H_2O + CrO_4^{2-} \rightarrow Cr(OH)_3 + 2OH^-.$$

Balance H's by adding three H's to right side. You have

$$\frac{3}{2} H_2 + H_2O + CrO_4^{2-} \rightarrow Cr(OH)_3 + 2OH^-$$

Oxidation: $SO_3^{2-} \rightarrow SO_4^{2-}$.

Charges are already balanced. To balance oxygen, add water to left side. As such,

$$H_2O + SO_3^{2-} \rightarrow SO_4^{2-}.$$

Now balance hydrogens to obtain

$$H_2O + SO_3^{2-} \rightarrow SO_4^{2-} + H_2.$$

In summary, the balanced half-reactions are

oxid: $\quad H_2O + SO_3^{2-} \rightarrow SO_4^{2-} + H_2$

red: $\quad \frac{3}{2} H_2 + H_2O + CrO_4^{2-} \rightarrow Cr(OH)_3 + 2OH^-$

So that no free H's appear in overall reaction, multiply the oxidation reaction by 3 and red by 2. You obtain

oxid: $\qquad\qquad 3H_2O + 3SO_3^{2-} \rightarrow 3SO_4^{2-} + 3H_2$

red: $\qquad 3H_2 + 2H_2O + 2CrO_4^{2-} \rightarrow 2Cr(OH)_3 + 4OH^-$

overall (oxid + red):

$$5H_2O + 3SO_3^{2-} + 2CrO_4^{2-} \rightarrow 3SO_4^{2-} + 2Cr(OH)_3 + 4OH^-.$$

Notice: The H_2's dropped out.

● **PROBLEM** 13-2

Balance the following reaction in acidic aqueous solution:

$$ClO_3^- + Fe^{2+} \rightarrow Cl^- + Fe^{3+}$$

Solution: Reactions in which electrons are transferred from one atom to another are known as oxidation-reduction reactions or as redox reactions. To balance this type of reaction, you want to conserve charge and matter, i.e., one side of the equation must not have an excess of charge or matter. To perform this balancing, you need to (1) Balance charge by adding H^+ (in acid) or OH^- (in base). (2) Balance oxygen by adding water. (3) Balance atoms (of hydrogen) by adding hydrogen to appropriate side. These three rules will balance the redox equation. These rules apply to balancing only the half-reactions. The overall reaction, the sum of these, will be balanced by their addition. Proceed as follows: Fe^{2+} goes to Fe^{3+}. It lost an electron thus, it's the oxidation half reaction. To balance charge, add H^+. Thus,

$$Fe^{2+} + H^+ \rightarrow Fe^{3+}.$$

To conserve mass, add an H atom to right. You obtain

$$Fe^{2+} + H^+ \rightarrow Fe^{3+} + \frac{1}{2} H_2.$$

The reduction must be $ClO_3^- \rightarrow Cl^-$. The charges are already balanced. To balance the 3 oxygen atoms on left side, add 3 water molecules on right side. You obtain

$$ClO_3^- \rightarrow Cl^- + 3H_2O.$$

To balance hydrogens, add 6 hydrogens (or $3H_2$ molecules) to left side.

$$3H_2 + ClO_3^- \rightarrow Cl^- + 3H_2O.$$

In summary, you have

oxid: $\qquad\qquad Fe^{2+} + H^+ \rightarrow Fe^{3+} + \frac{1}{2}H_2$

red: $\qquad\qquad 3H_2 + ClO_3^- \rightarrow Cl^- + 3H_2O.$

So that no free H's appear in the overall equation, multiply the oxidation reaction by six. You obtain

$$6Fe^{2+} + 6H^+ \rightarrow 6Fe^{3+} + 3H_2$$

Thus, oxid: $\qquad 6Fe^{2+} + 6H^+ \rightarrow 6Fe^{3+} + 3H_2$

red: $\qquad\qquad 3H_2 + ClO_3^- \rightarrow Cl^- + 3H_2O$

overall: $\qquad 6Fe^{2+} + ClO_3^- + 6H^+ \rightarrow 6Fe^{3+} + cl^- + 3H_2O$

Notice: The H atoms dropped out. This is the balanced e-quation for charge and mass are equal on both sides of the equation. H^+ comes from the acid; recall, it's in an acidic solution.

● **PROBLEM** 13-3

Balance the equation for the following reaction taking place in aqueous acid solution:

$$Cr_2O_7^{2-} + I_2 \rightarrow Cr^{3+} + IO_3^-$$

Solution: The equation in this problem involves both an oxidation and a reduction reaction. It can be balanced by using the following rules: (1) Separate the net reaction into its two major components, the oxidation process (the loss of electrons) and the reduction process (the gain of electrons). For each of these reactions, balance the charges by adding H^+, if the reaction is occurring in an acidic medium, or OH^- in a basic medium. (2) Balance the oxygens by addition of H_2O. (3) Balance hydrogen atoms by addition of H. (4) Combine the two half reactions, so that all charges from electron transfer cancel out. These rules are applied in the following example.

The net reaction is

$$Cr_2O_7^{2-} + I_2 \rightarrow Cr^{3+} + IO_3^-$$

The oxidation reaction is

$$I_2^0 \rightarrow 2IO_3^- + 10e^-$$

The I atom went from an oxidation number of 0 in I_2 to + 5 in IO_3^-, because O always has a - 2 charge. You begin with I_2, therefore, 2 moles of IO_3^- must be produced and 10 electrons are lost, 5 from each I atom. Recall, the next step is to balance the charges. The right side has a total of 12 negative charges. Add 12 H^+'s to obtain

$$I_2 \rightarrow 2IO_3^- + 10e^- + 12H^+$$

To balance the oxygen atoms, add $6H_2O$ to the left side, since there are 6 O's on the right, thus,

$$I_2 + 6H_2O \rightarrow 2IO_3^- + 10e^- + 12H^+.$$

Hydrogens are already balanced. There are 12 on each side. Proceed to the reduction reaction:

$$Cr_2O_7^{2-} + 6e^- \rightarrow 2Cr^{3+}$$

Cr began with an oxidation state of + 6 and went to + 3. Since $2Cr^{3+}$ are produced, and you began with $Cr_2O_7^{2-}$, a total of 6 electrons are added to the left. Balancing charges: the left side has 8 negative charges and right side has 6 positive charges. If you add 14 H^+ to left, they balance. Both sides now have a net + 3 charge. The equation can now be written.

$$Cr_2O_7^{2-} + 6e^- + 14H^+ \rightarrow 2Cr^{3+}.$$

To balance oxygen atoms, add $7H_2O$'s to right. You obtain

$$Cr_2O_7^{2-} + 6e^- + 14H^+ \rightarrow 2Cr^{3+} + 7H_2O.$$

The hydrogens are also balanced, 14 on each side. The oxidation reaction becomes

$$I_2 + 6H_2O \rightarrow 2IO_3^- + 10e^- + 12H^+$$

The reduction reaction is

$$Cr_2O_7^{2-} + 6e^- + 14H^+ \rightarrow 2Cr^{3+} + 7H_2O.$$

Combine these two in such a manner that the number of electrons used in the oxidation reaction is equal to the number used in the reduction. To do this, note that the oxidation reaction has $10e^-$ and the reduction $6e^-$. Both are a multiple of 30. Multiply the oxidation reaction by 3, and the reduction reaction by 5, obtaining

oxidation: $\qquad 3I_2 + 18H_2O \rightarrow 6IO_3^- + 30e^- + 36H^+$

reduction: $5Cr_2O_7^{2-} + 30e^- + 70H^+ \rightarrow 10Cr^{3+} + 35H_2O$

Add these two half-reactions together.

$$3I_2 + 18H_2O \rightarrow 6IO_3^- + 30e^- + 36H^+$$

$$+ \quad \underline{5Cr_2O_7^{2-} + 30e^- + 70H^+ \rightarrow 10Cr^{3+} + 35H_2O}$$

$$3I_2 + 18H_2O + 5Cr_2O_7^{2-} + 30e^- + 70H^+ \rightarrow 10Cr^{3+} + 35H_2O + 30e^- + 36H^+$$

Simplifying, you obtain:

$$3I_2 + 5Cr_2O_7^{2-} + 34H^+ \rightarrow 6IO_3^- + 10Cr^{3+} + 17H_2O$$

This is the balanced equation.

● **PROBLEM** 13-4

Balance the equation for the following reaction taking place in aqueous basic solution:

$$MnO_4^- + H_2O_2 \rightarrow MnO_2 + O_2$$

Solution: The equation in this problem involves both oxidation and reduction. When balancing it, you can use the following rules. Separate the net reaction into its two major components, the oxidation reaction (the loss of electrons) and the reduction reaction (the gain of electrons). For each half-reaction, balance the charges with H^+, if the medium is acidic, or OH^-, if the medium is basic. Next, balance the oxygens by the addition of H_2O. Balance total atoms by the addition of H atoms. Finally, combine the two half reactions, so that all charges from electron transfer cancel out.

You employ these rules as follows:

The net reaction is

$$MnO_4^- + H_2O_2 \rightarrow MnO_2 + O_2$$

The oxidation process is

$$H_2O_2 \rightarrow O_2 + 2e^-$$

The oxygen atoms in H_2O_2 go from -1 to zero in O_2. Thus, you have a loss of two electrons. To balance charges, add 2 OH^- to the left side, since there exist 2 negative charges on the right side. You obtain

$$H_2O_2 + 2OH^- \rightarrow O_2 + 2e^-$$

You now have 4 oxygens on the left, but only 2 on the right. Thus, add 2 water molecular ro the right, obtaining

$$H_2O_2 + 2OH^- \rightarrow O_2 + 2e^- + 2H_2O$$

There are the same number of H's on each side. Proceed, now, to reduction half-reaction. Here,

$$MnO_4^- + 3e^- \rightarrow MnO_2$$

Mn begins with a + 7 oxidation number and ends up with + 4 in MnO_2. Therefore, 3 electrons must be added to the left side of the equation. To balance the charges, add 4 OH^-

ions to right, since you have a total of 4 negative charges on left. Rewriting the equation

$$MnO_4^- + 3e^- \rightarrow MnO_2 + 4OH^-.$$

Add 2 water molecules to the left, so that oxygen atoms can be balanced, obtaining

$$2H_2O + MnO_4^- + 3e^- \rightarrow MnO_2 + 4OH^-.$$

The hydrogens are balanced. Thus,

oxidation: $H_2O_2 + 2OH^- \rightarrow O_2 + 2e^- + 2H_2O$

reduction: $2H_2O + MnO_4^- + 3e^- \rightarrow MnO_2 + 4OH^-$

To combine these two so that electrons cancel out. Select a multiple of 3 and 2, since these are the number of electrons involved in the half-reactions. This multiple is six. Multiply the oxidation by 3 and the reduction by 2, obtaining

oxidation: $3H_2O_2 + 6OH^- \rightarrow 3O_2 + 6e^- + 6H_2O$

reduction: $4H_2O + 2MnO_4^- + 6e^- \rightarrow 2MnO_2 + 8OH^-$

The net reaction is the total. Thus, adding you obtain:

$$3H_2O_2 + 4H_2O + 6OH^- + 2MnO_4^- + 6e^- \rightarrow 3O_2 + 6e^- + 6H_2O + 8OH^- + 2MnO_2$$

Cancel the electrons, subtract OH^- ions and H_2O's to obtain:

$$2MnO_4^- + 3H_2O_2 \rightarrow 2MnO_2 + 3O_2 + 2H_2O + 2OH^-$$

which is the balanced equation.

● **PROBLEM** 13-5

Determine the volume in milliliters of .20 M $KMnO_4$ required to oxidize 25.0 ml of .40 M $FeSO_4$ in acidic solution. Assume the reaction which occurs is the oxidation of Fe^{2+} by MnO_4^- to give Fe^{+3} and Mn^{2+}.

Solution: This problem can be solved by two methods: the mole and the equivalent methods. The mole method requires consideration of the balanced equation that illustrates the reaction. From the data provided, this equation becomes

$$5Fe^{2+} + MnO_4^- + 8H_3O^+ \rightarrow 5Fe^{3+} + Mn^{2+} + 12 H_2O.$$

Now 25.0 ml of .40 M $FeSO_4$ furnishes
$(.025$ liters$)(.40$ mol/liter$) = .010$ moles of Fe^{2+}, since
the definition of molarity is

$$M = \frac{number\ of\ moles\ of\ solute}{number\ of\ liters}.$$

The balanced equation indicates that the number of
moles of MnO_4^- will be 1/5 that of Fe^{2+}. As such, the number
of moles of $MnO_4^- = (.010)(1/5) = .002$ moles. Since the
$KMnO_4$ solution has a concentration of .2 M, then the number
of liters required is

$$\frac{.002\ mol\ of\ MnO_4^-}{.2\ mol/liter} = .01\ liters,\ which\ equals\ 10\ ml.$$

The equivalent method functions differently. An equivalent is defined as that mass of oxidizing or reducing
agent that picks up or releases the Avogadro number of
electrons. Normality is defined as the number of equivalents per liter. Since, in going from Fe^{2+} to Fe^{3+}, you
lose 1 electron, .40 M $FeSO_4$ is equal to .40 N $FeSO_4$.
Recalling the definition of normality, you have

$$(.025\ liter)(.40\ equiv/liter) = .01\ equiv.\ of\ Fe^{2+},$$

the reducing agent. In an oxidation-reduction reaction,
the number of equivalents of oxidizing agent must equal that
of the reducing agent. This means you must have .01 equiv.
of MnO_4^-. You know that for $KMnO_4$, there exists 1 equiv/liter.
Therefore, the number of liters equals

$$\frac{.01\ equiv.}{1.0\ equiv./liter} = .01\ liters\ or\ 10\ ml.$$

ELECTRODE POTENTIAL

● **PROBLEM** 13-6

Using the tables of standard electrode potentials, arrange the following substances in decreasing order of ability as reducing agents:
Al, Co, Ni, Ag, H_2, Na .

Solution: The tables of standard electrode potentials list substances
according to their ability as oxidizing agents. The greater the standard electrode potential, E°, of a substance, the more effective it is
as an oxidizing agent and the less effective it is as a reducing agent.
From the table of standard electrode potentials,

$$Al^{3+} + 3e^- \rightleftarrows Al(s) \qquad\qquad E^\circ = -1.66v$$
$$Co^{2+} + 2e^- \rightleftarrows Co(s) \qquad\qquad E^\circ = -0.28v$$
$$Ni^{2+} + 2e^- \rightleftarrows Ni(s) \qquad\qquad E^\circ = -0.25v$$

$$Ag^+ + e^- \xrightleftharpoons{} Ag(s) \qquad E^\circ = +0.80v$$
$$2H^+ + 2e^- \xrightleftharpoons{} H_2(g) \qquad E^\circ = 0 \text{ v}$$
$$Na^+ + e^- \xrightleftharpoons{} Na(s) \qquad E^\circ = -2.71v$$

Thus, in increasing ability as oxidizing agents,
$$Na^+ < Al^{3+} < Co^{2+} < Ni^{2+} < H^+ < Ag^+ .$$

But if Na^+ has a greater tendency to oxidize (gain electrons) than Al^{3+}, then, from looking at the reverse reactions, the "conjugate oxidant" Na must have a greater tendency to reduce (lose electrons) than the "conjugate oxidant" Al. Thus, Na, is a better reducing agent than Al, and so on. The substances, in order of decreasing ability as reducing agents, are therefore

$$Na > Al > Co > Ni > H_2 > Ag .$$

● **PROBLEM** 13-7

Using the tables, of standard electrode potentials, list the following ions in order of decreasing ability as oxidizing agents: Fe^{3+}, F_2, Pb^{2+}, I_2, Sn^{4+}, O_2.

Half-reaction	E°, V
$Li^+ + e^- \rightleftharpoons Li$	−3.05
$K^+ + e^- \rightleftharpoons K$	−2.93
$Na^+ + e^- \rightleftharpoons Na$	−2.71
$Mg^{2+} + 2e^- \rightleftharpoons Mg$	−2.37
$Al^{3+} + 3e^- \rightleftharpoons Al$	−1.66
$Mn^{2+} + 2e^- \rightleftharpoons Mn$	−1.18
$Zn^{2+} + 2e^- \rightleftharpoons Zn$	−0.76
$Cr^{3+} + 3e^- \rightleftharpoons Cr$	−0.74
$Fe^{2+} + 2e^- \rightleftharpoons Fe$	−0.44
$Cd^{2+} + 2e^- \rightleftharpoons Cd$	−0.40
$Co^{2+} + 2e^- \rightleftharpoons Co$	−0.28
$Ni^{2+} + 2e^- \rightleftharpoons Ni$	−0.250
$Sn^{2+} + 2e^- \rightleftharpoons Sn$	−0.14
$Pb^{2+} + 2e^- \rightleftharpoons Pb$	−0.13
$Fe^{3+} + 3e^- \rightleftharpoons Fe$	−0.04
$2 H^+ + 2e^- \rightleftharpoons H_2$	0 (definition)
$Sn^{4+} + 2e^- \rightleftharpoons Sn^{2+}$	0.15
$Cu^{2+} + 2e \rightleftharpoons Cu$	0.94
$Fe(CN)_6^{3-} + e^- \rightleftharpoons Fe(CN)_6^{4-}$	0.46
$I_2 + 2e^- \rightleftharpoons 2 I^-$	0.54
$O_2 + 2 H^+ + 2e^- \rightleftharpoons H_2O_2$	0.68
$Fe^{3+} + e^- \rightleftharpoons Fe^{2+}$	0.77
$Hg_2^{2+} + 2e^- \rightleftharpoons 2 Hg$	0.79
$Ag^+ + e^- \rightleftharpoons Ag$	0.80
$2 Hg^{2+} + 2e^- \rightleftharpoons Hg_2^{2+}$	0.92
$Br_2 + 2e^- \rightleftharpoons 2 Br^-$	1.09
$O_2(g) + 4 H^+ + 4e^- \rightleftharpoons 2 H_2O$	1.23

Reaction	
$Cr_2O_7{}^{2-} + 14\,H^+ + 6e^- \rightleftharpoons 2\,Cr^{3+} + 7\,H_2O$	1.33
$Cl_2 + 2e^- \rightleftharpoons 2\,Cl^-$	1.36
$MnO_4{}^- + 8\,H^+ + 5e^- \rightleftharpoons Mn^{2+} + 4\,H_2O$	1.51
$Ce^{4+} + e^- \rightleftharpoons Ce^{3+}$	1.61
$MnO_4{}^- + 4\,H^+ + 3e^- \rightleftharpoons MnO_2(s) + 2\,H_2O$	1.68
$H_2O_2 + 2\,H^+ + 2e^- \rightleftharpoons 2\,H_2O$	1.77
$O_3 + 2\,H^+ + 2e^- \rightleftharpoons O_2 + H_2O$	2.07
$F_2 + 2e^- \rightleftharpoons 2\,F^-$	2.87

<u>Solution</u>: The best oxidizing agent will be the one with the greatest ability to gain electrons (be reduced) and will therefore have the most positive standard electrode potential, E^o . From the tables,

$$Fe^{3+} + e^- \rightleftharpoons Fe^{2+} \qquad\qquad E^o = +0.77v$$

$$F_2(g) + 2e^- \rightleftharpoons 2F^- \qquad\qquad E^o = +2.87v$$

$$Pb^{2+} + 2e^- \rightleftharpoons Pb(s) \qquad\qquad E^o = -0.13v$$

$$I_2(s) + 2e^- \rightleftharpoons 2I^- \qquad\qquad E^o = +0.54v$$

$$Sn^{4+} + 2e^- \rightleftharpoons Sn^{2+} \qquad\qquad E^o = +0.15v$$

$$O_2(g) + 2H^+ + 2e^- \rightleftharpoons H_2O_2(\ell) \quad E^o = +0.68v$$

Thus the substances, in order of decreasing ability as oxidizing agents, are

$$F_2 > Fe^{3+} > O_2 > I_2 > Sn^{4+} > Pb^{2+} \quad .$$

● **PROBLEM** 13-8

Calculate ΔE^o for the following cells: (1) Cadmium and Hydrogen, (2) Silver and Hydrogen and (3) Cadmium and silver, using the following data:

Reaction	E^o volts
$Cd \rightarrow Cd^{+2} + 2e^-$	+ .403
$H_2 \rightarrow 2H^+ + 2e^-$	0.00
$Ag \rightarrow Ag^+ + e^-$	- .799

<u>Solution</u>: You are asked to calculate the standard cell potential (ΔE^o) for each of the given pairs. To do this, you must realize that in such cells, you have 2 half-reactions. Namely, an oxidation reaction (loss of electrons) and a reduction reaction (gain of electrons). The sum of these half-reactions yields the overall reaction and the ΔE^o of the whole cell. Thus, to find the ΔE^o for each of these pairs, you need to know the E^o of the half-reactions. There is one other important fact to be kept in mind.

In cells, if the reaction is to proceed spontaneously, ΔE^o must have a positive value. This means, therefore, that you must choose the half-reactions such that their sum always gives a positive ΔE^o . You are told the E^o of the oxidation half-reaction for each element in each pair. The reduction half-reaction is the reverse of the oxidation reaction for each element, with a change in sign of E^o . For example, if you have $A \rightarrow A^{+1} + e^-$ with an $E^o = B$ for oxidation, the reduction is $A^{+1} + e^- \rightarrow A$ with a $E^\circ = -B$.

With this in mind, the procedure is as follows:
(1) Cadmium (Cd) and hydrogen (H_2).

The reaction for this cell must be the sum of the oxidation and reduction such that the ΔE° is positive. This can only occur if the anode (oxidation) has the higher oxidation potential. Thus, you calculate ΔE° as $+ .403 - (0.000) = +.403v$. Similarly, for (2) and (3), a positive ΔE° can only be obtained with the anode having the higher oxidation potential. Thus, for (2), $E^\circ = (0.000) - (-.799) = + .799v$. For (3), $E^\circ = (.403)-(-.799) = +1.202v$.

For the following oxidation-reduction reaction, (a) write out the two half-reactions and balance the equation, (b) calculate ΔE°, and (c) determine whether the reaction will proceed spontaneously as written;

$$Fe^{2+} + MnO_4^- + H^+ \rightarrow Mn^{2+} + Fe^{3+} + H_2O.$$

(1) $\qquad Fe^{3+} + e^- \overset{\rightarrow}{\leftarrow} Fe^{2+}, \quad E^\circ = 0.77$ eV

(2) $\quad MnO_4^- + 8H^+ + 6e^- \overset{\rightarrow}{\leftarrow} Mn^{2+} + 4H_2O, \; E^\circ = 1.51$ eV.

Solution: (a) The two half-reactions of an oxidation-reduction reaction are the equations for the oxidation process (loss of electrons) and the reduction process (gain of electrons). In the overall reaction, you begin with Fe^{2+} and end up with Fe^{3+}. It had to lose an electron to accomplish this. Thus you have oxidation:

$$Fe^{2+} \rightarrow Fe^{3+} + e^-.$$

Notice: this is the reverse of the reaction given with $E^\circ = .77$. As such, the oxidation reaction in this problem has $E^\circ = - .77$ eV. The reduction must be

$$MnO_4^- + 8H^+ + 5e^- \rightarrow Mn^{2+} + 4H_2O,$$

since in the overall reaction, you see $MnO_4^- + H^+$ go to Mn^{2+}, which suggests a gain of electrons. This is the same reaction as the one given in the problem, $E^\circ = 1.51$ eV. To balance the overall reaction, add the oxidation reaction to the reduction reaction, such that all electron charges disappear. If you multiply the oxidation reaction by 5, you obtain:

$$5Fe^{2+} \rightarrow 5Fe^{3+} + 5e^-$$

$$MnO_4^- + 8H^+ + 5e^- \rightarrow Mn^{2+} + 4H_2O$$

$$\overline{\rule{0pt}{0pt}\qquad\qquad\qquad\qquad\qquad\qquad\qquad\qquad}$$

$$5Fe^{2+} + MnO_4^- + 8H \rightarrow 5Fe^{3+} + Mn^{2+} + 4H_2O$$

Notice: Since both equations contained 5e$^-$ on different sides, they cancelled out. This explains why the oxidation reaction is multiplied by five. Thus you have written the balanced equation.

(b) The ΔE° for the overall reaction is the sum of the E° for the half-reactions, i.e., $\Delta E^\circ = E_{red} + E_{oxid}$. You know that E_{red} and E_{oxid}; $\Delta E^\circ = 1.51 - .77 = 0.74$ eV.

(c) A reaction will only proceed spontaneously when $\Delta E^\circ =$ a positive value. You calculated a positive ΔE°, which means the reaction proceeds spontaneously.

ELECTROCHEMICAL CELL REACTIONS

For the following voltaic cell, write the half-reactions, designating which is oxidation and which is reduction. Write the cell reaction and calculate the voltage of the cell made from standard electrodes. The cell is Co; Co^{+2} ‖ Ni^{+2} ; Ni .

Solution: The cell reaction is the algebraic sum of the reactions that take place at the electrodes. Every cell has 2 electrodes an anode and a cathode. Oxidation, which is the loss of electrons, occurs at the anode. Reduction, which is the gain of electrons, takes place at the cathode.

The cell is always written as solid; ion in solution ‖ ion in solution; solid (anode)   (cathode)

Oxidation and reduction are the half reactions that take place in the cell. For this cell, they are

$$Co \rightarrow Co^{+2} + 2e^- \text{ (oxidation at anode)}$$
$$Ni^{+2} + 2e^- \rightarrow Ni \text{ (reduction at cathode)}$$

Sum: $Ni^{+2} + Co \rightarrow Ni + Co^{+2}$ (Cell reaction) .

Since Co is losing electrons, it provides the oxidation reaction and Ni^{+2} , gaining these electrons, takes part in the reduction reaction.

The voltage of a cell is the sum of the oxidation and reduction potentials in units of volts and is designated by E° (under standard conditions) .

$$E^\circ_{cell} = E^\circ_{oxidation} + E^\circ_{reduction} .$$

The voltages of half cell reactions are usually given as the reduction potentials. The oxidation potential is opposite in sign to the reduction potential. The potentials can be obtained from a table of standard reduction potentials.

For
$$Ni^{+2} + 2e^- \rightarrow Ni , \text{ the potential is } -.25 \text{ v}, E^\circ_{red} = -.25\text{v}.$$
$$Co^{+2} + 2e^- \rightarrow Co, \text{ the potential is } -.277 \text{ v}.$$

Since $Co \rightarrow Co^{+2} + 2e^-$ is the oxidation reaction, E^o_{ox} equals the negative of $-.277$ v, or $E^o_{ox} = .277$ v.

Substituting these values into the equation $E^o = E^o_{oxid} + E^o_{red}$, one obtains

$$E^o = +.277 + (-.25) = .027 \text{ v} .$$

Since E^o is positive, the reaction proceeds spontaneously and can be used to supply current.

● **PROBLEM** 13-11

For the following **voltaic cell**, write the half reactions, designating which is oxidation and which reduction. Write the cell reaction and calculate the voltage (E^o) of the cell from the given electrodes. The cell is

$$Cu; \; Cu^{+2} \; \| \; Ag^{+2} \; ; \; Ag .$$

Solution: In a voltaic cell, the flow of electrons creates a current. Their flow is regulated by 2 types of reactions occur concurrently, oxidation and reduction. Oxidation is a process where electrons are lost and reduction where electrons are gained. The equation for these are the half-reactions. From the cell diagram, the direction of the reaction is always left to right.

$$Cu \rightarrow Cu^{+2} + 2e^- \qquad \text{oxidation}$$
$$Ag^{+2} + 2e^- \rightarrow Ag \qquad \text{reduction} .$$

Therefore, the combined cell reaction is

$$Cu + Ag^{+2} \rightarrow Cu^{+2} + Ag .$$

To calculate the total E^o, look up the value for the E^o of both half-reactions as reductions. To obtain E^o for oxidation, reverse the sign of the reduction E_o. Then, substitute into $E^o_{cell} = E^o_{red} + E^o_{ox}$. If you do this, you find

$$E^o_{cell} = -(E^o_{red} \; Cu) + E^o_{red} \; Ag^{+2}$$
$$= -.34 + .80$$
$$= .46 \text{ volt} .$$

● **PROBLEM** 13-12

Calculate E^o for the cell in which the following reaction occurs.

$$2Al + 3NiCl_2 \rightarrow 2AlCl_3 + 3Ni.$$

First, indicate the direction of the electron flow.

Solution: This problem is solved by finding the oxidation and reduction reactions which occur. Knowing this, we can solve both questions.

First, we must determine the metals involved. They are Al and Ni, for which the half-reactions are

$$Al \rightarrow Al^{+3} + 3r^- \qquad E^o_{oxid} = 1.66$$
$$Ni^{+2} + 2e^- \rightarrow Ni \qquad E^o_{red} = -.25$$

Since Al is losing electrons (oxidation), and Ni is gaining electrons (reduction), the electron flow is from Al to Ni

E° , the standard electrode potential is the sum of the E°'s for the half-reactions listed above

$$E^{\circ} = E^{\circ}_{ox} + E^{\circ}_{red}$$
$$= 1.66 + (-.25)$$
$$= 1.41 \text{ volts}$$

● **PROBLEM** 13-13

Given the following standard electrode potentials at 25°C: $Sn^{4+} + 2e^{-} \rightarrow Sn^{2+}$, $E^{\circ} = 0.15$ ev and $Fe^{3+} + e^{-} \rightarrow Fe^{2+}$, $E^{\circ} = +0.77$ev will the reaction $Sn^{2+} + 2Fe^{3+} \overset{\rightarrow}{\underset{\leftarrow}{}} Sn^{4+} + 2Fe^{2+}$ proceed spontaneously?

Solution: A reaction will proceed spontaneously only if it has a positive ΔE° as written. Thus, to answer this question, you want to calculate the ΔE° and see whether it is positive. This can be done by considering its half-reactions. The sum of the electrode potentials for these reactions will be the ΔE°.
    The overall reaction is
$$Sn^{2+} + 2Fe^{3+} \overset{\rightarrow}{\underset{\leftarrow}{}} Sn^{4+} + 2Fe^{2+} .$$

The half-reactions are, oxidation (loss of electrons) and reduction (gain of electrons) reactions. You have then,

$$\text{oxidation: } Sn^{2+} \rightarrow Sn^{4+} + 2e^{-} .$$
This, has the reverse of the standard potential of the reaction given. Thus, its $E^{\circ} = -(0.15) = -.15$ev.

$$\text{Reduction: } Fe^{3+} + e^{-} \rightarrow Fe^{2+} .$$
This has the same standard potential as in the given reaction. Thus, its $E^{\circ} = 0.77$ev. Adding these two equations together, one obtains the desired net reaction.

$$
\begin{array}{rcl}
S_{n}^{2+} & \rightarrow & Sn^{4+} + 2e^{-} \\
2Fe^{3+} + 2e^{-} & \rightarrow & 2Fe^{2+} \\
\hline
2Fe^{3+} + Sn^{2+} & \rightarrow & Sn^{4+} + 2Fe^{2+}
\end{array}
$$

The $\Delta E^{\circ} = E^{\circ}_{oxid} + E^{\circ}_{red} = -.15 + .77 = +.62$ volt. The fact that it is positive means the reaction proceeds spontaneously.

● **PROBLEM** 13-14

Construct a galvanic cell based on the reaction
$$3Fe(s) + 2Au^{+3} \rightarrow 3Fe^{+2} + 2Au(s)$$
with ΔH negative.

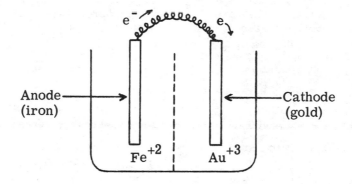

Solution: A galvanic cell may be defined as one in which spontaneous chemical reactions occur at each of the electrodes of the cell to produce an electric current.   Thus, to construct this cell, you need to know those reactions that occur at the electrodes.

The two electrodes are the anode and cathode.   At the anode oxidation occurs, which means you have the loss of electrons.   At the cathode, reduction occurs, which means you have the gain of electrons.   The oxidation and reduction reactions are each called half-reactions.   These are the reactions that occur at the electrodes.   From the given reaction, it becomes apparent that oxidation is given by $Fe(s) \rightarrow Fe^{+2} + 2e^{-}$ and reduction by $Au^{+3} + 3e^{-} \rightarrow Au(s)$.   Thus, the anode half-cell would consist of an iron electrode in a solution containing Fe^{+2} ions, while the cathode half-cell would consist of a gold electrode in a solution containing Au^{+3} ions.

A compound such as $FeSO_4$ could serve as a source of Fe^{+2} ions, and $AuCl_3$ as a source of Au^{+3} ions.

The cell might appear as in the figure shown .

CHAPTER 14

ATOMIC THEORY

ATOMIC WEIGHT

> If the atomic weight of carbon 12 is exactly 12 amu, find
> the mass of a single carbon-12 atom.

<u>Solution</u>: To solve this problem, one must first define
the mole concept. A mole is defined as the weight in grams
divided by the atomic weight (or molecular weight) of the
atom or compound.

$$\text{mole} = \frac{\text{weight in grams}}{\text{atomic or molecular weight}}$$

If one has a mole of carbon 12, then there are 12
grams of it present. One mole of any substance contains
6.022×10^{23} particles.

The mass of a single carbon atom is found by
dividing 12 g/mole by 6.022×10^{23} atoms/mole.

$$\text{mass of 1 C atom} = \frac{12 \text{ g/mole}}{6.022 \times 10^{23} \text{ atoms/mole}}$$

$$= 2.0 \times 10^{-23} \text{ g/atom.}$$

> The atomic weight of iron is 55.847 amu. If one has 6.02 g
> of iron, how many atoms are present?

<u>Solution</u>: A mole is defined as the weight in grams of a

substance divided by its atomic weight:

$$\text{mole} = \frac{\text{amount in grams}}{\text{atomic weight}}$$

If one calculates the number of moles of iron, then the number of atoms present can be calculated. There are 6.02×10^{23} atoms per mole.

$$\text{no. of moles of Fe} = \frac{6.02 \text{ g}}{55.847 \text{ g/mole}} = 1.08 \times 10^{-1} \text{ moles}$$

$$\text{no. of Fe atoms present} = (1.08 \times 10^{-1} \text{ moles}) \text{ x}$$

$$(6.02 \times 10^{23} \text{ atoms/mole})$$

$$= 6.49 \times 10^{22} \text{ atoms.}$$

● **PROBLEM** 14-3

Nitrogen **reacts** with hydrogen to form ammonia (NH_3). The weight-percent of nitrogen in ammonia is 82.25. The atomic weight of hydrogen is 1.008. Calculate the atomic weight of nitrogen.

<u>Solution</u>: When elements combine to form a given compound, they do so in a fixed and invariable ratio by weight.

In a given amount of NH_3, 82.25% of its weight is contributed by nitrogen. The weight-percent of hydrogen in ammonia is, then

$$100 - 82.25 = 17.75\%.$$

One mole of nitrogen and 3 moles of hydrogen combine to form one mole of ammonia. Therefore, one mole of nitrogen constitutes 82.25% and 3 moles of hydrogen constitute 17.75% by weight of one mole of ammonia. The atomic weight of an element is equal to the weight of one mole of that element. The following ratio can be set up to solve for the atomic weight (AW) of nitrogen:

$$\frac{AW_N}{3 \times AW_H} = \frac{\text{weight-percent N}}{\text{weight-percent H}}$$

Solving for AW_N

$$AW_N = \frac{(3 \times AW_H)(\text{weight-percent N})}{(\text{weight-percent H})}$$

$$= \frac{3(1.008)(18.25)}{17.75} = 14.01.$$

VALENCE AND ELECTRON DOT DIAGRAMS

● **PROBLEM** 14-4

On the basis of valence, predict the formulas of the
compounds formed between the following pairs of elements:
(a) Sn and F. (b) P and H. (c) Si and O.

Solution: Valence may be defined as a number which
represents the combining capacity of an atom or radical,
based on hydrogen as a standard.

For molecules containing two kinds of atoms, the
product of the number of times one kind of atom appears
in a molecule and the valence of that kind of
atom, must be equal to the product of the number of times
the other kind of atom appears multiplied by the valence
of this second kind of atom.

(a) The valence of Sn is 4 and that of F is 1. Hence,
the compound is SnF_4 (1 atom Sn × 4 = 4 atoms F × 1).

(b) The valence of P is 3 and that of H is 1. Hence,
the compound is PH_3 (1 atom P × 3 = 3 atoms H × 1).

(c) The valence of Si is 4 and that of O is 2. Hence,
the compound is SiO_2 (1 atom Si × 4 = 2 atoms O × 2). ,

● **PROBLEM** 14-5

The atomic weight of element X is 58.7. 7.34 g of X
displaces 0.25 g of hydrogen from hydrochloric acid
(HCl). What is the valence of element X?

Solution: Chlorine has a valence of -1, thus to
determine the valence of X, one must calculate the number
of moles of Cl^- that will bind to each mole of X. The
valence will be equal to this number. There are 2 moles
of Cl^- present for every mole of H_2 formed. To find the
number of moles of H_2 formed, one must divide 0.25 g by
the molecular weight of H_2 (MW of H_2 = 2).

$$\text{moles of } H_2 = \frac{0.25 \text{ g}}{2 \text{ g/mole}} = .125 \text{ moles of } H_2.$$

no. of moles of Cl^- = 2 × .125 = .250 moles.

One should now determine the number of moles of X
present. This is done by dividing the number of grams by
the molecular weight. (MW of X = 58.7).

$$\text{no. of moles} = \frac{7.34 \text{ g}}{58.7 \text{ g/mole}} = .125 \text{ moles.}$$

From this, one sees that .125 moles of X combines with .250 moles of Cl$^-$. The number of moles of Cl$^-$ that bind to each mole of X is equal to the number of moles of Cl$^-$ present divided by the number of moles of X.

$$\begin{array}{c}\text{no. of Cl}^- \text{ that combine} \\ \text{with each X}\end{array} = \frac{.250 \text{ moles of Cl}^-}{.125 \text{ moles of X}}$$

$$= 2 \text{ moles/Cl}^-\text{/mole X}$$

The formula for the resulting compound is XCL_2. Because Cl$^-$ has a valence of -1 and 2 Cl$^-$ combine with each X, X must have a valence of +2 for a neutral molecule to be formed.

● **PROBLEM 14-6**

The faint light sometimes seen over Marshland at night, the "will-o'-the-wisp", is believed to come about as a result of the burning of a compound of phosphorus (P) and hydrogen (H). What is the formula of this compound?

$$\begin{array}{c} \text{H} \\ \text{x} \bullet \\ \text{H} \; {}^{x}_{\bullet} \; \text{P} \; {}^{x}_{\bullet} \; \text{H} \\ \bullet\bullet \end{array}$$

Solution: To find the formula of this compound, it is necessary to determine the valence of the elements from which it is composed. The valence of an element is the number of electrons that are involved in chemical bonding.

To find the valence of phosphorus and hydrogen, consider their atomic number and electronic configuration.

Hydrogen: Atomic number = 1.

Electronic configuration = $1s^1$

Phosphorus: Atomic number = 15.

Electronic configuration = $1s^2 2s^2 2p^6 3s^2 3p^3$.

The outer electrons are $1s^1$ for hydrogen, and $3p^3$ for phosphorus. It takes one additional electron to fill hydrogen's s orbital; its valence is one. It takes 3 more electrons to fill phosphorus' p orbital; its valence is three. Elements react with the purpose of filling all their orbitals with the maximum number of electrons by either a transfer of electrons or by sharing electrons.

It would take three hydrogen atoms to complete phosphorus' outer orbital. In turn, each electron of phosphorus would serve to complete the outer orbital of each hydrogen atom. This can be pictured in an electron-dot formula as shown above.

In this figure, the X's represent the outer electrons of hydrogen and dots represent the electrons in the outer shell of phosphorus. The formula of this compound is, thus, PH_3.

● **PROBLEM 14-7**

H_2O_3, hydrogen trioxide, a close relative of hydrogen peroxide, has recently been synthesized. It is extremely unstable and can be isolated only in very small quantities. Write a Lewis electron dot structure for H_2O_3.

Solution: A Lewis dot structure of a compound shows the arrangement of valence electrons. Valence electrons are defined as an element's outer electrons which participate in chemical bonding. Thus, to write an electron dot structure for H_2O_3, calculate the total number of valence electrons.

This can be done by considering the electronic configurations of H (hydrogen) and O (oxygen).

Hydrogen possesses one valence electron while oxygen has 6 valence electrons. In H_2O_3, a total of $(2)1 + (3)6 = 20$ valence electrons are involved.

With this in mind, the Lewis electron dot structure becomes

$$H : \overset{..}{\underset{..}{O}} : \overset{..}{\underset{..}{O}} : \overset{..}{\underset{..}{O}} : H$$

Notice, you have represented the required 20 valence electrons.

● **PROBLEM 14-8**

Using electron-dot notation, show for each of the following the outer shell electrons for the uncombined atoms and for the molecules or ions that result:

(a)   H + H   →   hydrogen molecule
(b)   Br + Br   →   bromine molecule
(c)   Br + Cl   →   bromine chloride

(d) Si + F → silicon fluoride
(e) Se + H → hydrogen selenide
(f) Ca + O → calcium oxide

Solution: When electrons are transferred from one atom to another, ions are formed, which gives rise to ionic bonding. Two atoms, both of which tend to gain electrons, may combine with each other by sharing one or more pairs of electrons. These two atoms form a covalent bond.

To solve this problem, one must know the number of valence electrons, in each of the atoms in the equations. The valence number reflects the combining capacity of an atom. Next, one must know which atoms combine to form ionic bonds and which form covalent bonds. The only ionic bond formed in these equations is for Ca + O; the other bonds are covalent, and electrons are shared to form an isoelectronic electron cloud such as a noble gas.

Thus,

(a)   H• +   H•   →   H : H

(b) : Br : + : Br : →   : Br : Br :

(c) : Br : + : Cl : →   : Br : Cl :

(d) • Si • + : F : →   : F : S : F :
                                  : F :

(e) • Se : + H•   →   H : Se :
                                    H

(f)   Ca • + • O : →   Ca⁺⁺ : O̿ :

The sulfate ion consists of a central sulfur atom with four equivalent oxygen atoms in a tetrahedral arrangement. Keeping in mind the octet rule, draw the electronic structure for the ion. What should the internal O-S-O bond angle be?

Figure a

Figure b

Figure c

Figure d

Solution: The formula for the sulfate ion is $SO_4^=$. To write the electronic structure of the ion in this problem, one must consider the definition of valence and the octet rule. Valence electrons refer to those outer electrons that participate in chemical bonding. The octet rule states that for stability, there can be no more than eight electrons in the outer orbit of an atom, either as a result of transfer or sharing. Thus, after determining the number of valence electrons present, arrange them so that they obey the octet rule. The electronic configuration of sulfur is $1s^2 2s^2 2p^6 3s^2 3p^4$. It has 6 valence electrons; they are found in the 3s and 3p orbitals. The electronic configuration of oxygen is $1s^2 2s^2 2p^4$, which means it also has six valence electrons; the first orbital contains only 2 electrons. The electronic structure of each of these atoms can be represented as shown in figure a and figure b, where x's and **dots** indicate valence electrons. The electronic structure of the ion can be pictured as figure c. Here, one can see that the sulfur and two of the oxygen atoms are surrounded by eight electrons. Because two of the oxygen atoms are only surrounded by seven electrons, each of these atoms possesses a negative charge. This structure may also be drawn as shown in figure d.

For greatest stability the oxygen atoms must take positions as far apart as possible. It has been shown that when four atoms surround a fifth the most stable arrangement is tetrahedral. In this arrangement, the O-S-O bonds form a 109.5° angle.

IONIC AND COVALENT BONDING

> Distinguish a metallic bond from an ionic bond and from a covalent bond.

Solution: The best way to distinguish between these bonds is to define each and provide an illustrative example of each.

When an actual transfer of electrons results in the formation of a bond, it can be said that an ionic bond is present. For example,

$$2K° \quad + \quad \overset{..}{\underset{..}{S}}: \quad \rightarrow \quad 2K^+ \quad + \quad :\overset{..}{\underset{..}{S}}:^{2-} \quad \rightarrow \quad K_2S$$

| potassium atoms | sulfur atom | potassium ions | sulfur ion | ionic bond due to the attraction of unlike ions |

(unlike ions due to transfer of electrons from potassium to sulfur)

When a chemical bond is the result of the sharing of electrons, a covalent bond is present. For example:

$$:\overset{..}{\underset{..}{Br}} \cdot + \cdot \overset{..}{\underset{..}{F}}: \quad \rightarrow \quad :\overset{..}{\underset{..}{Br}}:\overset{..}{\underset{..}{F}}:$$

These electrons are shared by both atoms

A pure crystal of elemental metal consists of millions of atoms held together by metallic bonds. Metals possess electrons that can easily ionize, i.e., they can be easily freed from the individual metal atoms. This free state of electrons in metals binds all the atoms together in a crystal. The free electrons extend over all the atoms in the crystal and the bonds formed between the electrons and positive nucleus are electrostatic in nature. The electrons can be pictured as a "cloud" that surrounds and engulfs the metal atoms.

> An ionic bond is established between positive ion A and negative ion B. How would one expect the strength of the bond to be affected by each of the following changes: (a) Doubling the charge on A, (b) Simultaneously doubling the charge on A and B, (c) Doubling the radius of B, and (d) Simultaneously doubling the radius of A and B?

Solution: When two ions come together to form an ionic bond, energy is released. The more energy released, the stronger the ionic bond. The amount of energy released is determined by the equation

$$E = 1.44 \frac{q_1 q_2}{r}$$

where E = energy in electron volts, q_1 = charge on the positive ion, q_2 = charge on the negative ion, and r = the distance between the nuclear centers. If one changes one parameter, another must adjust to maintain this e-quality.

Solving:

(a) If the charge on A, the positive ion, is doubled, the energy released is doubled. That is,

$$2E = 1.44 \frac{2q_1 q_2}{r} \text{ is equivalent to } E = \frac{1.44\ q_1 q_2}{r}.$$

If E is doubled, the strength of the chemical bond is doubled.

(b) Using a similar line of reasoning, it is found that if one doubles both the positive and negative charges, four times E is released. The strength of the bond is, thus, 4 times as great as the original bond.

(c) If one increases the radius of the ions then, the distance between their nuclei must also increase. To maintain the equality, E must decrease because r is inversely pro-potional to E. Therefore, the bond strength decreases. When the ionic radius of one ion is doubled, E is halved.

(d) Both radii are doubled. E is diminished by a factor of 4 and the strength of the bond is decreased by a factor of 4.

● **PROBLEM 14-12**

Compare the ionic bond strength of NaCl to KF; assuming that the radii of Na^+, K^+, F^-, and Cl^- are, respectively, 0.097, 0.133, 0.133, and 0.181 NM.

Solution: The ionic bond strength is directly proportional to the energy released when positive and negative ions form chemical bonds. To solve this problem, therefore, compute how much energy is released when Na^+ and Cl^- ions form NaCl and when K^+ and F^- ions form KF. Employ the expression that relates energy to charge and radii:

$$E = 1.44 \frac{q_1 q_2}{r}$$

where E = energy in electron volts, r = distance between the nuclei of the ions in the molecule, and q_1 and q_2 are the charges on the ions. Note that the charge on each ion is the same. The distance between the nuclei, r, is the sum of the radii of the ions. With these facts in mind, one can determine the amount of energy released in the formation of NaCl.

$$E_{NaCl} = 1.44 \frac{q_1 q_2}{0.278} \text{ . For KF, } E_{KF} = 1.44 \frac{q_1 q_2}{0.266}$$

Comparing the amount of energy released in each case

$$\frac{E_{NaCl}}{E_{KF}} = \frac{0.266}{0.278}$$

$$\frac{0.266}{0.278} \times 100 = 95.6\%.$$

Thus, the bond strength of NaCl is 95.6% as strong as the bond strength of KF.

● **PROBLEM 14-13**

A chemist possesses KCl, PH_3, $GeCl_4$, H_2S, and CsF. Which of these compounds do not contain a covalent bond?

Solution: A covalent bond is defined as one in which electrons are shared. The stability of covalent bonds in molecules depends on the difference in electronegativity values of the two atoms which make up the molecule. Electronegativity refers to the tendency of an atom to attract shared electrons in a chemical bond. If the electronegativity difference of two elements is greater than 1.7, an ionic bond is formed; if it is less than 1.7, a covalent bond is formed.

To solve this problem, consult a table of electronegativity values, and compute the electronegativity difference of the atoms in each of the given compounds. Proceed as follows:

	Electronegativity Values		Difference
KCl	K = 0.8	Cl = 3.0	2.2
PH_3	P = 2.1	H = 2.1	O
$GeCl_4$	Ge = 1.8	Cl = 3.0	1.2
H_2S	H = 2.1	S = 2.5	0.4
CsF	Cs = 0.7	F = 4.0	3.3

Thus, only KCl and CsF exceed 1.7. They possess ionic bonds. The remainder of the molecules possess covalent bonds.

Consider a covalent bond between hydrogen and arsenic. It is known that the radii of hydrogen and arsenic atoms are respectively: 0.37 and 1.21 Angstroms. What is the approximate length of the hydrogen-arsenic bond?

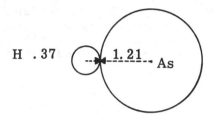

Solution: One may assume that the two atoms are spheres. Thus, as in the figure shown, the bond length defined as the distance between the two nuclei is the sum of the lengths of the two radii.

bond length = length of H radii + length of As radii.

bond length = $0.37 \overset{\circ}{A} + 1.21 \overset{\circ}{A} = 1.58 \overset{\circ}{A}$.

ELECTRONEGATIVITY

What is the meaning and significance of the Pauling electronegativity scale?

Solution: In any chemical bond, electrons are shared between the bonding atoms. In covalent bonds, the valence electrons are shared almost equally - the shared electrons spend about the same amount of time with each atom. In ionic bonds, the valence electrons are monopolized by one atom. The degree to which a bond will be ionic or covalent is dependent upon the relative electron-attracting ability of the bonding atoms.

The Pauling electronegativity scale provides a measure for the relative electron-attracting abilities or electronegativity of each element. The most electronegative element, fluorine, is assigned the highest number, 4.0. The least electron attracting elements (and consequently, those most willing to lose electrons), cesium and francium, are assigned the lowest number, 0.7. Numbers are assigned to the remaining elements so that no element has a higher number than an element more electronegative than it. Furthermore, the numbers are assigned so that the differences between the electronegativities of two elements is indicative of the ionic quality of the bond that forms between them. In particular, if the difference is 1.7 or greater, then the shared electrons are monopolized by the more electronegative atom to such a great extent that the bond is said to be ionic. If the difference is less than 1.7, the bond is covalent.

Thus, when given a compound, the Pauling electronegativity scale can be used to determine the species that acts as the electron donor, the species that acts as the electron acceptor, and the degree of electron polarization of the bond.

● **PROBLEM** 14-16

Classify the bonds in the following as ionic, ionic-covalent, covalent-ionic and covalent: I_2, LiCl, MgTe, Cl_2O, H_2S.

Solution: The bonds in these molecules can be classified by considering the electronegativities of the atoms involved.

The electronegativity of any element is the tendency of that element to attract electrons. The greater the electronegativity, the stronger the attraction. When 2 atoms join, the type of bond formed can be determined by calculating the difference in electronegativity of the two atoms involved. When the difference is greater than 1.7, the bond is classified as ionic, if less than 1.7, then the bond is covalent. An ionic bond involves the complete transfer of electrons from 1 atom to another, while in a covalent bond, the electrons are shared between like or similar atoms. Covalent-ionic indicates a mixed character which is more covalent in nature. Ionic-covalent bonds have more of an ionic character.

Consider the cases in point. For I_2, there is no difference in electronegativity because the 2 atoms involved in the bond are the same, and hence contains a covalent bond with equal sharing of the electrons.

In LiCl, the electronagetivities are Li = 1.0 and Cl = 3.0. (The electronegativity values are obtained from an electronegativity table). The electronegative difference is 2.0. Therefore, the bond is ionic.

One proceeds in a similar manner for the remainder of the compounds.

Compounds and Electronegativities of the Elements	Difference in Electronegativity	Type of Bond
Mg - Te 1.2　2.1	2.1 - 1.2 = 0.9	Covalent-ionic
Cl_2 - O 3.0　3.5	3.5 - 3.0 = 0.5	Covalent-ionic
H_2 - S 2.1　2.5	2.5 - 2.1 = 0.4	Covalent-ionic

● **PROBLEM** 14-17

40.0 kJ of energy is added to 1.00 gram of magnesium atoms in the vapor state. What is the composition of the final mixture? The first ionization potential of Mg is 735 kJ/mole and the second ionization potential is 1447 kJ/mole

Solution: Ionization potential may be defined as the energy required to pull an electron away from an isolated atom. The second ionization potential is the amount of energy required to pull off a second electron after the first has been removed.

The composition of the final mixture is determined by calculating the number of electrons that will be removed from the magnesium ions. To do this one must determine the number of moles of Mg present in 1 g. From this one can determine the number of electrons that will be liberated by using the values for the first and second ionization potentials of Mg.

The atomic weight of Mg is 24.3. Since moles = grams/atomic weight, there are in 1 gram of Mg, 1/24.30 or 4.11×10^{-2} moles present. The first ionization potential of Mg is 735 kJ/mole. Therefore, 4.11×10^{-2} moles of Mg requires 4.11×10^{-2} moles × 735 kJ/mole or 30.2 kJ to ionize all of the atoms once. 40 kJ was added to the system leaving 40 kJ - 30.2 kJ or 9.8 kJ to remove the second electron. If one has 9.8 kJ and 1447 kJ/mole is required to remove the second electron, then

$$\frac{9.8 \text{ kJ}}{1447 \text{ kJ/mole}} = 6.77 \times 10^{-3} \text{ moles of atoms can}$$

have their second electron removed. 4.11×10^{-2} moles of Mg are present.

$$\frac{6.77 \times 10^{-3}}{4.11 \times 10^{-2}} \times 100 = 16.5\%.$$

This means that 16.5% of the atoms can have a second electron removed. Therefore, the composition of the mixture

is: Mg^{++} 16.5%, Mg^+ 100 - 16.5 or 83.5%.

POLARITY OF BONDS

Determine which of the atoms in each pair possess a partial positive charge and which a partial negative. (a) the O-F bond, (b) the O-N bond, (c) the O-S bond. Electronegativity values for these elements can be found from a table of electronegativities.

<u>Solution</u>: Electronegativity is the tendency of an atom to attract shared electrons in a chemical covalent bond. Since electrons are negatively charged, to find the partial charge on each atom of the pair consult a table for the electronegativity values of the atoms in the molecules. The atom with the higher value will have a greater tendency to attract electrons, and will, thus, have a partial negative charge. Because the overall bond is neutral, the other atom must have a partial positive charge.

For part (a), F has a higher electronegativity than O, which means that F will have a partial negative charge (δ^-) and O will have a partial positive charge ($^+\delta$). To show this the molecule can be written $\begin{pmatrix} \delta^+ & \delta^- \\ O — F \end{pmatrix}$. Similar logic is used in working out parts b and c.

The electronegativity of O is 3.5 and of N is 3.0, thus O is more negative than N. The molecule is written $\begin{pmatrix} \delta^- & \delta^+ \\ O — N \end{pmatrix}$.

(b) O-N bond:

(c) O-S bond:

The electronegativity of O is 3.5 and of S is 2.5; therefore, O is the more negative of this pair, $\begin{pmatrix} \delta^- & \delta^+ \\ O — S \end{pmatrix}$.

Which molecule of each of the following pairs would
exhibit a higher degree of polarity. HCl and HBr, H_2O
and H_2S; BrCl and IF?

Solution: Polarity indicates that there is an uneven
sharing of electrons between 2 atoms. This creates a
charge distribution in the molecule where one atom is
partially positive and the other is partially negative.
The degree of polarity is measured by finding the
difference in the abilities of the two atoms to attract
electrons. This tendency to accept electrons is called
the electronegativity. The greater the electronegativity
difference, the greater the degree of polarity.

From the table of electronegativity values, the
following electronegativities can be obtained:

	Compounds	Electronegativity Difference
(1)	HCl	3.0 - 2.1 = .9
	HBr	2.8 - 2.1 = .7
(2)	H_2O	3.5 - 2.1 = 1.4
	H_2S	2.5 - 2.1 = .4
(3)	BrCl	3.0 - 2.8 = .2
	IF	4.0 - 2.5 = 1.5

In pair (1) (HCl and HBr), HCl has the larger
electronegativity. Hence, HCl has a greater degree of
polarity than HBr. For the same reasons, H_2O in pair (2)
and IF in pair (3) have the greater degrees of polarity.

Of the following pairs, which member should exhibit the largest dipole moment. Use the data from the accompanying table. (a) H-O and H-N; (b) H-F and H-Br; (c) C-O and C-S.

Pauling electronegativities
(H = 2.1)

Li	Be	B											C	N	O	F
1.0	1.5	2.0											2.5	3.0	3.5	4.0
Na	Mg	Al											Si	P	S	Cl
0.9	1.2	1.5											1.8	2.1	2.5	3.0
K	Ca	Sc	Ti	V	Cr	Mn	Fe	Co	Ni	Cu	Zn	Ga	Ge	As	Se	Br
0.8	1.0	1.3	1.5	1.6	1.6	1.5	1.8	1.8	1.8	1.9	1.6	1.6	1.8	2.0	2.4	2.8
Rb	Sr	Y	Zr	Nb	Mo	Tc	Ru	Rh	Pd	Ag	Cd	In	Sn	Sb	Te	I
0.8	1.0	1.2	1.4	1.6	1.8	1.9	2.2	2.2	2.2	1.9	1.7	1.7	1.8	1.9	2.1	2.5
Cs	Ba	La-Lu	Hf	Ta	W	Re	Os	Ir	Pt	Au	Hg	Tl	Pb	Bi	Po	At
0.7	0.9	1.1-1.2	1.3	1.5	1.7	1.9	2.2	2.2	2.2	2.4	1.9	1.8	1.8	1.9	2.0	2.2
Fr	Ra	Ac	Th	Pa	U	Np										
0.7	0.9	1.1	1.3	1.5	1.7	1.3										

The values given in the table refer to the common oxidation states of the elements. For some elements variation of the electronegativity with oxidation number is observed, for example, Fe(II) 1.8, Fe(III) 1.9; Cu(I) 1.9, Cu(II) 2.0; Sn(II) 1.8, Sn(IV) 1.9.

Solution: A dipole consists of a positive and a negative charge separated by some distance. Quantitatively, a dipole is described by giving its dipole moment, which is equal to the charge times the distance between the positive and negative centers. The polarity of a bond is measured as the magnitude of the moment of the dipole. Thus, to find which member has the higher dipole moment, determine which bond has the greatest polarity. The polarity of the bond is indicated by the difference in electronegativities of the atoms (i.e., the difference in their tendency to attract shared electrons in a chemical covalent bond). The greater the difference in electronegativities, the greater the bond polarity, giving it the greater dipole moment. From the table, note that in part

(a) the difference in electronegativities of H-O is 3.5 - 2.1 or 1.4. For H-N, the difference is 3.0 - 2.1 or 0.9. Therefore, H-O has the largest dipole moment. Using similar calculations, one can determine the bonds with the larger dipole moments in parts b and c.

(b) H-F and H-Br

For H-F: 4.0 - 2.1 = 1.9

For H-Br: 2.8 - 2.1 = 0.7.

Thus, H-F has the larger dipole moment.

(c) C-O and C-S

For C-O: 3.5 - 2.5 = 1.0

For C-S; 2.5 - 2.5 = 0.

Thus, C-O has the larger dipole moment here.

• PROBLEM 14-21

> Find the net dipole moment in Debyes for each of the following situations: (a) One + 1 and one - 1 ion separated by 2×10^{-8} cm, and (b) one +2 and one - 2 ion separated by 2×10^{-8} cm. One charge = 4.80×10^{-10} esu and 1 Debye = 1×10^{-18} esu-cm.

Solution: A dipole consists of a positive and a negative charge separated by a distance. Quantitatively, a dipole is described by its dipole moment, which is equal to the charge times the distance between the positive and negative centers. For both situations, substitute the values into this quantitative expression:

net dipole moment = charge × distance

(a) Net dipole moment

$$= (4.80 \times 10^{-10} \text{ esu})(2 \times 10^{-8} \text{ cm})$$

$$= 9.6 \times 10^{-18} \text{ esu-cm.}$$

1 Debye = 1×10^{-18} esu-cm.

$$\frac{9.6 \times 10^{-18} \text{ esu-cm}}{1 \times 10^{-18} \text{ esu-cm/Debye}} = 9.6 \text{ Debyes}$$

(b) Net dipole moment

$$= (2)(4.80 \times 10^{-10})(2 \times 10^{-8})$$

$$= 19.2 \times 10^{-18} \text{ esu-cm}$$

Converting to Debyes

$$\frac{19.2 \times 10^{-18} \text{ esu-cm}}{1 \times 10^{-18} \text{ esu-cm/Debye}} = 19.2 \text{ Debyes.}$$

• PROBLEM 14-22

> The net dipole moment of water is 1.84 debyes and the bond angle is 104.45°. What moment can be assigned to each O-H bond?

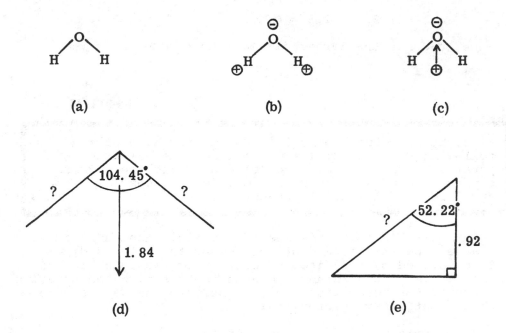

(a)

(b)

(c)

(d)

(e)

Solution: To answer this problem, consider the definition of a dipole, how it is expressed quantitatively, and the geometry of a water molecule.

A dipole consists of a positive and negative charge separated by some distance. Quantitatively, it is expressed as dipole moment, which is the charge times the distance between the positive and negative centers. The units are debyes.

The geometry of a water molecule is not linear. It is represented by FIG. a.

The oxygen atom shares its electrons with the hydrogen atoms; covalent bonding. Because the oxygen atom is electronegative, which means it has a tendency to attract electrons, the shared electrons will spend more time on the oxygen atom than on the hydrogen atoms. Thus, a polar covalent bond exists. The oxygen tends to develop a negative charge because the electrons spend more time on the oxygen atom. Since a water molecule is neutral (overall), the charge on the hydrogen atoms become positively charged (Fig. b). Therefore, a dipole exists. The net dipole is represented by Fig. c. As given, the dipole moment is 1.84 D. One is asked to compute the moment of each OH bond. One can represent the net moment and the OH moment as in Fig. d. The net dipole moment is the longer line and bisects the bond angle of 104.45°. The shorter lines represent the components of the net dipole, which comes from each bond.

This can be simplified and drawn as Fig. e. This

282

is the representation for one OH bond. The net dipole must be divided by two (1.84/2 = 0.92), since the total number O-H bonds is 2. The bisected angle of 104.45° yields 52.22°. To find X, the unknown OH dipole, use trigonometry.

The $\cos 52.22°$ is $= \dfrac{\text{adjacent leg}}{\text{hypotenuse}} = \dfrac{.92}{X}$, since

a right triangle is present. $\cos 52.22° = 0.6127$. Thus, equating $0.6127 = 0.92/X$. Therefore,

$$X = \frac{.92}{.6127} = 1.50 \text{ Debyes.}$$

● **PROBLEM 14-23**

Given that the electronegativities of F, Cl, Br, and I are, respectively, 4.0, 3.0, 2.8, and 2.5, account for the fact that the dipole moment decreases in the sequence HF, HCl, HBr, and HI, even though bond length and the number of electrons increase.

Solution: A dipole is defined as a molecule which is electrically unsymmetrical - that is, the centers of positive and negative charges are not located at the same point within the molecule.

Quantitatively, a dipole is described by its dipole moment, which is equal to the charge times the distance between the positive and negative centers. The decrease in dipole moment will reflect a decrease in either the value of the charges or the distance between them. It is given that the bond length increases in this sequence, which means that distance increases. This suggests an increase in dipole moment within the sequence. But the dipole moments decrease, this means that the charge must be decreasing. This can be explained by noting that the electronegativity values are decreasing within the sequence. Electronegativity measures the tendency of an atom to attract shared electrons in a molecule. By attracting these electrons, it develops a negative charge. If the electronegativity decreases, so does the charge, which would then account for the decrease in dipole moment.

CHAPTER 15

QUANTUM CHEMISTRY

PAULI EXCLUSION PRINCIPLE, HUND'S RULE AND ELECTRONIC CONFIGURATION

● **PROBLEM** 15-1

Explain the following: Pauli exclusion principle and Hund's rule.

Solution: An atom is described by four quantum numbers: the principal quantum number N, the angular momentum quantum number ℓ, the magnetic quantum number m, and the spin quantum number s. According to the Pauli exclusion principle, no two electrons in an atom can have the same four quantum numbers. If two electrons did, they would have identical fingerprints, a situation forbidden by nature.

Each orbital can accommodate a maximum of two electrons. With this in mind, Hund's rule states that once an electron is in an orbital, a second electron will not enter into that same orbital if there exist other orbitals in that subshell that contain zero electrons. In other words, all orbitals in a subshell must contain one electron, before a second one can enter. Hund's rule also states that single electrons in their separate orbitals of a given subshell will have the same spin quantum number.

● **PROBLEM** 15-2

Given the ground-state oxygen atom, tabulate each of the electrons by its quantum number.

Solution: Begin by writing the electronic configuration of the ground-state oxygen atom. An electron is in its ground state when it is in its lowest energy level, this is the normal state of the electrons. The atomic number of oxygen is 8. Thus, the oxygen atom has 8 electrons. The electronic configuration of the oxygen atom is $1s^2 2s^2 2p^4$. The quantum numbers are N, ℓ, M, and s. N is the principal quantum number which, in the electronic configuration, is the integer in front of the subshells (s and p) and corresponds to the energy level occupied by the electron. The other quantum numbers can be found once N is determined, ℓ is equal to 0, 1, 2, ... N-1, depending upon N. M is equal to $+ \ell$ to $-\ell$ and S is equal to $+\frac{1}{2}$ or $-\frac{1}{2}$. ℓ is the orbital quantum number which denotes the subshell and angular shape of electron distribution. M is the magnetic quantum number and s denotes the spin of electron. All four are needed to describe each electron. To tabulate the electrons according to their quantum numbers proceed as follows: the electron configuration is $1s^2 2s^2 2p^4$. Take the first shell, or N = 1, $1s^2$. The superscript indicates that 2 electrons are present in this shell. Thus, 2 sets of quantum numbers are needed. For both electrons, N = 1. Because ℓ = 0 ... n - 1, ℓ = 0 for both electrons in the s subshell. M + ℓ to - ℓ, thus, M = 0 for both also. The four quantum numbers for each electron must be different. Therefore, one electron has a spin of $+\frac{1}{2}$ and one has a spin of $-\frac{1}{2}$. The sets of quantum numbers for these two electrons are 1, 0, 0, $+\frac{1}{2}$ and 1, 0, 0, $-\frac{1}{2}$. For the second shell, N = 2. There are two subshells, s and p. Consider the s subshell first. In the $2s^2$ orbital, N = 2 and there are two electrons to be described. For both electrons ℓ = 0, because both are in the s subshell. M = 0, because M = $+ \ell$ to $- \ell$. For one electron $s = +\frac{1}{2}$, for the other s = $-\frac{1}{2}$. The sets of quantum numbers for these two electrons are 2, 0, 0, $+\frac{1}{2}$ and 2, 0, 0, $-\frac{1}{2}$. In the $2p^4$ orbital there are 4 electrons to be described. For all, N = 2, and ℓ = 1 (ℓ is always equal to 1 for a p subshell). M = $+ \ell$ to $- \ell$. Thus, one electron has M = + 1, the second electron has M = 0, and the third electron has M = - 1. The fourth electron will have an M = - 1, 0, or + 1. Whatever it is, it will differ in spin from the electron with the same M. The spins of the others can be $+ \frac{1}{2}$ or $- \frac{1}{2}$ The sets of the quantum numbers for the first three electrons in a 2p orbital can be written (2, 1, - 1, $+\frac{1}{2}$) (2, 1, 0, $+\frac{1}{2}$), and (2, 1, 1, $+ \frac{1}{2}$). The fourth might be written (2, 1, - 1, - $\frac{1}{2}$), (2, 1, 0, - $\frac{1}{2}$), or (2, 1, 1, - $\frac{1}{2}$).

● **PROBLEM** 15-3

Write possible sets of quantum numbers for electrons in the second main energy level.

Solution: In wave mechanical theory, four quantum numbers are needed to describe the electrons of an atom. The first or principal quantum number, n, designates the main energy level of the electron and has integral values of 1, 2, 3, ... The second quantum number, ℓ, designates the energy sublevel within the main energy level. The values of ℓ depend upon the value of n and range from zero to n - 1. The third quantum number, m_ℓ, designates the particular orbital within the energy sublevel. The number of orbitals of a given kind per energy sublevel is equal to the number of m_ℓ values ($2\ell + 1$). The quantum number m_ℓ can have any integral value from + ℓ to - ℓ including zero. The fourth quantum number, s, describes the two ways in which an electron may be aligned with a magnetic field (+ ½ or - ½).

The states of the electrons within atoms are described by four quantum numbers, n, ℓ, m_ℓ, s. Another important factor is the Pauli exclusion principle which states that no two electrons within the same atom may have the same four quantum numbers.

To solve this problem one must use the principles of assigning electrons to their orbitals.

If n = 2; ℓ can then have the values 0, 1; m_ℓ can have the values of + 1, 0 or - 1, and s is always + ½ or - ½.

Thus, the answer is:

		n	ℓ	m_ℓ	m_s
n = 2					
ℓ = 0, 1	2s	2	0	0	+ ½
		2	0	0	- ½
m_ℓ = + 1, 0, - 1					
		2	1	+1	+ ½
s = + ½, - ½		2	1	+1	- ½
		2	1	0	+ ½
	2p	2	1	0	- ½
		2	1	-1	+ ½
		2	1	-1	- ½

● **PROBLEM** 15-4

Apply Hund's rules to obtain the electron configuration for Si, P, S, Cl, and Ar.

Si	$3p^2$	↑	↑	___
P	$3p^3$	↑	↑	↑
S	$3p^4$	↑↓	↑	↑
Cl	$3p^5$	↑↓	↑↓	↑
Ar	$3p^6$	↑↓	↑↓	↑↓

<u>Solution</u>: The ground state of an atom is that in which the electrons are in the lowest possible energy level. Each level may contain two electrons of opposite spin. When there are several equivalent orbitals of the same energy, Hund's rules are used to decide how the electrons are to be distributed between the orbitals:

1) If the number of electrons is equal to or less than the number of equivalent orbitals, then the electrons are assigned to different orbitals.

2) If two electrons occupy two different orbitals, their spins will be parallel in the ground state. Hund's rules states that the electrons attain positions as far apart as possible which minimizes the repulsion obtained from interelectronic forces.

To solve this problem one must:

(1) Find the total number of electrons within the atom

(2) Determine the number of valence electrons

(3) Find the number of electrons in the highest equivalent energy orbital.

The total number of electrons in an atom is equal to that atom's atomic number.

Thus,   Si has 14 electrons

P   has 15 electrons

S   has 16 electrons

Cl has 17 electrons

Ar has 18 electrons.

Next, from the orbital configuration:

$_{14}$Si $1s^2 2s^2 2p^6 3s^2$ | $3p^2$

$_{15}$P $1s^2 2s^2 2p^6 3s^2$ | $3p^3$

287

$_{16}S$ $1s^2 2s^2 2p^6 3s^2 \mid 3p^4$

$_{17}Cl$ $1s^2 2s^2 2p^6 3s^2 \mid 3p^5$

$_{18}Ar$ $1s^2 2s^2 2p^6 3s^2 \mid 3p^6$

    One knows that the highest equivalent energy orbital is the 3p orbital. The number of electrons in this orbital increases by 1 starting with 2 for Si, then, 3 for P, 4 for S, 5 for Cl, and 6 Ar. Thus, Ar closes this orbital. Using Hund's rules, the electron configurations can be written as shown in the accompanying figure.

● **PROBLEM** 15-5

Predict the total spin for each of the following electronic configurations: (a) $1s^2 2s^2$; (b) $1s^2 2s^2 2p^3$; and (c) $1s^2 2s^2 2p^6 3s^2 3p^6 3d^5 4s^2$.

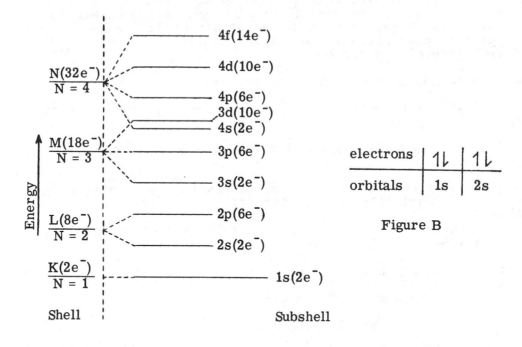

Figure A

Figure B

Figure C

<u>Solution</u>: One determines the total spin of an atom by calculating the sum of all the s quantum numbers of the electrons. There are four quantum numbers needed to describe each electron. They are the principal quantum number n, the azimuthal quantum number ℓ, the magnetic quantum number m and the spin quantum number s.

In each orbital of the atom two electrons can be accommodated. These electrons will have opposing spins of $+\frac{1}{2}$ and $-\frac{1}{2}$. The total spin is calculated by determining the total number of unpaired electrons and multiplying this number by $\frac{1}{2}$. It is assumed that all unpaired electrons will have the same spin. Solving for the total spins: Figure A shows the total number of electrons that can occupy each orbital.

(a) $1s^2 2s^2$. Filled s orbitals each contain 2 electrons. One writes this electronic configuration diagrammatically as shown in figure B.

Because there are no unpaired electrons the total spin for this atom is 0.

(b) $1s^2 2s^2 2p^3$. Here the two s orbitals are filled but the p orbital is only half filled. There are three subshells in the p orbital and there will be one electron occupying each of these. The configuration of lowest e- nergy is assumed when each of these 3 electrons has the same spin. This configuration is written diagrammatically as shown in figure C.

This configuration contains 3 unpaired electrons. The total spin is, thus $3 \times \frac{1}{2}$ or 3/2.

(c) $1s^2 2s^2 2p^6 3s^2 3p^6 3d^5 4s^2$. From figure A one sees that the only unfilled orbital in this configuration is the 3d. Therefore, unpaired electrons can only occur in this shell. From figure A, one sees that the 3d orbital can contain 10 electrons. Because each subshell contains 2 electrons, there are 5 subshells in this orbital. In this configuration there are 5 electrons occupying the 3d orbital, therefore, each subshell con- tains 1 electron and there are 5 unpaired electrons in the configuration. The total spin of this configuration is, thus, $5 \times \frac{1}{2}$ or 5/2.

● **PROBLEM** 15-6

Assuming all other orbitals to have zero net spin, what would be the net spin and the multiplicity of an atom having each of the following outer shell configurations: $2p^1$, $2p^3$, $2p^5$, $3d^1$, $3d^3$, $3d^5$? Rank these net spins in order of increasing paramagnetism.

<u>Solution</u>: We proceed by first defining "total spin" and

Configuration	Orbital Filling	$n\uparrow$	$n\downarrow$	$S = \left\lvert \dfrac{n\uparrow}{2} - \dfrac{n\downarrow}{2} \right\rvert$	$m = 2S + 1$
p^1	p_x (↑), p_y ( ), p_z ( )	1	0	1/2	2 (doublet)
p^3	p_x (↑), p_y (↑), p_z (↑)	3	0	3/2	4 (quartet)
p^5	p_x (↑↓), p_y (↑↓), p_z (↑)	1	0	1/2	2 (doublet)
d^1	d_{xy} (↑), d_{yz} ( ), d_{zx} ( ), $d_{x^2-y^2}$ ( ), d_{z^2} ( )	1	0	1/2	2 (doublet)
d^3	d_{xy} (↑), d_{yz} (↑), d_{zx} (↑), $d_{x^2-y^2}$ ( ), d_{z^2} ( )	3	0	3/2	4 (quartet)
d^5	d_{xy} (↑), d_{yz} (↑), d_{zx} (↑), $d_{x^2-y^2}$ (↑), d_{z^2} (↑)	5	0	5/2	6 (sextet)

"multiplicity". Let the number of electrons having "spin up" be denoted by $n_\uparrow$ and the total number of electrons having "spin down" be denoted by $n_\downarrow$. Assigning a value of + ½ to spin up and - ½ to spin down, the total spin s is given by the absolute value of $n_\uparrow (+ ½) + n_\downarrow (- ½) = n_\uparrow/2 + n_\downarrow/2$. The multiplicity is then defined as m = 2s + 1.

The configuration with the highest spin (highest multiplicity) will have the greatest paramagnetism. (Substances that are weakly attracted to magnets are paramagnetic.) The configuration with the lowest spin (lowest multiplicity), will be the least paramagnetic.

The p orbital can contain six electrons and the d orbital can contain 10 electrons. When these orbitals are filled, electrons are sequentially placed in each sub-orbital (e.g. the p_x or the d_{xy}) until there is one e-lectron in each suborbital, all electrons having the same spin. Only when there is one electron in each suborbital does another electron enter a suborbital already containing an electron, this time with a spin opposite to that of the electron already in the suborbital (the spins are then "paired") in accordance with the Pauli Exclusion Principle.

In the accompanying table we show the orbital filling corresponding to each configuration. Counting $n_\uparrow$ and $n_\downarrow$, we then calculate s and m.

The configurations p^1, p^5, and d^1 have the same electron paramagnetism (all have spin ½). The next most paramagnetic configurations are p^3 and d^3 (spin 3/2) and the most paramagnetic configuration is d^5 (spin 5/2).

● **PROBLEM 15-7**

Given the following electron configurations: (a) (Z = 11) $1s^2 2s^2 2p^6$, (b) (Z = 25) $1s^2 2s^2 2p^6 3s^2 3p^6 3d^5$, and (c) (Z = 29) $1s^2 2s^2 2p^6 3s^2 3p^6 3d^{10}$; provide the proper ionic symbol.

Solution: The ionic symbol of an atom is equal to the charge on the atom. This charge is determined by comparing the atomic number Z and the number of electrons as shown in the electronic configuration. The atomic number corresponds to the net positive charge on the nucleus and the number of electrons indicates magnitude of the negative charge of the electron cloud.

One writes the electronic configuration of hydrogen as $1s^1$, 1s indicates the atomic orbital and the superscript 1 indicates that there is one electron in the orbital. Thus, one can determine the number of electrons present by taking the sum of the superscripts. The net charge on an atom is found by adding the net negative charge (the sum of the electrons) and the net positive charge (the atomic number, which is equal to the number of protons) For hydrogen, (Z = 1) $1s^1$, the net negative charge is − 1 and the net positive charge is + 1, thus, the atom is neutral and no ionic symbol is used. One uses this method to determine the ionic symbols for the atoms described in the problem.

(a) (Z = 11) $1s^2 2s^2 2p^6$. The net negative charge is equal to (− 2) + (− 2) + (− 6) or − 10. The net positive charge is 11. The net charge on the atom is 11 − 10 = + 1. From the periodic table one sees that this atom is Na^+, because the atomic number of sodium is 11.

(b) (Z = 25) $1s^2 2s^2 2p^6 3s^2 3p^6 3d^5$. Total number of electrons in configuration is 2 + 2 + 6 + 2 + 6 + 5 = 23. The net charge on the atom is, then 25 − 23 or + 2. From the periodic table one can determine that this atom is Mn^{+2}.

(c) (Z = 29) $1s^2 2s^2 2p^6 3s^2 3p^6 3d^{10}$. Total number of electrons in configuration = 2 + 2 + 6 + 2 + 6 + 10 = 28. Z = 29 = number of electrons in a neutral atom. Difference: 29 − 28 = + 1. The atom is Cu^{+1}.

● **PROBLEM** 15-8

You are given H, N, O, Ne, Ca, Al, and Zn. Determine which of these atoms (in their ground state) are likely to be paramagnetic. Arrange these elements in the order of increasing paramagnetism.

Solution: Paramagnetic substances possess permanent magnetic moments. An electric current flowing through a wire produces a magnetic field around the wire. Magnetic fields are thus produced by the motion of charged particles. Then, a single spinning electron, in motion around the nucleus, should behave like a current flowing in a closed circuit of zero resistance and therefore should act as if it were a small bar magnet with a characteristic permanent magnetic moment. The magnetism of an isolated atom results from two kinds of motion: the orbital motion of the electron around the nucleus, and the spin of the electron around its axis. Two spin orientations are permitted for electrons, + ½ and − ½. Two electrons occupy each filled orbital and their opposing spins cancel out the magnetic moments, thus, for an atom to be paramagnetic it must contain unpaired electrons.

H (Z = 1): $1s^1$ → The subshell, s, has only 1 electron as indicated by the superscript number. In the s subshell, you have only 1 orbital. Each orbital can hold 2 electrons. Therefore, this electron is unpaired and H is paramagnetic.

N (Z = 7): $1s^2 2s^2 2p^3$ → The p subshell has 3 orbitals

that contain a total of 3 electrons. Because electrons have the same charge, they try to avoid each other, if possible. Thus, each electron is in a different orbital. Therefore, they are unpaired and N is paramagnetic.

O (Z = 8): $1s^2 2s^2 2p^4$ → The p subshell has 3 orbitals with 4 electrons. Recalling the information given above, this means that 1 orbital has two electrons. The other 2 orbitals possess one electron each. Thus, there are two unpaired electrons. O is paramagnetic.

Ne (Z = 10): $1s^2 2s^2 2p^6$ Here, all orbitals contain two electrons each. No electron is unpaired. Thus, Ne is not paramagnetic.

Ca (Z = 20): $1s^2 2s^2 2p^6 3s^2 3p^6 4s^2$. Again, all orbitals have two electrons. Therefore, calcium is not paramagnetic.

Al (Z = 13): $1s^2 2s^2 2p^6 3s^2 3p^1$ The 3p subshell has only 1 electron for three orbitals. It must be unpaired, as such. It is paramagnetic.

Zn (Z = 30): $1s^2 2s^2 2p^6 3s^2 3p^6 3d^{10} 4s^2$.Each orbital has two electrons. Thus, no paramagnetism exists.

The order of paramagnetism (increasing) is proportional to the number of unpaired electrons. Thus, H, Al, O and N is the order of increasing paramagnetism.

MOLECULAR ORBITAL THEORY

● PROBLEM 15-9

What is a sigma bond? What is a pi bond? What are their basic differences?

Solution: A molecular orbital that is symmetrical around the line passing through two nuclei is called a sigma (σ) orbital. When the electron density in this orbital is con-centrated in the bonding region between the two nuclei, the bond is called a sigma bond. The covalent bonds in H_2 and HF are sigma bonds.

In the formation of the bonding orbital between two fluorine atoms, the 2p orbitals overlap in a head-to-head fashion to form a sigma bond. However, there is a second way in which half-filled p orbitals of two different atoms may overlap to form a bonding orbital.

If the two p orbitals are situated perpendicular to the line passing through the two nuclei, then the lobes

of p orbitals will overlap intensively sideways to form
an electron cloud that lies above and below the two nuclei.
The bond resulting from this sideways or lateral overlap
is called a pi (π) bond; the bonding orbital is called a
pi orbital. It differs from a sigma orbital in that it is
not symmetrical about a line joining the two nuclei. Pi
bonds are present in molecules having two atoms connected
by a double or triple bond. The sigma bond has greater
orbital overlap and is usually the stronger bond; a pi bond,
with less overlap, is generally weaker.

● **PROBLEM** 15-10

Compare the bond order of He_2 and He_2^+.

Solution: The bond order, or number of bonds in a
molecule, is equal to the difference in the sum of the
number of bonding electrons and the number of antibonding
electrons divided by two.

$$\text{Bond order} = \frac{\text{no. of bonding electrons} - \text{no. of antibonding electrons}}{2}$$

This means that the number of bonding and antibonding
electrons must be determined. There are 2 electrons in He,
thus in He_2 there are 4. These electrons are all in the 1s
level. For each level, there exists bonding and antibonding
orbitals, each of which holds 2 electrons. Thus, in He_2,
2 electrons are bonding and 2 are antibonding. From this,
the

$$\text{Bond order} = \frac{2 - 2}{2} = 0.$$

Thus, there are no bonds in He_2; and two He atoms
will not bond together to form a molecule of He_2.

In He_2^+, one electron is removed from He_2, which
means that there are now three electrons present. They
are all in the 1s level. This is the lowest energy level
that an electron can assume. The three electrons are
distributed so that two are in bonding orbitals and one
is in an antibonding orbital. Thus,

$$\text{no. of bonds} = \frac{2 - 1}{2} = 0.5 = \text{bond order}.$$

Because the bond order is not zero, this molecule
can form.

How would one expect the bond strength of NO to compare with that of O_2?

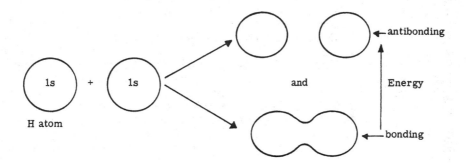

Solution: The molecular orbital is the sum of the atomic orbitals. For example, when two atomic orbitals are combined, two molecular orbitals are formed. One orbital is called a bonding orbital and the other is an anti-bonding orbital. The bonding orbital is at a lower energy level than the antibonding orbital. If possible, electrons seek out the bonding orbital rather than the antibonding orbital. The orbitals in the production of H_2 from H atoms can be visualized as shown in the accompanying figure.

The greater the number of antibonding orbitals in a molecule, the weaker the bond. Bond order is a quantity that indicates the strength of bonding orbitals. It is defined as half the number of bonding electrons minus half the number of antibonding electrons. Thus, the higher the bond order, the stronger the chemical bond.

To compare the bond strength of NO with O_2, compare their bond orders. To do this, consider the total number of valence electrons in each element. Valence electrons are the outer electrons, which participate in bonding. For NO, the total number of valence electrons is $3 + 4 = 7$. There exist 3 bonding p orbitals, which accommodate 6 e-lectrons. The 1 unpaired electron must be in an anti-bonding orbital. This means that the bond order of NO is $\frac{1}{2}(6) - \frac{1}{2}(1) = 3 - 0.5 = 2.5$.

In O_2 there is a total of 8 valence electrons. This means 2 electrons must be in antibonding orbitals, since the 3 bonding orbitals can accommodate only 6 electrons. The bond order of $O_2 = \frac{1}{2}(6) - \frac{1}{2}(2) = 2$. The bond order of NO is higher, which means, its chemical bond is stronger than that of O_2.

One electron is removed from O_2 and one from N_2. The bonding in O_2 is strengthened, while the bonding in N_2 is weakened. 1) Explain these findings, and 2) predict what happens if an electron is removed from NO.

Solution: There are two types of molecular orbitals: bonding and antibonding. A chemical bond is strengthened by electrons in bonding orbitals and weakened by electrons in antibonding orbitals. For every bonding orbital, there is a corresponding antibonding orbital. Each orbital can hold 2 electrons. Bond order measures bond strength by giving an indication of the number of electrons in bonding versus antibonding orbitals. Bond order is defined as one half the number of electrons in the bonding orbital less one half the number of electrons in the antibonding orbital. Thus, the higher the bond order, the stronger the bond.

To find the original bond order, consider the valence electrons, the outermost electrons, since they are the only ones that participate in bonding. For N, $Z = 7$. Its electron configuration is $1s^2 2s^2 2p^3$. The outermost electrons are in $2p^3$. This means that in N_2 there are a total of six valence electrons. There exist 3 bonding p orbitals. They can accommodate the six valence electrons. Since no electrons need be in antibonding orbitals, bond order $= \frac{1}{2}(6) - \frac{1}{2}(0) = 3$. When an electron is removed, the bonding orbitals have only 5 electrons. Thus, the bond order becomes $\frac{1}{2}(5) - \frac{1}{2}(0) = 2.5$. Since the bond order went from 3 to 2.5, the bond is weakened by removing the electron from N_2.

For O, $Z = 8$. Since its electron configuration is $1s^2 2s^2 2p^4$, each O atom has 4 valence electrons. O_2 has a total of 8 valence electrons. The three bonding p orbitals can hold only 6 of these electrons. Thus, two electrons are in antibonding orbitals. The bond order is $\frac{1}{2}(6) - \frac{1}{2}(2) = 2$. When one removes an electron, it is removed from the antibonding orbitals, if electrons exist in such orbitals. Therefore, the O_2, after removal of the electron, has only 1 electron in an antibonding electron. This means the bond order becomes $\frac{1}{2}(6) - \frac{1}{2}(1) = 2.5$. The bond increased from 2 to 2.5, which means that bond strength increases when one removes an electron from O_2.

To predict what happens to NO bond strength, consider the bond order before and after the electron removal. Recall, an O atom has 4 valence electrons and N has 3 valence electrons. The total in NO is seven. The 3 p bonding orbitals can hold six of these electrons. This means 1 electron is in on antibonding orbital. Bond order $= \frac{1}{2}(6) - \frac{1}{2}(1) = 2.5$. If one removes one electron, the antibonding orbitals contain zero electrons. Thus, the bond order becomes $\frac{1}{2}(6) - \frac{1}{2}(0) = 3$. The bond increased from 2.5 to 3, which

means the bond strength increases. Therefore, one can predict the chemical bond strength of NO increases when an
electron is removed.

Describe the bonding in linear, covalent $BeCl_2$ and planar,
covalent BCl_3. What is the difference in the hybrid
orbitals used?

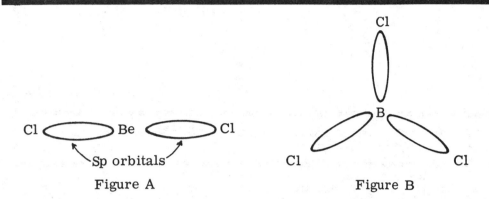

Figure A   Figure B

Solution: The solution to this problem involves the
hybridization of orbitals. Once this is clear, the bonding
in $BeCl_2$ and BCl_3 will follow.

Quantum theory deals with independent orbitals, such
as 2s and 2p. This can be applied to a species, like
hydrogen, with only 1 electron. However, with atoms that
contain more than one electron, different methods must be
used. For example, the presence of a 2s electron perturbs
a 2p electron, and vice versa, such that a 2s electron
makes a 2p electron take on some s-like characteristics.
The result is that the hydrogenlike 2s and 2p orbitals
are replaced by new orbitals, that contain the combined
characteristics of the original orbitals. These new
orbitals are called hybrid orbitals. The number of
hybrid orbitals resulting from hybridization equals the
number of orbitals being mixed together. For example, if
one mixes an s and p orbital, one obtains two sp hybrid
orbitals. One s and two p = three sp^2 orbitals. One s
with three p = four sp^3 orbitals. sp orbitals are linear.
sp^2 orbitals assume a planar shape and sp^3 orbitals
assume a tetrahedral shape.

Solving: It is given that $BeCl_2$ is linear and covalent. Since sp orbitals are linear, Be undergoes sp
hybridization. If something is linear, the bond angle
is 180°. By understanding hybridization, one also knows
the geometry of the molecule. A diagram of the bonding
resembles Fig. A.

Given that BCl_3 is planar, and since sp^2 hybridization yields a planar structure, B has sp^2 hybridized
bonding with angles of 120°(Fig. B).

CHAPTER 16

NUCLEAR CHEMISTRY

● **PROBLEM 16-1**

The mass of an electron is 9.109×10^{-28} g. What is the atomic weight of electrons?

Solution: Atomic weight is defined as the weight of one mole of particles. There are 6.02×10^{23}, or Avogadro's number, of particles in 1 mole. Therefore, the atomic weight of electrons is equal to 6.02×10^{23} times the mass of one electron.

atomic weight of electrons = 9.109×10^{-28} g $\times 6.02 \times 10^{23}$/mole

$$= 5.48 \times 10^{-4} \text{ g/mole.}$$

● **PROBLEM 16-2**

A chemist is given an unknown element X. He finds that the element X has an atomic weight of 210.197 amu and consists of only two isotopes, ^{210}X and ^{212}X. If the masses of these isotopes are, respectively, 209.64 and 211.66 amu, what is the relative abundance of the two isotopes?

Solution: The relative abundance of the two isotopes is equal to their fraction in the element. The sum of the fractions of the isotopes times their respective masses is equal to the total atomic weight of X. The element X is composed of only two isotopes. The sum of their fractions must be equal to one.

Solving: Let y = the fraction of the 210 isotope. Since, the sum of the fractions is one, $1 - y$ = the fraction of the 212 isotope. The sum of the fractions times their masses, equals the atomic weight of X.

$$209.64 y + 211.66(1 - y) = 210.197;$$

$y = 0.7242 =$ fraction of ^{210}X. $1 - y = 0.2758 =$ fraction of ^{212}X.

By percentage the relative abundance of ^{210}X is 72.42% and ^{212}X is 27.58%.

Chlorine is found in nature in two isotopic forms, one of atomic mass 35 amu and one of atomic mass 37 amu. The average atomic mass of chlorine is 35.453 amu. What is the percent with which each of these isotopes occurs in nature?

Solution: This is a mathematical problem, the solution to which centers on defining the average value properly. Consider a set of N observations or measurements, M_1, M_2, ..., M_N, Let the probability that the observation M_1 is made be p_1, the probability that the observation M_2 is made be p_2, and so on. Then, the average A is defined as:

$$A = p_1 M_1 + p_2 M_2 + \ldots + p_N M_N.$$

Since, by definition, the sum of the probabilities must be one, then:

$$1 = p_1 + p_2 + \ldots + p_N.$$

For this problem there are two observations, hence N = 2. Let the first observation be $M_1 = 35$ amu and the second observation be $M_2 = 37$ amu. The average A = 35.453 amu. Hence,

$$A = p_1 M_1 + p_2 M_2$$

$$35.453 \text{ amu} = p_1 \times 35 \text{ amu} + p_2 \times 37 \text{ amu}$$

where $1 = p_1 + p_2$.

One must determine p_1 and p_2 (the probabilities of occurrence of isotope 35 and 37, respectively).

From the second of these relationships, $1 = p_1 + p_2$ one obtains $p_2 = 1 - p_1$. Then

$$A = p_1 M_1 + p_2 M_2 = p_1 M_1 + (1 - p_1) M_2$$

$$= p_1 M_1 + M_2 - p_1 M_2$$

$$= M_2 + (M_1 - M_2) p_1$$

or, $p_1 = \dfrac{A - M_2}{M_1 - M_2} = \dfrac{35.453 \text{ amu} - 37 \text{ amu}}{35 \text{ amu} - 37 \text{ amu}} = 0.7735.$

Then, $p_2 = 1 - p_1 = 1 - 0.7735 = 0.2265$.

Thus, the isotope of mass 35 amu occurs with probability of 0.7735 or $0.7735 \times 100 \% = 77.35 \%$ and the isotope of mass 37 amu occurs with a probability of 0.2265 or $0.2265 \times 100 \% = 22.65 \%$.

In reality, the two isotopes do not have integral atomic masses, and the percent occurrences calculated above are not exactly correct.

● **PROBLEM** 16-4

Chromium exists in four isotopic forms. The atomic masses and percent occurrences of these isotopes are listed in the following table:

Isotopic mass (amu)	Percent occurrence
50	4.31%
52	83.76%
53	9.55%
54	2.38%

Calculate the average atomic mass of chromium.

Solution: We will make use of the definition of average:

$$A = p_1 M_1 + p_2 M_2 + \ldots + p_N M_N$$

where A is the average value, M_i is the atomic mass of isotope "i" and p_i is the corresponding probability of occurrence. For the four isotopes of chromium. we have:

$M_1 = 50$ amu $\quad p_1 = 4.31\% = 0.0431$

$M_2 = 52$ amu $\quad p_2 = 83.76\% = 0.8376$

$M_3 = 53$ amu $\quad p_3 = 9.55\% = 0.0955$

$M_4 = 54$ amu $\quad p_4 = 2.38\% = 0.0238$

Hence, the average atomic mass of chromium is

$A = p_1 M_1 + p_2 M_2 + p_3 M_3 + p_4 M_4$

$= 0.0431 \times 50$ amu $+ 0.8376 \times 52$ amu $+ 0.0955 \times 53$ amu

$\quad + 0.0238 \times 54$ amu

$= 2.155$ amu $+ 43.555$ amu $+ 5.062$ amu $+ 1.285$ amu

$= 52.057$ amu.

Given that the masses of a proton, neutron, and electron are 1.00728, 1.00867, and .000549 amu. respectively, how much missing mass is there in $^{19}_{9}F$ (atomic weight = 18.9984)?

Solution: The total number of particles in $^{19}_{9}F$ and their total weight can be calculated. The amount of missing mass in $^{19}_{9}F$ will be the difference of this calculated weight and the given atomic weight of $^{19}_{9}F$. The subscript number 9, in $^{19}_{9}F$, indicates the atomic number of fluorine (F). Because the atomic number equals the number of protons, there are 9 protons in F. The superscript, 19, indicates the total number of particles in the nucleus. Since the nucleus is composed of protons and neutrons, and there are 9 protons, there are 10 neutrons present. In a neutral atom, the number of electrons equals the number of protons. Thus, there are 9 electrons. The total number of particles is, thus, 28. The mass and quantity of each particle is now known. Calculating the total weight contribution of each type of particle:

Protons: $9 \times 1.00728 = 9.06552$

Neutrons: $10 \times 1.00867 = 10.0867$

Electrons: $9 \times .000549 = \underline{.004941}$

Total mass = 19.1572.

It is given that the mass of the fluorine atom is 18.9984. Therefore, the missing mass is 19.1572 − 18.9984 = 0.1588 amu.

Calculate ΔE for the proposed basis of an absolutely clean source of nuclear energy

$$^{11}_{5}B + ^{1}_{1}H \rightarrow ^{12}_{6}C \rightarrow 3\ ^{4}_{2}He$$

Atomic masses: $^{11}B = 11.00931$, $^{4}He = 4.00260$, $^{1}H = 1.00783$.

Solution: The energy of nuclear reactions, ΔE, is calculated from the difference between the masses of products and reactants in accordance with the Einstein Law. Einstein's Law can be stated $\Delta E = \Delta mc^2$, where Δm is the difference in the masses of the products and the reactants, and c is the speed of light (3×10^{10} cm/sec). The total reaction here can be written

$$^{11}_{5}B + ^{1}_{1}H \rightarrow 3\ ^{4}_{2}He.$$

Thus, Δm is equal to the mass of $^{11}_5B$ and ^1_1H subtracted from the mass of 3 ^4_2He. The mass of 3$\frac{1}{2}$He is equal to 3 times the mass of ^4_2He.

$$\Delta m = (3 \times m \text{ of } ^4_2He) - (m \text{ of } ^{11}_5B + m \text{ of } ^1_1H)$$

$$= (3 \times 4.00260) - (11.00931 + 1.00783)$$

$$= 12.0078 - 12.01714 = -9.34 \times 10^{-3} \text{ g/mole.}$$

One can now solve for ΔE by using Δm.

$$\Delta E = \Delta mc^2 = -9.34 \times 10^{-3} \text{ g/mole} \times (3.0 \times 10^{10} \text{ cm/sec})^2$$

$$= -9.34 \times 10^{-3} \text{ g/mole} \times 9.0 \times 10^{20} \text{ cm}^2/\text{sec}^2$$

$$= -8.406 \times 10^{18} \text{ g cm}^2/\text{mole sec}^2$$

$$= -8.406 \times 10^{18} \text{ ergs/mole.}$$

There are 4.18×10^{10} ergs in 1 Kcal, thus ergs can be converted to Kcal by dividing the number of ergs by the conversion factor 4.18×10^{10} ergs/Kcal.

$$\text{no. of Kcal} \doteq \frac{-8.406 \times 10^{18} \text{ ergs/mole}}{4.18 \times 10^{10} \text{ ergs/Kcal}}$$

$$= -2.01 \times 10^8 \text{ Kcal/mole.}$$

ΔE for this reaction is -2.01×10^8 Kcal per mole.

● **PROBLEM** 16-7

The first step in the radioactive decay of $^{238}_{92}U$ is $^{238}_{92}U = ^{234}_{90}Th + ^4_2He$. Calculate the energy released in this reaction. The exact masses of $^{238}_{92}U$, $^{234}_{90}Th$, and ^4_2He are 238.0508, 234.0437 and 4.0026 amu, respectively. 1.0073 amu = 1.673×10^{-24} g.

Solution: The energy released in this process can be determined from the change in mass that occurs. Energy and mass are related in the following equation,

$$\Delta E = \Delta mc^2$$

where, ΔE is the change in energy, Δm the change in mass and c the speed of light (3.0×10^{10} cm/sec). Δm is found by subtracting the mass of $^{238}_{92}U$ from the sum of the masses of $^{234}_{90}Th$ and ^4_2He.

$$\Delta m = (234.0437 \text{ amu} + 4.0026 \text{ amu}) - 238.0508 \text{ amu}$$

$$= -.0045 \text{ amu.}$$

Energy is expressed in ergs (g-cm^2/sec^2), therefore,

Δm must be converted to grams before solving for ΔE.

$$\Delta m = (-\ .0045\ \text{amu})\ \frac{(1.673 \times 10^{-24}\ \text{g})}{(1.0073\ \text{amu})}$$

$$= -\ 7.47 \times 10^{-27}\ \text{g}.$$

Solving for ΔE:

$$\Delta E = (-\ 7.47 \times 10^{-27}\ \text{g})(3.0 \times 10^{10}\ \text{cm/sec})^2$$

$$= -\ 6.72 \times 10^{-6}\ \text{g cm}^2/\text{sec}^2 = -\ 6.72 \times 10^{-6}\ \text{erg}$$

Therefore, 6.72×10^{-6} ergs are released.

● **PROBLEM** 16-8

What is the total binding energy of $_6C^{12}$ and the average binding energy per nucleon?

Solution: The mass of an atom, in general, is not equal to the sum of its component masses. The mass of the component parts (protons, neutrons, and electrons) is slightly greater than the mass of the atom. This difference in mass has an energy equivalent ($E = mc^2$), which is called the binding energy of the nucleus.

Although binding energy refers to the nucleus, it is more convenient to use the mass of the whole atom in calculations. Then, $M_n = M - ZM_e$, where M_n, M, and M_e are the nuclear, atomic, and electron masses, respectively, and Z is the atomic number. Since a carbon 6 atom, C_6^{12}, is made up of 6 protons and 6 electrons (or 6 H^1 atoms) plus 6 neutrons, then the binding energy, (b.e.) can be represented as follows:

$$\text{b.e.} = M_n + ZM_e - M$$

b.e. for $_6C^{12}$ = 6[mass of electron and proton (H^1) + mass of neutron] - atomic mass of $_6C^{12}$.

In other words, a mass difference equation can be written in terms of whole atom masses.

Mass of 6 H^1 atoms = 6 × 1.0078 = 6.0468

Mass of 6 neutrons = 6 × 1.0087 = <u>6.0522</u>

Total mass of component particles = 12.0990

Atomic mass of $_6C^{12}$ = <u>12.0000</u>

Loss in mass of formation of $_6C^{12}$ = 0.0990

Binding energy (931.5 MeV/Δmass)(.0990 Δmass) = 92.22 MeV

Since there are 12 nucleons (protons plus neutrons), the average binding energy per nucleon is

$$\frac{92.22\ \text{MeV}}{12\ \text{nucleons}} = 7.68\ \text{MeV}.$$

CHAPTER 17

ORGANIC CHEMISTRY I: NOMENCLATURE AND STRUCTURE

ALKANES

● PROBLEM 17-1

Explain the terms primary, secondary, and tertiary in regards to covalent bonding in organic compounds.

Solution: If a carbon atom is bound to only one other carbon atom, then the former carbon atom is called primary. If a carbon atom is bonded to two other carbon atoms, then that carbon atom is called secondary. If a carbon atom is bonded to three other carbon atoms, then that carbon atom is called tertiary.

Any group that is attached to a primary, secondary, or tertiary carbon is called a primary, secondary, or tertiary group. For example,

Carbons 1, 2, and 5 are primary, carbon 4 is secondary, and carbon 3 is tertiary. The hydrogen atoms attached to carbons 1, 2, and 5 are called primary hydrogens, those attached to carbon 4 are called secondary hydrogens, and those attached to carbon 3 are called tertiary hydrogens. This same principle applies to alcohols, and depending upon where the hydroxyl group (– OH) is attached (that is, primary, secondary, or tertiary carbon), the alcohol is called primary, secondary, or tertiary, respectively.

Name each of the following alkanes. Indicate which, if any, are isomers.

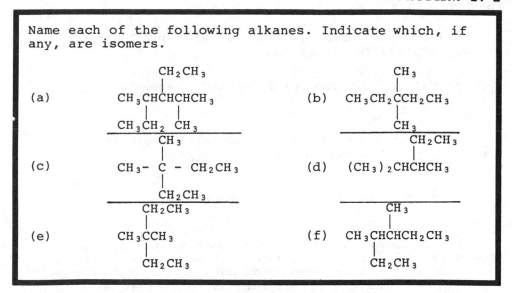

Solution: Isomers are related compounds that have the same molecular formula but different structural formulas.

Isomerism is not possible among the alkanes until there are enough carbon atoms to permit more than one arrangement of the carbon chain.

To name the above compounds, one uses a set rules to provide each compound with a clear name. These rules for nomenclature are the IUPAC rules (International Union of Pure and Applied Chemistry), and are referred to as systematic nomenclature.

One of the rules of the IUPAC system is to choose the largest chain of carbon atoms in the molecule and call it parent compound. Thus,

(a) has a 6 carbon parent chain with methyl groups bonded to the second and fourth carbon atoms of the parent chain. There exists, also, an ethyl group bonded to the third carbon atom.

As such, the name of this organic molecule is 2,4-dimethyl-3-ethylhexane.

(b) has 5 carbon parent molecule and 2 methyl groups on carbon number 3. Therefore, the name is 3,3-dimethylpentane.

(c) has a 5 carbon parent molecule with 2 methyl groups bonded to the third carbon of the parent chain. Therefore, the name of this structure becomes 3,3 di-methylpentane.

(d) has a 5 carbon parent molecule, and 2 methyl groups attached to carbon numbers 2 and 3.

Therefore, the name is 2,3-dimethylpentane.

(e) has a 5 carbon parent molecule, and 2 methyl groups attached to carbon number 3.

Therefore, the name is 3,3-dimethylpentane.

(f) has a 6 carbon parent molecule, and 2 methyl groups attached to carbon numbers 3 and 4.

Therefore, the name is 3,4-dimethylhexane.

To find which compounds are isomers, one counts the number of carbon and hydrogen atoms contained in the molecule. If the total number of both carbon and hydrogen atoms in one molecule is the same as in another molecule, but they have different structural formulas, they are isomers.

If the calculation of total carbon and hydrogen molecules is made, b, c, d, and e become isomers, with b and e being same compound.

● PROBLEM 17-3

Each of the following is an incorrect name for an alkane. Write a structural formula for each and provide the correct systematic name: (a) 2-ethylbutane; (b) 2-isopropylpentane; (c) 1,1-dimethylpentane; (d) 2,2-dimethyl-4-ethylpentane.

Solution: First, one writes the formula starting with the parent molecule. Next, one locates the number of the carbon on the parent molecule that is attached to a particular group by the number in front of that particular group in the compound's name.

Thus, (a) 2-ethylbutane becomes

(b) 2-isopropylpentane becomes

```
      H    H    H    H    H
      |    |    |    |    |
 H —— C —— C —— C —— C —— C —— H
      |    |    |    |    |
      H    |    H    H    H
           |
      H    |    H
      |    |    |
 H —— C —— C —— C —— H
      H    H    H
```

(c) 1,1-dimethylpentane becomes

```
           H
           |
      H —— C —— H
           |          H    H    H    H
           |          |    |    |    |
      H —— C —————————C —— C —— C —— C —— H
           |          |    |    |    |
           |          H    H    H    H
      H —— C —— H
           |
           H
```

(d) 2,2-dimethyl-4-ethylpentane

```
           H
           |
      H —— C —— H
           |
      H         H    H    H
      |         |    |    |
 H —— C —— C —— C —— C —— C —— H
      |    |    |    |    |
      H    |    H    H    H
           |
      H —— C —— H   H–C–H
           |         |
           H        H–C–H
                     |
                     H
```

Each name is incorrect in the same respect; the named parent molecule is not the longest chain of the compound. If a compound twists or bends in free space it must be taken into account when naming the compound.

Thus, the correct names are

(a) 3-methylpentane, since the longest chain has 5 carbons and a methyl group attached to carbon number 3.

(b) 2,3-dimethylhexane since the longest chain has 6 carbons and methyl groups are attached to carbon numbers 2 and 3.

(c) 2-methylhexane, since the longest chain has 6 carbons and a methyl group is attached to carbon number 2.

(d) 2,2,4-trimethylhexane, since the longest chain has 6 carbons and three methyl groups attached to carbons 2, 2 and 4; 1 methyl group attached to carbon 4 and 2 methyl groups attached to carbon 2.

● **PROBLEM** 17-4

Write the structural formulas for all chlorine derivatives having molecular formula $C_5H_{11}Cl$.

Solution: In hydrocarbon derivatives, the hydrogen atoms are replaced by other atoms or groups of atoms, such as oxygen, chlorine, hydroxyl (-OH), or nitro ($-NO_2$), which produce chemically active centers in an otherwise less active molecule.

To solve this problem, one first writes the structural isomers with five carbons in a continuous chain, in which each different hydrogen atom of the alkane has been replaced by a chlorine atom:

(a)

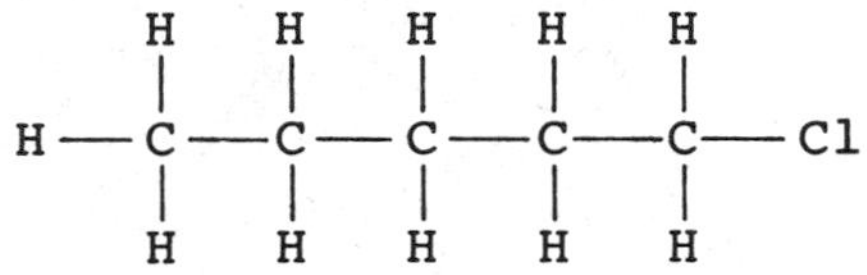

(b)

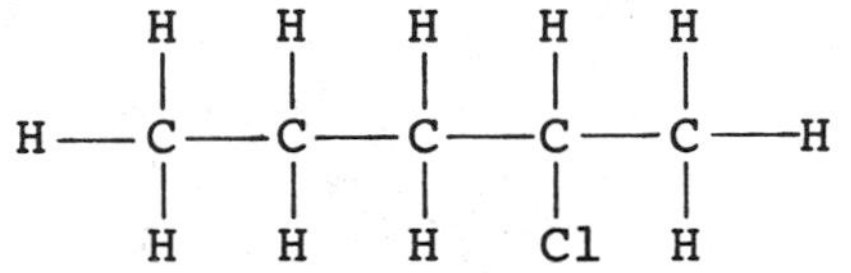

(c)

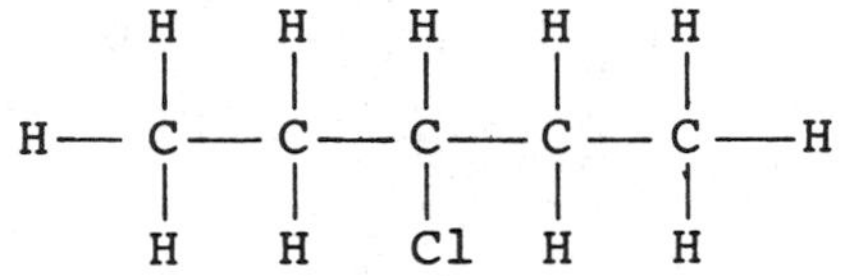

Their names are (a) 1-chloropentane, (b) 2-chloropentane, (c) 3-chloropentane.

Second, one writes the structural isomers with four carbons as the parent molecule, in which two hydrogen atoms have been replaced by a chlorine atom and a methyl group:

(d)

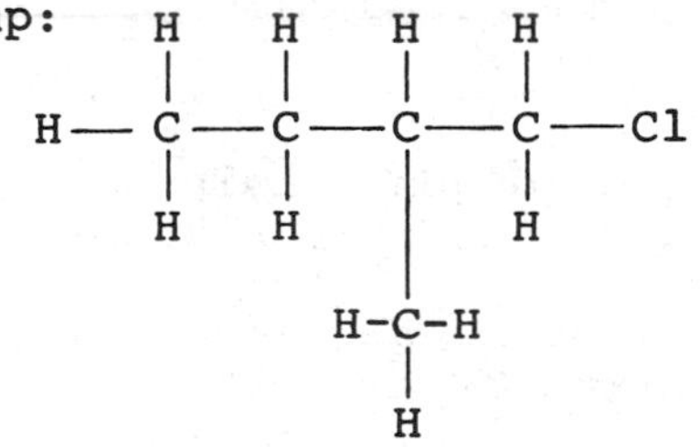

(e)

```
        H     H     H     H
        |     |     |     |
H ——— C ——— C ——— C ——— C ——— Cl
        |     |     |     |
        H     |     H     H
              |
            H-C-H
              |
              H
```

(f)

```
        H     H     Cl    H
        |     |     |     |
H ——— C ——— C ——— C ——— C ——— H
        |     |     |     |
        H     H     |     H
                    |
                  H-C-H
                    |
                    H
```

(g)

```
        H     H     Cl    H
        |     |     |     |
H ——— C ——— C ——— C ——— C ——— H
        |     |     |     |
        H     |     H     H
              |
            H-C-H
              |
              H
```

Their names are (d) 1-chloro-2-methylbutane, (e) 1-chloro —3-methylbutane, (f) 2-chloro —2-methylbutane, and (g) 2-chloro —3-methylbutane.

Third, one writes the structure of the isomer with three carbons for a parent molecule, in which three hydrogen atoms of the three carbon chain have been replaced by a chlorine atom and two methyl groups:

```
                    H
                    |
                  H-C—H
                    |
        H           |           H
        |           |           |
H ——— C ——————— C ——————— C ——— Cl
        |           |           |
        H           |           H
                    |
                  H—C-H
                    |
                    H
```

This compound's name is 1-chloro —2,2-dimethyl-propane or 1-chloro neopentane.

Hence, there are eight structural isomers with the molecular formula $C_5H_{11}Cl$.

A chemist has at his disposal the following hydrocarbons:
(a) 3,3-dimethylpentane, (b) n-heptane, (c) 2-methyl-
heptane, (d) n-pentane, and (e) 2-methylhexane. Arrange
these compounds in order of decreasing boiling points
(without referring to tables).

<u>Solution</u>: To rank the boiling points of these substances,
you must consider the rules which govern the property of
boiling points.

　　　Except for very small alkanes, the boiling point
rises 20 to 30 degrees for every carbon that is added to
the chain. (Alkanes are saturated hydrocarbons of the
general formula C_nH_{2n+2}, where n = number of carbon atoms.)
Alkanes of the same carbon number but different structures
(isomers) will have different boiling points. A branched-
chain isomer has a lower boiling point than a straight-
chain isomer. This is because the shape of a branched-
chain molecule tends to approach a sphere, decreasing the
surface area, so that the intermolecular forces are
easily overcome at a lower temperature. With this in mind,
you can proceed to solve the problem. Because these rules
pertain only to structures, you must write them out.

(a) 3,3-dimethylpentane:

$$H_3C - C - C - C - CH_3$$

(b) n-heptane:

$$H_3C - C - C - C - C - CH_3$$

(c) 2-metylheptane:

$$H_3C - C - C - C - C - CH_3$$

(d) n-pentane:

$$H_3C - C - C - CH_3$$

(e) 2-methylhexane:

$$H_3C - C - C - C - CH_3$$

　　　c. has the greatest carbon content, 8 carbon atoms,
which means it has the highest boiling point. a, b and e
all have 7 carbon atoms; thus carbon content is equal.
But only b is <u>not</u> branched, which means it has the
highest boiling point out of this group. e is the next

highest since it is less branched than a. d has the
lowest boiling point, since it has the lowest carbon
content (5 atoms). Thus, you rank them in order of decreasing boiling point as c, b, e, a, d.

ALKENES AND ALKYNES

Classify each of the following as a member of the methane
series, the ethylene series, or the acetylene series:
$C_{12}H_{26}$, C_9H_{16}, C_7H_{14}, $C_{26}H_{54}$.

Solution: Before beginning this problem, one should first
know the general formulas for each of the series. For the
alkanes (methane series), the general formula is C_nH_{2n+2},
where n is the number of carbon atoms and 2n + 2 is the
number of hydrogens. Molecules of the ethylene series,
also called the alkene series, have two adjacent carbon
atoms joined to one another by a double bond. Any member
in this series has the general formula C_nH_{2n}. The acetylene
series, commonly called the alkyne series, has two adjacent
carbon atoms joined to one another by a triple bond. The
general formula for this series is C_nH_{2n-2}. With this in
mind one can write:

$C_{12}H_{26}$	:	C_nH_{2n+2}	: alkane series
C_9H_{16}	:	C_nH_{2n-2}	: acetylene series
C_7H_{14}	:	C_nH_{2n}	: ethylene series
$C_{26}H_{54}$	:	C_nH_{2n+2}	: alkane series

Draw the structure of 4-ethyl-3,4-dimethyl-2-hexene.

Solution: To draw the structure of more complex compounds,
such as this one, certain steps must be followed.

(1) Identify the parent compound that associated with
the longest carbon chain that contains the functional
group. In 4-ethyl-3,4-dimethyl-2-hexene, the parent
compound is hexene.

(2) Draw the parent carbon skeleton, in this case,
a six carbon chain. Do not put any hydrogen atoms in yet.

$$C \!-\! C \!-\! C \!-\! C \!-\! C \!-\! C$$

(3) Number the carbon atoms starting at either end. This is important; otherwise it may get confusing when one adds the functionality.

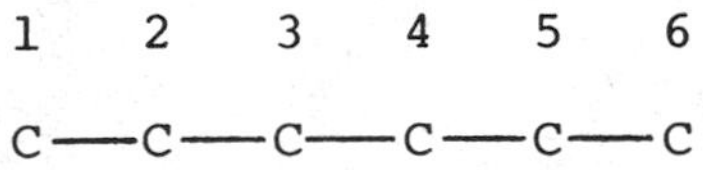

$$
\begin{array}{cccccc}
1 & 2 & 3 & 4 & 5 & 6
\end{array}
$$

$$C \!-\! C \!-\! C \!-\! C \!-\! C \!-\! C$$

(4) Add the suffix functionality, in this case -2-ene. "Ene" tells one that a double bond is present, while "2" indicates that it is at the second carbon.

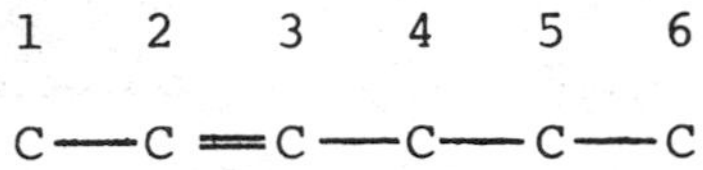

$$
\begin{array}{cccccc}
1 & 2 & 3 & 4 & 5 & 6
\end{array}
$$

$$C \!-\! C = C \!-\! C \!-\! C \!-\! C$$

(5) Add the prefix functionality, starting at the beginning of the name and continuing until the parent name is reached. Here, the prefixes are 4-ethyl-3,4-dimethyl-.

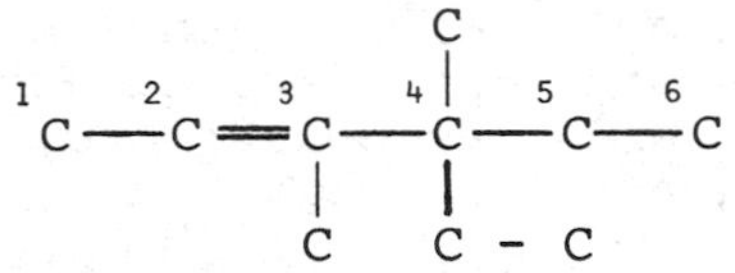

$$
\underset{1}{C} \!-\! \underset{2}{C} = \underset{3}{C} \!-\! \underset{4}{C} \!-\! \underset{5}{C} \!-\! \underset{6}{C}
$$

Now, the hydrogen atoms can be added to give a complete structure.

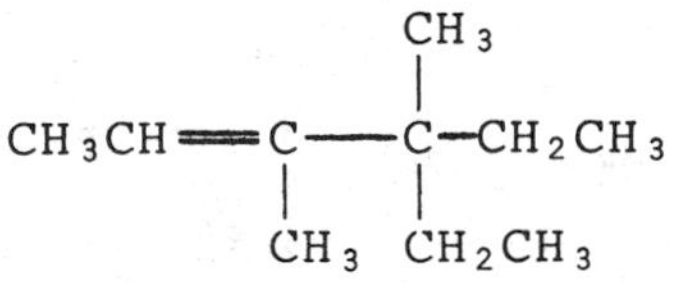

$$
CH_3CH = C \!-\! C \!-\! CH_2CH_3
$$

with CH_3 above, and CH_3 and CH_2CH_3 below.

● **PROBLEM** 17-8

Write condensed structural formulas for all the alkynes, i.e. unsaturated compounds with triple bonds, with a molecular formula of C_5H_8.

Solution: A condensed structural formula provides all the information represented by other structural formulas (i.e. Lewis diagrams, bond diagrams), but it is not as cumbersome.

To solve this problem, first write all the structural isomers with five carbons in a continuous chain:

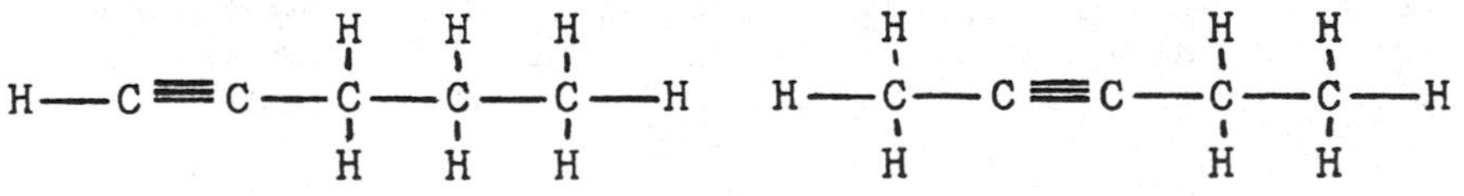

$$
H \!-\! C \equiv C \!-\! C \!-\! C \!-\! C \!-\! H \qquad H \!-\! C \!-\! C \equiv C \!-\! C \!-\! C \!-\! H
$$

Second, write all the structural isomers with a four

312

carbon parent molecule and one carbon in a branch:

$$H-\overset{\overset{\displaystyle H}{|}}{\underset{\underset{\displaystyle H}{|}}{C}}-\overset{\overset{\displaystyle H}{|}}{\underset{\underset{\displaystyle \underset{\displaystyle H}{|}}{H-\overset{|}{\underset{|}{C}}-H}}{C}}-C\equiv C-H$$

No other structural formulas are possible.

Thus, there are only three structural formulas possible for C_5H_8.

Next, one writes these formulas in the condensed form. Namely,

(a) $CH\equiv CCH_2CH_2CH_3$; (b) $CH_3C\equiv CCH_2CH_3$; (c) $CH_3\underset{\underset{\displaystyle CH_3}{|}}{CH}C\equiv CH.$

Which of the following compounds can exhibit geometric and/or optical isomerism? (a) $H_2C=C(Cl)CH_3$; (b) $ClFC=CHCl$; (c) $CH_3CH_2CH=CHCH(CH_3)_2$; (d) $CH_3CHClCOOH$; (e) $HC\equiv CCH=CHCl$; (f) $ClCH=CHCHClCH_3$; (g) cyclohexene; (h) $H_3CN=NCH_3$; (i) $[NH(CH_3)(C_2H_5)(C_3H_7)]^+Cl^-$.

Solution: Optical isomerism refers to the ability of a substance to rotate plane polarized light. Such substances exist as enantiomers (species which are interchangeable only by the breaking and the reforming of bonds and not by only the rotation about bonds). When a mirror is placed between enantiomers, it shows them to be mirror images of each other. If the mirror image of a compound is not equivalent to the original compound, the original compound and its mirror image are said to be non-superimposable or enantiomeric. If a certain compound possesses an enantiomer, it must possess a chiral center. For a molecule to be chiral, it must have a carbon atom attached to four different groups. Thus, you can identify optical isomerism by detecting whether there exists a chiral carbon atom in the molecule. Only (d), (f), and (i) fit into this general category:

(d) $CH_3-\overset{\overset{\displaystyle H}{|}}{\underset{\underset{\displaystyle Cl}{|}}{C^*}}-COOH$ (f) $ClCH=CH-\overset{\overset{\displaystyle H}{|}}{\underset{\underset{\displaystyle Cl}{|}}{C^*}}-CH_3$ and

313

similarly with (i). In (i) the nitrogen atom is the chiral center.

Geometric isomerism refers to cis-trans isomerism. When a compound possesses a double bond, it is possible for geometric isomerism to exist. A geometric isomer is said to exist when two different groups are bonded to each of the two carbon atoms forming the double bond. To determine whether a compound is the cis or the trans isomer, these groups are first assigned priority in order of atomic number. The atom with the highest atomic number is given highest priority. A plane is then imagined along the length of the double bond. If the atoms of greatest priority are both on one side of the plane the isomer is said to be cis. This can be seen in the diagram below. (The numbers indicate priority ratings.)

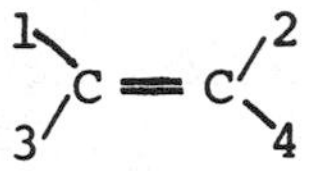

$$\underset{3}{\overset{1}{}}C=C\underset{4}{\overset{2}{}}$$

cis-isomer

$$\underset{4}{\overset{1}{}}C=C\underset{2}{\overset{3}{}}$$

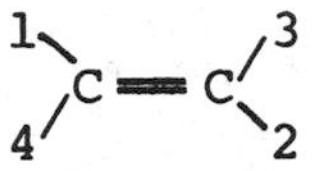

trans-isomer

Only (b), (c), (e), and (h) fit this definition. Notice:

(b)

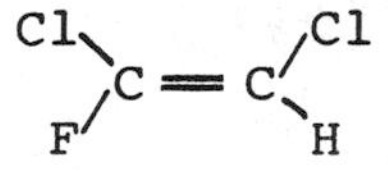

$$\underset{F}{\overset{Cl}{}}C=C\underset{H}{\overset{Cl}{}}$$ and $$\underset{Cl}{\overset{F}{}}C=C\underset{H}{\overset{Cl}{}}$$

cis   trans

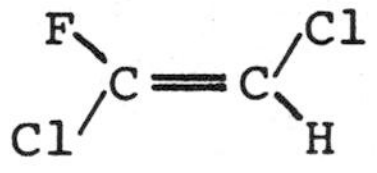

Similar results can be shown in the others.

(c) $CH_3CH_2CH=CHCH(CH_3)_2$

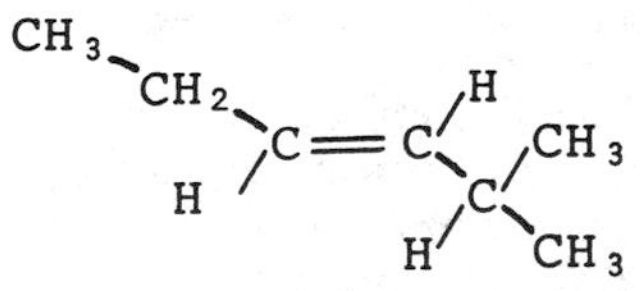

trans   or   cis

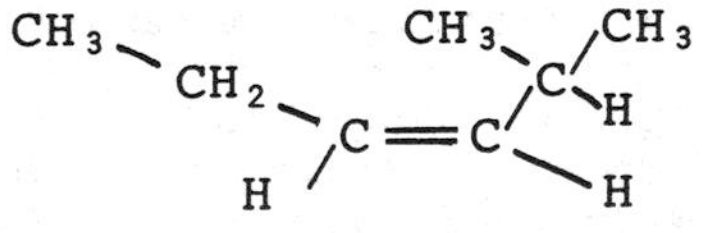

(e) $HC\equiv CCH=CHCl$

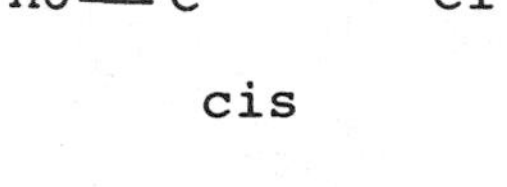

cis 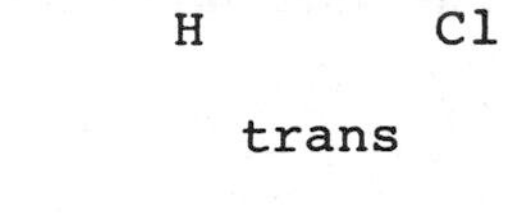   trans

(h) $H_3CN=NCH_3$

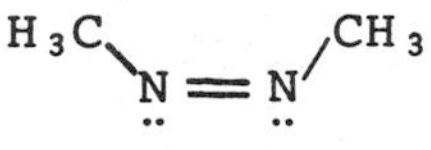

$$H_3C \diagdown N = N \diagup CH_3$$

cis

$$H_3C \diagdown N = N \diagdown CH_3$$

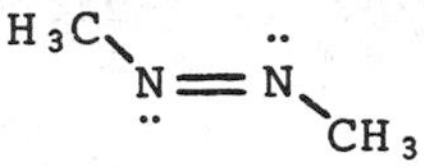

trans

ALCOHOLS

● **PROBLEM** 17-10

Name the following systematically:

(a) $CH_3CHOHCH_2CH_2CH_2CH_3$

(b) $CH_3CHCH_2CH_2OH$
      |
      CH_2CH_2

(c) $CH_3CH_2CH_2COHCH_3$
              |
          CH_3CHCH_3

(d) $CH_2OHCHCH_2CHCH_3$
              | |
          CH_3 CH_3

Solution: All of these compounds are alcohols; they fit into the general formula R-OH, where R is any alkyl group.

In the systematic naming of any alcohol, the following rules should be followed:

(1) The longest chain that contains the hydroxyl group (OH) is considered the parent compound.

(2) The ‾e ending of the name of this carbon chain is replaced by ‾ol.

(3) The locations of the hydroxyl and any other groups are indicated by the smallest possible numbers.

Thus, compound (a)

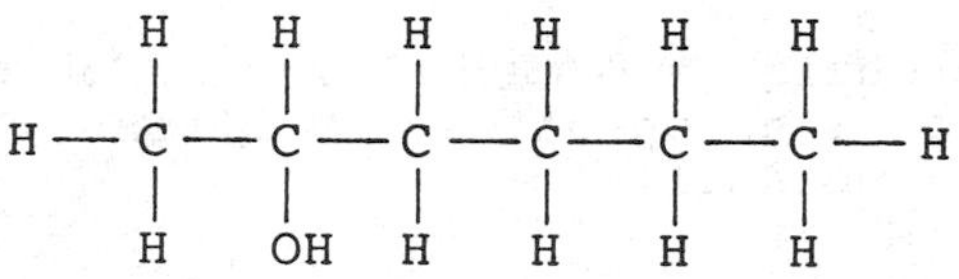

$$H - \overset{\overset{\displaystyle H}{|}}{\underset{\underset{\displaystyle H}{|}}{C}} - \overset{\overset{\displaystyle H}{|}}{\underset{\underset{\displaystyle OH}{|}}{C}} - \overset{\overset{\displaystyle H}{|}}{\underset{\underset{\displaystyle H}{|}}{C}} - \overset{\overset{\displaystyle H}{|}}{\underset{\underset{\displaystyle H}{|}}{C}} - \overset{\overset{\displaystyle H}{|}}{\underset{\underset{\displaystyle H}{|}}{C}} - \overset{\overset{\displaystyle H}{|}}{\underset{\underset{\displaystyle H}{|}}{C}} - H$$

has a 6-carbon chain and an hydroxyl group on carbon number 2. The name of this compound is 2-hexanol.

Compound (b) has a 5-carbon chain,

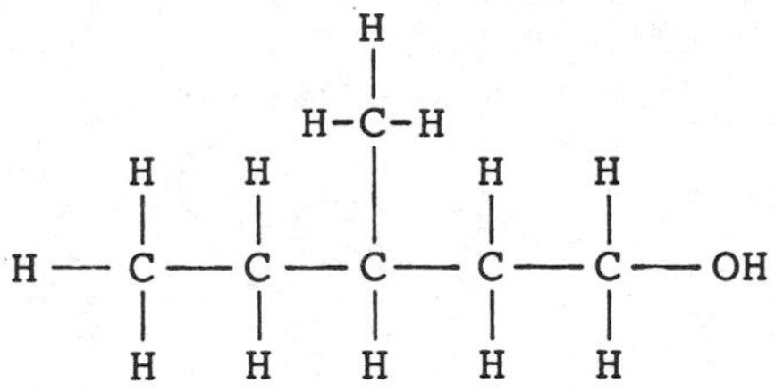

```
                    H
                    |
                  H-C-H
      H     H     |     H     H
      |     |     |     |     |
  H — C  —  C  —  C  —  C  —  C — OH
      |     |     |     |     |
      H     H     H     H     H
```

because this is the longest chain that contains the hydroxyl group. There is a methyl group on carbon number 3, and an hydroxyl group on carbon number 1. The name of this compound is, therefore, 3-methyl-1-pentanol.

Compound (c),

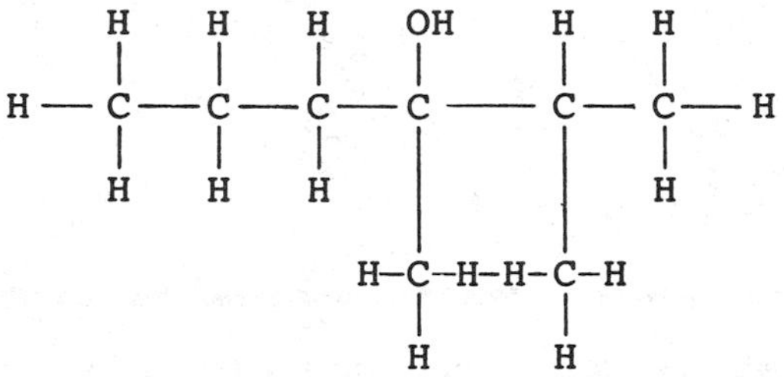

```
      H     H     H    OH     H     H
      |     |     |     |     |     |
  H — C  —  C  —  C  —  C  —  C  —  C — H
      |     |     |           |     |
      H     H     H           H     H

                  H-C–H-H-C–H
                    |       |
                    H       H
```

has a 6-carbon chain that contains the OH group, two methyl groups on carbons 2 and 3, and an hydroxyl group on carbon number 3. Thus, the name is 2,3-dimethyl-3-hexanol.

Compound (d)

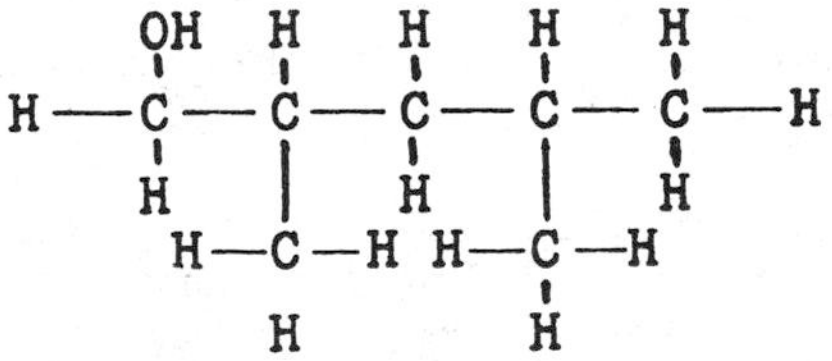

```
     OH    H     H     H     H
     |     |     |     |     |
  H — C  —  C  —  C  —  C  —  C — H
     |     |     |     |     |
     H     |     H     |     H
        H — C — H   H — C — H
            |           |
            H           H
```

has a 5-carbon chain, two methyl groups on carbons 2 and 4, and an hydroxyl group on carbon 1. Thus, the name is 2,4-dimethyl-1-pentanol.

● PROBLEM 17-11

Name the compound shown in figure A by the IUPAC system.

$$CH_3CH_2 \qquad\qquad CH_3$$

$$HC \text{————} CH \text{——} OH$$

$$CH_3CH_2CH_2CH_2 \text{—} C$$

$$CH_3CH_2 \text{—} C \text{—} CH_2CH_3$$

Figure A

Solution: In naming complex open chain organic compounds, first find the longest continuous chain containing the functional groups. Write down the parent name. The parent for this particular compound is heptene. Number the chain starting from the end that will give the smallest prefix numbers for the functional groups. This is shown in figure B.

$$CH_3CH_2 \qquad\qquad {}^1CH_3$$

$${}^3CH \text{————} {}^2CH \text{——} OH$$

$$CH_3CH_2CH_2CH_2 \text{—} {}^4C$$

$${}^7CH_3 {}^6CH_2 \text{—} {}^5C \text{—} CH_2CH_3$$

Add the suffix functionality with the appropriate numbering: 4-hepten-2-ol. Add the prefix functionality, remembering to group together like prefixes. Then, double check to make sure a substituent has not been forgotten or one substituent has not been included twice. By following these steps, one arrives at the name for the structure:

4-n-butyl-3,5-diethyl-4-hepten-2-ol.

● **PROBLEM** 17-12

Which of the following, if any, are not alcohols derived from the methane series of hydrocarbons: C_6H_5OH, $C_{17}H_{33}OH$, C_4H_8OH, $C_9H_{19}OH$?

Solution: Alcohols are derived from molecules whose hydrogen atoms have been replaced by one or more hydroxyl (-OH) groups. The simplest alcohols are derived from the alkanes or the methane series and contain only one hydroxyl group per molecule. These have the general formula ROH, where R is an alkyl group of composition, C_nH_{2n+1}. Thus, the alcohols to be derived from the methane series will follow this formula.

(a) C_6H_5OH has 6 carbons. Therefore, its hydrogen

content should be $2n + 1 = 2(6) + 1 = 13$. Because there exist only 5 hydrogens, excluding the H from OH, it cannot be derived from the methane series.

Compound (b), $C_{17}H_{33}OH$, also does not fit the general formula ($n = 17$, $2n + 1 = 35$), and thus, is not derived from the methane series. If it did fit, it would possess 35 hydrogens instead of 33.

Compound (c), C_4H_8OH, does not fit the general formula ($n = 4$, $2n + 1 = 9$) and, thus, is not derived from the methane series. If it did fit, the alkyl group it would posses 9 H instead of 8.

Compound (d), $C_9H_{19}OH$, does fit the general formula ($n = 9$, $2n + 1 = 19$), and is derived from the methane series.

OTHER FUNCTIONAL GROUPS

● PROBLEM 17-13

Name each of the organic compounds shown in Figure A below.

Figure A

(a) $CH_3 - CH = CH_2$

(b) $CH_3 - \underset{\underset{C_2H_5}{|}}{CH} - CH_2 - CH = CH - CH_3$

(c) $CH_3CH = CHCH_2CH_2CH_3$

(d) 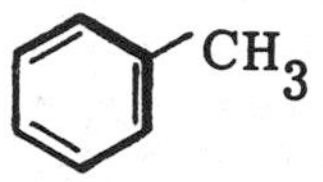 CH_3

Solution: A system of nomenclature called the IUPAC system has been formulated so that all organic molecules may have their structures defined adequately. In this system for hydrocarbons (i.e. compounds containing only hydrogen and carbon atoms) the longest chain is taken as the basic structure, and the carbon atoms are numbered from the end of the chain closest to a branch chain or other modification of simple alkane structure. The position of substituents in the chain are denoted by the number of carbon atom or

318

atoms to which they are attached. In the problem, you are
not given alkanes, you are given alkenes, compounds that
contain a double bond between a pair of carbon atoms (i.e.
unsaturated), and a ring compound. In unsaturated compounds,
the rules are the same, except that the position of the
double bond is indicated; the numbering starts at the end
of the chain nearest the double bond. For rings, name the
ring and any substituent present based on which carbon
is located. Thus, you proceed as follows:

(a) There is only one chain, and it possesses
three carbon atoms. The double bond is located on the
first carbon, not the second, since you want to use the
lowest possible number. As such, you form the molecule
propene. Three carbons suggest propane. It's an alkene,
so that you change ane to ene. Therefore, propane becomes
propene. You have no need to name the position of the
double bond here; the double bond can only be in two positions and both yield the same molecule. That is,
$CH_2 = CH - CH_3$ is equivalent to $CH_3 -CH = CH_2$.

(b) The longest chain containing the double bond has
7 carbon atoms, so that "hep" prefix is suggested. Because
it is a double bond, you add the suffix ene to obtain
heptene. The double bond is located on the second carbon,
not the third, since you want the lowest number. You have,
therefore, the 2-heptene. Using this numbering system, you
see that CH_3, a methyl group, is located on the fifth
carbon. Thus, the name of the molecule is 5-methyl 2 heptene.

(c) Has a six carbon chain, which suggests the prefix "hex". There is a double bond so that the molecule
has the suffix ene. Thus, you obtain hexene. The double
bond is located on the second carbon, which means the
name of the molecule is 2-hexene.

(d): This ring compound has a methyl group (CH_3)
positioned on a benzene ring. The compound can be called
methyl benzene. It is also given   the special name of
toluene.

● **PROBLEM 17-14**

Which of the following compounds are saturated? Which
are unsaturated? (a) $CH_3CH_2CH_2CH_3$, (b) $CH_2 = CHCH_2CH_3$,
(c) cyclohexane, (d) cyclohexene, (e) benzene.

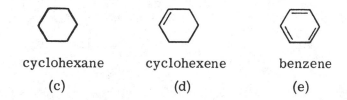

cyclohexane   cyclohexene   benzene

(c)   (d)   (e)

Solution: The most fundamental class of organic compounds is the saturated hydrocarbons. A hydrocarbon is a compound that contains only carbon and hydrogen. Saturated is used to describe the absence of double bonds and/or triple bonds. The term comes from the fact that these compounds do not react with hydrogen because they are saturated with hydrogen. When a double and/or triple bond is present, the compound is termed unsaturated.

Thus, compounds a and c are saturated and compounds b, d, and e are unsaturated.

APPENDIX

Names, Symbols, and Atomic Number of the Elements

Name	Symbol	Atomic number	Name	Symbol	Atomic number	Name	Symbol	Atomic number
Actinium	Ac	89	Gold (Aurum)	Au	79	Praseodymium	Pr	59
Aluminum	Al	13	Hafnium	Hf	72	Promethium	Pm	61
Americium	Am	95	Helium	He	2	Protactinium	Pa	91
Antimony	Sb	51	Holmium	Ho	67	Radium	Ra	88
Argon	Ar	18	Hydrogen	H	1	Radon	Rn	86
Arsenic	As	33	Indium	In	49	Rhenium	Re	75
Astatine	At	85	Iodine	I	53	Rhodium	Rh	45
Barium	Ba	56	Iridium	Ir	77	Rubidium	Rb	37
Berkelium	Bk	97	Iron (Ferrum)	Fe	26	Ruthenium	Ru	44
Beryllium	Be	4	Krypton	Kr	36	Samarium	Sm	62
Bismuth	Bi	83	Lanthanum	La	57	Scandium	Sc	21
Boron	B	5	Lead (Plumbum)	Pb	82	Selenium	Se	34
Bromine	Br	35	Lithium	Li	3	Silicon	Si	14
Cadmium	Cd	48	Lutetium	Lu	71	Silver (Argentum)	Ag	47
Calcium	Ca	20	Magnesium	Mg	12	Sodium	Na	11
Californium	Cf	98	Manganese	Mn	25	Strontium	Sr	38
Carbon	C	6	Mendelevium	Md	101	Sulfur	S	16
Cerium	Ce	58	Mercury	Hg	80	Tantalum	Ta	73
Cesium	Cs	55	Molybdenum	Mo	42	Technetium	Tc	43
Chlorine	Cl	17	Neodymium	Nd	60	Tellurium	Te	52
Chromium	Cr	24	Neon	Ne	10	Terbium	Tb	65
Cobalt	Co	27	Neptunium	Np	93	Thallium	Tl	81
Copper (Cuprum)	Cu	29	Nickel	Ni	28	Thorium	Th	90
Curium	Cm	96	Niobium	Nb	41	Thulium	Tm	69
Dysprosium	Dy	66	Nitrogen	N	7	Tin (Stannum)	Sn	50
Einsteinium	Es	99	Nobelium	No	102	Titanium	Ti	22
Erbium	Er	68	Osmium	Os	76	Tungsten (Wolfram)	W	74
Europium	Eu	63	Oxygen	O	8	Uranium	U	92
Fermium	Fm	100	Palladium	Pd	46	Vanadium	V	23
Fluorine	F	9	Phosphorus	P	15	Xenon	Xe	54
Francium	Fr	87	Platinum	Pt	78	Ytterbium	Yb	70
Gadolinium	Gd	64	Plutonium	Pu	94	Yttrium	Y	39
Gallium	Ga	31	Polonium	Po	84	Zinc	Zn	30
Germanium	Ge	32	Potassium	K	19	Zirconium	Zr	40

Length

	cm	m	km	in	ft	mi
1 centimeter =	1	10^{-2}	10^{-5}	0.3937	3.281×10^{-2}	6.214×10^{-6}
1 METER =	100	1	10^{-3}	39.3	3.281	6.214×10^{-4}
1 kilometer =	10^{5}	1000	1	3.937×10^{4}	3281	0.6214
1 inch =	2.540	2.540×10^{-2}	2.540×10^{-5}	1	8.333×10^{-2}	1.578×10^{-5}
1 foot =	30.48	0.3048	3.048×10^{-4}	12	1	1.894×10^{-4}
1 mile =	1.609×10^{5}	1609	1.609	6.336×10^{4}	5280	1

1 angstrom = 10^{-10} m
1 nautical mile = 1852 m
= 1.151 miles = 6076 ft

1 light year = 9.4600×10^{12} km
1 parsec = 3.084×10^{13} km
1 fathom = 6 ft

1 yard = 3 ft
1 rod = 16.5 ft
1 mil = 10^{-3} in

ELECTRONIC STRUCTURE OF THE ELEMENTS

Atomic No.	Element	K 1 s	L 2 s p	M 3 s p d	N 4 s p d f	O 5 s p d f	P 6 s p d f	Q 7 s p d f
1	H	1						
2	He	2						
3	Li	2	1					
4	Be	2	2					
5	B	2	2 1					
6	C	2	2 2					
7	N	2	2 3					
8	O	2	2 4					
9	F	2	2 5					
10	Ne	2	2 6					
11	Na	2	2 6	1				
12	Mg	2	2 6	2				
13	Al	2	2 6	2 1				
14	Si	2	2 6	2 2				
15	P	2	2 6	2 3				
16	S	2	2 6	2 4				
17	Cl	2	2 6	2 5				
18	Ar	2	2 6	2 6				
19	K	2	2 6	2 6 ..	1			
20	Ca	2	2 6	2 6 ..	2			
21	Sc	2	2 6	2 6 1	2			
22	Ti	2	2 6	2 6 2	2			
23	V	2	2 6	2 6 3	2			
24	Cr	2	2 6	2 6 5	1			
25	Mn	2	2 6	2 6 5	2			
26	Fe	2	2 6	2 6 6	2			
27	Co	2	2 6	2 6 7	2			
28	Ni	2	2 6	2 6 8	2			
29	Cu	2	2 6	2 6 10	1			
30	Zn	2	2 6	2 6 10	2			
31	Ga	2	2 6	2 6 10	2 1			
32	Ge	2	2 6	2 6 10	2 2			
33	As	2	2 6	2 6 10	2 3			
34	Se	2	2 6	2 6 10	2 4			
35	Br	2	2 6	2 6 10	2 5			
36	Kr	2	2 6	2 6 10	2 6			
37	Rb	2	2 6	2 6 10	2 6 ..	1		
38	Sr	2	2 6	2 6 10	2 6 ..	2		
39	Y	2	2 6	2 6 10	2 6 1	2		

Atomic No	Element	K 1 (s)	L 2 (s p)	M 3 (s p d)	N 4 (s p d f)	O 5 (s p d f)	P 6 (s p d f)	Q 7 (s p d f)
40	Zr	2	2 6	2 6 10	2 6 2 ..	2		
41	Nb	2	2 6	2 6 10	2 6 4* ..	1		
42	Mo	2	2 6	2 6 10	2 6 5 ..	1		
43	Tc	2	2 6	2 6 10	2 6 6 ..	1		
44	Ru	2	2 6	2 6 10	2 6 7 ..	1		
45	Rh	2	2 6	2 6 10	2 6 8 ..	1		
46	Pd	2	2 6	2 6 10	2 6 10* ..	0		
47	Ag	2	2 6	2 6 10	2 6 10	1		
48	Cd	2	2 6	2 6 10	2 6 10	2		
49	In	2	2 6	2 6 10	2 6 10	2 1		
50	Sn	2	2 6	2 6 10	2 6 10	2 2		
51	Sb	2	2 6	2 6 10	2 6 10	2 3		
52	Te	2	2 6	2 6 10	2 6 10	2 4		
53	I	2	2 6	2 6 10	2 6 10	2 5		
54	Xe	2	2 6	2 6 10	2 6 10	2 6		
55	Cs	2	2 6	2 6 10	2 6 10 ..	2 6	1	
56	Ba	2	2 6	2 6 10	2 6 10 ..	2 6	2	
57	La	2	2 6	2 6 10	2 6 10 ..	2 6 1 ..	2	
58	Ce	2	2 6	2 6 10	2 6 10 2*	2 6	2	
59	Pr	2	2 6	2 6 10	2 6 10 3	2 6	2	
60	Nd	2	2 6	2 6 10	2 6 10 4	2 6	2	
61	Pm	2	2 6	2 6 10	2 6 10 5	2 6	2	
62	Sm	2	2 6	2 6 10	2 6 10 6	2 6	2	
63	Eu	2	2 6	2 6 10	2 6 10 7	2 6	2	
64	Gd	2	2 6	2 6 10	2 6 10 7	2 6 1 ..	2	
65	Tb	2	2 6	2 6 10	2 6 10 9*	2 6	2	
66	Dy	2	2 6	2 6 10	2 6 10 10	2 6	2	
67	Ho	2	2 6	2 6 10	2 6 10 11	2 6	2	
68	Er	2	2 6	2 6 10	2 6 10 12	2 6	2	
69	Tm	2	2 6	2 6 10	2 6 10 13	2 6	2	
70	Yb	2	2 6	2 6 10	2 6 10 14	2 6	2	
71	Lu	2	2 6	2 6 10	2 6 10 14	2 6 1 ..	2	
72	Hf	2	2 6	2 6 10	2 6 10 14	2 6 2 ..	2	
73	Ta	2	2 6	2 6 10	2 6 10 14	2 6 3 ..	2	
74	W	2	2 6	2 6 10	2 6 10 14	2 6 4 ..	2	
75	Re	2	2 6	2 6 10	2 6 10 14	2 6 5 ..	2	
76	Os	2	2 6	2 6 10	2 6 10 14	2 6 6 ..	2	
77	Ir	2	2 6	2 6 10	2 6 10 14	2 6 7 ..	2	
78	Pt	2	2 6	2 6 10	2 6 10 14	2 6 9 ..	1	
79	Au	2	2 6	2 6 10	2 6 10 14	2 6 10 ..	1	
80	Hg	2	2 6	2 6 10	2 6 10 14	2 6 10 ..	2	
81	Tl	2	2 6	2 6 10	2 6 10 14	2 6 10 ..	2 1	
82	Pb	2	2 6	2 6 10	2 6 10 14	2 6 10 ..	2 2	
83	Bi	2	2 6	2 6 10	2 6 10 14	2 6 10 ..	2 3	
84	Po	2	2 6	2 6 10	2 6 10 14	2 6 10 ..	2 4	
85	At	2	2 6	2 6 10	2 6 10 14	2 6 10 ..	2 5	
86	Rn	2	2 6	2 6 10	2 6 10 14	2 6 10 ..	2 6	
87	Fr	2	2 6	2 6 10	2 6 10 14	2 6 10 ..	2 6	1
88	Ra	2	2 6	2 6 10	2 6 10 14	2 6 10 ..	2 6	2
89	Ac	2	2 6	2 6 10	2 6 10 14	2 6 10 ..	2 6 1 ..	2
90	Th	2	2 6	2 6 10	2 6 10 14	2 6 10 ..	2 6 2 ..	2
91	Pa	2	2 6	2 6 10	2 6 10 14	2 6 10 2*	2 6 1 ..	2
92	U	2	2 6	2 6 10	2 6 10 14	2 6 10 3	2 6 1 ..	2
93	Np	2	2 6	2 6 10	2 6 10 14	2 6 10 4	2 6 1 ..	2
94	Pu	2	2 6	2 6 10	2 6 10 14	2 6 10 6	2 6	2
95	Am	2	2 6	2 6 10	2 6 10 14	2 6 10 7	2 6	2
96	Cm	2	2 6	2 6 10	2 6 10 14	2 6 10 7	2 6 1 ..	2
97	Bk	2	2 6	2 6 10	2 6 10 14	2 6 10 9*	2 6	2
98	Cf	2	2 6	2 6 10	2 6 10 14	2 6 10 10	2 6	2
99	Es	2	2 6	2 6 10	2 6 10 14	2 6 10 11	2 6	2
100	Fm	2	2 6	2 6 10	2 6 10 14	2 6 10 12	2 6	2
101	Md	2	2 6	2 6 10	2 6 10 14	2 6 10 13	2 6	2
102	No	2	2 6	2 6 10	2 6 10 14	2 6 10 14	2 6	2
103	Lr	2	2 6	2 6 10	2 6 10 14	2 6 10 14	2 6 1 ..	2
104	—	2	2 6	2 6 10	2 6 10 14	2 6 10 14	2 6 2 ..	2

Work and Energy Conversions

Unit	Symbol	Conversion to Joule (J)
Foot-pound force	ft lbf	1.3558179
Foot-poundal	–	4.2140110×10^{-2}
Ton (nuclear equivalent of TNT)	tn	4.20×10^9
British thermal unit (IST current)	Btu	$1.055056 \times 10^{3*}$
Btu, IST before 1956	–	1.05504×10^3
Btu, mean	–	1.05587×10^3
Btu, thermochemical	–	1.054350×10^3
Btu (39°F)	–	1.05967×10^3
Btu (60°F)	–	1.05468×10^3
Calorie	cal	4.1868*
Calorie, mean	–	4.19002
Calorie, thermochemical	–	4.184**
Calorie (15°C)	–	4.18580
Calorie (20°C)	–	4.18190
Calorie kilogram	–	$4.1868 \times 10^{3*}$
Calorie kilogram, mean	–	4.19002×10^3
Calorie kilogram, thermochemical	–	$4.184 \times 10^{3**}$
Kilocalorie	kcal	$4.1868 \times 10^{3*}$
Kilocalorie, mean	–	4.19002×10^3
Kilocalorie, thermochemical	–	$4.184 \times 10^{3**}$
Electron volt	eV	$1.6021917 \times 10^{-19}$
Erg	–	$1.00 \times 10^{-7**}$
Joule (International of 1948)	J	1.000165
Watt hour	W h	$3.60 \times 10^{3**}$
Kilowatt hour	kW h	$3.60 \times 10^{6**}$
Kilowatt hour (International of 1948)	–	3.60059×10^6

*International steam table.
**Defined value.

Enthalpy Data

Substance	$\Delta H^\circ_f (298)$ kJ mol^{-1}	$\Delta H^\circ_f (0)$ kJ mol^{-1}
H	217.997	216.03
H_2	0	0
O	249.17	246.78
$O(^1D)$	438.9	436.6
O_2	0	0
$O_2(^1\Delta)$	94.3	94.3
$O_2(^1\Sigma)$	156.9	156.9
O_3	142.7	145.4
HO	39.0	38.7

Substance	$\Delta H°_f(298)$ kJ mol^{-1}	$\Delta H°_f(0)$ kJ mol^{-1}
HO$_2$	2 ± 8	5 ± 8
H$_2$O	−241.81	−238.92
H$_2$O$_2$	−136.32	−130.04
N	472.68	470.82
N$_2$	0	0
NH	343	343
NH$_2$	185	188
NH$_3$	− 45.94	− 38.95
NO	90.25	89.75
NO$_2$	33.2	36.0
NO$_3$	71 ± 20	77 ± 20
N$_2$O	82.05	85.50
N$_2$O$_4$	9.1	18.7
N$_2$O$_5$	11.3	23.8
HNO	99.6	102.5
HNO$_2$	− 79.5	− 74
HNO$_3$	−135.06	−125.27
HO$_2$NO$_2$	− 54 ± 20	
CH	594.1	590.8
CH$_2$	386	386
CH$_3$	145.6	149.0
CH$_4$	− 74.81	− 66.82
CO	−110.53	−113.81
CO$_2$	−393.51	−393.14
HCO	37.6	37.2
CH$_2$O	−108.6	−104.7
HCOOH	−378.6	−371.6
CH$_3$O	14.6	22.6
CH$_3$O$_2$	7 ± 8	
CH$_3$OH	−200.7	−189.7
CH$_3$OOH	−131	
CH$_3$ONO	− 65.3	− 52.6
CH$_3$ONO$_2$	−119.7	−103.4
C$_2$H$_5$	107.5	
C$_2$H$_6$	− 83.8	− 68.3
CH$_3$OOCH$_3$	−125.5	
S	276.98	274.72
S$_2$	128.49	128.20
HS	146 ± 4	145 ± 4
H$_2$S	− 20.63	− 17.70
SO	5.0	5.0
SO$_2$	−296.81	−294.26
SO$_3$	−395.7	−390
SOH	21 ± 17	
HSO$_3$	−481 ± 25	
CS	272	268
CS$_2$	117.2	116.6
OCS	−142	−142
F	79.39	77.28
F$_2$	0	0
HF	−273.30	−273.26
HOF	− 98 ± 4	− 95 ± 4
FO	109 ± 8	109 ± 8
FO$_2$	50 ± 12	52 ± 12
FONO	67	

Substance	$\Delta H°_f(298)$ kJ mol^{-1}	$\Delta H°_f(0)$ kJ mol^{-1}
FONO$_2$	10	18
CF$_2$	-182 ± 8	-182 ± 8
CF$_3$	-470 ± 4	-468 ± 4
CF$_4$	-933	-927
FCO	-170 ± 60	-170 ± 60
COF$_2$	-634.7	-631.6
Cl	121.30	119.62
Cl$_2$	0	0
HCl	-92.31	-92.13
ClO	102	102
ClOO	89 ± 5	91
OClO	97 ± 8	100 ± 8
Cl$_2$O	81.4	83.2
HOCl	-78	-75
ClNO	51.7	53.6
ClNO$_2$	12.5	18.0
ClONO	83	
ClONO$_2$	26.4	
FCl	-50.7	-50.8
CCl	502 ± 20	498 ± 20
CCl$_2$	238 ± 20	237 ± 20
CCl$_3$	79.5	80.1
CCl$_4$	-95.8	-93.6
CHCl$_3$	-102.9	-98.0
CH$_2$Cl	125	
CH$_2$Cl$_2$	-95.4	-88.5
CH$_3$Cl	-82.0	-74.0
ClCO	-17	
COCl$_2$	-220.1	-218.4
CFCl	30 ± 25	30 ± 25
CFCl$_2$	-96	
CFCl$_3$	-284.9	-281.8
CF$_2$Cl	-269	
CF$_2$Cl$_2$	-493.3	-489.1
CF$_3$Cl	-707.9	-702.9
CHFCl$_2$	-284.9	-279.5
CHF$_2$Cl	-483.7	-477.4
COFCl	-427 ± 33	-423 ± 33
C$_2$Cl$_4$	-12.4	-11.9
C$_2$HCl$_3$	-7.8	-4.3
CH$_2$CCl$_3$	45 ± 30	
CH$_3$CCl$_3$	-142.3	-145.0
Br	111.86	117.90
Br$_2$	30.91	45.69
HBr	-36.38	-28.54
HOBr	-80 ± 8	
BrO	125	133
BrNO	82.2	91.5
BrONO$_2$	20 ± 30	
BrCl	14.6	22.1
CH$_2$Br	163	
CH$_3$Br	-37.7	-22.3

THE PERIODIC TABLE

METALS

NONMETALS

TRANSITION METALS

KEY

112.40
Cd → Symbol
48 → Atomic number

Atomic weight → 112.40

PERIODS	IA	IIA	IIIB	IVB	VB	VIB	VIIB	VIII	VIII	VIII	IB	IIB	IIIA	IVA	VA	VIA	VIIA	O
1	1.0079 **H** 1																	4.00260 **He** 2
2	6.94 **Li** 3	9.01218 **Be** 4											10.81 **B** 5	12.011 **C** 6	14.0067 **N** 7	15.9994 **O** 8	18.9984 **F** 9	20.179 **Ne** 10
3	22.9898 **Na** 11	24.305 **Mg** 12											26.9815 **Al** 13	28.086 **Si** 14	30.9738 **P** 15	32.06 **S** 16	35.453 **Cl** 17	39.948 **Ar** 18
4	39.098 **K** 19	40.08 **Ca** 20	44.9559 **Sc** 21	47.90 **Ti** 22	50.9414 **V** 23	51.996 **Cr** 24	54.9380 **Mn** 25	55.847 **Fe** 26	58.9332 **Co** 27	58.71 **Ni** 28	63.546 **Cu** 29	65.38 **Zn** 30	69.72 **Ga** 31	72.59 **Ge** 32	74.9216 **As** 33	78.96 **Se** 34	79.904 **Br** 35	83.80 **Kr** 36
5	85.4678 **Rb** 37	87.62 **Sr** 38	88.9059 **Y** 39	91.22 **Zr** 40	92.9064 **Nb** 41	95.94 **Mo** 42	98.9062 **Tc** 43	101.07 **Ru** 44	102.9055 **Rh** 45	106.4 **Pd** 46	107.868 **Ag** 47	112.40 **Cd** 48	114.82 **In** 49	118.69 **Sn** 50	121.75 **Sb** 51	127.60 **Te** 52	126.9046 **I** 53	131.30 **Xe** 54
6	132.9054 **Cs** 55	137.34 **Ba** 56	57–71 *	178.49 **Hf** 72	180.9479 **Ta** 73	183.85 **W** 74	186.2 **Re** 75	190.2 **Os** 76	192.22 **Ir** 77	195.09 **Pt** 78	196.9665 **Au** 79	200.59 **Hg** 80	204.37 **Tl** 81	207.2 **Pb** 82	208.9804 **Bi** 83	(210) **Po** 84	(210) **At** 85	(222) **Rn** 86
7	(223) **Fr** 87	(226.0254) **Ra** 88	89–103 †	(260) **Ku** 104	(260) **Ha** 105													

* LANTHANIDE SERIES

138.9055 **La** 57	140.12 **Ce** 58	140.9077 **Pr** 59	144.24 **Nd** 60	(145) **Pm** 61	150.4 **Sm** 62	151.96 **Eu** 63	157.25 **Gd** 64	158.9254 **Tb** 65	162.50 **Dy** 66	164.9304 **Ho** 67	167.26 **Er** 68	168.9342 **Tm** 69	173.04 **Yb** 70	174.97 **Lu** 71

† ACTINIDE SERIES

(227) **Ac** 89	232.0381 **Th** 90	231.0359 **Pa** 91	238.029 **U** 92	237.0482 **Np** 93	(242) **Pu** 94	(243) **Am** 95	(245) **Cm** 96	(245) **Bk** 97	(248) **Cf** 98	(253) **Es** 99	(254) **Fm** 100	(256) **Md** 101	(253) **No** 102	(257) **Lr** 103

INDEX

Numbers on this page refer to <u>PROBLEM NUMBERS</u>, not page numbers

The High School Tutors

The **HIGH SCHOOL TUTORS** series is based on the same principle as the more comprehensive **PROBLEM SOLVERS**, but is specifically designed to meet the needs of high school students. REA has recently revised all the books in this series to include expanded review sections, new material, and newly-designed covers. This makes the books even more effective in helping students to cope with these difficult high school subjects.

If you would like more information about any of these books,
complete the coupon below and return it to us or go to your local bookstore.